KT-419-380

Parkinson's
Disease Society

The problems faced in mental retardation are frequently heightened by the concomitance of psychiatric illness. For some time, the prevalence of such dual diagnosis has been underestimated and poorly understood. The process of resettlement from long-stay institutions into community care, however, has led to more widespread recognition. Care strategies are changing and, with emphasis on consumer choice and community care remaining the preferred option for service provision, the need for specialist professional input increases.

A multidisciplinary and truly international team of professionals offer their perspectives on a wide range of current and evolving aspects in this field. Key issues in aetiology and assessment include acknowledgement of, and adaption to, the difficulties inherent in psychiatric diagnosis of people with non-verbal communication. Recent advances in Fragile-X syndrome, premature aging in Down's syndrome, the taxonomy of autism, sexuality, challenging behaviour and cognitive therapy are amongst the many issues discussed in detail. Contemporary treatment interventions, service systems and delivery are all addressed including an overview of the variety of international strategies currently employed in connection with issues of mental retardation in mental health.

This uniquely international and authoritative work which encompasses such a wealth of current knowledge and techniques is sure to be welcomed by mental retardation and mental health professionals alike including psychiatrists, psychologists, social workers, nurses, service providers, administrators and managers.

MENTAL HEALTH IN MENTAL RETARDATION
RECENT ADVANCES AND PRACTICES

MENTAL HEALTH IN MENTAL RETARDATION

Recent advances and practices

Edited by
NICK BOURAS
Division of Psychiatry, Guy's Hospital, London, UK

CAMBRIDGE
UNIVERSITY PRESS

Published by the Press Syndicate of the University of Cambridge
The Pitt Building, Trumpington Street, Cambridge, CB2 1RP
40 West 20th Street, New York, NY 10011-4211, USA
10 Stamford Road, Oakleigh, Melbourne 3166, Australia

First published 1994

Printed in Great Britain at the University Press, Cambridge

A catalogue record for this book is available from the British Library

Library of Congress cataloguing in publication data

Mental health in mental retardation: recent advances and practices/
  edited by Nick Bouras.
      p.   cm.
    Includes index.
    ISBN 0–521–43495–5 (hardback)
    1. Mentally handicapped – Mental health.   2. Mentally handicapped –
Mental health services.   I. Bouras, Nick.
    [DNLM: 1. Mental Retardation – complications.   2. Mental Disorders –
complications.   WM 307.M5 M5487 1994]
RC451.4.M47M466   1994
616.85′88 – dc20
DNLM/DLC
for Library of Congress   93-28359   CIP

ISBN 0 521 43495 5 hardback

TAG

In memory of Frank Menolascino

Contents

List of Contributors

Tony Attwood PhD
Specialist Services Coordinator, Division of Intellectual Disability Services, Department of Family Services and Aboriginal and Islander Affairs, GPO Box 806, Brisbane 4001, Australia

Angela Barnicoat MD
Waldurg Research Fellow, Department of Medical and Molecular Genetics, Guy's Hospital London SE1 9RT, UK

Nehama Baum PhD
Executive Director, Muki Baum Association, 111 Anthony Road Downsview, Ontario M3K 1B7, Canada

Betsy A. Benson PhD
Director, Dept. of Psychology (M/C 285), Institute for Study of Developmental Disabilities, University of Illinois, Box 4348, Chicago IL 60680, USA

German E. Berrios MD
Consultant Psychiatrist and University Lecturer, Addenbrooke's Hospital, Hills Road, Cambridge CB2 2QQ, UK

Joan Bicknell MD
Emeritus Professor, Psychiatry of Disability, St. George's Hospital Medical School, Blackshaw Road, London SW17 0RE, UK

Nick Bouras MD
Consultant Psychiatrist and Senior Lecturer, Section Psychiatry of Learning Disabilities, United Medical and Dental Schools, Guy's Hospital, London SE1 9RT, UK

David Brooks MD
Consultant Psychiatrist in Mental Handicap, Bexley Health District and

Section Psychiatry of Learning Disabilities, United Medical and Dental
Schools, Guy's Hospital, London SE1 9RT, UK

Hilary Brown
*Senior Lecturer in Mental Handicap, Centre for the Applied Psychology of
Social Care, Beverley Farm, University of Kent, Canterbury CT2 7LZ, UK*

Diane Cox-Lindeubaum ACSW
*Clinical Consultant/Clinical Supervisor, 109 Scodon Drive, Ridgefield,
CT 06877, USA*

Henry Crabbe MD
*Medical Director, Psychiatric Medicine Center, New London, Connecticut
06320, USA*

Kenneth Day MD
*Consultant Psychiatrist, Northgate Hospital and Senior Lecturer University
of Newcastle upon Tyne, Morpeth, Northumberland NE61 3PB, UK*

Anton Dosen MD
*Director Treatment, Nieuw Sprareland, Clinic for Psychiatric and Be-
havioural Disorders in the Mentally Retarded, Wanssumweg 14, 5807 AE
Oostrum, Netherlands*

Katie Drummond MD
*Senior Lecturer, Psychiatry of Disability, St.George's Hospital Medical
School, Blackshaw Road, London SW17 0RE, UK*

William Fraser MD
*Professor of Psychiatry of Mental Handicap, University of Wales College of
Medical Academic Department of Mental Handicap, Ely Hospital, Cow-
bridge Road, Ely, Cardiff, S Glamorgan CF5 5XE, UK*

Stephen French Gilson PhD
*School of Social Work, Virginia Commonwealth University, Richmond,
Virginia, USA*

William Gardner PhD
*Chairman and Professor Rehabilitation Psychology Programme and Head
Treatment Processes Section, Waisman Center on Mental Retardation and
Human Development, University of Wisconsin, Maddison, Wisconsin 53705,
USA*

Shaun Gravestock MD
*Lecturer and Senior Registrar, Section Psychiatry of Learning Disabilities,
United Medical and Dental Schools, Guy's Hospital, London SE1 9RT, UK*

Janice Graeber
Waisman Center on Mental Retardation and Human Development, University of Wisconsin, Maddison, Wisconsin 53705, USA

Randi J. Hagerman MD
Associate Director, Child Development Unit (7451-B140), The Children's Hospital, 1056 East 19th Avenue, Denver, Colorado 80218–1088, USA

Anthony J. Holland MD
Lecturer and Honorary Consultant Psychiatrist, Academic Department of Psychiatry, University of Cambridge, Addenbrooke's Hospital, Hills Road, Cambridge CB2 2QQ, UK

Sheila Hollins MD
Professor, Psychiatry of Disability, St.George's Hospital Medical School, Blackshaw Road, London SW17 0RE, UK

Geraldine Holt MD
Consultant Psychiatrist, Greenwich Health Authority and Section Psychiatry of Learning Disabilities, United Medical and Dental Schools, Guy's Hospital, London SE1 9RT, UK

Ron Joachim
Executive Director, Active Foundation Inc., 116 Jersey Street, GPO Box 446, Jolimont WA6014, Australia

John Johnson PhD
Assistant Professor, Department of Early Childhood and Special Education, 339 Teachers College, Cincinnati, Ohio 45221–0002, USA

Chris Kiernan PhD
Professor of Behavioural Studies in Mental Handicap, Director Hester Adrian Research Centre, Manchester M13 9NG, UK

Paul Kymissis MD
Associate Professor of Psychiatry, Dept. of Psychiatry and Behavioral Sciences, New York Medical College, Valhalla NY10595, USA

Andrew Levitas MD
Medical Director Division of Prevention and Treatment of Developmental Disorders, Department of Psychiatry, University of Medicine and Dentistry of New Jersey, Stratford, New Jersey 08002, USA

Len Leven MD
Director of Psychiatry at the Mental Retardation Research Institute, New York Medical College, Valhalla, New York 10595, USA

Louis Lindenbaum Ed.D
Associate Executive Director/Director, Putnam Association for Retarded Citizens, Kent Centre, Rt. 52, Carmel, NY 10512, USA

John McEvoy PhD
Honorary Senior Fellow, School of Psychology, University of Birmingham, Edgbaston Birmingham B15 2TT, UK

Jim Mansell
Professor of the Applied Psychology of Mental Handicap, University of Kent, Canterbury, Kent CT2 7LZ, UK

Frank Menolascino MD
+(Deceased), Late Professor of Psychiatry, Department of Psychiatry, Creighton, Nebraska, 2205 South 10th Street, Omaha NE68108, USA

Jack Piachaud MD
Consultant Psychiatrist, Paddington Community Hospital, 7A Woodfield Road, London W9 2BB, UK

Alice Puddephatt BA
Developmental Disabilities Programme, University of Western Ontario, Health Sciences Addition, London, Ontario, N6A 5C1, Canada

Steve Reiss PhD
Professor, Nisonger Centre, Ohio State University Medical School, 1581 Dodd Drive, Columbus, Ohio 43210–1297, USA

Frank R. Rusch PhD
University of Illinois at Urbana-Champaign 110 Education Building, 1310 South Sixth Street, Champaign, IL 61820, USA

Valerie Sinason
Principal Psychotherapist in Child/Family and Adult Department, The Tavistock Clinic, 120 Belsize Lane, London NW3, UK

Ludwik Szymanski MD
Director Childrens Hospital and Associate Professor, Department of Psychiatry, Harvard University Medical School, Boston, MA, USA

Sam Sussman PhD
Director of Social Services, London Psychiatric Hospital, 850 Highbury Avenue, PO Box 2532, Station A, London Ontario, N6A 4H1, Canada

Akihito Takahashi MD
Director, Kisen Centre for Developmental Disabilities, 1–30–9 Funabaghi, Setagaye-ku, Tokyo 156, Japan

Sophie Thompson MD
Consultant Psychiatrist and Psychotherapist, Merton Community Mental Handicap Team, Birches House, 1 Birches Close, Mitcham, Surrey, UK

Jeremy Turk MD
Wellcome Research Training Fellow and Honorary Senior Registrar, Department of Child Psychiatry, Institute of Child Health, Great Ormond Street, London WC1N 1EH, UK

Vicky Turk PhD
Head of Clinical Psychology Services, Bexley Health Authority and formerly Senior Research Fellow at the University of Kent, Canterbury CT2 7LZ, UK

Steven A. Weisblatt MD
Clinical Assistant Professor of Psychiatry, Albert Einstein Hospital, Department of Psychiatry, 25–56 1825 Eastchester Road, Bronx 10461–2372, New York, USA

Lorna Wing MD
Centre for Social and Communication Disorders, Elliot House, 113 Masons Hill, Bromley, Kent BR2 9HT, UK

Acknowledgements

I am grateful to Dr Yan Kon for her invaluable help with the editing of this volume. I also thank Dr Brendan McCormack and Dr Joanna Mulvey for their assistance. Mrs Kay Scutt deserves my gratitude for typing the manuscript.

Introduction

The principles of care for people with mental retardation have undergone radical changes over the past 20 years. The recognition of their right to live as normal a life as possible, the closure of long stay institutions, the development of community-based facilities, the influence of families in the direction of services, and the self advocacy movement have been some of the main issues which have affected the planning and implementation of care for people with mental retardation. The new prevailing ideology is based on a holistic approach, and places increasing emphasis on consumer choice and satisfaction as well as outcome. People with mental retardation are supported to live and work in the environment of their choice and enabled to develop their potential. Participation, choice, integration and contribution are the principles guiding the individually tailored programmes of services.

Mental health has always been an important factor for people with mental retardation. The provision of mental health services for people with mental retardation has received a new impetus from the current ideology and philosophy of care. We have witnessed, over the past decade, the emergence of advances in aetiology, diagnosis, treatment and models of service for people having both conditions; mental retardation and mental health problems. These developments for people with mental retardation and the recent advances in the mental health field are presented in this book. Emphasis is placed on current and evolving aspects of diagnosis and therapeutic methods as well as service systems.

The volume is divided into six Parts. Part I deals with the historical aspects, the aetiological concepts, and the incidence; a view on the psychosocial development of children and adolescents with mild mental retardation, the psychological process of the inner world of a person with mental retardation and the direction for future research are also discussed.

Part II focuses on the complexities of assessment and diagnosis. The use of reliable assessment methods is described, together with the manifestations of characteristic psychiatric conditions in mental retardation and the diagnostic challenges faced by the practising clinician. The needs of adolescents are mentioned separately and the fact that they have attracted less attention both clinically and in terms of research is pointed out. The progress made in understanding autism and related conditions is outlined and the issues on challenging behaviour are discussed. Part III presents current knowledge on special issues such as Fragile-X syndrome, the relation between Down's syndrome and Alzheimer's disease and highlights views and research findings related to sexuality. Part IV emphasises the role of treatment methods and the growing interest in pharmacotherapy, the use of specific behavioural techniques and the increasing application of individual, group and family psychotherapy for people at all levels of mental retardation. 'Sand play' is illustrated with practical examples. Part V addresses the issues surrounding the delivery of service systems supported by research on community based residential facilities and specialist services. The monitoring of quality is also covered from a clinical and service perspective.

Part VI provides an international overview on similarities and differences in the perception of the problem and the provision of service between USA, Canada, Australia, some European countries, Japan and the third world with the case study of Zimbabwe.

An effort has been made to keep the term mental retardation throughout the book as authors, reflecting their orientation and country of origin, used terms such as mental handicap, developmental handicap, developmental disabilities, learning difficulties, learning disabilities (currently officially used in Britain) interchangeably. There are, however, some instances where the contributor's term of preference was kept, as it was felt to be more in line with the expressed views.

Most of the chapters are based on an International Conference held at the University of Kent Canterbury, under the auspices of the Mental Handicap Section of the World Psychiatric Association. It is very sad that Frank Menolascino, the great pioneer in the field and a driving force behind this publication, died before the book was completed. His chapter included in this volume is the last he contributed in his professional life. His work will guide for years to come professionals and others to further advance a much needed field.

Part I
Overview and the nature of the issues

1

Mental illness and mental retardation: history and concepts

GERMAN E. BERRIOS

Introduction

Existing historical work on the concept of mental retardation (as opposed to its management) is limited, particularly in its association with the notion of mental illness. Whether undertaken by Séguin (1846), Barr (1904), Kanner (1964), Lewis (1961) or Scheerenberger (1983), historical accounts appear as presentistic,[1] and yet a contextualised historical analysis should offer an unique opportunity to study the combined operation of concepts such as cognition, mental disorder, development, and psychometry.[2] Indeed, on a wider canvas, it may even throw light on the history of child psychiatry (Walk, 1964), infantile psychosis (Gineste, 1983) and the vexed question of the definition of man as a rational or cognitive being.[3] Most of this work has not yet been carried out, so this chapter will limit itself to mapping the process whereby the concept of mental retardation was constructed in European psychiatric thinking during the first half of the nineteenth century. Historical changes before the 1860s will be barely mentioned.

Matters historiographical

The biographical approach has been extensively used in this context, and the ghosts of Pereira, Itard, Esquirol, Belhomme, Guggenbühl, Séguin, Howe, and Morel, comfortably inhabit most of the historical works mentioned above. This technique, however, works only when it avoids anachronistic interpretation: otherwise, as in Séguin's book,[4] it can be unduly harsh with earlier figures because no attempt is made to determine the boundary conditions within which they made their claims.

Likewise, little effort is made to separate the history of: 1. the words used for naming phenomena (semantic history), 2. the behaviours in question (behavioural palaeontology), and 3. the concepts created throughout the ages to understand such behaviours (conceptual history). Confusing these three levels has led to historical error such as the claim that it was Esquirol who first *distinguished* idiocy from dementia (Scheerenberger, 1983). The assumption behind the historical approach suggested here is that, whatever the name or conceptual interpretation used, the behaviours in question – because they are biologically determined – have existed for a long time (Rushton, 1988). History tells that their *medicalisation* probably started by the seventeenth century, and their *psychiatrisation* by the nineteenth. This is probably the reason why Esquirol – who was writing from the point of view of mental alienism – is credited with creating the notion of idiocy.

This brief historiographical excursion is meant to provide some conceptual tools with which the early nineteenth century debate on the boundaries of mental retardation can be usefully analysed.

Mental retardation before the 19th century

Clear operational distinctions between idiocy and dementia have, in fact, existed since before the nineteenth century. For example, they were used by Medieval Courts where idiocy is associated with qualifiers such as congenital and irreversible. By the seventeenth century, legal definitions even included tests (based on the assessment of everyday behaviour, such as handling money) to decide on the level of mental retardation. From a medical viewpoint, these definitions were first sharpened by Thomas Willis, and later by Vicenzo Chiarurgi (1987), both of whom distinguished between insanity, dementia, and mental retardation. There was also an awareness that the latter was congenital and irreversible (James, 1991).

Cullen

To understand recent changes in the meaning of mental retardation one must take up the story at the time of Cullen whose class II, neuroses had as its Order IV the Vesaniae, defined as: 'lesions of the judging faculty without fever or coma'. This rubric included four genera: Amentia, Melancholia, Mania, and Oneirodynia. Amentia, the category relevant to mental retardation, was defined as: 'imbecility of the judging faculty with inability to perceive or remember', and classified into three species: congenital, senile, and acquired – the latter two corresponding roughly to dementia. Under Amentia, Cullen brought together a number of eighteenth century nosological categories: Amentia, Stupidity, Morosis and Fatuity (Vogel), Amentia and Amnesia (Sauvages and Sagar), and Morosis and

Oblivio (Linne).[5] Amentia congenita is particularly important to the subsequent history of mental retardation because it was specifically defined by Cullen 'as a condition present from birth and which included Amentia morosis and microcephala, both types of idiocy'. Indeed, the Latin term amentia was translated into the vernacular by Cullen's students as folly or idiotism.

French views
Pinel

Apart from being the translator of one of the French versions of Cullen's Nosology,[6] Pinel composed a Nosography himself. His Class IV, Neuroses, included neuroses affecting the senses, cerebral function, locomotion, voice, nutritive function, and generation.[7] Idiotisme appears as one of the categories classified under the Névroses des fonctions cérébrales, where it is defined as an 'abolition, more or less absolute, of the functions of understanding and feeling' which may be acquired or congenital (originaire). Pinel did not deviate from this definition which he linked to the views expressed by the 'auteur of Synonymes français' on a 'échelle de graduation de la raison'. Thus, in 1801, Pinel defined ideotism as 'total or partial obliteration of the intellectual powers and affections: universal torpor: detached half articulated sounds; or entire absence of speech from want of ideas: in some cases, transient and unmeaning gusts of passion'[8] and continued defending the view that it was acquired or congenital. The same was repeated in the second and last edition of the Traité.[9]

Thus, Pinel's conception of idiotism can be described as fully medical (for example, it was included in his nosography), psychiatric (it featured together with mania, melancholia and dementia), and based upon his notion of disorder of reason or the intellectual faculty.[10] Like Cullen (he also considered idiotism as a synonym of Amentia), Pinel proposed that this condition may be either acquired or congenital. However, for the first time, he used the word Démence (Berrios, 1987) to refer to Cullen's acquired amentias, and included a discussion of cretins which shows his awareness of the variety of cases that might fall under the category idiotism.

Esquirol

This great French alienist had the advantage of writing in the context of the much reduced psychiatric nosological system created by Pinel, and in the wake of the French Revolution, whose progressism required that the distinction between idiocy and dementia (as we have seen already present in Cullen) was emphasised. In his later writings on L'idiote, Esquirol seems, however, to have been influenced by Georget (see below), although he does not mention him by name. Thus, whilst in his 1814 and 1817 entries to the Panckoucke dictionary,[11] Esquirol stated that mental retardation was a disease, for their 1828 reprinting he made important changes, the most important being, perhaps, his criticism of the célébre professeur Pinel for 'not distinguishing between idiocy and dementia' and his claim that: 'idiocy is not a disease but a state in which the intellectual faculties are never manifested or developed for lack of education'. In spite of the fact that chronology indicates that the developmental view originated in Georget, it is difficult to be positive about the origin of this idea. After all, the young man – who was close to his teacher (he is said to have died in Esquirol's arms) could have borrowed it from him. Esquirol seems also to have left a door open to the possibility, in some cases, of mental retardation resulting from pure cultural influence: for example, he discusses this in relation to the cagots[12] who were supposed to have a higher rate of mentally retarded children.

Esquirol (1838) provided a psychological account of dementia and idiocy. Influenced by faculty psychology, he considered the latter as a disorder of intellect, and hence, as a problem with which alienists ought to be concerned. He did not, however, consider idiocy as a form of insanity (folie) for the latter condition was, at the time, narrowly defined in terms of délire.[13] Esquirol, however, saw no difficulty in considering it as a mental illness (maladie mentale). This did not reflect therapeutic pessimism: indeed, imbued by the optimism of the French Revolution, he had encouraged Itard in his quest to educate the boy of Aveyron.[14]

But those who followed Esquirol, particularly after the 1850s, when the doctrine of degeneration began to take hold,[15] did not share in his optimism. There is little doubt that it was this fatalism, and all the negative consequences it engendered, that fuelled the challenge to the view that idiocy was yet another form of mental illness. This questioning, born out of the altruism of educators, such as Séguin and others, was motivated by practical reasons as it was felt that accepting the 'psychiatric' view would lead to suffering and hardship amongst the mentally retarded. Current arguments concerning the separation between idiocy and mental illness are, therefore, redolent of those rehearsed during the nineteenth century. The problem then, as now, was not totally created by semantic confusion. There was, in fact, a substantive point, to wit, whether or not the mentally retarded were on a continuum with normal subjects. This was interpreted by some to mean that mental retardation *per se*, was not a form of mental illness although the mentally retarded, like anyone else, might develop mental illness. The fact was also known that the more severe the idiocy, the more frequent was the presence of psychiatric or neurological disease.

Georget and the developmental hypothesis

An important departure from the 'disease concept' took place in 1820 when Georget defined idiocy as 'failure in the development of the intellectual faculties'. Aware of his own originality Georget went on to state: 'idiocy should not be made into a type of insanity (délire) for a failure to develop cannot be properly considered as a disease (maladie)' . . .'idiots must be classified as monsters (monstres)' (Georget, 1820). The expression of such unorthodox views by a man barely aged 25 at the time needs explanation, particularly as he was a disciple of Esquirol who considered idiocy and imbecility as forms of alienation mentale, and who, in general, paid little attention to the developmental aspects of mental disorder.

Onésime Edouard Séguin

By the middle of the century, French views on mental retardation had divided between those who continued supporting the medical views of Esquirol and those who, like Séguin (soon to emigrate to America) took an antimedical stance. For example, in the full review that appeared in Fabre's popular encyclopaedia,[16] the anonymous author starts its narrative with Esquirol and then quotes Belhomme and Séguin (the latter in his more medical or physiological vein). The same can be said of Guislain, another popular author of the period, who in his Leçons accepted the conventional distinction between idiots and imbeciles but also argued that he saw no reason to make of this group and different variety of mental illness.[17] Views on mental retardation during this period, however, are dominated by the work of Séguin.

A rather controversial figure, a lawyer turned educator and then physician, Séguin was also interested in metrication and thermometry (Martin, 1981). After siding with the republicains de la veille in the 1848 revolution, he felt (groundlessly) insecure in the France of Louis Napoleon and escaped to the USA in 1850. The first account of his work with idiots appeared in 1838 in joined authorship with Esquirol (Résumé de ce que nous avons fait pendant 14 mois). He claimed that he had found 'in his soul the resources' needed to develop a theory which was not only important for 'idiocy but for education'. It is unlikely, however, that these ideas were original (Kraft, 1961). Likewise, for all his aggressive comments on the medical approach,[18] he remained ambivalent on the question of whether mental retardation was a form of mental illness.[19]

The medical view, however, remained unaltered. For example, Foville

(1874) repeated the old concepts except that, under the new Morelean banner, emphasised the degenerative taint. The same can be said of Chambard (1888) who confirmed the medical approach, and stated that both idiocy and imbecility should be discussed under the rubric of mental dysgenesis. Thus, it is not surprising that when Ball (1890) published his great work on mental disorder he called these states morphological insanities (folies morphologiques).

German views
Hoffbauer

During the first half of the nineteenth century, Hoffbauer[20] dealt with the issue of legal responsibility in the mentally retarded and the deaf and dumb. He considered feeble-mindedness (Verstandschwäche) as a form of pathology of intellect which could affect its level (imbecility – Blödsinn) or extension (stupidity – Dummheit). Both subtypes, in turn, could be congenital or acquired; in other words, mental retardation proper or dementia.[21]

Heinroth

Heinroth[22] made idiocy (anoia) into a Genus of mental disorder (Störungen des Seelenlebens) and divided it into four subtypes. He characterised idiocy as a disorder in which: 'the senses, especially the higher senses, cannot comprehend or grasp, and the intellect cannot collect any ideas from the sensations. The spirit is quite empty and is merely vegetating. The animal feelings and instincts, such as hunger or the sexual instinct, are however, stronger, and the patient can easily be excited into anger, which may become rage...'.[23] The distinction between the four subtypes of idiocy was made in terms of accompanying symptoms: anoia simplex was the pure form; anoia melancholica, was accompanied by agitation and partial insight into the condition; anoia abyole, by lethargy, inactivity and lack of responsiveness; and anoia catholica, which was the more severe form.

Griesinger

W. Griesinger has been described as sponsoring a nineteenth century form of unitary psychosis (Vliegen, 1980). This is because he seemed to suggest that melancholia, mania and dementia were clinical states which could appear successively in the same individual, thereby reflecting the fact that he was suffering from a disease characterised by a march of organic events starting with neurophysiological depression (Depressionszunstände) and proceeding to excitation (Exaltationszustände) to end up in weakness (Schwächezustände) (Griesinger, 1861). Idiocy fitted in well into Griesinger's clinical cascade and was made (together with chronic insanity (partielle Verrücktheit), confusion (Verwirrtheit) and stupor or terminal dementia (apathische Blödsinn) the central example of psychischen Schwächezustände. Whilst the other three states were acquired, and constituted what, nowadays, would be called the defect states, idiocy was congenital: 'By the term idiocy (Idiotismus), we understand conditions in which the state of mental weakness exists from birth or early infancy, and in which psychological development has been impeded or prevented'. Griesinger postulated a strong organic and hereditary hypothesis for such states of mental weakness, considering all social explanations as 'shallow' (flache Auffassung). His account is interesting for it shows, as it had done Cullen's the previous century that, although there was awareness of the congenital nature of mental retardation, theoretical and social considerations led to its being conflated with acquired defect states such as dementia. It also sets in perspective the relevance of Esquirol's 'discovery'.

Von Feuchtersleben

Von Feuchtersleben (1845)[24] wrote: 'Idiocy proceeds, as a psychopathy,[25] proximately from anaesthesia, weakness of attention, amnesia, and want of images. It represents, in some measure, an approximation of the human character to that of animals, and is characterized by an incapacity of judging, or even, in its higher degree, of contemplating. The alteration is more prominent in the direction of thought than in that of feeling and will, though, in the higher degrees, both feeling and will are also wanting (Abulia, Heinroth)...the lowest degree, which Hartman calls stupidity, is characterised by an incapacity of comprehending, judging, and concluding, even in affairs of what is called common sense...the higher degree, idiocy *sensu strictiori*, shows total incapacity for mental activity'. This wider definition of mental retardation includes changes in all mental functions.

British views

Prichard

James Cowles Prichard, the great British alienist and anthropologist (Stocking, 1973), wrote an important book on mental disorders in which the influence of Continental views, particularly Esquirol's, can be detected. Prichard (1835) did not consider idiotism or mental deficiency as a form of insanity, and hence treated these states in a separate chapter. Idiotism he defined as: 'a state in which the mental faculties have been wanting from birth, or have not been manifested at the period at which they are usually developed. Idiotism is an original defect, and is by this circumstance, as well as by its phenomena, distinguished from that fatuity that results from disease or from protracted age'. Prichard quotes Esquirol, Fodéré, and Georget, discusses cretinism at length, and supports Esquirol's continuity view: 'there is no exact line of demarcation between idiotism and a degree of weakness which is generally termed imbecility'; but goes one step further in linking these states to normality: 'There are different degrees and varieties of mental deficiency, which scarcely amount to what is termed either idiotism, or, in general language, imbecility. Persons so affected are commonly said to be weak in character, stupid, or of mean capacity...'.

Bucknill and Tuke (1858) also criticised Esquirol's pessimism: 'it would no longer be right to speak of the faculties of the idiot being doomed to remain stationary',[26] and found contradiction between what he lists in a table showing that decrease in the size of the heads of idiots and what he states in the text.

The second half of the nineteenth century

Views on mental retardation during the second half of the nineteenth century are characterised by a transformation of the categorical approach: for example, quantitative bridges begin to be established between normal children and the mildly retarded. This required a major change in theory. Thus, Netchine has suggested that, up to this period, whilst mental retardation itself was graded into sub categories, there was no general quantitative dimension to include the various levels of normality. This was to occur only after the important work of Sollier (1891) (sadly neglected) and that of Binet and Simon (often quoted) who introduced the first workable concept of intellectual coefficient.

Paul Sollier

Sollier trained under Bourneville at Bicêtre, and was for a while in charge of the Pathological Museum. His aim was to deal with the general psychological characteristics of idiocy rather than with specific or rare cases. He complained that writings on this category were 'poor' in France as compared with America or England. The first problem he encountered was that 'idiocy is not a clinical entity... that the idiot is an abnormal being but that its abnormality varies in many dimensions... [on the other hand] he is not a separate category but merges with the milder forms of the disorder'. To sort this out he suggests that it might be possible to 'measure their mental state by seeking to compare it to a particular age in the normal child'. Sollier finds an important obstacle: 'for this principle to apply it would be needed that the cause of idiocy was the same in each case... unfortunately this is not the case'. To collect his data, Sollier made use of a modified version of a structured interview schedule developed by Voisin (1843) which included sections on instincts, feelings and affections, perceptual functioning, psychomotor skills, intellect, and physiological and psychological functions. In spite of discussing quantification, Sollier's book includes no numerical data; indeed, it is not even clear how many cases were studied. His principles as much as his conclusions, however, are modern in outlook and break with categorical thinking, to the point that Binet and Simon did not need to think out a justification for their work.

Binet and Simon

In their classical paper of 1905,[27] these authors simply repeated Sollier's view that there was a 'need to establish a scientific (quantitative) diagnosis of the states of lower intelligence'. One year before Binet's death he published his final manifesto on the nosology of l'arriération.[28] After complaining for the way in which alienists had neglected the detailed study of these conditions, they attacked the anatomo-pathological classifications (à la Bourneville)[29] and also Sollier's suggestion that imbecility was not accompanied by brain pathology. They reaffirmed the value of quantitative groupings but criticised Régis and Kraepelin for not providing adequate operational definitions. Finally, Binet and Simon commented negatively on suggestions by psychologists that only one mental function was primarily disorder in mental handicap, stating that, in fact, all are. During the 1930s new ingredients were added to the definition, particularly Lewis's (1933) notion of 'subcultural deficiency'. Current views, well reflected in the criteria of DSM III-R, include quantitative criteria, genetics, physical disability, behavioural adaptation, and social competence. This form of Chinese menu system has improved the reliability of the descriptors but does not guarantee validity nor does it offer a theory to unify the various strands involved in the clinical expression of mental retardation. What is worse, it does not offer a conceptual framework to tackle the question: is mental retardation a form of mental illness?

Summary

The view that mental retardation was a defect of intellectual function different from insanity or dementia became well established during the first half of the nineteenth century. It was also during this period that mental retardation became burdened with an important ambiguity, the question of whether it was a form of mental illness. This was not only due to definitional confusions. In fact, encouraged by the semantic logic of faculty psychology, and the categorical view of idiocy, nineteenth century alienists felt entitled to claim that most forms of mental retardation were diseases. But following protestations by educators and antimedical men such as Séguin, a compromise developed during the second half of the century which suggested a human variation type of continuum between normality, imbecility and idiocy (leading to the claim that members of the latter two groups could not be considered as mentally ill). This hypothesis was heuristic in that it encouraged the development of a quantitative view which first with Sollier, and then Binet and Simon, led to the creation of the abstract notion of intellectual coefficient. Since early in the nineteenth century, however, there had also been awareness of the possibility that the frequency of neurological and psychiatric pathology increased *pari passu* with the depth of the mental retardation. The tensions that this observation created within the continuum model were not solved during the 19th century, and might not have been alleviated even today.

Notes

1 By 'presentistic' is meant here a form of historiography that describes events chronologically and as relentlessly progressive, i.e. it makes the assumption that the most recent development is necessarily superior. It has also been called by Herbert Butterfield 'the Whig interpretation of history'.

2 On this see the penetrating study: Netchine, G. (1973). Idiotas, débiles y sabios en el siglo XIX. In Zazzo, R. (ed.) *Los débiles mentales*, Fontanella, Barcelona, pp. 77–117 (translation of *Les débilités mentales*, Colin, Paris, 1969). See also Pichot, P. (1948). French pioneers in the field of mental deficiency. *American Journal of Mental Deficiency* **53**, 128–37; Lang, J. L. (1965). Situation de l'infance handicapée. *Esprit*, **33**, 588–99; and Mahendra, B. (1985). Subnormality revisited in early 19th century France. *Journal of Mental Deficiency*, 29, 391–401.

3 See, for example, Sir Frederic Bateman's evocative title: *The Idiot; his Place in Creation and his Claims on Society*, 2nd Ed., London, Jarrold & Sons; or the debate initiated by Georget that the mentally handicapped were a type of monster: Georget E. J. (1820) *De la Folie. Considérations sur cette maladie*, Paris, Crevot. On the concept of monster and its relationship to the definition of man, see: Davaine, C. (1874) Monstres. Monstruosité. In Dechambre, A. & Lereboullet, L. (eds.) *Dictionnaire encyclopédique des sciences médicales*, vol. 61, Paris, Masson, pp. 201–264. After the 1860s, the notion of monstrosity became entangled with degeneration theory: see Talbot, E. S. (1898). *Degeneracy, its Causes, Signs and Results*. London, Walter Scott, Ltd. The same ideological background inspired the debate on a classification of idiots based upon the physiognomic features of the 'great Caucasian family' which led to the coining of mongolism: see Down, J. L. (1866). Observations on an ethnic classification of idiots. *London Hospital Reports*, **3**, 259–62.

4 See Séguin, 1846, *op. cit.* The English version of this rare book, carried out by Séguin and his son for the American market (*Idiocy: and its Treatment by the*

Physiological Method, New York, William Wood & Co., 1866) did not include a large and telling section entitled: Définitions de l'Idiotie antérieures a mes travaux (pp. 23–71), in which the French writer describes and criticises earlier definitions and classifications.

5 Cullen, W. (1803). *Synopsis nosologiae methodicae*. Edinburgh, W. Creech. Cullen's contemporaries were already aware of the fact that his category Amentia resulted from lumping together a number of previous disparate clinical states. For example, the great Italian nosologist Chiarugi stated: 'in his nosology, Cullen combined them in the same way' (Chiarurgi, 1987, *op. cit.*).

6 Cullen, W. (1785). *Institutions de médicine pratique*. 2 vols, French Translation of Ph. Pinel, Paris, Duplain. This translation seems to have been a financial failure due, apparently, to the fact that E. Bosquillon, the Royal lecturer, published another the same year.

7 Pinel, Ph. (1818). *Nosographie Philosophique ou la méthode de l'analyse appliquée à la médicine. Paris, vol 1, 6th ed., J. A. Brosson (First Edition 1798)*.

8 Pinel, Ph. (1806). *A Treatise of Insanity*. (translation of D. D. Davis), Sheffield, W. Tood, p. 172, (First edition: (1801) (Year IX)) *Traité médico-philosophique sur l'aliénation mentale ou la manie*. Paris, Richard, Caille et Ravier.

9 Pinel Ph. (1809). *Traité médico-philosophique sur l'aliénation mentale*. Paris, Brosson, pp. 181–190

10 Although influenced by Cabanis and the French ideologues, Pinel used a common sense form of faculty psychology which he is likely to have borrowed from Dugald Stewart. On Pinel's psychological influences see Riese, W. (1969). *The Legacy of Philippe Pinel*, New York, Springer; Staum, M. (1980). *Cabanis*, Princeton, Princeton University Press; Postel, J. (1981). *Genèse de la Psychiatrie*, Paris, Le Sycomore; d'Istria, F. C. (1926). La Psychologie de Bichat. *Revue de Metaphysique et de Morale*, **23**, 1–38.

11 Esquirol first dealt with the notions of idiotism and imbécillité in 1814, in the context of démence (*Dictionnaire des sciences médicales*, Paris Panckoucke, vol 8, pp. 280–294) where he quotes Pinel, 1809, op. cit.:'dementia should not be confused with imbecility or idiotism. The faculty of reasoning in the imbecile is undeveloped and weak; the dement has lost his... idiots and cretins are not able to have sensations, memory or judgement and show only few animal instincts; their external shape shows that they are not organised to think' (p. 284). In the same entry, he stated that imbécillité was a species of aliénation mentale. The entry on Idiotisme appeared in the same dictionary in 1817 and was to be reprinted in an expanded form in 1838 (*Des maladies mentales considérées sous les rapports médical, hygiénique et médico-légal*. vol. 2, Paris, Baillière, pp. 283–397).

12 Les cagots, referred to by Michel as one of the accursed races (races maudites), include groups of peoples who, since the Medieval period, were ostracised into various areas of Northern Spain and Western France, and forbidden to enter into social contact with the rest of the population (see Lagneau G. (1869) Cagots. In Dechambre A. & Lereboullet L. (eds.) *Dictionnaire encyclopédique des sciences medicales*, vol. 11, Paris, Masson (pp. 534–557). Whether through inbreeding or social isolation and lack of education, it is claimed that mental retardation was highly prevalent in this group. Esquirol claims that this improved once their ostracism ended (pp. 370–372).

13 The French term délire (like the German Wahn) names a complex psychiatric phenomenon which is not totally rendered into English by the word 'delusion'. This has caused much difficulty over the years.

14 Nothing else will be said in this chapter about the boy of Aveyron and its relevance to the conceptual debate on idiocy and its treatment in early nineteenth century France. Particularly important works on this topic are: Malson, L. (1964). *Les Enfants Sauvages*. Paris, Union Générale d'Editions; Lane, H. (1977). *The Wild Boy of Aveyron*. London, George Allen & Unwin; Sánchez, R. (1982) Comentarios del Traductor. In *Jean Itard, Victor de L'Aveyron*. Madrid, Alianza, pp. 99–251); and Swain, G. (1976). The Wild boy of Aveyron de H. Lane. *L'evolution psychiatrique*, **41**, 995–1011.

15 The notion of degeneration was introduced into psychiatry by Morel in 1857. Literature on this topic is now very large; for three different historical approaches see: Genil-Perrin, G. (1913). *Histoire des origines et de l'évolution de l'idée de dégénérescence en médicine mentale*. Paris, A. Leclerc; Huertas, R. (1987). *Locura y degeneración: psiquiatria y sociedad en el positivismo francés*. Madrid, Consejo Superior de Investigaciones Cientificas; Pick, D. (1989) *Faces of Degeneration: A European Disorder, c1848–1918*. Cambridge, Cambridge University Press.

16 pp. 553–576 in Fabre, J. (ed.) (1849). *Bibliothéque du médicin-practicien*, vol. 9, Paris, J. B. Baillière.

17 p. 343 in Guislain, J. (1852). *Leçons orales sur les phrénopathies*, vol. 1, Gand, Hebbelynck.

18 He started his medical training only in 1843, and had to quit the Bicêtre Hospital after entering into conflict with its physicians. His writings on the education of the idiot were praised by the Académie des Sciences and ignored by the Académie de Médicine. This may partly explain his antimedical stance (see Martin, 1961, op. cit.) Likewise, Séguin was displeased about a certificate issued by Esquirol & Guersant: 'The undersigned have the pleasure of acknowledging that Mr Séguin has started with success the training of a child almost mute and seemingly retarded ...' The use of the word 'seemingly' irked Séguin who felt that this betrayed Esquirol's belief in the incurability of idiocy (p. 14, Séguin, 1846, *op. cit*). In the same work, Séguin mounted a savage attack on Esquirol and his disinterest in idiocy (see. pp. 24–30 in Séguin, 1846, *op. cit*.). This text was omitted from the American translation: Séguin E. (1866). *Idiocy and its Treatment by the Physiological Method*. New York, Wood & Company.

19 For example he wrote: 'I hereby formally accuse physicians ... of having confused idiocy with other analogous chronic conditions, of confusing it with concomitant pathological states that are not part or consequence of idiocy, of not dedicating sufficient time to their study ...'. Séguin goes on to say that physicians entertain too theoretical a view, that their definitions are negative, and that there is too much emphasis on the intellectual defect. (pp. 69–71 in Séguin, 1846, op. cit.)

20 J. C. Hoffbauer (1766–1827) was a professor of Philosophy and Law at Halle University from which he had to retire early on account of deafness. He collaborated with the German alienist Reil.

21 See pp. 42–85 Hoffbauer, J. C. (1827). *Médicine légale relative aux aliénés et aux sourds-muets ou les lois appliquées aux désordres de l'intelligence* (translated by A. M. Chambeyron with notes by Esquirol and Itard) Paris, Bailliere (First German Edition 1808) This curious translation includes frequent critical notes from both translator, a disciple of Esquirol, and the great man himself which clearly misses the point of Hoffbauer's work by deriding his efforts to carry out a psychological analysis, in terms of Faculty Psychology, of the subtypes of feeblemindedness (see, for example, pp. 43–44). Instead, Chambeyron and

Esquirol wanted clinical and frequential analyses of the phenomena involved, tasks which were irrelevant to Hoffbauer's brief. A useful historical point, however, is made in a table comparing Hoffbauer's classification of mental disorder with French views; it is therein concluded that: 'imbecility, idiocy and dementia are confused by the Germans under the general heading of feeblemindedness which they divide into imbecility and stupor'. It was, perhaps, wrong of the footnoters to generalise to all 'Germans' alienists as others, such as Heinroth (see below), had a different view.

22 Historical misreading has created the myth that Heinroth believed that 'the ultimate cause of mental disturbance is sin' (see p. 141 in Alexander, F. G. & Selesnick, S. T. (1966). *The History of Psychiatry*. New York, Harper and Row). For a timely correction see Cauwenbergh, L. (1991). J. Chr. A. Heinroth (1773–1843): psychiatrist of the German Romantic era. *History of Psychiatry*, **2**, 365–83.

23 p. 195 of Heinroth, J. C. (1975). *Textbook of Disturbances of Mental Life. Or Disturbances of the Soul and their Treatment*. Vol. 11, Baltimore, Johns Hopkins University Press (First German Edition 1818).

24 Feuchtersleben Baron von, E. (1845). *Lehrbuch der ärztlichen Seelenkunde*. Wien, Carl Gerold (English translation by H. E. Lloyd and B. G. Babington (1847). *The Principles of Medical Psychology*, London, Sydenham Society).

25 A clarification is indicated here: circa 1845, the term 'psychopathy' simply meant mental disorder and had nothing to do with the usage it was to acquire after 1890 (on this see Berrios, G. E. (1993). European views on personality disorders: a conceptual history. *Comprehensive Psychiatry* **34**, 14–30.

26 p. 93 in Bucknill & Tuke, 1858, *op. cit.*

27 Binet, A. & Simon, Th. (1905). Sur la nécessité d'établir un diagnostic scientifique des états inférieurs de l'intelligence. *L'année psychologique*, **11**, 163–90. Binet has received far more attention than Simon. For a general introduction see: Wolf, T. H. (1973). *Alfred Binet*. Chicago, Chicago University Press.

28 Binet, A. & Simon, Th. (1910). L'Arriération. *L'année psychologique*, **16**, 349–60.

29 Désiré Magloire Bourneville (1840–1909), a protégé of Charcot's, spent most of his creative career at Bicêtre, where he became the leading French specialist in mental retardation.

References

Ball, B. (1890). *Leçons sur les maladies mentales*. 2nd ed., Paris, Asselin et Houzeau (first edition 1880) p. 934.

Barr, M. W. (1904). *Mental Defectives, their History, Treatment and Training*. Philadelphia: Blackiston's Son & Co.

Berrios, G. E. (1987). Dementia during the seventeenth and eighteenth centuries: a conceptual history. *Psychological Medicine*, **17**, 829–37.

Chambard, E. (1888). Idiotie. In A. Dechambre & L. Lereboullet (eds). *Dictionnaire encyclopédique des sciences médicales*, vol. 51, pp. 507–527. Paris: Masson.

Chiarurgi, V. (1987). *On Insanity and its Classification*, Translation of G. Mora, Canton, Watson, p. 230 (1st edn. 1793, Della Pazzia in genere, e in specie. Trattato medicoanalitico. Firenze, Luigi Carlieri).

Esquirol, E. (1838). *Des maladies mentales considérées sous les rapports médical, hygiénique et médico-légal*. Paris: Baillière.

Foville, A. fils (1874). Idiotie, Imbecillité. In B. Anger *et al.* (eds.), *Noveau dictionnaire de médicine et de chirurgie pratiques*, vol. 18, pp. 363–375. Paris: Baillière.

Georget, E. J. (1820). *De la Folie*, Paris: Crevot.

Gineste, T. (1983). Naissance de la psychiatrie infantile (destins de l'idiote, origine des psychoses). In J. Postel & C. Quetel (eds.). *Nouvelle histoire de la psychiatrie*. pp. 499–516. Paris: Privat.

Griesinger, W. (1861). *Die pathologie und therapie der psychischen krankheiten* pp. 22–59. Stuttgart: Krabbe (1st edn 1845).

James, F. E. (1991). Some observations on the writings of Felix Platter (1539–1614) in relation to mental handicap. *History of Psychiatry*, **2**, 103–8.

Kanner, L. (1964). *A History of the Care and Study of the Mentally Retarded.* Charles C. Thomas, Illinois: Springfield.

Kraft, I. (1961). Edouard Séguin and the 19th century moral treatment of idiots. *Bulletin of the History of Medicine*, **35**, 393–418.

Lewis, A. (1961). The study of defect. *American Journal of Psychiatry*, **117**, 289–305.

Lewis, E. O. (1933). Types of mental deficiency and their social significance. *Journal of Mental Science*, **79**, 298–304.

Martin, J. (1981). Une biographie française (1812–1850) d'Onésime Édouard Séguin, premier thérapeute des enfants arriérés, d'aprés ses écrits et les documents historiques. *Thus de médecine*, Saint Antoine, Paris.

Neugebauer, R. (1989). A doctor's dilemma: the case of William Harvey's mentally retarded nephew. *Psychological Medicine*, **19**, 569–72.

Prichard, J. C. (1835). *A Treatise on Insanity*. pp. 318–327. London: Sherwood, Gilbert and Piper.

Rushton, P. (1988). Lunatics and idiots: mental disability, the community, and the poor law in North-East England, 1600–1800. *Medical History*, **32**, 34–50.

Scheerenberger, R. C. (1983). *A History of Mental Retardation.* Baltimore: Brookes.

Séguin, E. (1846). *Traitement moral, hygiéne et éducation des idiots et des autres enfants arriérés.* Paris, Baillière.

Sollier, P. (1891). *Psychologie de l'idiot et de l'imbécile.* Paris, Alcan.

Stocking, G. W. (1973). Introduction. In J. C. Prichard, *Researches into the Physical History of Man*, pp. ix–cvxiii, Chicago: Chicago University Press.

Voisin, F. (1843). *De l'idiotie chez les enfants.* Paris, Baillière.

Vliegen, J. (1980). *Die Einheitspsychose. Geschichte und Problem.* Stuttgart: Enke.

Walk, A. (1964). The pre-history of child psychiatry. *British Journal of Psychiatry*, **110**, 754–67.

2

Mental retardation and mental health: concepts, aetiology and incidence

LUDWIK S. SZYMANSKI

Introduction

A considerable amount of professional time and writing has been spent on discussions as to whether people with mental retardation can have mental disorders, how one can define such disorders in this population, and what types of disorders are encountered. Yet, we rarely pause and ask ourselves why this should be an issue at all. It is accepted, without much discussion that, for example, persons who are deaf may also, have mental disorders, like everyone else. What is special, then, about mental retardation, in this respect?

This chapter will be devoted primarily to the discussion of this dilemma: the concept of comorbidity of mental disorder and mental retardation. This is not only a theoretical, but also a practical issue. One of the most common questions posed to a consultant psychiatrist is whether a disturbed person who has mental retardation has a mental illness or merely a 'behaviour' problem. In fact, only those judged to have the former are usually referred for a psychiatric consultation. Thus the clarification of the concept of the interrelationship of mental retardation and mental illness may have implications for provision of health services and for planning social policy for people with mental retardation. For instance, many community residences refuse to accept clients labelled as having a mental disorder, but will accept persons with 'behaviour disorders'. To accommodate these new market demands, specialised group homes for 'the dually diagnosed' are being developed in some localities.

In the recent two decades the issue of mental illness in persons who have also mental retardation has been given increasing attention. There are at least two reasons for this. First, it is part of the general recognition of the right of people with mental retardation to appropriate medical care. In the past, it was common for a person with mental retardation behaving in a manner unacceptable to the caregivers, to be given large doses of psychotropics (usually antipsychotics), without concern about diagnosis, side effects or follow-up. Fortunately, such practice is not accepted any more, and appropriate medical assessment, diagnosis and follow up (although not necessarily by a psychiatrist), are usually required. Secondly, following the normalisation principles (Wolfensberger, 1972), persons with mental retardation are expected to live in the community and to use community facilities. Disturbed behaviours are one of the main (if not the main) reasons of the failure of their integration into the community.

The problems of integrating the concepts of mental retardation and mental illness

Problems with the definitions

Mental retardation as a mental disorder

The Diagnostic and Statistical Manual of Mental Disorders, 3rd edn., Revised (DSM III R) (APA 1987), as well as other classifications, list mental retardation as a mental disorder. Obviously, mental retardation is different from the 'standard' mental illnesses. It is, rather, a description of a developmental state, characterised by functioning below a certain arbitrarily defined level. It has been called an 'administrative concept' (Rutter, 1975), yet listing mental retardation as a mental disorder has been sometimes a source of confusion for mental health practitioners. It had been quite common that retarded patients referred because of definite psychopathology, would receive only the diagnosis of mental retardation, since the clinician would not know how to assess a person with limited intelligence and language. The diagnosis of mental retardation (listed by the earlier *Diagnostic and Statistical Manual of Mental Disorders*, 3rd edn. (DSM III) (1980) on Axis I (major mental disorders), was a convenient way to satisfy a requirement for making some diagnosis. This practice has been markedly diminished since in the DSM III R the diagnosis of mental retardation was transferred to Axis II (personality and developmental disorders), thus putting more pressure on the professionals to make separately a statement about Axis I diagnosis.

Overlap in the definitions

One of the major problems confounding the concepts of mental illness and mental retardation is that both, to a large extent, are recognised by their behavioural symptoms. In the past no differentiation was made between mental illness and mental retardation. However, in the eighteenth century, Locke noted, 'In short, herein lies the difference between retarded persons and madmen: that madmen put the wrong ideas together and so make erroneous propositions, but argue and reason rightly from them: but retarded persons make very few or no propositions and reason scarcely at all' (quoted by Szymanski & Crocker, 1989). The earliest definitions of mental retardation were based on retarded persons' lack of ability to perform tasks expected for their age. This approach is still the centre of the current definitions. While there is no 'standard' definition of mental illness, the *Diagnostic and Statistical Manual of Mental Disorders*, 3rd edn., Revised (APA, 1987), conceptualises mental disorders as '...a clinically significant behavioural or psychological syndrome or pattern that occurs in a person and that is associated with present distress (a painful symptom) or disability (impairment in one or more important areas of functioning)...'. The diagnostic criteria for mental retardation in the same manual include significantly subaverage general intellectual functioning, deficits in adaptive functioning and onset before the age of 18. Thus, in summary although these definitions do not say it explicitly, mental retardation seems to be conceptualised as a condition in which the level of behavioural and psychological processes is below what is expected (for person's age and background), while in the mental disorders the quality of these processes is impaired. These differences cannot be, however, so simplified in all cases. In many mental disorders the level of cognitive functioning may be impaired as well and in some, such as in dementia, its deterioration is the primary feature.

Largely due to this definition overlap, many psychiatrists regarded all unusual behavioural patterns of persons with mental retardation as part and parcel of mental retardation, due to 'organicity' (Philips, 1966).

Professionals' ignorance of mental retardation

The second obstacle to the acceptance of the concept of mental disorder in persons with mental retardation has been the ignorance of mental health professionals, including psychiatrists. This, however, was not always so, as noted in a historical reviews of the roles of psychiatry in mental retardation (Donaldson & Menolascino, 1977). In the middle of the last century, the care of persons with mental retardation was considered to be part of psychiatry's responsibilities. Later, most of the psychiatrists lost interest in mental retardation. In part, this was due to the therapeutic pessimism that followed the developments in neuropathology (which saw mental retardation as an incurable brain disorder), and in part to domination of psychiatry by psychoanalysis, that saw normal intellectual and language abilities as a prerequisite to the success of psychoanalytic treatment. Mental retardation virtually vanished from the psychiatric training curricula and generations of psychiatrists did not see patients with mental retardation at all, or at the most for administrative purposes or to prescribe medication to make them more docile. Thus the progress in psychiatry, including better understanding, diagnosis and treatment of mental disorders, did not include persons who were functioning below normal developmental level.

On the other hand, there were always some psychiatrists who were interested in mental retardation from the psychiatric point of view. In the United States, already at the end of the last century Hurd (1888), writing about 'imbecility with insanity' recognised that mental illness can coexist with mental retardation. In the early part of this century quite a number of studies were published on mental health issues of persons with mental retardation. For instance, Lowrey (1928), pointed out that behaviour problems of children with mental retardation and of children with normal intelligence, do not differ. In the 1920s, Howard Potter started his crusade for psychiatrists' involvement with people with mental retardation, and the recognition of their mental health needs. Although mental retardation, related topics have been gradually included in psychiatric training curricula, there is still a shortage of trained psychiatrists to work in this field (American Psychiatric Association, 1991).

Difficulties in the diagnosis of mental disorders in persons with mental retardation

Traditionally psychiatric diagnosis is based to a considerable extent on the evaluation of psychological processes, emotions and affect. This is mostly done through direct communication with the patients, who thus need to have language skills sufficient for such communication, as well as cognitive skills enabling some degree of conceptual thinking. Many lower functioning persons with mental retardation will have difficulties with such communication, making psychiatric diagnosis difficult, especially of the more specific disorder subtypes. For instance, Reid (1972) found that, while one could diagnose a subtype of psychosis in individuals with verbal communications and mild mental retardation, this was not possible in persons with non-verbal communication. These difficulties are parallel to those encountered with younger children. In fact, until recently, it was not recognised that children could suffer of certain mental disorders, especially depression. However, now the DSM III-R permits substitution of caregivers' observations of depressed mood (and other symptoms) for the patients' subjective reports. Still, many psychiatrists feel uncomfortable making a psychiatric diagnosis on a non-verbal patient. (This topic is further discussed in Part II.)

Behaviour–mental illness dichotomy

Many professionals in mental retardation and some in mental health fields tend to divide persons who have mental retardation and also appear to be disturbed, into those who have 'behaviour' problems and those who have mental, or 'psychiatric' illness. No satisfactory definitions of these entities have been established. Usually, by 'behavioural' it is meant that the behaviours in question are a learned response, such as to environmental situation, caregivers' management, etc. In fact, such division is not justified nor necessary. The DSM III-R describes mental disorder as a '... behavioural or psychological syndrome'. Thus its manifestations can be behavioural and/or psychological. Furthermore, the DSM III-R is '... atheoretical with regard to etiology or pathophysiologic process...' (p. XXIII). The aetiology of a disorder is not a part of its definition, except for disorders in which it is well established (such as organic mental disorders or adjustment disorders). Thus there is no basis for dichotomising 'behaviours' and psychiatric illness. If the diagnostic criteria for a certain mental disorder are met, the diagnosis is justified. The more appropriate question should be, of which recognised mental disorder syndrome are the behaviours in question a part? The DSM III-R also includes a number of disorders which could be called 'monosymptomatic', characterised by a single symptom (such as stereotypy/habit disorder, or impulse control disorders). For unusual clinical presentations, the Not Otherwise Specified categories can also be used.

Theoretical underpinnings of diagnostic controversies

While the DSM III-R is descriptive and atheoretical, for some pro-fessionals the psychiatric diagnosis is linked to their view of the aetiology of the disorder in question. Thus it will be difficult for them to diagnose a disorder in a situation in which, according to their beliefs, such disorder could not arise (even if its clinical manifestations are seen). For example, psychoanalytically rooted clinicians may find it difficult to diagnose a mental disorder caused, in their opinion, by failed defence mechanisms against an internal conflict, if they do not believe that a person has sufficient intelligence to develop such conflict. For instance, it had been once proposed that persons with mental retardation could not develop depression, since their low intelligence prevented them from perceiving their deficiencies and developing low self esteem. (An opposing view held that all people with mental retardation experienced maternal rejection owing to their retardation and thus all had to be depressed.) No data support such views. In the other camp, many behaviourists see all behaviours of persons with mental retardation as simply learned and 'attention getting' and oppose the use of psychiatric diagnoses.

These controversies are not only theoretical, but have also practical implications. Since certain schools of thought are often associated with certain disciplines, acceptance of one of them may mean that treatment of mental disorders (or 'behaviours') is the province of a particular discipline, which in turn should get increased staffing, funding, etc. This is well illustrated by the following episode:

Some years ago this author was given the responsibility of organising psychiatric services in a large, old-fashioned state institution for persons with mental retardation. In their first meeting, the institution's medical director announced that the psychiatrists will be, of course, responsible only for prescribing psychotropic drugs, since the psychologists are customarily responsible for 'behaviours'. The psychiatrist's answer that he would follow an interdisciplinary, collaborative approach, was met with disbelief, equal to the disbelief 15 years later, when the medical director was reminded of this episode.

On the other hand, e.g. a pronouncement that a patient (usually a difficult one) has a mental illness and not 'behaviour' problems may mean that the treatment (and its failure) should be the responsibility of a psychiatrist. This is, of course, a moot issue for modern mental health professionals who utilise an interdisciplinary team approach, in which several disciplines collaborate and share the responsibility.

Aetiology

There is no reason to expect that mental disorders comorbid with mental retardation have different aetiologies from the same disorders in a person with normal intelligence. Furthermore, the final clinical presentation and its severity, especially the functional disability and subjective distress, cannot simply be seen as the result of a single aetiology, even if such can be found. Rather, it is a result of an interaction between many contributing factors and mechanisms, which ultimately determine the person's psychosocial adaptation. This can be exemplified in a case of a person with mental retardation due to congenital rubella, who was referred because of severe self-injurious behaviour (SIB). While the rubella virus was the original aetiological factor, the SIB could be due to, or at least be modified by, the following factors: sensory isolation (due to blindness and deafness), degree of retardation and lack of communicative language, presence of a mood or psychotic disorder, responses of caregivers to the SIB, etc.

These mechanisms are well illustrated by the scheme developed by Garrard and Richmond (1965) and modified by Szymanski (1980). According to it, three groups of factors: biological, psychological and sociocultural continuously interact with each other and jointly determine the ultimate psychosocial adaptation of the individual, in a continuously changing, transactional mechanism. Its elements will be reviewed briefly.

Biological factors

Brain dysfunction that results in mental retardation might also predispose the individual to a mental disorder (Szymanski, Rubin & Tarjan, 1989). Some mental retardation syndromes are known to be associated with behavioural aberrations and psychopathology. Fragile X syndrome has been described to be associated with pervasive developmental disorders (Meryash, Szymanski, Gerald, 1982; Brown *et al.*, 1982; Gillberg & Wahlstrom, 1985), although this connection has been disputed (Einfield, Molony & Hall, 1989; Piven *et al.*, 1991). Persons with fragile-X often tend to exhibit behavioural patterns such as self-injury, overactivity and tendency to anxiety. Self-injury is a characteristic feature of certain congenital syndromes associated with mental retardation especially the Lesch–Nyhan syndrome (Harris, in press). Congenital rubella syndrome has been associated with attention-deficit like presentation and autistic disorder. Seizure disorders, increased with mental retardation, may be associated with psychopathology. Physical handicaps may lead to low self-image and psychological and behavioural defences against it. Medications may also have behavioural side effects, e.g. methylphenidate may cause tics, phenobarbital may cause short attention span and impulsivity.

Psychological factors

This group includes the factors that contribute to individual's low self-image on one hand, and limit the repertoire of available defences on the other hand. For instance most persons with mental retardation, are aware of their deficiencies, failures and rejection. However, due to their deficiencies in conceptual thinking and in communicative and other skills, they may have problems in developing constructive, compensatory defences. Instead, behavioural problems and/or psychopathology (e.g. depression) may ensue. Inappropriate behaviours may lead to social rejection, which has been linked to depression (Reiss & Benson, 1985). The social adaptation may be further impaired by temperamental factors, such as difficulties in tolerating changes (Rutter, 1975). The communication difficulties are often a crucial factor in poor impulse control and social maladaptation. It is not uncommon that when an aggressive individual with mental retardation acquires effective means of communication, verbal or non-verbal, the aggressive behaviour abates.

Environmental–sociocultural factors

Persons with mental retardation are subjected to various environmental stresses, perhaps even more than persons without mental retardation. These may include disturbances in the relationship with their parents (confusing and inappropriate expectations, overprotection, rejection), inconsistent care by multiple caregivers, rejection by the society (especially peers), poor access to community resources, and to mental health services. Even quite capable persons with mild mental retardation usually have little to say about their lives and are subjected to constant manipulation by multiple caregivers as decision makers. For non-verbal individuals, who live in a group setting where conformity and 'compliance' is demanded, behavioural outbursts may be the only way of communicating their feelings and assuming some control.

Epidemiology

The prevalence of mental disorders among persons with mental retardation has been studied by numerous researchers, yet there are few reliable data. Several reasons for that have been identified (Szymanski, 1980; Szymanski & Crocker, 1989; Russell, 1988). Most studies focused on selected populations, such as patients referred to clinics, or patients in institutions.

The diagnostic criteria for mental disorders have been also different from one study to another, with some using rather idiosyncratic classifications. Commonly, the patients were identified as having 'behaviour problems', rather than a defined mental disorder.

Detailed tabulations of literature are available (Bruininks, Hill & Morreau, 1988; Bregman, 1991). The more representative studies will be reviewed here.

Studies on selected populations

Menolascino (1965, 1966) in evaluating 616 children found 24.5% with both mental retardation and emotional disorder. Philips (1966) evaluated 170 referred children and noticed that 'it was uncommon to see a child without moderate or severe emotional maladjustment'. Webster (1970) evaluated 159 young children in a nursery for children with mental retardation and diagnosed disturbance in emotional development in all, and psychosis (not defined further) in 18%. Philips and Williams (1975) reviewed records of 100 children referred to a psychiatric clinic. Psychiatric diagnoses were given to 87%, and the most common ones were: psychosis 38%, behavioural disorders 26%, personality disorders 16%, neurosis 5%. The symptoms were the same as in a comparison group of children without mental retardation. Szymanski (1977) in 132 children referred to a mental retardation clinic found a mental disorder comorbid with mental retardation in 54%. Wright (1982), among 1507 residents in an institution, found serious mental disorders in 7.3% Among them, schizophrenia was diagnosed in 1.8%, affective disorder in 2.8%, early childhood psychosis in 2.7%. Eaton and Menolascino (1982) reported on 168 children and adults, 6 to 76 years of age, evaluated in a mental health clinic for people with mental retardation; 67% were given a psychiatric diagnosis besides mental retardation. The DSM III classification was employed. Organic brain syndrome with behavioural reaction was diagnosed in 18.4% and with psychotic reaction in 11.4%. Symptoms judged to be indicative of schizophrenia were seen in 14.3%. No diagnosis of pervasive developmental disorders or affective disorders was made. Szymanski (unpublished data) in a developmental disabilities clinic conducted detailed diagnostic assessment on 277 children with mild/moderate mental retardation and 123 adults. A DSM III Axis I diagnosis of a mental disorder was made in 74% of adults and 70% of children. Among adults, the most common diagnoses were: adjustment disorder 15%, affective disorder 15%, psychotic disorder 13%, pervasive developmental disorder

11 %. Among children, the most common diagnoses were: pervasive developmental disorders 22%, affective disorders 12%, adjustment disorders 10%.

Linaker and Nitter (1990) screened 164 residents of an institution for persons with mental retardation using a screening instrument PIMRA (Psychopathology Instrument for Mentally Retarded Adults) and case notes review. Schizophrenia was diagnosed by these means in 48 cases, anxiety disorder in 94, personality disorder in 85, affective disorder in none. In 11 cases no DSM III Axis I or II disorders were made. These results have to be taken with caution, as no clinical psychiatric assessment was done. It is unclear why no cases of affective disorders were found.

Deb and Hunter (1991) studied 150 adults with mental retardation and epilepsy. They were compared with a matched group of persons with mental retardation but without epilepsy. A mental disorder was diagnosed in 25%.

Studies on unselected populations

Rutter, Graham and Yule (1970) studied the entire age group of 9 to 11 year old children on the Isle of Wight through parent/teacher question-naires and direct interviews. Only IQ scores were used for diagnosis of mental retardation (in contrast to DSM III that also uses the criterion of adaptive behaviour). A psychiatric disorder was diagnosed in about 7% of total study cohort, but in 30% to 42% of children with IQ under 70. Koller *et al.* (1983) in a longitudinal study followed up a cohort of persons with mental retardation born in an English city during a period of five years. Retrospective data indicated that 61% were considered to have a behavioural disorder in childhood. Lund (1985) in a study of a random sample of 302 adults with mental retardation found, using modified diagnostic DSM III criteria, 28% to have a mental disorder. The most frequent diagnosis was behaviour disorder (11%), (not a formal DSM III diagnosis), followed by psychosis of uncertain type (5%), dementia and autism (3.6% each), neurosis (2%), not a DSM III diagnosis), affective disorder (1.7%) and schizophrenia (1.3%).

Gostason (1985) studied a random sample of adults with mental retardation. The DSM III diagnostic criteria were reportedly used, (although some non-DSM III categories were cited). Mental illness was diagnosed in 55% of people with severe and in 17% of people with mild mental retardation, and in 8% of controls without mental retardation.

Gillberg *et al.* (1986) reported on a representative sample of 149 adolescents 13–17 years of age (83 with mild, 66 with severe retardation), assessed by child psychiatrists. Sixty four per cent of persons with severe and 57% with mild mental retardation were judged to have a 'handicapping psychiatric condition'. Fourteen per cent of mildly and 50% of severely retarded persons had 'psychotic behaviour' (which included autism, social impairment and schizophrenia). DSM III diagnostic criteria were not used, therefore it is difficult to compare these results with other studies.

Reiss (1990) reported on 205 randomly selected persons with mental retardation attending community based day programmes. Of them, 59 selected by a psychopathology screening test were clinically assessed by a psychologist. Of those selected by the screening instrument, 86.7% or about 39% of the total, were judged to have symptoms of a mental disorder besides the mental retardation. No standard diagnostic categories were used and the clinical evaluation was conducted 6 to 12 months after screening. While the cases were selected randomly, it should be kept in mind that usually severely disturbed individuals are not accepted into community programmes: thus the prevalence of mental disorders could be even higher in a fully random sample. Interestingly, in spite of these differences, the available studies agree on two essential points: that mental retardation is a risk factor for developing a mental disorder and that all categories of 'usual' mental disorders are seen in this population.

Roles of psychiatrists

There are two misconceptions about the roles of psychiatrists in the field of mental retardation, both of which have had a rather destructive effect, preventing consumers from seeking psychiatric help and preventing psychiatrists from entering the field of mental retardation.

The first misconception is that all psychiatry can offer to the persons with mental retardation and mental illness, is psychotropic drugs prescribed to control disturbing behaviours. This misconception ignores the fact that persons with mental retardation may have all kinds of 'usual' mental disorders and that the behaviours in question may be symptoms of such disorders, as described above. Thus a careful and comprehensive diagnostic assessment by a clinician trained and experienced with this population is a prerequisite to any treatment, and this is probably the most important role of a psychiatrist. Next, as discussed further in this book, people with mental retardation can benefit from various psychiatric treatment modalities, besides medications. Last but perhaps most importantly, considering the multihandicapping nature of mental retardation, the treatment has to be comprehensive, eclectic, utilising pharmacological, psychological, milieu and medical modalities. Thus, a number of professionals have to be involved, as an interdisciplinary team.

The second misconception is that the field of mental retardation is an uninteresting one for psychiatrists, in which they cannot gather constructive experience and enrich their professional skills. This view has been perpetuated mostly by older psychiatrists, often with psychoanalytic orientation, who themselves did not have an opportunity to train and acquire experience in this field. The reality seems to be quite opposite. The field of mental retardation is an ideal one to study the interaction of the biomedical and the psychosocial factors in producing the clinical presentation of a mental disorder. With the high prevalence of physical problems, psychiatrists will have to exercise their medical as well as their psychiatric skills. Furthermore, the psychiatrist acts to draw the various strands of the interdisciplinary mental retardation team to produce a coherent management plan. This has been documented in a long term follow up study of psychiatric residents trained in psychiatry of mental retardation (American Psychiatric Association, 1991).

Summary

The main points discussed in this chapter can be summarised as follows: Mental retardation is not a specific disease, but a behavioural syndrome, reflecting the levels of a person's functioning. Persons with mental retardation are not a homogenous group but represent a wide spectrum of abilities, clinical presentations and behaviour.

Persons with mental retardation are at a heightened risk for mental disorders, which are the same as those seen in non-retarded persons. Aetiology of psychopathology in persons with mental retardation is as multivaried as in persons without mental retardation.

Primary responsibilities of psychiatrists in the field of mental retardation are diagnosis, treatment, prevention and research of mental disorders within an interdisciplinary setting.

References

American Psychiatric Association (1991). *Task Force Report No. 30: Psychiatric Services to Adult Mentally Retarded and Developmentally Disabled Persons.* Washington, DC: APA.

Bregman, J. D. (1991). Current developments in the understanding of mental retardation Part II: psychopathology. *Journal of the American Academy of Child and Adolescent Psychiatry*, **30**, 861–72.

Brown, W. T., Jenkins, E. C., Friedman, E., Brooks, J., Wisniewski, K.,

Raguthu, S. & French, J. (1982). Autism is associated with the fragile-x syndrome. *Journal of Autism and Developmental Disorders*, **12**, 303–8.

Bruininks, R. H., Hill, B. K. & Morreau, L. E. (1988). Prevalence and implications of maladaptive behaviors and dual diagnosis in residential and other service programs. In J. A. Stark, F. J. Menolascino, M. H. Albarelli, V. C. Gray, eds. *Mental Retardation and Mental Health: Classification, Diagnosis, Treatment and Services*. New York: Springer-Verlag.

Deb, S. & Hunter, D. (1991). Psychopathology of people with mental handicap and epilepsy II: psychiatric illness. *British Journal of Psychiatry*, **159**, 826–30.

Diagnostic and Statistical Manual of Mental Disorders, 3rd edn. (1980). Washington, DC: American Psychiatric Association.

Diagnostic and Statistical Manual of Mental Disorders, 3rd end. Revised (1987). Washington, DC: American Psychiatric Association.

Donaldson, J. Y. & Menolascino, F. J. (1977). Past, current and future roles of child psychiatry in mental retardation. *Journal of the American Academy of Child Psychiatry*, **16**, 38–52.

Eaton, L. F. & Menolascino, F. J. (1982). Psychiatric problems in the mentally retarded: types, problems and challenges. *American Journal of Psychiatry*, **139**, 1297–303.

Einfield, S., Molony, H. & Hall, W. (1989). Autism is not associated with the Fragile-X syndrome. *American Journal of Medical Genetics*, **34**, 187–93.

Garrard, S. D. & Richmond, J. B. (1965). Diagnosis in mental retardation and mental retardation without biological manifestations. In C. H. Carter, ed. *Medical Aspects of Mental Retardation*. Springfield, Ill., Charles C. Thomas.

Gillberg, C. & Wahlstrom, J. (1985). Chromosome abnormalities in infantile autism and other childhood psychoses: a population study of 66 cases. *Developmental Medicine and Child Neurology*, **27**, 293–304.

Gillberg, C., Persson, E., Grufman, M. & Themner, U. (1986). Psychiatric disorders in mildly and severely mentally retarded urban children and adolescents: epidemiological aspects. *British Journal of Psychiatry*, **149**, 68–74.

Gostason, R. (1985). Psychiatric illness among the mentally retarded. A Swedish population study. *Acta Psychiatrica Scandinavica* (Suppl. 318), **71**, 1–117.

Harris J. C. (in Press). Neurobiological factors in self-injurious behavior. In J. Luiselli, J. Matson & N. N. Singh, eds. *Assessment, Analysis and Treatment of Self-Injury*. New York: Springer-Verlag.

Hurd, H. M. (1928). Imbecility with insanity. *American Journal of Insanity*, **45**, 261–9.

Koller, H., Richardson, S., Katz, M. & McLaren, J. (1983). Behavior disturbance since childhood among a 5-year birth cohort of all mentally retarded young adults in a city. *American Journal of Mental Deficiency*, **87**, 386–95.

Linaker, O. M. & Nitter, R. (1990). Psychopathology in institutionalised mentally retarded adults. *British Journal of Psychiatry*, **156**, 522–5.

Lowrey, L. G. (1928). The relationship of feeblemindedness to behaviour disorders. *Journal of Psycho-Asthenics*, **23**, 96–100.

Lund, J. (1985). The prevalence of psychiatric morbidity in mentally retarded adults. *Acta Psychiatrica Scandinavica*, **75**, 563–570.

Menolascino, F. J. (1965). Emotional disturbance and mental retardation. *American Journal of Mental Deficiency*, **70**, 248–56.

Menolascino, F. J. (1966). The facade of mental retardation. *American Journal of Psychiatry*, **122**, 1227–35.

Meryash, D. L., Szymanski, L. S. & Gerald, P. S. (1982). Infantile autism associated with the Fragile-X syndrome. *Journal of Autism and Developmental Disorders*, **12**, 295–300.

Monfils, M. J. & Menolascino, F. J. (1981). Modified individual and group therapy approaches for the mentally retarded–mentally ill. In F. J. Menolascino, J. A. Stark, eds. *Handbook of Mental Illness in the Mentally Retarded*. New York: Plenum Press.

Philips, I. (1966). Children, mental retardation and emotional disorder. In I. Philips, ed. *Prevention and Treatment of Mental Retardation*. New York: Basic Books.

Philips, I. & Williams, N. (1975). Psychopathology and mental retardation: A study of 100 mentally retarded children. *American Journal of Psychiatry*, **132**, 1265–71.

Piven, J., Gayle, J., Landa, R., Wzorek, M. & Folstein, S. (1991). The prevalence of Fragile X in a sample of autistic individuals diagnosed using a standardized interview. *Journal of the American Academy of Child and Adolescent Psychiatry*, **30**, 825–30.

Reid, A. H. (1972). Psychoses in adult mental defectives: II. schizophrenic and paranoid psychoses. *British Journal of Psychiatry*, **120**, 213–18.

Reiss, S. (1990). Prevalence of dual diagnosis in community-based day programs in the Chicago metropolitan area. *American Journal of Mental Retardation*, **94**, 578–585.

Reiss, S. & Benson, B. A. (1985). Psychosocial correlates of depression in mentally retarded adults: I Minimal social support and stigmatization. *American Journal of Mental Deficiency*, **89**, 331–7.

Russell, A. T. (1988). The association between mental retardation and psychiatric disorder: epidemiological issues. In J. A. Stark, F. J. Menolascino, M. H. Albarelli & V. C. Gray eds. *Mental Retardation and Mental Health: Classification, Diagnosis, Treatment and Services*. New York: Springer-Verlag.

Rutter, M. (1975). Psychiatric disorder and intellectual impairment in childhood. *British Journal of Psychiatry*, Special Publication No. 9, 344–8.

Rutter, M., Graham, P. & Yule, W. (1970). *A Neuropsychiatric Study in Childhood*. London: Spastics International Medical Publications.

Szymanski, L. S. (1977). Psychiatric diagnostic evaluation of mentally retarded individuals. *Journal of American Academy of Child Psychiatry*, **16**, 67–87.

Szymanski, L. S. (1980). Psychiatric diagnosis of retarded persons. In L. S. Szymanski & P. E. Tanguay, eds. *Emotional Disorders of Mentally Retarded Persons*. Baltimore: University Park Press.

Szymanski L. S. & Crocker A. C. (1989). Mental Retardation. In H. I. Kaplan & B. J. Sadock eds. *Comprehensive Textbook of Psychiatry IV*. Baltimore: Williams & Wilkins.

Szymanski, L. & Grossman H. (1984). Dual implications of 'dual diagnosis'. *Mental Retardation*, **22**, 155–6.

Szymanski, L. S. & Kiernan, W. E. (1983). Multiple family group therapy with developmentally disabled adolescents and young adults. *International Journal of Group Psychotherapy*, **33**, 521–34.

Szymanski, L. S., Rubin, I. L. & Tarjan, G. (1989). Mental retardation, *Annual Review of Psychiatry*, vol. 8, Washington, DC: American Psychiatric Association.

Webster, T. G. (1970). Unique aspects of emotional development in mentally retarded children. In F. J. Menolascino ed. *Psychiatric Approaches to Mental Retardation.* New York: Basic Books.

Wolfensberger W. (1972). *The Principle of Normalization in Human Services.* Toronto: National Institute on Mental Retardation.

Wright, E. C. (1982). The presentation of mental illness in mentally retarded adults. *British Journal of Psychiatry,* **141**, 496–502.

3

Psychosocial development of children and adolescents with mild mental retardation

ANDREW LEVITAS AND
STEPHEN FRENCH GILSON

Introduction

An exclusive focus upon intellectual development avails us little when we attempt to address the mental health issues presented by children and adults with mild and moderate retardation. Nihira, Meyers and Mink (1980); Mink & Meyers (1981) linked behavioural disturbance to upbringing and home environment; Richardson, Koller and Katz (1985) isolated 'instability of upbringing', excluding cognitive and neurological impairment, as the significant factor in the high rate of behavioural disturbance in their population. Crnic, Friedrich and Greenberg (1983) proposed the interaction of factors intrinsic and extrinsic to the retardation to account for some facets of developmental outcome. Much literature on psychotherapy for persons with mental retardation (Thorne, 1948; Abel, 1953; Lott, 1970; Szymanski, 1980; Levitas & Gilson, 1989) finds issues of autonomy and dependency central to the lives and personalities of retarded patients. Various theoretical schools link these preoedipal issues to comfort with risk (Erikson 1968), or to replacement of self-object needs with true object needs (Baker & Baker, 1987). The current authors undertook to bring together observations of caregiver/retarded child interaction, psychosocial dimensions of the retardation syndrome, and clinical observations of persons with mild and moderate mental retardation in psychotherapy, with the separation–individuation scheme (Mahler, Pine & Bergman, 1975; Mahler & McDevitt, 1980; McDevitt & Mahler, 1980). This scheme is represented graphically in Fig. 3.1 to produce a proposed scheme of development for individuals with mild and moderate mental retardation (Levitas & Gilson, 1990). We propose that a primary psychosocial deficit intrinsic to the phenomenon of mental retardation, through interaction with variables common if not inevitable in the

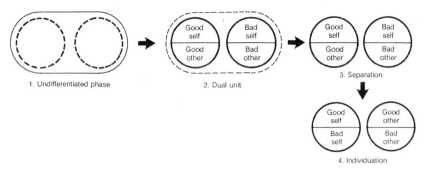

Fig. 3.1. Development of object relations by the normal child: infancy through establishment of a sense of self

responses of caregivers and the habilitation establishment, produce a secondary psychosocial deficit that is the core of the personality for adults with mild or moderate mental retardation. This personality structure has many implications for the diagnosis and treatment of psychiatric disorders in people with mild and moderate mental retardation (Levitas & Gilson, 1990).

The Primary psychosocial deficit

Webster (1970) suggested 'the primary psychopathology of mental retardation' consisted of more than just a cognitive deficit signified by subnormal intelligence quotient. Common to all children with mental retardation in his study population, and present proportional to the degree of retardation, he found what he called 'benign autism', passivity, avoidance of novelty, and 'simplicity of emotional response'. When retarded and nonretarded children of comparable developmental age are compared as to active involvement in object play, frequency and duration of object play are less in retarded than non-retarded children (Gowen *et al.*, 1992) as predicted by this scheme. We prefer to update and clarify these terms, and include in the primary psychosocial deficit the delay in developmental milestones, relative self-absorption, passivity, novelty avoidance, and relative lack of emotional nuance (Levitas & Gilson, 1987, 1990).

Parental grief, parental activity

Family grief at the birth or recognition of a child with mental retardation was described by Solnit and Stark (1961), accompanied by 'disappoint-

ment...[a] feeling of helplessness and sense of failure'; a set of feelings
mirrored by medical and habilitative personnel (p. 534). These latter may
be the source of the zeal to speed developmental milestones (Levitas &
Gilson, 1990; Zigler & Hodapp, 1986). This guilt does not run a
conventional course to resolution; rather, Olshansky (1962) describes
'chronic sorrow', which Wikler, Wasow and Hatfield (1981) describe as
activated at each developmental crisis. Soon after birth, grief and parental
activity appear to be reciprocal, with the mother becoming more actively
involved with her Down Syndrome child with each sign of 'normality'
(Emde & Brown, 1978). However, mothers of stigmatized, physically
handicapped (but non-retarded) infants develop atypical active strategies
of interaction, compensating for their children's deficits (Wasserman *et al.*,
1987) resulting in secure attachment similar to controls by Ainsworth's
(Ainsworth *et al.*, 1978) measure.

This parental activity in mother and child with mental retardation dyads
continues into the individuation phase to the point of maternal domination
of the interaction, with virtual inattention to the child's initiatives, in
dramatic contrast with mother/nonretarded child dyads (Eheart, 1982;
Kogan, Wimberger & Bobbitt, 1969; Terdal, Jackson & Garner, 1976;
Breiner & Forehand, 1982; Selfer, Clark & Sameroff, 1991).

These observations strongly suggest that parental grief either gives rise
to, or is not incompatible with, development of interactive strategies
compensating for the child's primary psychosocial deficit, resulting in
secure attachment at the cost of domination of the parent/child interaction
during the period of developing autonomy (Levitas & Gilson 1990).

Separation–individuation: the mediated self

A more detailed treatment of this process is available in Levitas and
Gilson (1990). The following is a summary of the main effects of maternal
domination of interaction (i.e. caregiver domination) during the separation–individuation process. During the undifferentiated phase, a combination of Mahler's normal autistic and symbiotic phases (Mahler &
McDevitt, 1980) the child with mental retardation may be comparatively
undemanding, failing to signal needs and experiencing 'organismic
distress' (Mahler & McDevitt, 1980). Grieving parents rebound from
initial withdrawal with active involvement compensating for the child's
interactional deficits.

This active intrusion, so necessary to the evolution of secure attachment,
separation, and development of object permanence, becomes the 'domi-

nance' of the mother, other caregivers, and therapists, of the interaction with the retarded toddler, attenuating the child's initiative in exploration. The beginning of locomotion, delayed in the retarded toddler, leaves him or her perhaps clumsily propelling a larger body. More passive, with a preference for routine over novelty, and with much of their time for free exploration occupied by directed therapeutic interventions, their exploration of the world is attenuated. Mahler's process of 'hatching' occurs, but the 'expansion beyond the symbiotic orbit' (Mahler & McDevitt, 1980) is limited and its character is different. The exploration the child does accomplish is mediated by parents or therapists, replacing the mother's normal 'mirroring' frame of reference (Mahler & McDevitt, 1980) to which the child's still-primitive self adjusts, with what is, for the retarded child a 'screen' through which the world is filtered.

Throughout the practising subphase, the two tracks of separation and individuation, normally intertwined, continue to diverge as caregiver domination of interaction persists. The toddler's normal narcissism is attenuated by parental direction, and parental 'screening' of the outside world. On-time developmental milestones may thus be approximated at the cost of the child's initiative. Object permanence is achieved, but pleasure in the exercise of autonomy is lessened to the point of ambivalence. It is possible that efforts to 'stimulate' the child are redoubled in response.

The rapprochement subphase may be blurred for children with mental retardation, since (1) the child may have achieved little actual distance and (2) the developmental delay shifts rapprochement and true individuation into the early school years. Development of self-representation in a child away from home, with academic demands which can cause dependence on parents and teachers for narcissistic gratification (e.g. help in achieving success), and who has received most if not all, experience through the filter of the executive ego of caregivers, must follow an atypical path. During the rapprochement subphase the parents' (and teachers') reactions become even more of a focus for the child than heretofore; the caregivers evolve from a screen through which the world is filtered, as the child turns actively to the caregiver, into a screen in the sense of a television screen, on which the world is viewed. Such initiative as the child is able to pursue becomes the foundation for such autonomy as the child develops: the self-representation of children with mental retardation (Fig. 3.2) includes the executive ego functions of caregivers, since caregivers are the mediators of the child's experience. This atypical self-representation, the mediated self, is the first component of a secondary psychosocial deficit.

The need for proximity to a caregiver depends upon the extent to which

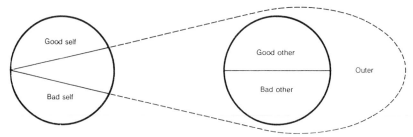

Fig. 3.2. Individuation achieved by the retarded child

the child (later, the adult) must meet new or novel challenges. Dependence may take the form of simply having a caregiver in the room when a task requiring initiative or decisions presents itself. True autonomy, initiative, and narcissistic gratification from mastery appear to be missing and must be 'borrowed' through the executive ego functions of a nonretarded person. The mediated self preserves for the child with mental retardation some of the 'magical solutions of closeness and merging' (Mahler & McDevitt, 1980); it is a stable self-representation which nonetheless lacks some elements of self-constancy open to nonretarded children.

Note that this formulation is also consistent with Kohut and Wolf's description of the 'overburdened personality' (Kohut & Wolf, 1978) and the failure to replace self-object needs with true object needs: any caregiver may mediate the child's or adult's with mental retardation experience; this is a self-object need. Note also the intactness of ego boundaries; only certain executive ego functions are borrowed from objects or object representations. There may however be failure to identify another's point of view, or an objective point of view, with ongoing egocentricity (Bernstein, 1970), 'outer-directedness' (Zigler, 1967), and poor self-esteem and lack of a sense of competence (Aleksandrowicz & Aleksandrowicz, 1987). The self-system is thus stable as long as a mediator is present, or need for initiative and decision-making is not encountered; when novelty is encountered a mediator must be sought and found.

The mediated super-ego

Continued unavailability of time, place and circumstances in which to practise such autonomy as may be open to the school-age retarded child, and concentration on cognitive achievement or 'socialisation' (that is, play as a guided experience in learning to be with others) plus the limits to experimentation imposed by the mediated self, deprive the retarded child

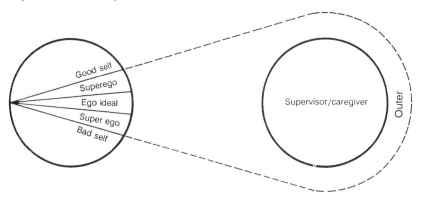

Fig. 3.3. Ego and superego development of the retarded child

of the opportunity to develop self-regulation and values by free practice in a world of peers, that is, within a group of children with similar developmental issues and solutions (Levitas & Gilson, 1987). Formation of an ego-ideal based on modelling of adults and introjection of their values may be on the one hand attenuated by the child's image of him or herself as 'faulty' or 'broken', and on the other unrealistically strengthened by defensive perfectionism and literal copying of the dominating adult. For the older school-age child, modelling and imitation of non-familial adults (sports and entertainment figures, military heroes) is the norm; the child with mental retardation may seem to have oedipal-appearing 'crushes' on teachers, therapists and other caregivers. Adult omnipotence is not challenged by fantasy and peer play (Levitas & Gilson, 1990). The mediated self, coupled with a relatively unmodified omnipotent superego, lead to failure to develop stable and integrated processes of self-regulation. Rather, the child regulates his or her activity by constant reference to the wishes and emotional states of others; harsh superego and omnipotent ego-ideal are experienced as part of an 'outer', neither wholly integrated into the self nor clearly part of an autonomous object (Figure 3.3). The caregiver is not only a guide to experience, but to how to feel about experiences.

Developmental tasks of adolescence

Through successive subphases, adolescents develop acceptable drive regulation, sexual relationships, active sexuality, true autonomy and integration of sexuality and intimacy. The onset of puberty finds

adolescents with mental retardation with scant experience of self-regulation, little private time, and few true peer contacts. Mediation of drive
regulation by others, who now can include idealised chronological (but not
developmental) peers, leaves the adolescent with mental retardation
vulnerable to exploitation. With peer relations and sexual expression
limited by prior development and societal and parental fears, and
individuation incomplete, the capacity to develop long-term, intimate
relations is perforce limited. Romantic 'crushes', may survive long into
middle and late adolescence. Or family prohibitions may be experienced as
demands to act asexually, setting the stage for conflict between the still-
harsh superego and the new drive. Masturbation may be the only outlet
possible, sometimes accompanied by fetishistic activity (Levitas & Gilson,
1990).

A similar combination of factors presents barriers to preparation for
true autonomy in a world of peers. Adolescent rites of passage (driving,
owning possessions, drinking, other kinds of adolescent experimentation
with peers) are seldom open to adolescents with mental retardation.
Special Olympics, a 'special' prom, or graduation, may bolster self-esteem
(Zeitlin & Turner, 1985) but do not have the experimentation, practising,
and mastery components inherent in true extracurricular activities such as,
for example, the school newspaper. Adolescents with mild and moderate
mental retardation are also aware of their exclusion from the activities of
chronological peers and siblings, and of their inability to make the
sophisticated social judgments precluded by the mediated self (Zeitlin &
Turner, 1985). Stated desires for autonomy are balanced by profound
fears; attempts at autonomy may require rescue by caregivers. Decisions
made by caregivers may be met only with acquiescence or futile, angry
defiance (Zeitlin & Turner, 1985).

The secondary psychosocial deficit

The syndrome of mental retardation, then, begins with a primary
psychosocial deficit characterised by developmental delays, passivity,
relative self-absorption, preference for routine and avoidance of novelty,
and lack of nuance in emotional communication and comprehension.
Interaction with caregivers results in caregiver dominance of the separation–individuation process, giving rise to a secondary psychosocial deficit
consisting of:

1. An atypical sense of self, the mediated self (Fig. 3.2). Continued
   interaction of the mediated self with an environment characterised by

supervision, relative lack of access to true peers, and lack of opportunity to experiment in a world of peers, results in the emergence of:

2. Primitive superego and omnipotent ego-ideal, both poorly integrated into the self (Fig 3.3).
3. Resulting deficits in self-regulation: mediated regulation.
4. Prohibitions experienced as inhibitions.
5. Development to a point analogous to early adolescence, characterised by primarily autoerotic sexual focus and profound ambivalence toward autonomy.

Thus the normal developmental trajectory for the mildly or moderately retarded child is atypical, and object relations and daily interactions of people with mental retardation are at risk for being seen as pathological. Aman has referred to the mentally retarded, from the standpoint of psychiatric diagnosis, as a subculture, whose differences in development must be taken into account when attempting to recognise familiar psychiatric disorders (Aman, 1991; Levitas & Gilson, 1990; Menolascino, Gilson & Levitas, 1986; Sovner, 1986; Sovner & Hurley, 1983).

Implications for psychiatric diagnosis and treatment

Before proceeding to a description of psychopathology in people with mild and moderate mental retardation, we must first understand and recognise the atypical but normal personality structure resulting from uncomplicated mental retardation. The secondary psychosocial deficit creates a dependency on the presence of non-retarded people, when decision making or response to novelty is required, sometimes approaching and easily confused with more conventional forms of dependency. Responses to loss and to fears generated by environmental demands for increased autonomy, and to threats to self-esteem generated by the unmodified superego are at risk for being mistaken for psychopathology. The normal adaptation of a person with mild or moderate mental retardation is a dependent posture; there is a risk of mistaking an adjustment disorder for Dependent Personality Disorder (a diagnosis meaningless in this context) (Levitas & Gilson, 1990). Resort to external supports and expression of conflict and loss in the context of relationship may render familiar psychiatric disorders difficult to recognise. Anxiety may manifest as demanding or clinging; sadness may manifest as withdrawal or irritability. Verbal expressions of sadness may be concrete and expressed in the context of relationships. Where the non-retarded person might say 'I'm depressed', the person with mental retardation might say, 'My mother doesn't love me' or 'My counsellor is angry at me'. Projective identification and projection are defenses to which the mediated self is especially vulnerable (Levitas & Gilson, 1990).

All of these defensive manoeuvres involve the family or caregiving system; the life cycle creates predictable developmental crises in the lives of people with mild and moderate mental retardation people (Wikler *et al.*, 1981; Gilson & Levitas, 1987; Levitas & Gilson, 1989), and the contribution of the caregiving system to the adjustment disorder must be assessed through comprehensive evaluation (Levitas & Gilson, 1989, 1990). When the signs of distress are ignored, misread, or misattributed the retarded person's incomplete internalisation of self-regulation may open the way for acts of aggression, destruction, or self-injury. Extreme anxiety resulting from sudden loss or need to adapt to novelty (e.g. change in a long-accustomed transit route, a sudden medical illness) may result in a catastrophic reaction, a brief psychotic-like reaction from which the individual will recover more or less rapidly when a trusted 'other' comes on the scene. All of these situations are at risk for being mistaken for psychosis. It must also be stressed that concrete expressions of sadness such as 'my father is dead', in the presence of a live father, may also be manifestations of mood congruent delusion in an episode of major depression. The usual biological features will be present (Menolascino *et al.*, 1986; Sovner, 1983; Levitas & Gilson, 1990).

Summary

Interaction of biological, psychological and social variables results in an atypical path of development for persons with mild and moderate mental retardation. The components of the resulting secondary psychosocial deficit are:

1. Atypical sense of self (the mediated self).
2. primitive superego and omnipotent ego-ideal, poorly integrated into the self.
3. deficits in self-regulation (Mediated Regulation).
4. prohibitions experienced as inhibitions.
5. primarily autoerotic sexual focus.
6. profound ambivalence toward autonomy.

The secondary psychosocial deficit leaves adults with mental retardation more vulnerable than their non-retarded counterparts to loss and demands for increased autonomy. Responses can be misread as indicative of more severe psychopathology, or can be mistaken for a more mild problem than in fact exists.

References

Abel, T. M. (1953). Resistances and difficulties in psychotherapy of mental retardates. *Journal of Clinical Psychology*, **9**, 107–9.

Ainsworth, M. D., Blehar, M. L., Walters, E. & Wall, S. (1978). *Patterns of Attachment*. New York: Wiley.

Aleksandrowicz, D. R. & Aleksandrowicz, M. K. (1987). Psychodynamic approach to low self-esteem related to developmental deviations: growing up incompetent. *Journal of the American Academy of Child and Adolescent Psychiatry*, **26**, 1583–5.

Aman, M. G. (1991). *Assessing psychopathology and Behavior Problems in Persons with Mental Retardation: A Review of Available Instruments*. Rockville, MD: US Department of Health and Human Services.

Baker, H. S. & Baker, M. N. (1987). Heinz Kohut's self psychology: an overview. *American Journal of Psychiatry*, **144**, 1–9.

Bernstein, N. (1970). *Diminished People: Problems and Care of the Mentally Retarded*. Boston, MA: Little, Brown.

Breiner, J. & Forehand, R. (1982). Mother–child interactions: a comparison of a clinic-referred developmentally delayed group and two non-delayed groups. *Applied Research in Mental Retardation*, **3**, 175–82.

Crnic, K. A., Friedrich, W. N. & Greenberg, M. T. (1983). Adaptation of families with mentally retarded children: A model of stress, coping, and family ecology. *American Journal of Mental Deficiency*, **88**, 125–38.

Eheart, K. B. (1982). Mother–child interactions with non-retarded and mentally retarded preschoolers. *American Journal of Mental Deficiency*, **87**, 20–25.

Emde, R. N. & Brown, C. (1978). Adaptation to the birth of a Down syndrome infant: Grieving and maternal attachment. *Journal of the American Academy of Child Psychiatry*, **17**, 299–323.

Engel, G. L. (1977). The need for a new medical model: a challenge for biomedicine. *Science*, **196**, 129–36.

Erikson, Erik. (1968). *Childhood and Society*. New York: Norton.

Gilson, S. F. & Levitas, A. S. (1987*a*). Normalization, a biopsychosocial approach. In: Gilson, S., Faulkner, E. & Goldsbury, T., eds. *Three Populations of Primary Focus: Medically Fragile/Mentally Retarded, Elderly/Mentally Retarded, and Mentally Ill/Mentally Retarded*, pp. 37–47, Omaha: University of Nebraska Medical Center/Creighton University School of Medicine.

Gilson, S. F. & Levitas, A. S. (1987*b*). Psychosocial crises in the lives of retarded people. *Psychiatric Aspects of Mental Retardation Reviews*, **6**, 27–32.

Gowen, J. W., Johnson-Martin, N., Goldman, B. D. & Hussey, B. (1992). Object play and exploration in children with and without disabilities: a longitudinal study. *American Journal on Mental Retardation*, **97**(1), 21–38.

Kogan, K. L., Wimberger, M. C., & Bobbitt, R. A. (1969). Analysis of mother–child interaction in young mental retardates. *Child Development*, **40**, 799–812.

Kohut, H. & Wolf, E. S. (1978). The disorders of the self and their treatment: an outline. *International Journal of Psycho-analysis*, 59, 413–425.

Levitas, A., & Gilson, S. F. (1987). Emotional and developmental needs of mentally retarded individuals. In: *Three Populations of Primary Focus: Medically Fragile/Mentally Retarded, Elderly/Mentally Retarded, and Mentally Ill/Mentally Retarded*, pp. 157–161, Omaha: *University of Nebraska Medical Center/Creighton University School of Medicine*.

Levitas, A. S. & Gilson, S. F. (1989). Psychotherapy with mildly and moderately retarded patients. In F. J. Menolascino and R. Fletcher (eds.), *Mental Retardation and Mental Illness: Assessment, Treatment and Service for the Dually Diagnosed*. Lexington, MA: Lexington Books.

Levitas, A. & Gilson, S. F. (1990). Toward the developmental understanding of the impact of mental retardation on the assessment of psychopathology. In E. Dibble & D. B. Gray eds. *Assessment of Behavior Problems in Persons with Mental Retardation Living in the Community*, pp. 71–106, Rockville, MD: US Department of Health and Human Services.

Lott, G. (1970). Psychotherapy of the mentally retarded: Values and cautions. In F. J. Menolascino Ed. *Psychiatric Approaches to Mental Retardation*, pp. 227–250, New York: Basic Books.

Mahler, M., Pine, F. & Bergman, A. (1975). *The Psychological Birth of the Human Infant*. New York: Basic Books.

Mahler, M. S. & McDevitt, J. B. (1980). The separation-individuation process and identity formation. In S. I. Greenspan & G. M. Pollock, eds. *The Course of Life: Psychoanalytic Contributions Toward Understanding Personality Development*, vol. 1, Infancy and Early Childhood, pp. 395–406, Rockville, MD: National Institute of Mental Health.

McDevitt, J. B. & Mahler, M. S. (1980). Object constancy, individuality and internalization. In S. I. Greenspan & G. M. Pollock, eds. *The Course of Life: Psychoanalytic Contributions Toward Understanding Personality Development*, vol. 1. *Infancy and Early Childhood*, pp. 407–423, Rockville, MD: National Institute of Mental Health.

Menolascino, F., Gilson, S. & Levitas, A. (1986). Issues in the treatment of mentally retarded patients in the community mental health system. *Community Mental Health Journal*, 22, 314–27.

Nihira, K., Meyers, C. E. & Mink, I. T. (1980). Home environment, family adjustment, and the development of mentally retarded children. *Applied Research in Mental Retardation*, 1, 5–24.

Nihira, K. Mink, I. T. & Meyers, C. E. (1981). Relationship between home environment and school adjustment of TMR children. *American Journal of Mental Deficiency*, 86, 8–15.

Olshansky, S. (1962). Chronic sorrow: a response to having a mentally defective child. *Social Casework*, 43, 190–3.

Richardson, S. A., Koller, M. & Katz, M. (1985). Relationship of upbringing to later behavior disturbance of mildly mentally retarded young people. *American Journal of Mental Deficiency*, 90, 1–8.

Selfer, R., Clark, G. N. & Sameroff, A. J. (1991). Positive effects of interaction coaching on infants with developmental disabilities and their mothers. *American Journal on Mental Retardation*, 96 (1), 1–11.

Solnit, A. J. & Stark, M. H. (1961). Mourning and the birth of a defective child. *Psychoanalytic Study of the Child*, 16, 523–7.

Sovner, R. (1986). Limiting factors in the use of DSM-III criteria with mentally retarded persons. *Psychopharmacology Bulletin*, 22, 1055–9.

Sovner, R. & Hurley, A. (1983). Do the mentally retarded suffer from affective illness? *Archives of General Psychiatry*, **40** 61–7.

Szymanski, L. S. (1980). Individual psychotherapy with retarded persons. In L. S. Szymanski & P. E. Tanguay eds. *Emotional Disorders of Mentally Retarded Persons: Assessment, Treatment, and Consultation*, pp. 131–147, Baltimore, MD: University Park Press.

Terdal, L., Jackson, R. M. & Garner, A. M. (1976). Mother–child interactions: a comparison between normal and developmentally delayed groups. In E. J. Mash, C. K. Hammerlynk & L. C. Handy, eds. *Behavior Modification and Families*, pp. 249–264, New York: Brunner Mazel.

Thorne, F. C. (1948). Counselling and psychotherapy with mental defectives. *American Journal of Mental Deficiency*, **52**, 263–71.

Waisbren, S. E. (1980). Parents' reactions after the birth of a developmentally disabled child. *American Journal of Mental Deficiency*, **84**, 345–51.

Wasserman, G. A., Lennon, M. C., Allen, R. & Shilansky, M. (1987). Contributors to attachment in normal and physically handicapped infants. *Journal of the American Academy of Child and Adolescent Psychiatry*, **26**, 9–15.

Webster, T. G. (1970). Unique aspects of emotional development in mentally retarded children. In F. J. Menolascino, ed. *Psychiatric Approaches to Mental Retardation*, pp. 3–54, New York: Basic Books.

Wikler, L., Wasow, M. & Hatfield, E. (1981). Chronic sorrow revisited: Parent vs. professional depiction of the adjustment of parents of mentally retarded children. *American Journal of Orthopsychiatry*, **51**, 63–70.

Zeitlin, A. G. & Turner, J. L. (1985). Transition from adolescence to adulthood: perspectives of mentally retarded individuals and their families. *American Journal of Mental Deficiency*, **89**, 570–9.

Zigler, E. (1967). Familial mental retardation: a continuing dilemma. *Science*, **155**, 292–8.

Zigler, E. & Hodapp, R. M. (1986). *Understanding Mental Retardation*. Cambridge: Cambridge University Press.

4

Psychological process: the inner world of people with mental retardation

JOAN BICKNELL

Introduction

The high prevalence of additional problems in people with mental retardation (learning disabilities) such as personal distress, psychiatric illness or behaviour disturbance remains largely unexplained. Although epidemiological studies are vital to furthering our understanding, the study of the 'inner world' of the person with disability may provide valuable insights (Varma, 1992). Counselling, psychodynamic psychotherapy, family and group therapy or a combination of these may help us to be more aware of uncommunicated needs and feelings. Such work needs to be constantly evaluated and refined to ensure therapeutic effectiveness.

'Inner worlds' of thoughts and feelings do exist however handicapped the person, and these can be explored by the person with mental retardation, with the therapist.

The chapter is divided into four sections:

1. The person with disability and the outside world.
2. The relationship of the person with disability to himself.
3. The person with disability and his therapist.
4. The person with disability and the institution.

The person with disability and the outside world

The person with mental retardation may experience an interface between himself and others where there is often a double message. His early and close relationships are with his family. Later on, school teachers and youth club leaders play their part. In adult life there may be more losses than he can manage. At any time in life he may be confused by what he sees and feels. His parents may be loving, but sad and angry with others.

Grandparents may disagree with parental decisions such as keeping him within the family or the choice of mainstream education. Siblings may be angry that 'he gets away with everything', or 'I can't come out tonight – I'm sitting for my brother. No – he's not a baby'. The child may be a centre for conflict and the wish that he wasn't there brings no peace to parents but only guilt. The adult gives reason for ongoing concern for continued vulnerability.

One way of handling a wish to protect and reject is to rise above it all and families may then always put the handicapped child first. Such sublimation may only intensify the sense of unfairness, which spills over onto siblings who may be used as 'parental children' if one parent becomes ill or the marriage breaks. Primary maternal preoccupation which occurs universally between mother and baby is usually shortlived if the child is not handicapped. When he becomes mobile he discovers that his small world, including his mother, is not perfect and not always under his command but he copes by the use of his developing faculties. Primary maternal preoccupation for a handicapped baby may continue into childhood and even into adulthood and create grotesque omnipotence as a result. Sometimes unusual sexual arrangements between a widowed elderly mother and her handicapped son may be explained as a continuation of maternal preoccupation which might also explain suicide and euthanasia pacts.

An elderly couple with an autistic son, Ben, sampled local services and did not find what they wanted. They became his permanent caregivers to do his bidding, and wobetide anyone who insisted on alternative care! Ben had never separated from his parents and knew they allowed him total power. Small wonder that he has little concept of sympathy, empathy, death or morality. Such a skewed dependency leads to great vulnerability should any break in the relationship occur.

For a long time it was assumed that parents were often responsible for the behavioural problems of their handicapped son or daughter and the 'overprotective parent' was often inflicted as a punitive label. This term was applied to caring parents, who were reluctant to expose their child to the risks of adulthood. They had received inadequate help from professionals from the start, conflicting advice and, as the parents grew more cautious around adolescence, they were judged as overprotective. When this happens, families feel attacked by professionals who fail to understand their real needs and how they survived until then.

When family stability is threatened, it is easy to see how blame may be put on the one who is handicapped. Sometimes such blame is distorted into scapegoating in which the responsibility for a lot of unrelated happenings are carried by the handicapped person. Such off-loading may keep the marriage together and the family at home. At other times one parent carries an unfair burden of work and blame and 'martyrdom'.

Some families get into a downward spiral of tension and tiredness. The handicapped person feels this tension and reacts by becoming more disturbed, making the family more tired. One mother in such a predicament said 'All I need is someone in the house to look after Lillian if she knocks me unconscious'. Perhaps the hallmark of such families is that expectations are low, from their son or daughter, from their own management skills and from outside agencies.

The concept of loss for the family or the person with disability is now a familiar one (Bicknell, 1983). The 'loss' of the perfect child that does not arrive is well understood but there are other losses, of promotion for one or other parent who cannot uproot the family, loss of status among local families and similarly for siblings in the playground.

Some young adults with mental retardation living in an institution were in a psychoanalytical group. When their group leader was leaving, they expressed their sadness and when he expressed his, they were shocked. They had no idea that staff could have sad feelings or could possibly be sad about leaving them. It was as if handicapped members had some monopoly on sadness. Recent work (Oswin, 1991) has enabled a greater understanding of the way in which real loss, mostly by death, can be understood and accepted by people with mental retardation, and can be for them as for others, a time of personal growth.

People with mental retardation are often aware that it is hard to have real control in any part of their world. Much teaching in school and in further education is about having cognitive skills to reach this goal; by managing money, learning to tell the time, to write, count or travel on a bus. High levels of anxiety may be related to inability to have some control of the environment. This impotence is more honest but a far cry from the omnipotence generated if primary maternal preoccupation has continued for too long.

It may be thought that the child at special school and the adult in sheltered employment has a good time. No exams, no deadlines, no responsibility for what he does or doesn't do, forgiven if he is late and bathed if he does not make it to the toilet. There are no gangs in the playground and the journey home is from door to door. He is unlikely to be mugged or exploited.

But vulnerability does not pass him by. More and more sexual and physical abuse is being discovered (Brown & Craft, 1989). Financial trickery is common. Even housework skills may be exploited. Veronica, a young adult with mental retardation, was raped by her brother regularly, her money taken and she was refused the right to make decisions. Her mother beat her and made her do all the housework in their squalid accommodation. Her pet cat was killed in front of her because she had not worked hard enough. Her low self-esteem made it impossible for her to gain the courage to speak out and move on and when offered the chance, did not take it but chose to stay in the squalor she knew best.

Sally, with mild mental retardation, lived with her extended family that housed a brothel. There were no family boundaries or rules. Sally became pregnant but she did not know by whom. Counselling helped her to choose the baby's future care by adoption but, on the birth of her child, she changed her mind. The baby was then removed against her wish and Sally was heartbroken. A girl, used by others, was denied the ultimate joy of her own child in her arms.

The world is a complicated place and quick thinking helps to avoid exploitation and reduce frustration. Someone with mental retardation often has a low tolerance threshold. Diana, a girl with mental retardation saved up to buy her own television, but could not tune it to all the channels and neither could the staff of her group home. Tears of rage followed and objects were thrown around her room before she collapsed sobbing. Is this immaturity, a spoilt girl, or does she require medication? Or is this part of a universal feeling that the world is getting too complicated?

Sometimes gaps in social knowledge maybe filled in by paranoid fantasy. Stephen, a young man with severe mental retardation and epilepsy did not know the concept of banking. When handing back some of his money each week, he believed that the head of the home used it for himself. This engendered so much bitterness that a lot of difficult behaviour resulted. A simple but repeated explanation was all that was needed.

So far this section has looked at the person with disability as an individual and the world as peopled by individuals. However, the disabled person has many formidable attitudes to confront, which belong in the world either through history or to contemporary thought and belief. One of these philosophies is 'death making'.

Throughout the generations, society has tried different ways to rid the population of people with disabilities. It was said that the events of the Second World War would never be repeated but many would label the death through inaction of new born handicapped babies as containing the same ingredients of racial hygiene. If death in infancy is aided then so will death later on. 'Death making' situations can be found in services for adults with mental retardation. One current idea causing grave concern is that residential care is so expensive that some euthanasia may be necessary so that the national economy is not threatened. Why should 'death making' occur? Financial and moral arguments will continue to rage until people with handicaps are seen as having more in common with us than otherwise. Until then, those with mental retardation inherit a legacy that their lives are less valuable than ours (Brandon, 1989).

To come back to the individual, many families have death wishes in the process of coming to terms with handicap in their child. They have a glimpse of the freedom without him and the guilt is overwhelming.

A mother, who was struggling to put on the coat of her very handicapped daughter Amy, said, 'I wish you were dead' in her anger. Those who heard her wished they had not. No one felt able to tell the mother that her feelings were understood. When the child died two weeks later of pneumonia, the grief and guilt of the parents were overwhelming. Others have said 'if you were a dog I would have put you down'. A nice reversal of this was given by Sandra, who said that babies with epilepsy are very expensive but babies without handicaps cost nothing. Presumably comments like 'we have paid a high price for you' were heard in the first place.

The effect of labels has been well argued in the sociology literature. Some create adverse responses (e.g. mental, demented, epileptic) and others create positive responses (middle class, graduates). The continual change of label in the field of mental retardation is an ineffectual way of dealing with stigma. A letter that started, 'Her Down's Syndrome started to trouble her' suggested that it was some sort of appendage rather than the very being of her person! Too easily does the person with disability become disenfranchised by his label and his self-esteem is threatened once again.

The relationship of the person with disability to himself

Before counselling can be effective, the person with disability must want to communicate, whether through words, movement, play or actions, and must feel 'good enough' about himself to feel that he can do this. He also needs to know his world sufficiently well to see the importance of working on problems even if these are identified by someone else. Much preparatory work by the therapist may be needed to both identify the problems and to raise the self-esteem of the client before work can begin.

Some people with mental retardation have problems in separating fact from fantasy. This may be a developmental problem or it may have arisen as a defence against boredom or helplessness. By the age of 5 years a normal child can sort out dreams and daydreams and enjoy stories for what they are. Some people with mental retardation are still at this level, although they may have had many years of life experience, may have lost parents and for years not been allowed comfort objects. Her little finger was a friend to Sarah with Down's Syndrome and she talked to it quietly. Sometimes she would scold. She was referred because it was thought she was hallucinating. Michael came to the author's attention, when he tried to sell the family silver. He had many autistic features, although highly skilled in other ways, but was unacceptable to the day centre because he had so many preoccupations that prevented him from working. In his boredom he developed a vivid visual hallucination of the devil siting on an orange cloud just above his head in bed. He must do whatever the devil told him. Much of his imagery was persecutory and represented his overwhelming anxiety to be perfect in what he did, especially for his parents and if not, then punishment would destroy him by fire or by hanging. Ronald, a partially sighted young man, spoke very slowly and many carers completed his sentences for him. This led to passivity on his part and a deterioration in his self-help skills such that schizophrenia was diagnosed. He rightly felt that he was being controlled, for even his sentences were completed by others. To add to his difficulties, he had not distinguished between fact and fantasy and was teased that birds would nest in his hair as it was long. He believed it and became fearful, going out less and rocking as a self-comforting gesture. Counselling consisted in the main of letting him finish his sentences and teaching him to reality test everything he heard.

Some fantasies are clearly wish fulfilment that boost seif-esteem and draw attention and applause. Graham spent much of the day in fantasy. 'See that man on that motorcycle? He gave me a lift.' 'See that old lady, I took her across the road and she gave me a pound but I gave it back and said, give it to the blind'. His stories cannot be true but continued for most of his waking hours. People close to him became tired or confused as to what was real and started scolding, confronting or ignoring. None of these responses helped. Graham lost touch with his parents and both have since died. He was not told of their deaths and did not go to their funerals (Hollins & Sireling, 1989). He had no mementoes. In moments of despair when he was in touch with his sad-self, he said 'I may as well have died with them'. Clearly in his fantasies he imagines himself to be the caring, daring grown up that he wants to be.

The main risk in fact and fantasy confusion is that the mental state will be considered psychotic and medication given, which will reduce the capacity for thinking through and learning more adult patterns of thinking, while keeping a fantasy world for enjoyment.

Sometimes the handicapped person is faced with complex contradictory information and acts out with behaviour that removes him/her from the need to face the cognitive problem. Often the antecedents are forgotten and only the behaviour is remembered. Christine was given two different appointments for her therapy and one of these coincided with her youth club. She was anxious, flushed and upset when she saw her therapist. 'I think I'm going to break a window' was the opening comment. Having made it clear that, while this was an option, there were other more useful options to consider, the reason for the anxiety was quickly uncovered. She had a poor concept of time and a poor memory. In these settings, she found it easier to be a 'helpless victim' where others made the decision or sorted the confusion. If she was put to bed or sedated because of the broken window, she would have handed over the responsibility for herself to others. The 'helpless victim', model is learned as a way of avoiding personal problem solving that might otherwise lead to personal growth. Learning to make the choices from an early age would help to avoid the 'helpless victim' strategy but the environment also needs to be supportive of developing appropriate autonomy.

Splitting, that is separating the good and the bad, and projecting the bad into someone or something is a mechanism used in particular when young and at times of stress. As the person matures, the good and the bad can be held together. Some people with mental retardation continue to 'split' into adulthood in ways that are not helpful. Elizabeth, a school leaver had major behaviour problems. She set fires, stole from cars and shops and absconded. She had behaviour programmes, medication and morality training to little avail. She accepted counselling and after a year, a break-through occurred. She said that she was two different people, one good and boring and one bad and exciting. She used two chairs to illustrate this. Clearly all efforts had been directed towards the good and boring part! In the process of recovery, she became deeply depressed when she saw the reality of the bad part of her. After some time, she was discharged from a psychiatric unit to live successfully and independently in the community. Louise's problems were different. A very handicapped young lady in a caring family, she started to hear voices that were distressing in some way. These seemed to be her own thoughts, externalised and rejected because of her own conflicts about growing up and becoming a sexual adult. When she 'heard' her thoughts, she was frightened, felt out of control and her idyllic child-like environment threatened. Secondary gain was obtained through the comforting of her parents. By working in both a counselling medium and using behavioural principles, the hallucinations were resolved.

Denial is a universal defence mechanism used to deal with reality which is too painful such as a bereavement. People with handicaps may deny their own disability. Sonia had severe athetosis and the first time she saw herself was in photos taken on her 21st birthday. She tore up those photos in distress and began to hate herself. The sudden awareness that her body was twisted and her face grimacing was too much for her. The depression that followed allowed the fantasy of the normal body to be worked through and a sense of reality took its place after the mourning for the perfect body that was not there. She then became more aware of her attributes, making the most of them with eventual peace of mind. Later she married and found further happiness.

If there are cognitive difficulties with time and number concepts, then denial seems more easily used in these areas. Malcolm did not want to leave his school and so decided that, when he reached the age of age of 18, his age would 'go backwards' until he was 7 again. This denial could not be dismantled by a cognitive approach. His foster mother was not going to get any older and neither was his social worker. All this hinged on his anxiety to keep the few adults that he knew for ever. In sessions with him, he started to examine the therapist's grey hair and then tentatively approach the whole question of ageing. He had come to accept this as inevitable when, several sessions later, in a game of dominoes he announced that, at her death, he would put flowers on his foster mother's grave.

The concept of permanence of objects has usually developed in a 12 month old child. Some people with disabilities only partially acquire this concept and may loose it at times of stress or illness. The idea that the table in the next room exists, even though it can't be seen, is the basic concept but in a more mature form it extends to the realisation that loved ones exist in the next town or on the other side of the globe. These beliefs can be tested by letter and by telephone. But when speech and writing are difficult, then there is little left to try out to reinforce the concept that loved ones exist, let alone finding out how they are feeling and whether there are good feelings for the handicapped person.

Some people with mental retardation put into respite care, may mourn for their home and loved ones. Behaviour problems may develop and the cause not understood. Every move, even if explained, must be seen as a potential psychological trauma, minimised only by using the utmost care such as the use of photographs and mementos and never by medication. Others also may benefit from the same techniques such as people with short term memory loss after a head injury or treatment for a brain tumour.

Sometimes psychological mechanisms are insufficient to contain feelings of anxiety and depression and somatisation occurs. In people with mental retardation these are often copies of a particular disability such as a hemiplegia, epilepsy or blindness or may take the form of the magnification of normal aches and pains. Some may examine their fingers and hands for the therapist to see. Some will just point to a spot and say that it hurts. Christine, who pointed to a tiny spot on her finger, said 'See that, my dog did that and I had twenty stitches'. While this could not have been true, her inner reality was that it had happened. Does one honour her inner reality and ignore her dishonesty? By allowing her to have her fantasy, more useful material followed about her vulnerability, in particular, when having epilepsy in public places, the epilepsy being 'the dog' that tears at her body.

Projection of the bad part of oneself onto someone else and then attacking that other person may be done by people with mental retardation in a particularly powerful way. When in therapy, Martin loved to call his therapist 'stupid' after everything that she said. It was said with all the disgust that he could muster! After a while, the therapist began to say stupid things or at least self evident comments and felt helpless in Martin's hands. This gave him even more opportunity to downgrade his therapist who then felt what it was like for Martin.

The person with disability and his therapist

In psychotherapy but not so much in counselling, transference and countertransference set the scene for the psychological work to be done. Transference requires an understanding of the 'as if' principle. For example, the therapist may see the person with disability 'as if' he were his own son and the person with disability might see him 'as if' he were his father. Many people with mental retardation do not have the 'as if' concept and the therapist, by default, might accept the invitation to become the client's best friend. If this happens, therapy ceases to be useful and termination is heartbreaking for the person with disability.

In counselling, a sense of equality is ideal and the therapist needs to look for ways in which equality can be fostered and applauded, in a game of chess perhaps or when fixing the times of appointments. John had just started to see his therapist, when in one session the door was opened twice. He was furious and wrote a note and stuck it on the door. 'Piss off', it said. His quick response earned gratitude, although some collaboration over wording may have been advisable!

Many people with disability in therapy have terrible stories to tell of loss and abuse (Hollins & Sinason, 1992). Further loss may have been incurred by the institutions responding punitively to unacceptable behaviour caused by the initial unhappiness. Pity can be evoked in the therapist, often leading to compulsive helping which deskills the client and stifles the relationship. 'I can cry here and know you won't do anything', suggests a creative level of mutual understanding. Counselling must leave room for expression of other emotions such as love in all its guises. Neil was found one day clutching the bonnet of his therapist's car 'I love her, I even love her car'. A boy with a long history of sexual abuse and loss dares to love again, dares to feel a boy and dares also to look for happiness. What better place to start!

The person with disability and the institution

Within any institution, be it a hospital or school, there are rules which provide structure and avoid chaos. Part of this structure is the efficient communication of knowledge to many people who 'need to know' and it can be hard to fit the issue of confidentiality into such an organisation. Those in therapy must have some expectation of confidentiality, otherwise treatment will not progress. The therapist must have the agreement of the person before he passes particular information. Other material such as suicidal thoughts may be passed on without the agreement, but this happens very rarely. A careful resumé and agreement at the end of the session, as to what remains confidential and what can be passed on, will enable the person with disability to feel more in control about information exchange in his intimate and extended world.

Taking someone into counselling is not done lightly. There must be an agreement from the person and if he is accompanied to the session then he may only show his real wishes by whether or not he cooperates. Even those who might wish to leave early, as a way of showing that they do not wish to be counselled, may need supervision, because of severe epilepsy or someone to push their wheelchair. This becomes an object lesson for the therapist as to the difficulties that some have, to be independent.

The one attending counselling may become the butt of jokes in school, in the hospital ward or at home, often because of ignorance or jealousy. 'Why does he go and not me? He must be daft', and his ordinariness is removed. But the resilience of those with disabilities must not be underestimated and many who have been distressed or regressed in therapy, put themselves together as they leave the room and return to the real and unkind world outside.

Summary

This chapter has explored some of the insights that may develop for both the person with mental retardation and the therapist, when the two enter into a counselling relationship. It is known from the high rate of psychiatric illness and challenging behaviours that people with mental retardation are vulnerable to personal distress. But there is now evidence that this vulnerability may diminish, as the disabled person explores his inter-personal relationships, thoughts and feelings with a therapist he can trust, who respects the person he is and the work he is doing (Waitman & Conboy-Hill, 1992).

References

Bicknell, J. (1983). Inaugural Lecture; The psychopathology of handicap. *British Journal of Medical Psychology*, **56**, 167–78.
Brandon, D. (1989). *Mutual Respect*. Surrey: Good Impressions Publishing Ltd.
Brown, H. & Craft, A. (1989). *Thinking the Unthinkable*. London: FPA Education Unit.
Hollins, S. & Sinason, V. (1992). *Jenny Speaks Out*. London: St George's Mental Health Library, The Sovereign Series.
Hollins, S. & Sireling, L. (1989). *When Mum Died*. London: St George's Hospital Medical School in association with Cambridge: Silent Books. (Also *When Dad Died: An Alternative to Separation*)
Oswin, M. (1991). *Am I Allowed to Cry*? London: Souvenir Press (Education & Academic) Ltd.
Varma, V. P. (1992). *The Secret Life of Vulnerable Children*. London: Routledge.
Waitman, A. & Conboy-Hill, S. (1992). *Psychotherapy and Mental Handicap*. London: Sage Publications Ltd.

5

Tomorrow's research

CHRIS KIERNAN

Introduction

One of the goals of tomorrow's research should be to extend research to
people with mild mental retardation, for whom there are no adequate
services. This has been a neglected group in research terms. They have, in
general, been marginalised in specialist services, at least in UK, but they
have needs which are not necessarily being met in generic services such as
forensic psychiatry and social work.

The chapter will be organised roughly around the WHO categories of
impairment, disability and handicap (WHO, 1989) and the notions of
prevention and amelioration. This is not a perfect framework, some areas
like service research do not fit well, but the framework is broadly
convenient.

Impairment

A prime goal of research should be to further the understanding of the
impairments of physiological functioning underlying mental retardation.
Advances in genetics are leading to the identification of genetic anomalies
underlying mental retardation and the isolation of new syndromes and
more precise delineation of others (Evans & Hamerton, 1985). This
research is giving increasing power to genetic counselling and, thereby,
increasing information to parents and opportunities for them to make
informed choices.

Understanding the mechanisms through which genetic anomalies relate
to handicap should surely be a further target for active research. Advances
are likely to emerge from several directions. First, from research on

disordered metabolism in well defined syndromes, e.g. PKU, Rett syndrome (Berg & Gosse, 1990). Secondly, research on the amelioration of behavioural signs may lead to understanding of underlying mechanisms. For example, the effect of naltrexone–naloxone on self-injury may lead to further understanding of the theoretical formulations implicating the dopamine system in syndromes characterised by self-injury (Oliver and Head, 1990).

Hopes that knowledge of biological mechanisms underlying disorders may lead to genetic engineering and thereby to amelioration seem to be remote. However remote, they may occur in the next decades, although they are unlikely to have an impact on people with existing syndromes.

Research on behavioural phenotypes is burgeoning. This is a fascinating area, which will undoubtedly develop further, especially given the interest of parent groups. However, there are dangers in this research of confusing common characteristics, which show in existing child or adult populations with genotypically determined behaviours. The phenotype, of course, reflects the interaction of genetically determined characteristics with developmental history. There is a danger of saying that a common characteristic is genotypically determined, e.g. self-injury, without recognising the function which behaviour may have acquired in development. Here there is a need for sophisticated interdisciplinary research to produce the picture of development.

Tuberose sclerosis (TS), for example, is characterised behaviourally by hyperactivity and aggression (Hunt and Dennis, 1987). People with TS may require more sensitive approaches than in other cases of hyperactivity and aggression, but basically are susceptible to common methods of management. There is no evidence to suggest that, because these behaviours are associated with the syndrome, they are not functional for individuals.

Disabilities

Disabilities involve physical and psychological loss or anomalies of function arising from impairment. In terms of cognitive function, there was a notable research effort, based in psychology, in the 1960s and 1970s. This led to the formulation of sophisticated models of the cognitive differences/deficits underlying mental retardation (O'Connor, 1987).

Work in this area has concentrated on constructs like selective attention and primary memory, which are likely to represent important sources of structural deficiencies in information processing in people with mental retardation. Other constructs, such as strategies, executive functioning and metacognition are developmental constructs, which are influenced by environmental contingencies as well as motivational and attributional components. There is extensive research work which suggests that people with mental retardation show structural deficiencies but that, in terms of strategies and other environmentally influenced components, it may be possible to offset these deficiencies through training (Justice, 1985).

This work, although theoretically sound, has had little or no impact on practice. There are several possible explanations of this failure. In terms of research, practice has been most influenced by behaviour modification, possibly to the exclusion of the less well 'marketed' cognitive research (Kiernan, 1991). Secondly, much of the research on cognitive disabilities was, at least initially, a quest for the 'philosopher's stone', the element of information processing which, once identified, would provide the key to understanding cognitive disability. In practice, the research suggests that pretty well all elements of processing can be affected in people with mental retardation. As a consequence, there is no single key which will affect functioning. Finally, this research has provided understanding of processes, in other terms has been 'enlightenment' research, rather than research which has direct practical outcomes or 'linear' research (Weiss, 1977). As such, it requires painstaking translation to everyday practice and that translation has not occurred. Without doubt, this area of research should be revisited in the next decade by researchers, and the possible consequences for practice drawn out.

Research on the social and emotional development of people with mental retardation has been relatively sparse and there has been a general decline in research on personality. This, probably, reflects the vagueness of many concepts in fields of study of emotion, motivation and personality. However, social development and functioning has been highlighted in work on 'social impairment' (Clements, 1987).

This is a growing field, stemming from autism research and research in child development, which should be extended more fully to studies of people with mental retardation. Amongst other benefits, it is likely to be of value in the understanding of challenging behaviour.

Research on motivation has again been sparse, although considerable attention has been given to the relatively poor intrinsic motivation of people with mild mental retardation (Haywood & Switzky, 1986). Intrinsic motivation relates to the degree to which learning is motivated by intrinsic rewards, such as curiosity and attainment of self-esteem, rather than by extrinsic rewards. Research suggests that people with mild mental retardation respond more to extrinsic than intrinsic motives. However, this research also suggests that responsiveness to intrinsic motivation may be enhanced by suitable educational programmes (Haywood & Switzky, 1986).

The de-emphasis on social–emotional development is also seen in the relative failure, to date, to research anxiety states and phobic disorders in people with mental retardation.

Whole areas of mental illness and mental retardation have also been neglected in research. This is partly a problem of lack of adequate diagnostic instruments which are now being developed. Research leading to more accurate diagnosis should also lead to more appropriate treatment.

Amelioration of disability is the function of education and the therapies, including psychotherapy. Several points need investigation through well controlled evaluations. These include investigation of effectiveness, in particular the effectiveness of psychotherapy and the plethora of 'special' therapies, such as the Peto method and holding therapy. In addition, new techniques, for example based on analyses of social impairment, need to be developed and evaluated. Prostheses, such as sign language, again need further investigation in terms of methods of teaching and long-term impact.

Handicap

Handicap represents the failure of people with mental retardation to fill expected roles in society. Service provision is mainly directed at this area, although only sometimes informed by knowledge of nature of disabilities. We need to adopt and develop an ecological model in relation to handicap (Bronfenbrenner, 1979). The elements of the model, the individual, the family, formal and informal settings with which individuals and families interact and the framework provided by policies, are widely agreed. Ecological models are essentially interactive. Changes in policies affect settings in which individuals and families have experiences and, correspondingly, the experience of providers within settings affect attitudes to individuals and families, and policy development.

In the US and UK, and to some degree in Western European and other countries, changes in policy are focusing key issues for research. Normalisation is predicated on the notion that society must change and cease to define people with mental retardation as deviant. In order to be effective, policies based on normalisation require attitude change, accepting people with mental retardation as full human beings with their own contributions to make, and support of people with mental retardation within communities alongside other members of society.

New policies place emphasis on the individual being within the family unit and being within a local community setting. This has re-focused several critical research issues for tomorrow. It is now clear that the presence of a person with mental retardation in a family does not lead to a 'pathological' family situation (Byrne, Cunningham & Sloper, 1988). However, this in turn emphasises questions concerned with the utilitarian, social, and psychological resources needed by families to care for a person with mental retardation and the interaction of these resources with the strategies used by families to cope with the additional pressures brought by the presence of a person with mental retardation (Crnic, Friedrich & Greenberg, 1983). We already know a good deal about these factors but we need further research to refine our models and, in particular, to translate research findings into methods of intervention.

One form of family resource concerns intervention to help families to facilitate development in early years. Early intervention research has been somewhat de-emphasised, again following failure of its early promise. Much of the early work was, however, based on models of development which were fairly primitive. There has been much development, for example in relation to understanding of the development of communication skills, which now offers greater promise of successful early intervention, especially within families (Kiernan, 1985).

Research on the effects of integration in school, work, and community leisure facilities is also critical. To date the largest amount of research has gone into the investigation of the impact of integration in school situations (Gulliford, 1985). This work has shown little advantage in terms of academic achievement in integrated education. However, both in education and in work and community settings, greater attention should be given not only to skill development but to the changes in self perception and the impact of integration on the attitudes of peers.

In theory, desegregation should lead to the lessening of handicap, as result of individuals having more opportunity to learn appropriate behaviour and of greater acceptance of difference without difference being labelled as deviance. We urgently need to know whether attempts to manage this dual function of desegregation are successful.

Surprisingly little research effort has been invested in the area of community attitudes and perceptions of people with mental retardation given its potential importance as a measure of the success or otherwise of policies based on normalisation. The approach adopted by service providers appears to be very much one of engineering integration and then hoping that attitudes will change. We need to monitor new policies and to analyse factors involved in attitude change, in order to ensure that adverse effects are not being produced.

Challenging behaviour represents a particular problem for integration in that it is possibly the most likely breakdown point of new models (Blunden & Allen, 1987). The general policy model in the UK requires that people with mental retardation should be treated as individuals with rights and worth. This has led, for example, to controversy over the use of aversive procedures (Repp & Singh, 1990). There is general agreement that a massive research effort needs to go into development of non-aversive procedures. Within this framework, the extensive use of antipsychotic drugs on the basis of clinical experience and traditional practice, rather than proven worth in their specific effects, also needs urgent attention. Community backlash is also likely to develop if people with mental illness and mental retardation are not adequately diagnosed and treated, giving extra urgency to the development of means for effective diagnosis and treatment of mental illness in people with mental retardation.

Again, if the goals of the overall policy are to be adequately evaluated, we need to monitor effects of changes on self-perception by people with mental retardation and on public attitudes. These changes are not necessarily going to be positive. One problem may be that the public will perceive that excessive resources are going into helping individuals who are perceived as 'less needy' than others in society.

Policy

New policies have a variety of aims, including more effective service delivery based on satisfaction of individuals with mental retardation, satisfaction of parents and carers, meeting needs and being cost-effective (NHS and Community Care Act, 1990). The importance of cost-effectiveness, a relatively new dimension of thinking in human services, is clearly significant, given the need to 'justify' expenditures to, possibly, sceptical politicians, service providers and the public. The effectiveness of new policies should clearly be a major focus for research.

Summary

During the coming decade there will be massive opportunities for research to enhance understanding and practice. However, we need to focus also on more effective translation of research into practice. There appears to be a growing antiintellectualism in services and in political thinking which may, in part, be a result of the failure to translate enlightenment research, e.g. on cognitive disabilities, into 'tangible deliverables'. Antiintellectualism is a dangerous trend which needs to be countered by more effective demonstrations of the value of academic research.

Decisions on the funding of research depend upon a number of factors. These include consideration of what is seen as most promising line of research at the time, e.g. cognitive psychology or behaviour modification. Prioritisation clearly changes as approaches are perceived as not living up to what may have been initially overambitious claims. Decisions are also political, informed in relation to the attitudes of the professions and public attitudes. Again, it is important to 'sell' the field. Support will also, in part, depend on how people with mental retardation are perceived relative to other 'deserving' groups.

Two final points. First of all research and service development in English speaking countries tends to have been insular. Little attention has been paid to date even to continental European countries. This trend should be reversed, especially in light of the opportunities opened up by developments in European Commission funding and in the former Communist dominated European countries. Secondly, there are substantial advantages to be seen in crossdisciplinary research. There is an unfortunate tendency to professional isolation in research. Different professions need each other in this field and advances are likely to be made in areas of overlap amongst disciplines.

References

Berg, J. M. & Gosse, G. C. (1990). Specific mental retardation disorders and problem behaviours. *International Review of Psychiatry*, **2**, 53–60.

Blunden, R. & Allen, D. (1987). *Facing the Challenge: An Ordinary Life for People with Learning Difficulties and Challenging Behaviour*. London: Kings Fund.

Bronfenbrenner, U. (1979). *The Ecology of Human Development*. Harvard: Harvard University Press.

Byrne, E. A., Cunningham, C. C. & Sloper, P. (1988). *Families and their Children with Down's Syndrome: One Feature in Common*. London: Routledge.

Crnic, K. A., Friedrich, W. N. & Greenberg, M. T. (1983). Adaptation of families with mentally retarded children: a model of stress. *American Journal of Mental Deficiency*, **28**, 125–38.

Clements, J. (1987). Units and teams: challenges in common. Quoted in Newman and Emmerson (1991) Specialised treatment units for people with challenging behaviours. *Mental Handicap*, **19**, 113–9.

Community Care: Caring for People. (1990). H.M.S.O. London.

Evans, J. A. & Hamerton, J. L. (1985). Chromosomal abnormalities. In
A. M. Clarke, A. D. B. Clarke and J. M. Berg (Eds.), *Mental Deficiency:
The Changing Outlook*. 4th edn. (pp. 213–266). London: Methuen.
Gulliford, R. (1985). Education. In A. M. Clarke, A. D. B. Clarke and
J. M. Berg (eds.), *Mental Deficiency: The Changing Outlook*. 4th edn.,
pp. 639–685, London: Methuen.
Haywood, H. C. & Switsky, H. N. (1986). Intrinsic motivation and behaviour
effectiveness in retarded persons. In N. R. Ellis and N. W. Bray (eds.),
International Review of Research in Mental Retardation. vol. 14, pp. 2–46,
New York: Academic Press.
Hunt, A. & Dennis, J. (1987). Psychiatric disorders among children with
tuberous sclerosis. *Developmental Medicine and Child Neurology*, **29**, 190–8.
Justice, E. M. (1985). Metamemory: an aspect of metacognition in the mentally
retarded. In N. R. Ellis (ed.), *International Review of Research in Mental
Retardation*. vol. 13, New York: Academic Press.
Kiernan, C. C. (1985). Communication. In A. M. Clarke, A. D. B. Clarke and
J. M. Berg (eds.), *Mental Deficiency: The Changing Outlook*. 4th edn.,
pp. 584–638, London: Methuen.
Kiernan, C. C. (1991). Research: progress and prospects. In S. S. Segal and
V. P. Varma (eds.), *Prospects for People with Learning Difficulties*,
pp. 170–185, London: David Fulton.
O'Connor, N. (1987). Cognitive psychology and mental handicap. *Journal of
Mental Deficiency Research*, **31**, 329–36.
Oliver, C. & Head, D. (1990). Self-injurious behaviour in people with learning
disabilities, determinants and interventions. *International Review of
Psychiatry*, **2**, 101–16.
Repp, A. C. & Singh, N. N. (1990). *Perspectives on the Use of Nonaversive and
Aversive Interventions for Persons with Developmental Disabilities*.
Sycamore, Il: Sycamore Publishing Company.
Weiss, C. (1977). *Using Social Research in Public Policy-Making*. Lexington,
Mass: Lexington Books.
WHO (1989). *Mental Disorders*. World Health Organisation: Geneva.

Part II

Assessment and diagnosis

6

Psychopathology in mental retardation
STEVEN REISS

Introduction

The assessment of psychiatric disorders in people with mental retardation
is relevant to clinical, research, and public policy concerns. In clinical
work, there is a need to screen for mental retardation and psychiatric
disorder (dual diagnosis) in large populations, to evaluate who is eligible
for treatment interventions, and the effects of behavioural or drug
therapies. In research, there is a need for valid measures to support
scientific inquiry on the causes and nature of psychopathology and in the
public policy arena, for epidemiological studies to plan appropriate mental
health services for people with mental retardation.

Concept of dual diagnosis

Historically, the central issue in the assessment of dual diagnosis (joint
occurrence of mental retardation and psychiatric disorder) was to
distinguish between primary and secondary handicaps (Cutts, 1957). Does
the person have primarily mental illness or primarily mental retardation?
The issue was important because it decided responsibility for funding
services. If it was determined that the person has primarily mental
retardation, services were provided by developmental centres.

Unfortunately, the distinction between primary versus secondary
handicaps has led to inadequate mental health services (Reiss, Levitan &
McNally, 1982). A practical consequence of labelling psychiatric disorders
as 'secondary' in importance is that the needed mental health services are
less likely to be funded. Many developmental disabilities advocates
consider themselves fortunate when they obtain services for all of their

client's 'primary' needs. If a clinician labels a handicap as 'secondary' in nature or importance, many government agencies will not fund the indicated services and instead will cite a lack of financial resources.

Another problem with the distinction between primary and secondary handicaps is that it is arbitrary. There are no criteria for making the distinction. There are no psychological tests to help decide which handicaps are primary and which handicaps are secondary.

Both mental retardation and psychiatric disorder constitute 'primary' service needs for people who have dual diagnosis. Consider the hypo-thetical case of a man with mild mental retardation who lives in-dependently but requires residential care after developing an affective disorder (depression). In this case, what is the primary handicap? Is the primary handicap the mental retardation that created the fragility of the man's adjustment to independent living, or is the primary handicap the depression that led to a deterioration in functioning and precipitated placement with a residential agency? One could argue the issue forever, because there are no criteria for determining which handicap is primary and which handicap is secondary. While clinicians and service agencies debate the issue of primary and secondary handicaps, the client's needs remain unmet.

The concept of dual diagnosis provides an alternative to the concepts of primary and secondary handicaps. Instead of trying to guess whether the primary problem is emotional or intellectual, both disorders are diagnosed and appropriate services are recommended for each. No effort is made to suggest that it is more important to serve one set of needs rather than the other. The person is given services for both mental retardation and mental illness. The underlying diagnostic philosophy is that all debilitating handicaps should be diagnosed and all critical service needs should be assessed.

Diagnostic overshadowing

Although the concept of dual diagnosis suggests that clinicians should identify both intellectual and emotional handicaps as primary service needs, there is a tendency for them to underestimate the importance of emotional handicaps in persons with mental retardation. Just as a six-inch line appears smaller than it really is when viewed next to a 12-inch line, some debilitating emotional problems may appear less important than they actually are when viewed in the context of debilitating effects of mental retardation. For example, consider the way people often construe behaviour problems in boys who do and who do not have mental retardation. When a boy with average intelligence displays grossly inappropriate behaviour, it is recognised that the boy has a behaviour problem. When a boy with mental retardation shows the same inappropriate behaviour, people presume that the inappropriate behaviour is a result of the mental retardation. Although there is no scientific evidence to support such presumptions, there is a natural tendency to explain behaviour in terms of salient factors (Bem, 1972; Weisz, 1981). There is a tendency to assume that aberrant behaviour is a manifestation of mental retardation rather than an indication of an accompanying psychiatric disorder.

The phenomenon of diagnostic overshadowing refers to instances in which the presence of the mental retardation decreases the diagnostic significance of an accompanying behaviour problem (Reiss, Levitan, & Szyszko, 1982; Reiss & Szyszko, 1983). In the first experiment on diagnostic overshadowing, Reiss *et al.* (1982*a, b*) presented a case description of a debilitating fear to two groups of psychologists. The groups differed only in terms of the information that was added to the description of a debilitating fear. One group was told that the individual had an IQ of 60, and the other group was told that the individual had an IQ of 102. Both groups were then asked to diagnose the fear and recommend an appropriate intervention. The results indicated that the same debilitating fear was less likely to be diagnosed as a phobia, and less likely to be referred for appropriate therapy, when the individual had mental retardation versus no mental retardation. In other words, the presence of mental retardation overshadowed the accompanying presence of abnormal behaviour usually considered indicative of psychopathology. Subsequent research extended diagnostic overshadowing to cases of dual diagnosis involving either schizophrenia or personality disorder (Reiss & Szyszko, 1983).

Assessment of depression

The phenomenon of diagnostic overshadowing suggests that there may be a tendency to underdiagnose psychiatric disorders for people with mental retardation. There is substantial evidence that this is true. For a sample of 205 assessed persons served by community agencies, Reiss (1990*a*) found a psychiatric diagnosis in the case files for only about one in four people who actually had a psychiatric disorder. The study provided evidence for a substantial rate of underdiagnosis of psychiatric disorders.

Depression is an excellent example of the tendency to overlook psychiatric disorders in persons with mental retardation. The prevalence rate for depression among people with mental retardation has been estimated to be between 3 and 6 per cent (Reiss, 1990*a*), which is a substantial rate for a psychiatric disorder. Yet except for Reid (1972) and a few others, the field has virtually ignored the occurrence of depression in people with mental retardation. There were no published research studies on depression in persons with mental retardation until the mid-1980s (Benson *et al.*, 1985; Kazdin, Matson & Senatore, 1983). The first measures of depression adapted for persons with mental retardation did not appear until the 1980s for adults (Matson, 1988; Reiss, 1988a; Reynolds & Baker, 1988) and the 1990s for children (Reiss & Vanelti-Hein, 1990).

Reiss and his colleagues have found that depression in persons with mental retardation is strongly associated with both low levels of social support and with poor social skills (Benson et al., 1985; Laman & Reiss, 1985; Reiss & Benson, 1985). In a longitudinal study, Laman (1989) found some evidence that poor social skills may lead to low levels of social support and subsequent depressed mood. Apparently, the people who became depressed were not necessarily those who faced the most adversity in their lives; the people who became depressed were those who were isolated and alone with nobody to support them through times of adversity.

Assessment of aggression

Theoretically, some aggressive behaviour problems in people with mental retardation should be associated with psychiatric disorder (Reiss, 1992*a*; Reiss & Rojahn, 1992). Specifically, aggressive behaviour problems may be associated with depression, paranoid ideas, personality disorder or psychosis. Some people with depression behave aggressively out of frustration and anger and/or to escape from their misery. Some people with paranoid ideas overinterpret innocent events as personal insults and counterattack or strike preemptively. People with personality disorder behave aggressively for the excitement it causes, whereas some people with psychosis behave aggressively because they hear voices saying 'strike'.

The assessment of psychiatric disorders associated with aggressive behaviour should have implications for treatment. The drugs that would be tried for aggressive behaviour associated with psychosis are different from those that would be tried for aggressive behaviour associated with depression. Although cognitive–behavioural therapists would likely use social skills training and anger management programmes to treat both psychosis and depression, they would not use social skills training to treat aggression associated with psychopathy (thrill-seeking).

Reiss and Rojahn (1992) summarised data on the relationship between aggression and depression for 528 adults, adolescents, and children with mental retardation. The subjects had been rated on either the adult or children's version of the Reiss screen for maladaptive behaviour (Reiss, 1988*a*; Reiss & Valenti-Hein, 1990). Criterion levels of depression were evident in about four times as many aggressive as non-aggressive subjects. Anger management problems were significantly associated with both sadness and aggressive behaviour. The findings provided support for the hypothesis that some instances of aggressive behaviour in persons with mental retardation are associated with depression.

Reiss (1992*b*) reported a case study of a 22-year old man who had a history of occasional violent outbursts. Because of his behaviour problem, the man had been asked to leave about a dozen residential placements since childhood. The results of the Reiss Screen, the Apperceptive Personality Test (Karp, Holmstrom & Silber, 1989), and an interview with the subject all indicated the presence of paranoid personality traits. For example, on the Apperceptive Personality Test, the man generated fantasy characters and then rated the characters in his stories as untrustworthy. On the Reiss Screen, the average ratings from four caretakers indicated a high score on the scale for 'paranoia'. When the caretakers paid attention to the intentional insult, he felt demeaned and jealous, and threatened violent behaviour.

These findings suggest the importance of assessing when aggressive behaviour is associated with psychopathology. It is no longer sufficient to assess aggressive behaviour solely in terms of a functional analysis of the frequency and the intensity of the behaviour problem. There also should be an evaluation of the person's feelings, mood, cognitive status, and mental state.

Principles of assessment

One of the challenges in diagnosis and assessment is how to evaluate when a behaviour problem is a symptom of mental retardation as opposed to a symptom of mental illness? For example, suppose that Mr. Smith does not bath and stay clean. Is unkempt behaviour an example of mental retardation in which there is a failure to acquire self-help skills, or is unkempt behaviour an example of regressive behaviour that is a symptom of schizophrenia? Reiss (1992a) has suggested the following four principles for deciding when behaviour is symptomatic of psychiatric disorder.

1. Diagnose patterns of symptomatology

By itself, a behaviour problem is insufficient evidence of psychopathology; for a dual diagnosis to be made, the behaviour problem should be one symptom in an overall pattern of symptoms that is described as a psychiatric disorder in the American Psychiatric Association's (1987) Diagnostic and Statistical Manual. For example, one way to evaluate the significance of unkempt behaviour is to assess the possible presence of a number of symptoms of psychosis. Unkempt behaviour would be part of an entire pattern of psychotic symptoms that is recognised as schizophrenia if a man shows bizarre behaviour, delusions, hallucinations, avoidance of others, and inappropriate affect. Under such circumstances, the unkempt behaviour would be part of an entire pattern of symptomatology that is recognised in the DSM-III R.

When diagnosing patterns of symptomatology, it is not essential that every symptom be present. It is sufficient for a diagnosis if there is a preponderance of relevant symptoms.

2. Diagnose changes in behaviour

With the notable exception of personality disorders, psychiatric disorders have periods of onset and represent deteriorations in behaviour from the premorbid state. Usually the deterioration in functioning is sufficiently severe to be obvious to care-staff.

The principle of change is especially relevant for deciding when symptoms such as unkempt behaviour are indications of mental retardation versus psychiatric disorder. If the individual is currently showing about the same level of self-care skills as he/she did in the past, such that self-care skills were never mastered, unkempt behaviour might be considered a sign of mental retardation. If the individual experienced a decline in self-care behaviour, so that in the past there was a noticeably higher level of self-care behaviour, unkempt behaviour may be considered a sign of a psychiatric disorder.

3. Make allowances for the impact of intellectual handicaps on the expression of symptomatology

When assessing psychopathology in persons with mental retardation, it is important to make allowances for the individual's intellectual handicaps and the circumstances under which people with mental retardation live. People with mental retardation sometimes express symptoms in direct and poorly disguised ways. Occasionally the residential environment impacts the expression of a symptom. Consider the following case examples:

(a) In avoidant disorder the client withdraws from interpersonal situations because of a fear of rejection. Sometimes this fear is so great that the person will not even pay attention to others who are talking to him/her ('spaced out'); however, the non-mentally retarded individual pretends to be listening to the person who is talking. For subjects who have mental retardation, the avoidance is sometimes so transparent that there is an actual looking away from people who approach.

(b) In somatoform disorder (hysterical neurosis), the client uses physical illness to obtain sympathy and support from others. In extreme cases, clients have sought numerous surgical operations to treat pains and complaints that had no physical basis. This required a great deal of 'doctor shopping', because after a doctor operated and found no basis to the complaint, the clients had to go to another doctor for a similar or second operation. People with mental retardation who live in residential facilities cannot shop around for doctors and are not likely to be given operations without physical evidence to support their verbal complaints. What might they do instead? In one extreme case, a young man developed the habit of swallowing ping pong balls. Every time he did this, he was rushed to hospital and had his stomach pumped. By swallowing ping pong balls, he induced a 'phoney' illness. Whereas the average client with somatoform disorder can gain sympathy and attention by repeatedly complaining of a 'phoney' illness to different doctors, the person with mental retardation sometimes has to induce a phoney illness to obtain the same effect.

4. Admit limitations of knowledge

Sometimes the behaviour problems of a person with severe or profound mental retardation cannot be diagnosed with any confidence. In such cases, the best one can do is to acknowledge the diagnostic ambiguity and to make no diagnosis at all. One should not provide diagnostic opinions beyond what can be based on knowledge of psychopathology and dual diagnosis.

Psychometric instruments

There has been need for screening instruments to identify psychiatric symptoms seen in persons with mental retardation by care staff, work supervisors, teachers etc. The Reiss Scales for Maladaptive Behaviour (1988*a*) for use with clients aged 14 and older and the Reiss Scales for Children's Dual Diagnosis (Reiss & Valenti-Hein, 1990) for use with children and adolescents between the ages of 4 and 18 are two such instruments feature similar formats and are standardised with populations of persons with mental retardation.

The Reiss screen has 36 items and the Reiss Scales have 60 items. Each item refers to a psychiatric symptom or behavioural category, rather than to a specific behaviour. The ratings are made by staff members who know the client well enough to report maladaptive behaviour. The informants rate the degree to which each category of maladaptive behaviour is currently *no problem*, *a problem*, or *a major problem* in the life of the person being evaluated.

The items are presented in three parts: the name of the symptom (such as withdrawn); a non-technical definition ('avoids personal contact with other people'); and common behavioural examples ('excessively shy, doesn't participate in group activities, prefers to be alone, socially isolated'). The common behavioural examples are intended to help the carer, who in most instances is not a mental health professional, understand the items.

The items on each instrument cover the full range of psychopathology.

Each Reiss instrument provides scores for psychometric scales, aggressive behaviour problem, anger, attention deficit disorder with hyperactivity, autism, avoidant disorder, anxiety disorder, conduct disorder, depression, paranoia, poor self-image, psychosis, personality disorder, and withdrawal.

The Reiss instruments also provide scores for significant behaviour problems. These include crying spells, hallucinations, pica, self-injury, sexual problems and suicidal tendencies.

The total score on each Reiss instrument is interpreted as a measure of the severity of psychopathology. The basic idea is that the more severe examples of psychopathology are more likely to exhibit a wide range of symptoms and more likely to result in ratings of 'major problems' rather than 'problems'. High total scores, however, must be judged in reference to the norms because almost nobody obtains a total score anywhere near the maximum possible score.

The most reliable scores on the Reiss instruments are the total scores. Cronbach's coefficient alpha has been estimated at .84 for the adult instrument and .91 for the child instrument. These findings indicate an adequate to high degree of internal reliability. The greater internal reliability for the child instrument is probably related to the greater number of items.

The Reiss instruments were found to have factor content validity. In other words, the results of factor analyses suggested scales that are consistent with psychiatric diagnosis and the basic concepts of psychopathology. The factor analytic findings imply that care staff using the Reiss instruments tend to group symptoms/items in ways that are consistent with psychiatric diagnosis.

Personality assessment

Personality assessment is widely used to help understand the psychological basis of a behaviour problem. These data are relevant to understanding such 'why' issues as: Why is Jones depressed? Why does Smith sometimes become explosively violent? The most widely used personality instrument is the Minnesota Multiphasis Personality Inventory (Hathaway & McKinley, 1943).

Projective assessment provides an alternative to true/false questions in the assessment of personality. An example of a widely-used projective test is the Thematic Apperceptive Test (TAT) (Morgan & Murray, 1935).

The Thematic Apperceptive Test has been probably the most widely used personality test for persons with mild mental retardation. This is because people with mental retardation are more comfortable telling stories than responding to direct questions about their personality or behaviour (Hurley & Sovner, 1985; Sarason, 1943). However, the TAT is outdated. The cards depict scenes with little contemporary relevance; minorities are not depicted in the cards; the cards have a gloomy, depressive tone. Interpretations of the TAT lack objectivity and rely too much on the subjective opinion of the examiner.

The Apperceptive Personality Test (APT) represents a promising alternative to the TAT (Karp *et al.*, 1989). The APT provides a set of eight new stimulus cards depicting contemporary scenes. However, the unique feature of the APT is that the subject completes a questionnaire about each story. In the questionnaire, the client identifies the characters, indicates how the characters feel and behave toward one another, indicates if the story has a happy ending and rates each character on a series of bipolar scales. The client's responses to the questionnaire are typed directly into a computer.

Steven Reiss, Betsy Benson, and Joe Szyszko are adapting the APT for use with persons with mild mental retardation. Four changes are being made. First, the administration time for a person with mild mental retardation is being reduced to about 30 to 40 minutes. The number of stimulus cards are being reduced from eight to four, and the length of the questionnaire is being reduced. Secondly, two stimulus cards were developed explicitly to relate the test to common psychological themes among people with mental retardation. Thirdly, the questionnaire rating scales are presented in two steps rather than one. For example, instead of asking the client to rate a story character as happy/sad on a 4-point scale, Question 1 might be; 'Is this man happy or sad'? If the client said 'sad', Question 2 would be; 'Is this man a little sad or a lot sad'? The response to the two questions are then transformed into a 4-point rating of happy/sad. Fourth, the test is being normed on people with mental retardation.

Summary

In the last decade, some progress has been made regarding the assessment of psychiatric disorders in persons with mental retardation. Today, there is some awareness that people with mental retardation are vulnerable to psychiatric disorders. The concept of dual diagnosis has been recognised; under this concept, all important service needs are assessed and no effort is made to label one set of needs as 'secondary' handicaps. The phenomenon of diagnostic overshadowing has helped explain findings that psychiatric disorders have been underdiagnosed for people with mental retardation. There is growing evidence that some cases of aggressive behaviour are associated with psychiatric disorders. For particularly ambiguous cases, criteria have been proposed to help decide when a behaviour is a symptom of mental retardation versus mental illness. Standardised screening instruments have been developed and have been widely distributed throughout the United States. Research continues on the development of the APT/MR as a new personality instrument explicitly designed for use with people with mental retardation.

References

American Psychiatric Association (1987). *Diagnostic and Statistical Manual of Mental Disorders*. 3rd edn., rev. Washington, DC.

Bem, D. J. (1972). Self-perception theory. In L. Berkowitz, ed. *Advances in Experimental Social Psychology*, vol. 6. New York: Academic Press.

Benson, B. A., Reiss, S., Smith, D. C. & Laman, D. C. (1985). Psychosocial correlates of depression in mentally retarded adults II: Poor social skills. *American Journal of Mental Deficiency*, **89**, 331–7.

Cutts, R. A. (1957). Differentiation between pseudo-mental defectives with emotional disorders and mental defectives with emotional disturbances. *American Journal of Mental Deficiency*, **61**, 761–2.

Hathaway, S. A. & McKinley, J. C. (1943). *Minnesota Multiphasic Personality Inventory Manual*. New York: The Psychological Corporation.

Hurley, A. D. & Sovner, R. (1985). The use of the thematic apperception test in mentally retarded persons. *Psychiatric Aspects of Mental Retardation*, **4**, 9–12.

Karp, S. A., Holmstrom, R. W. & Silber, D. E. (1989). *Apperceptive Personality Test Manual*. Worthington, OH: International Diagnostic Systems, Inc.

Kazdin, A. E., Matson, J. E. & Senatore, M. S. W. (1983). Assessment of depression in mentally retarded adults. *American Journal of Psychiatry*, **140**, 1040–3.

Laman, D. S. (1989). A longitudinal investigation of the relationship among depressed mood, social support and social skills in mentally retarded adults. Doctoral Dissertation, Department of psychology, University of Illinois at Chicago.

Laman, D. L. & Reiss, S. (1985). Social skills deficiencies associated with depressed mood in mentally retarded adults. *American Journal of Mental Deficiency*, **92**, 224–9.

Matson, J. L. (1988). *The PIMRA Manual*. Worthington, OH: International Diagnostic Systems, Inc.

Morgan, C. & Murray, H. (1935). A method for investigating fantasies: the thematic apperception test. *Archives of Neurology and Psychiatry*, **434**, 289–306.

Reid, A. H. (1972). Psychoses in adult mental defectives. I. Manic depressive psychoses. *British Journal of Psychiatry*, **120**, 205–12.

Reiss, S. (1988*a*). *Test Manual for the Reiss Screen for maladaptive behavior*. Worthington, OH: International Diagnostic Systems, Inc.

Reiss, S. (1988*b*). Dual diagnosis in the United States. Australia and New Zealand *Journal of Developmental Disabilities*, **14**, 43–50.

Reiss, S. (1990*a*). Prevalence of dual diagnosis in community-based day programs in the Chicago metropolitan area. *American Journal of Mental Deficiency*, **94**, 578–85.

Reiss, S. (1990*b*). The development of a screening measure for psychopathology in people with mental retardation. In E. Dibble and D. B. Gray, eds. *Assessment of Behavior Problems in Persons with Mental Retardation Living in the Community*, pp. 107–118. Rockville, MD: National Institute of Mental Health.

Reiss, S. (1992). Assessment of man with dual diagnosis. *Mental Retardation*, **30**, 1–16.

Reiss, S. (1993). Assessment of dual diagnosis. In J. L. Matson and R. P. Barrett (eds.), *Psychopathology in the Mentally Retarded*. 2nd edn., pp. 17–40, Boston: Allyn & Bacon.

Reiss, S. & Benson, B. A. (1985). Psychosocial correlates of depression in mentally retarded adults I: minimal social support and stigmatization. *American Journal of Mental Deficiency*, **89**, 331–7.

Reiss, S., Levitan, G. W., & McNally, R. J. (1982). Emotionally disturbed, mentally retarded people: an underserved population. *American Psychologist*, **37**, 361–7.

Reiss, S., Levitan, G. W. & Szyszko, J. (1982). Emotional disturbance and mental retardation: Diagnostic overshadowing. *American Journal of Mental Deficiency*, **86**, 567–74.

Reiss, S., Reiss, M. & Reppucci, N. D. (1978). Rejection of success in two severely retarded children. *Cognitive Therapy and Research*, **2**, 293–7.

Reiss, S. & Rojahn, J. (1992). Joint occurrence of depression and aggression in children and adults with mental retardation. Unpublished manuscript, Nisonger Centre, Ohio State University.

Reiss, S. & Szyszko, J. (1983). Diagnostic overshadowing and professional experience with mentally retarded persons. *American Journal of Mental Deficiency*, **87**, 396–402.

Reiss, S. & Valenti-Hein, D. (1990). *Test Manual for the Reiss Scales for Children's Dual Diagnosis*. Worthington, OH: International Diagnostic Systems, Inc.

Reynolds, W. M. & Baker, J. A. (1988). Assessment of depression in persons with mental retardation. *American Journal of Mental Deficiency*, **103**, 93–8.

Sarason, S. B. (1943). The use of the thematic apperception test with mentally deficient children: II. A study of high grade girls. *American Journal of Mental Deficiency*, **47**, 415–21.

Weisz, J. R. (1981). Effect of the 'mentally retarded' label on adult judgments about child failure. *Journal of Abnormal Psychology*, **90**, 371–4.

7

Psychiatric disorders in mental retardation

WILLIAM FRASER AND MARY NOLAN

Introduction

People with mental retardation exhibit the full range of psychiatric disorders found in the non-handicapped population. Many reviews have indicated that psychiatric disorder is more frequently reported in this group than in the general population. However, prevalence figures vary enormously from one study to another. Most estimates of the prevalence of serious psychiatric disorder, including both personality disorders and the psychoses, range from 8% to 15%. When minor emotional disorders are included, estimates are over 50%. Little is known about the natural history of mental disorders in the people with mental retardation.

Distinguishing behaviour disturbance from psychiatric disorder

The initial presentation to a psychiatrist is usually one of a behaviour disturbance which is causing management problems. Behaviours are labelled disturbed and reacted to as disturbed because 1) the disturbed person reacts in an idiosyncratic or inappropriate manner, i.e. the behaviour is difficult to understand; 2) their actions conflict with the smooth function and norms of the relevant social groups. Obviously the norms of contact between social groups vary and therefore individual perception of behaviour disturbance contains a subjective element. It should also be acknowledged that such behaviours negatively affect the long-term character of interactions with the disturbed person.

In any assessment we have to take into account both environmentally dependent factors, such as failed communications and aberrant behaviours which have been inadvertently reinforced, and environmentally inde-pendent factors, such as stage of development, preservation of homeostasis or habitual state of arousal of the individual, organic or functional mental illness (Baumeister, 1989). Behaviour disturbance by itself is thus insufficient for a psychiatric diagnosis.

Psychiatric diagnoses do not correlate well with behaviour disturbances. Behaviour disturbances may be due to any or all of the psychiatric disorders and these disorders may present as any or all of the behaviour disturbances commonly seen and identified in checklists, i.e. aggressive conduct, mood disturbances, withdrawal, antisocial conduct, idiosyncratic mannerisms and self injurious behaviours (Fraser *et al.*, 1986). The methods for assessing socially instigated aberrant behaviours include structured interviews (e.g. motivation assessment of self injurious behaviour, Durand & Crimmins, 1988), structured questionnaires (e.g. Aide to Functional analysis, Willis and LaVigna, unpublished manual), and direct observation either purely ethological or under evocative conditions (e.g. Iwata *et al.*, 1982; Sturmey *et al.* 1988). Checklist/inventory approaches have their limitations; they may be insensitive to minor behavioural changes, although the aberrant behaviour checklist (Aman *et al.* 1985) is sensitive enough for use in quite subtle medication engineering; they are relatively insensitive to environmental factors and to frequency, intensity and severity of behaviours (although the behaviour disturbance scale, Leudar & Fraser 1987, does take account of such factors). For proper analysis of the setting events that alter the reinforcing properties of environmental stimuli (and such 'setting events' include very important mental states), there is no substitute for direct observation in the natural environment. Repp and Felce (1990) have developed a system which allows the recording of up to 45 events on a portable computer, the Epson HX20. This allows environment/behaviour sequences to be analysed rather than just summary estimates of the frequency/duration of behaviour disturbances. The Lag analysis procedure (Box & Jenkins, 1970) can be used to determine the consistency of any event (variable) following any other event (variable), no *a priori* judgments are made as to which variables are independent and dependent, and may shed light on whether, for instance, a stereotype movement is environmentally independent or a sign of anxiety. Clinicians will not all have access to such aides, and must have a starting point to separate such a matrix of causes and consequences. That starting point should be developmental. The centrality of a developmental history and an examination of behaviour from a developmental perspective is paramount. The clinician must ask: do we need further explanations to account for this behaviour beyond developmental arrest? Quite often we do not, the behaviour is appropriate to the person's mental and emotional age.

The developmental perspective

However complex the interplay of environmental and intrinsic factors, their impact should be considered taking account of the individual's stage of development.

A thorough developmental history will reveal attention deficit disorder, developmental language disorder and pervasive developmental disorder, in addition to unspecified mental retardation. Such knowledge is crucial to the formulation of the predicament of a person with mental retardation and mental illness 'dual diagnosis'. Within a thorough developmental history supported by antenatal and birth history, and wherever possible, by Griffiths assessments or other forms of developmental quotients in early childhood, particular attention will be paid to social and language development as being the most sensitive indicators among the developmental milestones of subsequent psychological problems. There must be close questioning about reciprocal social interaction in infancy especially questions about intersubjectivity between mother and infant at the turn-taking stage; marked lack of awareness of others; abnormal seeking of comfort in the first year of life against the background of impairment in social play and peer friendships; and close questioning also on whether the child was abnormally fretful or placid, lacked early communication vocal or non-vocal, and the presence of a markedly restrictive repertoire of activities and interests, and if and when stereotyped body movements appeared. Similar questions about sleep problems and longstanding presence of continuous overactivity conduct will, if asked in a sensitive way, gradually build information towards a complete inventory of DSM IIIR criteria for, e.g. autistic disorder, other 'pervasive developmental disorders', developmental language disorders, attention deficit/hyperactivity disorder (ADDH), conduct disorder, oppositional defiant disorder and pathological avoidant disorder of childhood; all of which will be important factors in subsequent superimposed clinical conditions. It is likely that the clumsy term 'pervasive developmental disorder', which is approximately equivalent to the old term 'childhood psychosis', will fall into disuse and be replaced by the term 'autistic disorder or autistic spectrum disorder', although it, too, lacks specificity and is simply a clinical presentation of a final common path for many aetiologies.

Slow language development is part and parcel of mental retardation. However, children with uncomplicated mental retardation do their best to obey the maxims of conversation (that is, they try to take turns and co-operate in conversation, make their intentions known and be as clear as they can). People with 'childhood psychosis', whatever the cause, infringe many aspects of language. They violate the rules of language whilst straightforward children with mental retardation are simply slow in their acquisition of language. People with Pervasive DDs and psychosis sometimes violate the rules of syntax, phonology, prosody and pragmatics. Most of all, their language seems inappropriate. Bishop and Adams (1989) have made a start in disentangling the concept of inappropriacy in speech, broadly dichotomising it into due to linguistic difficulties and due to social and cognition difficulties. If people with mental retardation are inappropriate, it is mostly due to social cognition deficits. They are also inappropriate to a variable extent due to their linguistic difficulties. Rapin and Allen (1983) introduced the term 'semantic pragmatic deficit syndrome' as part of a subcategorisation of developmental language disorder in children. The main difficulty with children with semantic pragmatic disorder is that their language is structurally well formed but they have difficulty with including meaning relevant to the conversational situation.

Pathogenesis of psychiatric disorders

Many possible explanations have been proposed for the increased prevalence of psychiatric disorders in people with mental retardation:

1 Brain damage may cause both mental retardation and the psychiatric disorder. Neuroepileptic conditions give rise to a fivefold increase in the psychiatric disorders of childhood when compared with normal children (Rutter, Graham & Yule, 1970). Rutter (1989) also describes a chain of constraining environmental effects set in motion by a single negative event in infancy or childhood.
2 Repeated loss/separations.
3 Communication difficulties.
4 Low intelligence leading to poor coping mechanisms and vulnerability to exploitation.
5 Family difficulties, parental ill health, marital discord, inadequate discipline.
6 Failure to acquire social, interpersonal and recreational skills may impair relationships and predispose to ill health.
7 Low self-esteem from repeated failure, true/rejection from family, perceived repeated dysmorphic/unattractive appearance.
8 Labelling/adverse environments/adverse life events.

In summary, brain dysfunction interacts with other psychological, psychodynamic and environmental stresses and abnormalities to cause a psychiatric disorders.

Schizophrenia

It is now generally accepted that the point prevalence of schizophrenia in those with mental retardation is 3 % as compared with a 1 % prevalence in non-handicapped population. There is no agreed explanation for these figures. If anything, there is a tendency to see these figures as an underestimate across the whole population. Swedish studies from the 1950s give some indirect support to this view with a finding of 10.5 % rate of 'mental deficiency' amongst as registered cohort of schizophrenics. The exclusion of those people with organic illnesses (including mental retardation) from defined cohorts of schizophrenics in clinical studies hamper the delineation of this condition in this group. As yet there are no longitudinal/outcome studies, although Reid (1972) reported that the natural history was the same as in the non-disabled.

Differential diagnosis

The differentiation of schizophrenia from depression in people who have non-verbal communication is extremely difficult as there is no defined constellation of non-verbal symptoms of schizophrenia and it would be difficult to diagnose with an IQ much below the upper end of the moderate range. This does not mean that those with severe mental retardation do not suffer from schizophrenia, and there is a risk of under diagnosis and subsequently providing inadequate treatment for this group.

There may be problems in differentiating between the symptoms of mental retardation from those associated with negative symptoms of schizophrenia, i.e. amotivation, slowness of thought and action, poverty of speech and emotional blunting (Murray, 1986). Only a careful developmental history can separate pervasive developmental disorders (e.g. Autism, Asperger's) from schizophrenia, especially the negative forms (Clarke *et al.*, 1989; Turner, 1989).

Clinical features

It is generally accepted that the presentation of schizophrenia in those with mild mental retardation is very similar to that in the non-intellectually handicapped. This was confirmed in a recent study by Meadows *et al.* (1991) which compared clinical phenomena of 25 patients with 'mild mental handicap' and a diagnosis of schizophrenia with 26 schizophrenics of normal intelligence using the lifetime version of the schedule for affective disorders and schizophrenia. The results showed that both quantitatively and qualitatively the clinical phenomena elicited were the same in both study groups. There was a suggestion, however, that persecutory delusions and formal thought disorder may be less commonly encountered in the 'dual diagnosis' group. They also found that the mean age at first episode of schizophrenia was significantly earlier in the group with 'mental handicap', 22.5 years vs. 26.8 years $p < 0.05$. This finding supports earlier work which has linked earlier onset of schizophrenia with poorer academic performance (Aylward, Walker & Bettes, 1984). The reasons for this are as yet unclear; however, various suggestions have included that the co-existence of schizophrenia in a person with mental retardation represents a neurodevelopmental disorder, the severity of which is reflected by an earlier presentation. Alternatively, it has been proposed that this group are less able to cope with the early symptoms of a psychosis and hence present earlier.

The moderately handicapped may present with withdrawal, fearfulness, sleep disturbance and hallucinations without complex delusional systems, but may be able to express simple paranoid ideation (Heaton-Ward, 1977). Eaton and Menolascino (1982) were able to diagnose paranoid schizo-phrenia in both verbal and non-verbal communication of people with mental retardation. They reported that paranoid and catatonic features were the hallmarks of acute/chronic undifferentiated schizophrenia in this group.

As in any psychiatric evaluation, a longitudinal history can be invaluable in supporting a diagnosis of schizophrenia made on cross-sectional data, especially in those with limited communicative functioning. Such illnesses may produce a decrease in intellectual functioning as assessed on intelligence testing.

Affective disorder

People with mental retardation manifest the full range of affective disorders with depressed mood being amongst the commonest of psy-chiatric symptoms in this (Sovner & Hurley, 1983; Szymanski & Biederman, 1984).

Most changes tend to be poorly sustained and in the manic lacking in the quality of infectious gaiety typical of the normally intelligent manic. Associated delusions tend to be naive. For those functioning in the mild/moderate range standard diagnostic criteria can usually be used, (Sovner & Hurley 1983), aided by modified standard depression inventories (Kazdin, Matson & Senatore, 1983). A clinically useful diagnosis can be made, even in those with absent language development, based on behavioural and biological changes, especially when supported by a knowledge of mental illness in the family (Sovner, 1989). This may require a prolonged period of study of behaviour, levels of motor activity, weight and sleep patterns. It has been suggested that the presence of severe mental retardation may contribute to an early presentation of affective illnesses even in childhood or adolescence (Reid, 1980) and that states of severe depression may be encountered in childhood autism (Wing & Wing, 1976).

Not surprisingly, depressed mood has, as in the non-handicapped population, been found to be associated with poor social skills and low levels of social support (Laman & Reiss, 1985).

Suicidal behaviour has been rarely studied in those with mental retardation and such behaviour is perceived as rare to non-existent in the more severely handicapped. Reported suicides tend to be by less disabled individuals, often with definite superimposed psychiatric disorders. Walters (1990) reported four cases with IQs below 50 who clearly exhibited behaviour deemed suicidal or self endangering. These were gathered over 20 years, thus suggesting it to be a rare phenomenon in this group.

Manic depressive illness is marginally easier than schizophrenia to diagnose in people with mental retardation. Features associated with mania include increased motor output, vocalisation, aggression and sleeplessness; and of depression, decreased motor activity (or, para-doxically, wandering), poor appetite, sleeplessness or hypersomnolence. Taking longitudinal accounts of the behaviour, weight, sleep patterns based on reports by care givers, and using Spectral Analysis can help to establish complex periodicity on a periodogram to define a pattern of mood swings or behaviour (Tyrer & Shakour, 1990).

Evidence from communication about mental states

The careful analysis of communicative patterns of people with mental retardation can reveal a good deal about their mental state beyond assigning them to a specific developmental disorder. The developmentally delayed speaker/listener has not only problems with understanding what is going on but has difficulties in making his/her intentions known, obeying the conventions of communication and in saving face when things are going wrong in conversation. Much behaviour in people with mental retardation can be portrayed as the 'management of a spoiled identity' (Leudar, 1991).

The communicative encounter with a person with mental retardation should start with the questions: 1. What is his developmental age? 2. What is his Communicative age (comprehension and production), 3. What are the communicative demands made on him by his environment? 4. Is he making his intentions clear? 5. If not, is it his syntax or phonology or pragmatics (practical management of communication)? 6. If there is a problem of pragmatics, which conventions (maxims) of language does he infringe? The *maxim of quantity*: speakers should make their contribution as informative as required and not more or less so. The *maxim of quality*: speakers try not to say what they believe to be false or where they lack evidence. The *maxim of relevance*: speakers try to make contributions that are relevant. The *maxim of manner*: speakers try to avoid obscurity, be brief and orderly (Grice's Cooperative Principle, 1975). Leach (1983) describes the 'politeness principle' in detail and its maxims of tact, generosity, application and modesty, all of which are potential problems for people with mental retardation. Such people, when in trouble with the police, are likely to have problems with explanatory discourse, and when a mental illness supervenes, with the maxim of relevance.

Just observe for some of the interview what is going on. How does the person with mental retardation greet the interviewer (e.g. the gaze avoidance and gait/posture of the person with Fragile-X)? How does the speaker initiate verbal activity, gain/regain attention, request, give feedback, give general information. In taking turns how does the speaker indicate that he wants to yield the floor? How are silences/overlaps/ interruptions dealt with? How does the person with mental retardation link together his discourse i.e. ideas and thoughts (coherence), and how does he structure his text and 'bind' expressions together (cohesion)? How informative is he? Can the person with mental retardation locate and spontaneously 'repair trouble spots in the conversation? Can he do repairs in response to a request for clarification? Can he use presequences to orientate listeners to a later target sequences? Are insertion of topics potentially troublesome to him? Can he work with the listener to accomplish acceptable opening and closing routines? Can he signal to the listener topic change, response, distress, surprise, acknowledgment or agreement?

Schizophrenia, mania and other causes of inappropriacy in communication, can be differentiated, and perhaps confirmed by computer assisted language analysis, in mild mental retardation. By close attention to these questions, the clinician can really start to appreciate the difficulties the person with mental retardation faces even though he may have superficially good grammar and vocabulary. If the clinician does detect incoherence, he/she should proceed to test for thought disorder using Andreasen's (1986) scale for the assessment of thought, language and communication.

Neurotic disorders

Establishing the prevalence of neurotic disorders in people with mental retardation is extremely difficult, especially so in those with moderate and severe learning disabilities. In Day's 1983 study of admissions over a 5 year period, 28% were diagnosed as neurotic, of which only 4% were moderately and none severely disabled. With the resettlement of people with mental retardation into the community, it might be anticipated that more neuroses will occur with the exposure to the stress of ordinary life.

Acute anxiety states may develop in people with mental retardation as a response to stress in the same way as in the normally intelligent individual. Those unable to verbalise their feelings may present with low mood, self-injury or various types of acting out behaviours.

The prevalence of obsessive compulsive disorders (OCD) in the general population has been estimated to be 1%. In Vitiello, Spreat and Behar's (1989) study of institutions with mentally retarded people in, a prevalence of 3.5% was reported. There was also a suggestion that the clinical manifestations of this disorder differed in this group with ordering being the commonest compulsion, with no instances of hand washing which is the commonest amongst the intellectually normal. The diagnosis of OCD can be made in people with mental retardation based on external observation of repetitive, ritualistic behaviour and its functional consequences. Anxiety and subjective feelings may be unnecessary for a reliable diagnosis. It is often impossible to distinguish Asperger's and OCD in the developing child.

Some authors suggest that hysterical phenomena are common and sometimes 'gross' in handicapped people and probably a function of increased suggestibility with the meaning and gain being readily apparent. Such symptoms may occur as a response to stress or be associated with an affective disorder.

Personality disorder

Very little attention has been paid to the problems of personality disorder in this population. One of the problems has been that personality disorder is hard to specify and define and classifications tend to be arbitrary. However, this area is of increasing importance since personality factors are of great relevance in determining the success of the individual's introduction into the community.

Reid and Ballinger's (1987) survey of hospitalised mild/moderately handicapped adults using a standard assessment of personality, reported 56% of their group having features of abnormal personality and, in 22%, this abnormality was felt to be of a severity to suggest a personality disorder. This compares with an earlier community based study which found 27.1% of their sample to have personality disorder (Eaton & Menolascino, 1982). Day's 1985 study reported that personality disorder was the commonest psychiatric diagnosis in people with mental retardation amongst first admission psychiatric patients, and there was a strong correlation between these disorders and the adult male patient.

Obviously there are considerable problems studying such disorders in this group and the majority of the studies have failed to report personality disorder other than in people with mild/moderate mental retardation (Lund, 1985; Menolascino & Potter, 1989). Whether the diagnosis of personality disorder is possible or even relevant in the severely disabled is unclear, and it has been suggested that a personality typology rooted more in developmental concepts might be more appropriate (Gostason, 1985). Examples of phenotype personalities are Fragile-X syndrome and Prader–Willi syndrome.

There is considerable variability in the extent and severity of the clinical manifestations of Prader–Willi syndrome; there are some common behavioural and personality problems. In addition to the disturbed behaviour related to hyperphagia, psychosocial adjustments and relationships are often impaired partly because of sensitivity about physical appearance and also feelings of worthlessness and inferiority (Berg & Gosse, 1990). In questionnaire surveys, the following characteristics have been noted: skin picking, belligerence, stubbornness, irritability and impulsiveness (Greenswag, 1987).

Differential diagnosis

In the more disabled individuals it can be difficult to distinguish personality factors from the long-term consequences of psychotic illnesses. The operational definitions of some disorders include symptoms which may be difficult to identify as separate from the features of mental retardation e.g. passivity, inadequacy.

The diagnostic category of schizotypal personality has received attention in relation to its diagnosis in those with mental retardation and specifically its relationship with the autistic spectrum disorders. One approach to distinguish schizotypal personalities from high functioning autistics (HFA) or Asperger's in adult life is by psycholinguistic analysis. The HFA has abnormal prosody or bizarre stress contours in speech, the Asperger's less so, and the schizotypal personality has normal stress contours. Pilot studies of pragmatic skills suggest that HFA pays less attention to the listener's needs, Asperger's make an attempt, and the schizotypal person can do but may not choose to.

Organic psychoses

The effects of organic cerebral disease are more marked in people with mental retardation than in the general population.

Acute organic brain syndromes

An important cause of acute confusional states in people with mental retardation are drug side effects. Not only are they susceptible to the toxic effects of anticonvulsants but also antidepressants and tranquillisers. Chronic organic brain syndromes include people with Down's syndrome who survive into middle age are prone to develop a dementia whose neuropathology is identical to that of Alzheimer's disease, (see Part III).

Summary

In conclusion, 'dual diagnosis' is a useful term but also a crude simplification. Behaviour disturbances in people with mental retardation have complex origins, with psychiatric disorder being just one possibility. 'Challenging behaviour' is a final common path with many causes and contributory factors. Professionals have conceptualised 'Challenging behaviour' restrictively from their own discipline's typologies, practices and perspectives. This may be necessary to make sense of what is often a bewildering interplay of causes and effects. In this chapter we make a plea that clinicians start from a developmental perspective, and become better acquainted with socio- communicative aspects of learning disability.

References

Aman, M. G., Singh, N. N., Stewart, A. W. & Field, C. J. (1985) The aberrant behaviour checklist: a behaviour rating scale for the assessment of treatment effects. *American Journal of Mental Deficiency*, **89**, 485–91.

Andreasen, N. (1986). Scales for the assessment of thought, language and communication. *Schizophrenia Bulletin*, **12**(3), 473–81.

Aylward, E., Walker, E. & Bettes, B. (1984). Intelligence in schizophrenia: meta-analysis of the research. *Schizophrenia Bulletin*, **10**(3), 430–59.

Baumeister, A. A. (1989). Causes of severe maladaptive behaviour in persons with severe mental retardation: a review of hypotheses. Presentation given to the National Institutes of Health, Bethesda, MD.

Berg, J. M. & Gosse, G. C. (1990). Specific mental retardation disorders and problem behaviours. *International Review of Psychiatry*, **2**, 53–60.

Bishop, D. V. M. (1989). Autism, Asperger's syndrome and semantic–pragmatic disorder : Where are the boundaries? *British Journal of Disorders of Communication*, **24**, 107–21.

Bishop, D. V. M. & Adams, C. (1989). Conversational characteristics of children with semantic-pragmatic disorders. II. What features lead to a judgement of inappropriacy? *British Journal of Disorders of Communication*, **24**, 241–63.

Box, G. & Jenkins, G. (1970). *Time Series Analysis. Forecasting and Control.* San Francisco: Holder Day.

Clarke, D. J., Littlejohns, C. S., Corbett, J. A. & Joseph, S. (1989). Pervasive developmental disorders and psychoses in adult life. *British Journal of Psychiatry*, **155**, 692–9.

Corbett, J. A., Harris, R. & Robinson, R. G. (1975). In J. Wortis, ed. *Mental Retardation and Developmental Disabilities*. Vol. VII, pp. 79–111. New York: Brunner Mazel.

Day, K. (1983). A hospital-based psychiatric unit for mentally handicapped adults. *Mental Handicap*, **11**, 137–40.

Day, K. (1985). Psychiatric disorder in the middle-aged and elderly mentally handicapped. *British Journal of Psychiatry*, **147**, 660–7.

Durand, V. M. & Crimmins, D. (1988). Identifying the variables maintaining self injurious behaviour. *Journal of Autism and Developmental Disorders*, **17**, 17–28.

Eaton, L. F. & Menolascino, F. J. (1982). Psychiatric disorders in the mentally retarded: types, problems and challenges. *American Journal of Psychiatry*, **139**, 1297–303.

Fraser, W. I., Leudar, I., Gray, J. & Campbell I. (1986). Psychiatric and behaviour disturbance in mental handicap. *Journal of Mental Deficiency Research*, **30**, 49–59.

Greenswag, L. R. (1987). Adults with Prader–Willi syndrome: a survey of 232 cases. *Developmental Medicine and Child Neurology*, **29**, 145–52.

Grice, P. (1975). Logic and conversation. In Cole, P., Morgan, J., eds. *Syntax and Semantics. III Speech Acts.* Academic Press, New York.

Heaton-Ward, A. (1977). Psychosis in mental handicap. *British Journal of Psychiatry*, **130**, 525–33.

Iwata, B., Dorsey, N., Slifer, K., Bauman, K. & Richman, G. (1982). Towards a functional analysis of self-injury. *Analysis and Intervention in Developmental Disabilities*, **2**, 3–20.

Kazdin, A. E., Matson, J. L. & Senatore, V. (1983). Assessment of depression in mentally retarded adults. *American Journal of Psychiatry*, **140**, 1040–3.

Laman, D. S. & Reiss, S. (1985). Social skill deficiencies associated with depressed mood of mentally retarded adults. *American Journal of Mental Deficiency*, **92**, 224–9.

Leach, G. N. (1983). *Principles of Pragmatics.* Longman, London.

Leudar, I. Fraser, W. & Jeeves, M. A. (1987). Theoretical problems and practical solutions to behaviour disorders in retarded people. *Health Bulletin*, **45**, 347–55.

Leudar, I. (1991). Discourse in people with Handicaps. A lecture at the Forum on Mental Retardation. Royal Society of Medicine. London

Leudar, I. & Fraser, W. (1987). Behaviour disturbance and its assessment. In *Assessment in Mental Handicap*. Hogg, J. and Raynes, N. V., eds., pp. 107–28, Croom Helm.

Lund, J. (1985). Mentally retarded admitted to psychiatric hospitals in Denmark. *Acta Psychiatrica*, **72**, 202–5.

Matson, J. L., Gardner, W. I., Coe, D. A. & Sovner, R. (1991). A scale for evaluating emotional disorders in severely and profoundly mentally retarded persons. *British Journal of Psychiatry*, **159**, 404–9.

Meadows, G., Turner, T., Campbell, L., Lewis, S. W., Reveley, M. A. & Murray, R. M. (1991). Assessing schizophrenia in adults with mental retardation: a comparative study. *British Journal of Psychiatry*, **158**, 103–5.

Menolascino, F. J. & Potter, J. F. (1989). Mental illness in the elderly mentally retarded. *Journal of Applied Gerontology*, **8**, 192–202.

Murray, R. (1986). Schizophrenia. In P. Hill, R. Murray & A. Thorley, eds. *Essentials of postgraduate psychiatry*, pp. 3–36. London: Grune & Stratton.

Rapin, I. & Allen, D. (1983). Developmental language disorders: nosologic considerations. In U. Kirk, ed. *Neuropsychology of Language, Reading and Spelling*. New York: Academic Press.

Reid, A. H. (1972). Psychoses in adult mental defectives : manic depressive psychoses. *British Journal of Psychiatry*, **120**, 205–12.

Reid, A. H. (1980). Diagnosis of psychiatry disorder in the severely and profoundly retarded patient. Journal of the Royal Society of Medicine. 73, 607–609.

Reid, A. H. & Ballinger, B. R. (1987). Personality disorder in mental handicap. *Psychological Medicine*, **17**, 983–9.

Reiss, S. (1992). Assessment of psychopathology in persons with mental retardation. In J. L. Matson & R. P. Barrett (Eds). *Psychopathology and Mental Retardation*. 2nd edn. New York: Grune Stratton.

Repp, A. & Felce, D. (1990). A micro-computer system used for evaluative and experimental research in mental handicap. *Mental Handicap Research*, **3**, 21–32.

Rutter, M. (1989). Pathways from childhood to adult life. *Journal of Child Psychology and Psychiatry*, **30**, 23–53.

Rutter, M., Graham, P. & Yule, W. (1970). *A Neuropsychiatric Study in Childhood*. Spastics International Medical Publications. London.

Senatore, V., Matson, J. L. & Kazdin, A. E. (1985). An inventory to assess psychopathology of mentally retarded adults. *American Journal of Mental Deficiency*, **89**, 459–66.

Sovner, R. (1989). The use of Valproate in the treatment of mentally retarded persons with typical and atypical bipolar disorders. *Journal of Clinical Psychiatry*, **50**, 40–3.

Sovner, R. & Hurley, A. D. (1983). Do the mentally retarded suffer from affective illness? *Archives of General Psychiatry*, **40**, 61–7.

Sturmey, P., Carlson, A., Crisp, A. & Newton, J. I. (1988). The functional analysis of Aberrant responses. A refinement and extension of Iwata *et al.*'s (1982) methodology. *Journal of Mental Deficiency Research*, **32**, 31–46.

Szymanski, L. S. & Biederman, J. (1984). Depression and anorexia nervosa of persons with Down syndrome. *American Journal of Mental Deficiency*, **89**(3), 246–51.

Turk, J. (1992). The Fragile-X syndrome: on the way to a behavioural phenotype. *British Journal of Psychiatry*, **160**, 24–35.

Turner, T. H. (1989). Schizophrenia and mental handicap: an historical review, with implications for further research. *Psychological Medicine*, **19**, 301–14.

Tyrer, S. & Shakour, Y. (1990). The effect of lithium in the periodicity of aggressive episodes. In W. I. Fraser (Ed). *Key Issues in Mental Retardation Research*, pp. 121–129, London: Routledge.

Vitiello, B., Spreat, S. & Behar, D. (1989). Obsessive–compulsive disorder in mentally retarded patients. *Journal of Nervous and Mental Disease*, **17**(4), 232–236.

Walters, R. M. (1990). Suicidal behaviour in severely mentally handicapped patients. *British Journal of Psychiatry*, **157**, 444–6.

Wing, L. & Gould, J. (1979). Severe impairments of social interactions and associated abnormalities in children: epidemiology and classification. *Journal of Autism and Developmental Disorders*, **9**, 11–29.

Wing, J. K. & Wing, L. (1976). In L. Wing ed. *Early Childhood Autism*, p. 313, Oxford: Pergamon Press.

Wright, E. C. (1982). The presentation of mental illness in mentally retarded adults. *British Journal of Psychiatry*, **141**, 496–502.

8

Diagnosis of psychiatric disorders in persons with mental retardation

STEVEN A. WEISBLATT

Introduction

Until the fairly recent past, the psychiatric 'treatment' of individuals with developmental disorders consisted largely of sedation and restraint. This 'treatment' was often applied whether or not the individual had a comorbid mental disorder. As discrete treatments (e.g. pharmacological, behavioural, dynamic) have been proven effective for specific mental illnesses, it becomes critical to both recognise the presence of a mental disorder and make an accurate diagnosis.

Recognition of the presence of a 'dual diagnosis' (mental retardation and mental illness) hinges foremost on being able to distinguish behaviour that is 'state-dependent' from behaviour that is 'trait dependent'. Thus, for example, a constellation of behaviours (symptoms) including decreased sleep, decreased appetite, frequent tearfulness and anhedonia that are present for several weeks must be recognised as a state dependent syndrome superimposed upon a background of an individual's particular, trait dependent, characteristic way of being. Whether the patient is a person with mild mental retardation and good interpersonal relationships, who is living in a community residence, or a profoundly retarded autistic individual, who makes no eye contact living in an institution, the constellation of symptoms described above could not be attributed to their developmental disability.

Differentiating between state and trait dependent syndromes enables a more accurate and comprehensive understanding of an individual's difficulties. It enables the design of a holistic, habilitative treatment approach. Utilising an integrated biopsychosocial perspective to arrive at a differential diagnosis and working hypothesis, a team is far more likely to be 'on target' when applying multimodal biopsychosocial interventions.

Recognition of mental disorders is critical

Just as medicine has changed enormously over the last century, so has psychiatry. In the early part of the century, the guiding principle in the care of people with mental retardation was symptom management. If medication was used it was for sedation. As we approach the end of the century, however, the guiding principle has become one of maximising the individual through habilitative therapies. Medications are used in the treatment of syndromes of mental disorder, rather than being used to palliate symptoms. In order to use medications in this highly specific way, a correct diagnosis becomes essential.

Difficulties of diagnosis

It is first necessary to recognise that there is a comorbid mental disorder, before one can attempt to diagnose or treat that disorder. Recognition is relatively less difficult, if the mental disorder changes the individual's level of function in a substantial way. Recognition is far more complicated, though, in those individuals who are already significantly compromised in their level of function by the very nature of their developmental handicap, (Laman & Reiss, 1989).

Sovner (1986) led the way in defining the variables which confound the diagnostic process in persons with developmental disabilities. Intellectual distortion, psychosocial masking, cognitive disintegration and baseline exaggeration are variable that can decrease both the sensitivity and specificity of diagnosis:

Intellectual distortion is the difficulty the individual has in communicating his or her internal feeling state owing to decreased intellect and impaired language ability. Thus, there is decreased effectiveness of the usual diagnostic tool, the clinical interview. There is also less ability by any individual clinician to elicit subjective symptoms and an increased necessity to rely on the observations of others to report observable signs. Notably, this same variable may be part of the aetiology of self-injurious behaviours and aggression.

Psychosocial masking describes the impoverished social skills and life experiences that are typical of the population, wherein a psychiatric symptom may not appear as 'rich' as it may appear in a person without disabilities. For example, an individual with mild mental retardation living in a community residence who tells staff that he is going to call his lawyer and sue the staff may be displaying the grandiosity of mania.

Cognitive disintegration is the lowered threshold, in developmentally delayed individuals, for anxiety to become overwhelming and to act as a disorganiser of cognitive function. Transient breaks in reality testing and decompensation with 'small' stressors are examples of this phenomenon.

Baseline exaggeration describes the increase in maladaptive behaviour that may occur as a result of the superimposition of a mental disorder. Instead of being recognised as a possible harbinger of comorbidity, the increase in baseline symptoms may instead be ascribed to a fluctuation in previously observed behaviours. It is important, therefore to observe for exacerbation of baseline behaviours in addition to looking for the onset of new behaviours.

[handwritten annotation: + psychosocial masking – behav. prob. attrib to pgrt of LD]

Signs and symptoms of mental disorders

Signs and symptoms of mental disorders can be classified into five broad categories changes:

Psychotic
Cognitive
Affective
Behavioural
Biological

It is extremely difficult to diagnose psychotic symptoms in this population and often psychoses are over diagnosed. This is the result of attempting to diagnose 'breaks' in reality testing in someone who cannot easily communicate to the interviewer their view of reality. In the non-handicapped population, an inappropriate belief is not thought to be psychotic if it is due to lack of knowledge. Also, a non-reality based percept generally requires language for the patient to inform us of its presence. In all of these, the 'standard' of determining whether or not a psychotic symptom truly exists requires the presence of more than rudimentary communication. As most individuals with mental retardation have major deficits in communication, this determination becomes more difficult.

Signs of attention to internal stimuli can be observed, for example, instances where a patient is pushing away at an imagined tormenter or screaming at a wall and seeming to have a dialogue with it, or covering his or her ears in a quiet room as if warding off an intrusive auditory stimulus. However, even with signs of psychosis, speech is normally used to confirm the presence of a symptom. When speech is absent or inadequate, a diagnosis of psychosis must be made with caution and only in the presence of definitive signs. All too often the diagnosis is made without adequate data.

Cognitive changes, unlike those observed in the population of individuals with normal intelligence, require more extensive knowledge of the individual's premorbid level of cognition. In 'normals', there are more easily obtained cognitive baselines, such as job description and educational level, that can assist in determining a baseline of function. In the population with mental retardation, a baseline may only be known if it has been recorded or a caregiver can supply the information. The diagnostic sensitivity and specificity of a change from baseline is also somewhat compromised by impairments in language function.

Biological changes differ the least from those symptoms usually observed in 'normals'. Changes in sleep, appetite and weight are easy to note, if they are observed.

Affective changes, though more sensitive and specific when reported by the patient as symptoms, are often readily observable as signs. For example, sadness, crying, anhedonia, apathy, and withdrawn behaviour, as well as irritability, elevated mood, and hypersexuality are all observable signs. They must be observed, though, through an observational 'eye' that corrects for possible psychosocial masking of mood states.

Behavioural changes are also readily observed. Changes in work performance, concentration, distractibility, fearfulness, ADL skills, self injurious behaviour, pica, rumination and aggression are often harbingers of a mental disorder. Psychomotor agitation or retardation, as well as increased or decreased volume, frequency, rate, and quantity of verbalisation are also clues to the presence of 'dual diagnosis'.

Prevalent mental disorders

Several studies have attempted to establish relative prevalence of discrete mental disorders in the population of individuals with mental retardation. However, it should be noted that it is difficult to establish conclusions about prevalence without consensus about diagnostic categories and validation of diagnostic criteria. Until definitive studies are published, a working hypothesis that relative prevalences are similar to those seen in the 'normal' population may be appropriate.

Delirium is likely to be increased in incidence in mental retardation as the brain is already structurally compromised and may be more sensitive to systemic medical illness, much as in 'normal' individuals with early dementia. Also, patients are less able to communicate physical complaints earlier in the course of their medical illness and the illness may progress prior to recognition that the patient is ill. In fact, a change in mental status can be the first symptom of medical illness in these individuals.

Dementia is currently viewed as being of increased incidence and prevalence only in the population of individuals with Down's syndrome. Although actual prevalence in the remainder of the population is likely to be similar to that found in 'normals', there tend to be fewer dementias noted in records. This may in part be due to the increased difficulty of diagnosis, but may also reflect inadequate efforts at diagnosis.

Schizophrenic disorders are generally viewed as consisting of a psychotic process of significant duration following a prodrome of decompensation, with onset before the third decade of life, and displaying a chronic, deteriorating life course. It is also generally accepted that the recognition of prominent mood or affective symptoms juxtaposed with psychotic symptoms speaks against the diagnosis of schizophrenia. Nevertheless, with or without an affective picture, there has been a persistent, inaccurate, clinical bias to 'think schizophrenia first' in the presence of psychotic symptoms.

Schizophrenia has had a long history of overdiagnosis, both in Europe and in the US. Although a corrective swing has taken place in the last decade toward recognising more disorders as affective rather than 'schizophrenic' in the population of 'normals', this shift has not occurred as adequately in the mental health care of individuals with mental retardation. For many who are misdiagnosed, the 'diagnosis' of 'schizophrenia' has followed them through the decades and the persistence of the diagnostic error has continued to limit the effectiveness of both pharmacological and habilitative therapies.

Although the lifetime prevalence of schizophrenic disorders in the population worldwide is approximately 1 %, and the lifetime prevalence of affective disorders is ten to fifteen percent or greater, the overwhelming majority of individuals with a 'dual diagnosis' carry a 'diagnosis' of schizophrenia. Tragically for many of these individuals who are mis-diagnosed, their 'treatment' continues to be (mis)guided by their (mis)-diagnosis. Far too many individuals are sedated unnecessarily on anti-psychotics, while being deprived of possibly effective treatments for their mood disorder.

It is critical to understand how this diagnostic error can occur. In the people with mental retardation, the affective symptom equivalents evi-denced by changes in behaviour are frequently missed. Decreased sleep accompanied by increased yelling, self injurious behaviour, and masturbation, may not be recognised as behavioural equivalents of signs of mania. Maladaptive behaviours are mislabelled as psychotic signs and as psychotic signs are seen as pathognomonic of a schizophrenic disorder. As the affective symptom equivalents go unrecognised, the diagnosis of schizophrenia is made. Thus schizophrenia continues to be overdiagnosed.

Given the statistics noted above, it would appear that diagnosing most behavioural syndromes accompanied by biological features as affective disorders would yield more diagnostic specificity than the current tendency to overdiagnose schizophrenia. In fact, given the difficulty of being sure a patient is truly psychotic, as well as the difficulty of being sure there are no behavioural symptoms that are affective equivalents, one could even argue that the diagnosis of schizophrenia in an individual with mental handicap is a diagnosis of exclusion.

Affective disorders tend to present as cycling affective phenomena with, or without, psychotic symptoms in the context of periods of relatively stable intercurrent function. Critical to the diagnosis is the recognition of behavioural symptoms or changes as possible affective symptom equivalents. It must also be remembered that mixed affective states have been reported to occur in up to 40 % of normals and must be presumed to occur in individuals with mental retardation as well. A careful family history, including the immediate and extended family, can often help guide the diagnosis, as can diurnal or seasonal variability. Organic mood syndromes may be considered in the face of relatively constant mood symptoms or symptom equivalents over a long period of time with limited or no cycling.

Anxiety as a symptom is best seen in light of an individual's developmental and environmental history. Anxiety can, as well, exist as a 'depressive equivalent'. What may appear as state dependent generalised anxiety disorder may in fact be trait dependent interpersonal and sameness anxiety of an autistic individual. As well, what appears as new onset anxiety could be a post traumatic reaction, especially given the institutional histories of some individuals. Although it is likely that obsessive compulsive disorder occurs in individuals with mental retardation, it is prudent to consider in the differential trait dependent need for sameness and comorbidity of obsessive behaviour with major depressive illness.

Improving accuracy in differential diagnosis

Diagnostic accuracy hinges as much on the availability of sufficient, valid data and its' correct integration and organisation,as it does on the clinical insistence on diagnosing disorders rather than symptoms. Ultimately though, an accurate differential produces not an iron clad, precise fact, but a working hypothesis. This hypothesis may be confirmed or contradicted as the client is followed over time and more data is collected and/or by response to treatment.

One of the best ways to prevent missing diagnoses is to obtain comprehensive biopsychosocial assessments at baseline. This helps delineate if a change in behaviour has occurred and what the nature of the change is. Given a change from baseline or a static constellation of signs, a comprehensive psychiatric history should be taken.

In the history, one would want to first confirm that the symptoms and signs are as they have been described. Is it a psychotic symptom or is the patient just observably anxious. Is symptom presentation random or associated with demand avoidance or other secondary gain. One would also want to be cognisant of secondary gain phenomena within the care system. Has there been a real change in the client or merely a change in staff reporting. It is critical to gather data from all of the environments the client interacts with in order to establish interreporter reliability.

An example of data distortion may be seen in the following case. A 19 year old male with autistic disorder was being given pharmacotherapy and behaviour therapy to decrease the interpersonal anxiety that impeded his willingness to verbalise. The protocol was in effect in a community setting and after approximately one month on the protocol the individual was seen as progressing significantly. Shortly thereafter, an urgent call from the day programme stated that the client was having a medication side effect. Emergent phone calls were made only to determine that the day programme was panicking because, for the first time in years, the client was making verbal demands.

Early history often provides a glimpse into the individual's character style. Psychiatric history, both personal and familial, often provides a clue as to the genetic predisposition to certain disorders. Often, questions about early history and psychiatric history can be seen by family members as blaming. It is critical, therefore, to explain the reason for the questions. A family history often helps to 'dilute' the interviewees potential for feeling blamed and often assists in jarring a memory of a cousin or uncle with a history of a mental disorder.

In establishing the medical history a model must be used that is sufficiently thorough to differentiate, when medical conditions are masquerading as behavioural problems. A complete baseline history including medications, allergies, surgical history, medical history and trauma is often critical in helping focus the physical examination in a patient who is unable to say what hurts and may also be uncooperative.

Baseline laboratory testing should include: CBC with differential, erythrocyte sedimentation rate, fluorescent antinuclear antigen, SMA-6, SMA-12, VDRL, B-12, folate, thyroid function tests, thyroid stimulating hormone, U/A, and an EKG. Optional tests such as serum ceruloplasmin and a lupus erythematosis Preparation may also be helpful. If available, the actual electroencephalographic or CT report should be reviewed, as abnormalities are sometimes reported as an overall 'negative' report.

The need to constantly be suspicious of underlying medical illness cannot be overly stressed as indicated in the following example: Mary, a 22 year old moderately retarded woman was brought to the psychiatric area of an urban emergency room shortly after midnight by the staff of her community residence. The staff with her noted that she was extremely agitated and had been that way for almost two weeks. They were unaware of any precipitating factors and noted that there had been no recent medication changes except for an increase in her antipsychotic medication on the previous day designed to curb her agitation. Mary was so agitated that the emergency room staff could not even obtain vital signs. After she was sedated, a complete physical examination was done, as well as routine bloods, a chest film and a suprapubic tap. All findings were negative except for the urine retrieved from the tap which revealed a severe urinary tract infection. As Mary was unable to tell the staff she was in discomfort, her agitation was assumed to be 'behavioural' in origin.

Biopsychosocial interventions, whether used alone or together, can be both therapeutic and diagnostic. If a client is hypothesised to have mania and is unresponsive to behavioural interventions, but responds quickly to lithium, one may consider the working hypothesis supported. However, one must be cautious of such a 'confirmation' when antipsychotics are used. If a person with a symptom of agitation is non-specifically medicated with an antipsychotic and 'gets better' by displaying less agitation, it does not necessarily mean that they have been appropriately treated. If the client, in fact, had an agitated depression and remains quietly depressed one would not consider that a treatment success.

Summary

Caregivers to the population of individuals with mental retardation are developing and honing clinically practical approaches to the recognition, diagnosis and treatment of mental disorders. Within this holistic, bio-psychosocially integrated approach, a differentiation is made between state and trait dependent syndromes. Once signs and symptoms of a comorbid mental disorder are identified, further diagnostic assessment permits the differential diagnosis of, and specific aetiological treatment for discrete mental disorders. Using this 'state of the art' approach for differential diagnosis is critical in the design and implementation of effective treatment programmes.

References

Laman, D. & Reiss, S. (1989). The Illinois-Chicago Mental Health Program. In R. Fletcher & F. Menolascino, eds. *Mental Retardation and Mental Illness.* Massachusetts: Lexington Books.
Sovner, R. (1986). Limiting factors in the use of DSM-III criteria with mentally ill/mentally retarded persons. *Psychopharmacology Bulletin*, **24**(4), 1055–9.

9

Adolescents with mental retardation and psychiatric disorders

PAUL KYMISSIS AND LEN LEVEN

Introduction

The field of mental retardation is a common ground where the disciplines of neurology, psychiatry, sociology, genetics, paediatrics, and public health meet and share many concerns, goals, and responsibilities. Sometimes, these areas of overlap are clear; however, quite often they are not well separated or clearly defined. This may account for why there seems to be confusion in defining which discipline takes overall responsibility for the care of people with mental retardation. Another important factor is the complexity of mentally retarded people, requiring several disciplines to work together in order to understand and meet their needs.

The interest of psychiatry in mental retardation has undergone a dynamic evolution. When the American Association of Mental Deficiency was founded in 1876, all of its charter members were psychiatrists (Menolascino, 1983). By the turn of the century, mental health professionals showed little interest in mental retardation owing to the prevailing therapeutic nihilism of the times (Vail, 1966).

During the past three decades, as a result of scientific, political and economic changes, mental retardation has returned to the realm of mental health, not so much as a central issue but occupying 'a peripheral position' (Menolascino, 1983). Many hospitals, clinics, universities and academic departments within medical schools now teach, conduct research and provide services for people with mental retardation.

Adolescents with mental retardation

Studies of adolescents with mental retardation are scarce, while most of them have been done with children or adults. Some of the reasons are:

102

Adolescence is a relatively short period of life and the adolescents are constantly in flux; few practitioners have been trained to work with adolescents; adolescence is a highly complex stage of development and its study is extremely difficult. Finally, because adolescents can be so difficult to deal with, professionals prefer working with and studying, more tractable, compliant children or adults.

Adolescents are neither children nor adults. They are somewhere in between, special and unique. During adolescence, humans experience a change in their physical, behavioural and psychological characteristics. They struggle to establish their identity and move from dependency to independence and autonomy. Girls experience menarche, a single defining point of the entry into adolescence. Boys, however, do not quite have the same critical event traversing a series of maturational milestones.

Adolescents with mental retardation call less attention to themselves than adolescents with normal intelligence. Often, classical adolescent issues are less obvious or even non-existent: a wheelchair-bound, adolescent girl with moderate mental retardation will not strive for autonomy and individuation in the same attention-capturing way as her normal counterpart.

Mentally retarded youth enter adolescence with fewer resources and limited adaptive abilities. Their goals in the struggle for identity and autonomy cannot be as ambitious as their normal IQ peers. They are ambivalent about separation and they can only take a peripheral role in the social group. It is interesting to note that adolescent gangs nearly always have some mildly retarded among their members, who are unaware of their limited judgment and, therefore, exploited by the others.

It has been said that there is a continuous struggle between the adolescent and the adult world (Knobel, 1968). This is true also with adolescent mental retardation, although the form of the struggle may be different. Hopes that the condition will improve disappears as they get older; acceleration of physical strength makes it more difficult for parents or caregivers to control their violent outbursts, and, increased interest in sexuality, raises doubts in those surrounding them as to whether they will be able to continue to handle their behaviour. Although these factors can make for tumultuous times, often leaving the adolescent feeling more stigmatised, worthless and guilty than in the relatively calm period of middle childhood preceding this.

The family of the adolescent with mental retardation experiences complex problems. In addition to meeting the needs of the mentally retarded, they have to cope with the social stigma which is attached to the whole family. Also, the siblings may feel angry, frustrated, impatient and stigmatised as well. When the retarded adolescent develops sexual curiosity and interest, this could create the problem of supervision and protection of the other children in the family.

At times, there are families who become focused and centre around the retarded child, who becomes a connective link and a positive element in the life of the family.

The question of identity formation and identity crisis of the adolescent with mental retardation presents a great challenge for the adolescent psychiatrist. The adolescent with severe mental retardation does not go through the usual identity crisis, which is seen in adolescents with normal intelligence. The adolescents with moderate and mild mental retardation experience the identity crisis later on in life. As a result of their struggle to establish their identity, and move toward autonomy, they become very frustrated; as their goal to completely break away from their families is unattainable they may become depressed, or act out aggressively. Consequently, their families find it very hard to cope with this because, although they want to assist them to gain more autonomy and independence, they also want to remain supportive and nurturing.

Adolescents with mental retardation and psychiatric disorders

It has been estimated that 20–35% of children and adolescents with mental retardation suffer from a psychiatric illness (Eaton & Menolascino, 1982; Parsons, May & Menolascino, 1984, Ruedrich & Menolascino, 1984). In the Isle of Wight, the prevalence rate of emotional disorders among retarded children was 30.4% using a teachers' questionnaire, and 41.8% using the parents' questionnaire. Among the non-retarded, the prevalence was 7.7% and 9.5% (Rutter & Graham, 1970). Longitudinal studies in the general population have shown that low IQ in early childhood is related to emotional problems, and delinquency in adolescence (Douglas, Ross & Simpson, 1968).

Menolascino (1969) studied 256 emotionally disturbed children and adolescents with mental retardation. Some of their symptoms were: hyperkinesia, impulsivity, stereotyped movements, withdrawal, and panic attacks. Fifty-eight of these children and adolescents had adjustment reactions caused partly perhaps by their parents' dissatisfaction with their slow development, which created multiple interpersonal problems in the family.

A study to determine the presence of psychiatric disorders in 52 children with mental retardation found 21 had no psychiatric diagnosis; 18 had reactive behaviour disorder; 1 had neurotic behaviour disorder; 11 had cerebral dysfunction, and 1 had psychosis (Chess & Hassibi, 1970).

Treatment issues

Most of the treatment modalities available to the non-retarded, psychiatric patient can also be used with the mentally retarded adolescent. Special consideration should be given to the developmental level of the patient, diagnostic criteria, the presence of other illnesses or handicaps, and drug interactions. Medication should be started on lower doses and increased gradually to achieve maximum benefit with minimal side effects as these people seem to have greater susceptibility. Psychiatric medications should not be used only to control behaviour but should also address target diagnostic symptoms, e.g. psychosis, anxiety, depression. Neuroleptic medication may help to control hyperactivity, impulsivity, destructive and assaultive behaviour. Note that studies of people with mental retardation show high rates of placebo response (Rivinus, 1980). Stimulants should be used with caution as they can produce stereotypic or psychotic behaviour. Antidepressants and lithium are used to treat mood disorders as with non-retarded people. Lithium, carbamazepine and other mood stabilising agents may help in the management of challenging behaviour. Beta-blockers have also been used with some success. Benzodiazepines can help on a short-term basis to relieve anxiety, although there are increased chances of disinhibition.

Various types of psychotherapeutic approaches are used for the adolescent with mental illness and mental retardation. However, there has been some scepticism regarding psychotherapy, based most often on ignorance (Loft, 1970). Therapeutic obstacles, such as problems with abstract thinking, impulse control, and self-reflection, can be managed in the same fashion as with other children and adolescents in treatment (LaVietes, 1978).

In planning for psychotherapeutic interventions for adolescents with mental retardation, four criteria should first be considered (Lubin, 1983): intellectual aptitude, personality capacity for relationships, organic brain integrity, and communication skills.

One should not expect that the patients' improvement could go beyond the adaptive handicap, and techniques should be adapted to the patients' developmental level. Therapy with patients of the lowest intellectual functioning should focus primarily on behavioural techniques in contrast to patients of higher intelligence who should be assisted in learning how to recognize and communicate their feelings (Szymanski, 1980). The goals of therapy should be realistic and may need to be readjusted. Techniques available include verbal, non-verbal, art, play, music, movement, and dance therapies. An important objective in psychotherapy is to improve the concept of the self: 'Whatever a person does and how he behaves is determined by the concept he has about himself and his abilities' (Snygg & Combs, 1949). Most of the studies on the self-concept of people with mental retardation done with individuals having IQs from 50–80 have been encouraging (Lawrence & Winschel, 1973).

Group psychotherapy has also been used successfully. Various group modalities, such as films, psychodrama, art groups, analytic groups and multiple family groups have been utilised. Other variations on the traditional models have included: time-limited groups focusing on special topics, indefinite duration groups, mostly used with people in community residences, and mixed groups where therapy, education, and other programmes are combined (Szymanski, 1980). Adolescents do especially well in groups where they learn interpersonal skills and can express their feelings about being handicapped. It is important that the group leaders are adequately trained.

In order to assist the adolescent with moderate and mild mental retardation to navigate successfully through their identity crisis, which occurs later in their life, the combination of family therapy and group therapy could be particularly useful. It may, however, be difficult to engage other members of the family in therapy. In addition, other parameters, such as residential treatment, special education classes, vocational training, provide important beneficial effects.

Summary

Much has been accomplished for adolescents with mental retardation and psychiatric problems, and much remains to be done. These people increasingly have joined the universe of general psychiatry and are benefitting from the diagnostic and therapeutic advantages this offers, as well as increased social status, with all that it entails. The future will require efforts as diligent as those of the past, to bring to bear the appropriate resources so that they can move from the margins to the mainstream.

References

Chess, S. & Hassibi, M. (1970). Behavior deviations in the mentally retarded children. *Journal of the American Academy of Child Psychiatry*, **9**(2).

Douglas, T. W. B., Ross, J. M. & Simpson, H. R. (1968). *All our Future*. Peter Davis, London.

Eaton, L. F. & Menolascino, F. J. (1982). Psychiatric disorders in the mentally retarded: types, problems and challenges. *American Journal of Psychiatry*, **138**, 1297–303.

Knobel, M. (1968). Psychotherapy and Adolescence. In B. F. Ries, ed. *New Directions in Mental Health*, pp. 17–37, New York: Grune & Stratton.

Lanzkren, J. (1957). The concept of pfropfschizophrenia and its prognosis. *American Journal of Mental Deficiency*, **61**, 544–7.

LaVietes, R. (1978). Mental retardation psychological treatment. In B. Wolman *et al.* eds. *Handbook of Mental Disorders in Childhood and Adolescence*. Englewood Cliffs, NJ: Prentice-Hall.

Lawrence, E. A. & Winschel, J. F. (1973). Self-concept and the retarded: research issues. *Exceptional Children*. **39**(2), 310–8.

Loft, G. (1970). Psychotherapy of the mentally retarded: values and cautions. In F. J. Menolascino (ed.), *Psychiatric Approaches to Mental Retardation*. New York: Basic Books.

Lubin, R. L. (1983). Bridging the gap through individual counselling and psychotherapy with mentally retarded people. In F. J. Menolascino, ed. *Mental Health and Mental Retardation: Bridging the Gap*, pp. 119–128, Baltimore: University Park Press.

Menolascino, F. J. (1969). Emotional disturbances in mentally retarded children. *American Journal of Psychiatry*, **126**(2), 168–76.

Menolascino, F. J. (1983). Overview: bridging the gap between mental retardation and mental health. In F. Menolascino & B. McCann, eds. *Mental Health and Mental Retardation: Bridging the Gap*, Chap. 1, Baltimore: University Park Press.

Parsons, J. A., May, J. G. & Menolascino, F. J. (1984). The nature and incidence of mental illness in mentally retarded individuals. In F. J. Menolascino & J. A. Stark eds. *Handbook of Mental Illness in the Mentally Retarded*, pp. 3–43, New York: Plenum Press.

Rivinus, T. M. (1980). Psychopharmacology and the mentally retarded. In L. Szymanski & P. E. Tanguay, eds. *Emotional Disorders of Mentally Retarded Persona, Treatment and Consultation*, Chap. 13, Baltimore: University Park Press.

Ruedrich, S. & Menolascino, F. J. (1984). Dual diagnosis of mental retardation and mental illness: an overview. In F. Menolascino & J. Stark, eds. *Handbook of Mental Illness in the Mentally Retarded*, pp. 45–81, New York: Plenum Press

Rutter, M. & Graham P. (1970). *A Neuropsychiatric Study in Childhood*. London: Spastics International Medical Publications.

Snygg, D. & Combs, A. (1949). *Individual Behavior*. New York: Harper and Brothers.

Szymanski, L. S. (1980). Individual psychotherapy with retarded persons. In L. S. Szymanski & P. E. Tanguay, eds. *Emotional Disorders of Mentally Retarded Persons Assessment, Treatment and Consultation*, pp. 131–147, Baltimore: University Park Press.

Vail, D. (1966). *Dehumanization and the Institutional Career*. Springfield, IL: Charles C. Thomas.

10

The austistic continuum

LORNA WING

Introduction

Mental retardation tends to be associated with a variety of specific disabilities of cognitive or motor skills that stand out against the background of general developmental delay. Among these is the cluster of impairments of reciprocal social interaction, communication and imagination that is associated with a narrow, stereotyped, repetitive pattern of behaviour. This cluster is referred to as the 'triad of social impairments' (Wing & Gould, 1979). It occurs in up to half of all children with severe mental retardation, around 1–2% of those who are mildly retarded and in a tiny minority of those in the average or above range of ability (Akinsola & Fryers, 1986; Gillberg & Gillberg, 1989; Gillberg et al., 1986; Wing & Gould, 1979).

The best known subgroup of those with the triad is early childhood autism. However, this represents only about one quarter or less of the full range (Wing & Gould, 1979). In order to emphasise the similarities with typical autism, the whole group will be referred to as the 'autistic continuum'; it is roughly equivalent to the 'pervasive developmental disorders' as defined in DSM-III-R (American Psychiatric Association, 1987) and ICD-10 (World Health Organization, 1992).

It is important for workers in the field of mental retardation to recognise the triad of social impairments when it occurs, first, because it underlies much of the most serious and intractable challenging behaviour found in people who are severely mentally retarded (Wing & Gould, 1979; Wing, 1989) and, secondly, its presence has major and special implications for education, environmental planning and helping the individuals concerned.

In this chapter, the nature of autism will be discussed, the different manifestations of the autistic continuum and their prevalence will be described and ways of helping will be briefly outlined.

Historical background

Individual accounts of children and adults who were very probably autistic can be found in the historical literature, the most famous being that of Victor, the boy found wandering wild in the woods of Aveyron in central France in 1797 and educated by Itard (Lane, 1977). It was not until the end of the nineteenth century that psychiatrists slowly began to be interested in strange behaviour in children. At the beginning of the twentieth century, a number of workers tried to define subgroups of children they referred to as 'psychotic'. The only one of these to become widely known and accepted was the subgroup described by Leo Kanner (1943). He chose the term 'early infantile autism ' (from the Greek 'autos', meaning self) because psychiatrists had used it to refer to the state of being withdrawn into oneself. Nowadays, the name 'childhood autism' is used in preference to 'infantile autism'.

One year after Kanner's first paper on autism appeared, Hans Asperger (1944) described another subgroup with many similarities to autism, now known as Asperger's syndrome (Gillberg & Gillberg, 1989; Frith, 1991; Wing, 1981a).

Autism is now generally considered to be a disorder of certain aspects of childhood development resulting from biological causes (Coleman & Gillberg,1985; Schopler & Mesibov, 1987; Wing, 1988b). Its very frequent association with all degrees of mental retardation has been recognised (Gillberg, Steffenburg & Schaumann, 1991; Rutter, 1970; Wing and Gould, 1979). Many workers agree that typical autism is part of a wider continuum of conditions characterised by the triad of social impairments (Gillberg & Gillberg, 1989; Wing, 1988a) which includes Kanner's and Asperger's syndromes and other subgroups as yet unnamed.

The nature of autistic conditions

In order to plan education and care for people with conditions in the autistic continuum, it is necessary to understand the nature of the psychological dysfunctions underlying the overt behaviour. These are mostly present from early infancy.

Early developmental problems

In order for an infant to become a fully functioning independent adult, he or she has to develop many skills. These include all the obvious functions such as sucking and chewing, sitting up, crawling and walking, understanding and using speech, visual–spatial abilities, self-care, academic work and so on. But there are other skills that are much less obvious and well known and which have been examined and defined only in the last few decades. These are the skills of social interaction, social empathy, communication and imagination (Bullova, 1979; Frith, 1989; Schaffer, 1974; Ricks & Wing, 1975; Trevarthen, 1974). Just as with the more obvious skills, these aspects of development unfold in a more or less predictable sequence because the human brain is preprogrammed.

From the beginning of life, babies give out signals that attract adult care givers. They also respond to the sounds, facial expressions and physical contacts of parents and others. They recognise without teaching that other human beings are the most interesting features of the environment, and are eager to make eye contact almost from birth. As time goes on the complexity of cooing and babbling increases and babies, from 2 to 3 months onwards, 'converse' with others, especially their mothers, the pair taking turns to contribute with the timing the same as that of adult conversations.

There is an eager demand for social interaction and communication. Speech develops in the second year and is used enthusiastically to chatter to parents and any other familiar trusted person who will join in.

Also, in the second year, the development of the imagination begins to be apparent (Lowe, 1975; Sheridan, 1969; 1977). The child plays pretend games with miniature toys, and, most significantly, begins to use one object to represent another. Much imaginative play consists of pretending to be someone or something other than oneself, and to act out the thoughts and feelings as well as the actions of another person. All these aspects of development become more complex and sophisticated with increasing age, but their roots are present from birth. They are extraordinarily resistant to damage from even extreme deprivation for years at a time, unless there is some physical dysfunction of the relevant aspects of brain function (Clarke & Clarke, 1976). It is not yet known for certain which parts of the brain are involved in these skills but there is some tentative evidence to suggest that the hypothalamus, limbic system and the medial surface of the cortex may be important in this context (Damasio & Maurer, 1978).

The essence of the autistic continuum conditions is absence or impairment of these social and communication and imaginative skills. This can, rather rarely, occur on its own, giving rise to a person who is autistic but who has normal skills in other areas, and tests in the normal or even high ranges of intelligence on psychological tests.

More often, the parts of the brain responsible for the obvious skills–motor, self-care, and academic abilities–are affected, together with the social and communication skills, resulting in a person who is both autistic and generally mentally retarded. More often still, the parts of the brain responsible for the obvious skills can be impaired, leaving social and communication skills relatively intact. This is the case in mental retardation without autism, such as is usually, though not always, found in Down's syndrome (Wing & Gould, 1979).

The difference between 'speech' and 'communication' should be emphasised. The development of vocabulary, grammar and the physical mechanics of speaking are all aspects of speech, but the interest in and ability to use speech and non-verbal body language in order to communicate ideas and feelings, not just to ask for needs, are aspects of communication. In autistic conditions, it is possible to have speech without communication (Ricks & Wing, 1975). In non-autistic mental retardation it is possible to have communication (through body language) without speech.

'Theory of mind'

Recently, work has shown that typically autistic children lack a 'theory of mind' (Baron-Cohen, 1989; Frith, 1989). This skill normally develops over the preschool years. When fully developed, it is the ability to understand that other people have thoughts and feelings, can have true or false beliefs, and can deceive. This lack in autistic children could reasonably be predicted from the nature of their social and imaginative impairments. As Frith (1989) suggests, the absence of a theory of mind is probably one important aspect of a general inability to put individual events into a wider context. Thus, autistic children are unable to make coherent sense of their experiences.

It would be of great interest to examine 'theory of mind' in the whole range of autistic continuum conditions as well as those with typical autism.

The effects of the impairments on behaviour

The consequence of the psychological impairments is that the individual concerned lives in an unpredictable and therefore frightening world. Any change is unexpected and raises anxiety. The response to this is to cling to objects and routines that are familiar and to resist change in them. 'Challenging behaviour', such as aggression, screaming, self injury, running away, occurs when the familiar routines are disturbed or when unexpected events occur.

Possible causes

Although it seems likely that abnormality of a particular part of the brain is necessary to produce autism, there is now no doubt that a wide range of different initial causes can produce the relevant pathology (Coleman & Gillberg, 1987; DeMyer, 1975; Gillberg, 1988; Schopler & Mesibov, 1987; Wing, 1988b; Wing & Gould, 1979). It is no longer believed by serious workers in the field that parental mishandling gives rise to autism (DeMyer, 1975; 1979). A variety of conditions known to affect the brain have been found in the history of people with autism, in about one-third to one-half of the cases, especially those with most severe handicaps. These include maternal rubella, untreated phenylketonuria, tuberose sclerosis, lack of oxygen at birth, and, paradoxically, too much oxygen at birth, and encephalitis. Twin studies, and studies of families with more than one autistic child have shown that genetic factors are important (Folstein & Rutter, 1988). There is still much to learn about the causes, but at least a start has been made in collecting relevant clinical information.

Clinical pictures

There are wide variations in the clinical pictures within the autistic continuum, though all share the triad of social impairments. The two best known named syndromes will be described because, in many ways, they represent different extremes of the continuum. Then the full range of variations in manifestations will be outlined.

Kanner's autism

The picture Kanner described in young children with his syndrome has come to be known as typical, classic, or nuclear autism. Children of this kind appear to be aloof and indifferent to other people, though they do approach others to obtain things they want. They also enjoy being bounced up and down, tickled, swung round and round, but do not usually accept being cuddled or sitting quietly on someone's lap, unless they themselves choose to do so for a short time. As babies they do not engage in little games involving reciprocal actions while sitting on mother's lap, and do not point things out to others in order to share the interest, though some will point to things they want.

As toddlers they do not bring toys to show to people, and do not want others to be involved in their activities, except as passive tools. They do not run to greet parents on their return home, nor follow mother around the house, babbling or chattering, and trying to join in her activities. Eye contact is characteristically very poor.

Understanding and use of speech are slow in developing. About half remain mute, and those who do speak show characteristic abnormalities, especially parrot-like echoing of other people's words, and exact repetition, out of context, of words or phrases heard or used in the past. Where there is enough speech, there tends to be confusion over words the meaning of which change with the speaker or circumstances, such as I and you, up and down, words for relationships (for example, sister, uncle) and for times and dates (for example, before, yesterday) and so on. In general, there is marked difficulty with abstract, complex meanings and a strong tendency to interpret words in an immediate literal and often inappropriate way that has nothing to do with the context; thus a child told to 'walk on ahead' stopped, looked puzzled and touched her head.

The use of non-verbal communication (gesture, mime, 'body language') is markedly impaired. Unlike a deaf child, an autistic child does not use gesture to make up for poor speech. Vocal intonation is characteristically flat or peculiar.

Imaginative play does not develop. Instead, the pattern of activities is dominated by repetitive, stereotyped routines, such as switching lights on and off, flicking objects, putting objects into long straight lines, listening to the same record over and over again. There is a strong tendency for the child to build up a number of 'habits' or 'rituals', which he or she insists should be performed every day. These include, for example, a lengthy bedtime routine, insisting on following the same route to the shops each day, amassing large numbers of certain objects and carrying them around everywhere, insisting that members of the family sit at the same place at table. Attempts to change these routines usually lead to intense resistance. However, many autistic children may ignore or even enjoy changes that do not directly affect their own routines or possessions.

The impairments of reciprocal social interaction, communication and imagination and the repetitive stereotyped pattern of activities are central to the autistic picture and are clearly directly related to the underlying developmental disorders described above. Some other problems are frequently associated with the main features and are less obviously predictable from the developmental disorders.

Abnormalities of movement, including facial grimaces, flapping of hands and arms, jumping, tiptoe walking, self-spinning, rocking back and forth or side to side while standing are common. They are made worse by anger or excitement, as if there is an uncontrolled discharge of tension throughout the whole body. Posture and gait may appear odd and clumsy especially in adolescents and adults. Young autistic children may be agile in climbing and balancing, but are clumsy if asked to copy other people's movements.

Odd responses to simple sensory stimuli, fascination, distress or indifference, may be seen. Hypersensitivity to certain sounds, a tendency to smell objects and people, and lack of overt reaction to pain and to cold are common examples.

Peculiarities of autonomic function may be noted. Examples are excessive drinking of fluids, and disturbance of sleep or appetite.

Given the difficulties an autistic child has in understanding the world, and especially other people, it is not surprising that emotional and behavioural problems are frequent. Autistic children may be anxious and fearful of harmless things, such as bathing, or a particular colour, but oblivious to real dangers. Temper tantrums, screaming, destructiveness, aggression, restlessness, running away, the aimless creation of chaos, occur at home or in public and can make life a nightmare for the parents.

Around two-thirds or more of children with typical autism are also mildly or severely mentally retarded.

Asperger's syndrome

Asperger described children who are naive or odd and inappropriate in social interaction. They can speak but they are longwinded and literal in the language they use. They tend to deliver long monologues on subjects of interest to them regardless of the response of the listener. Their vocal intonation is monotonous or peculiar. Their body language is limited or inappropriate.

They typically have one or two subjects, such as railway timetables, varieties of British birds, padlocks, numbers on lampposts, hubcaps on cars, prime numbers, in fact, virtually anything that can be made into a list, which absorb them to the exclusion of almost everything else. They collect facts on these topics, but do not seem interested in or able to understand the wider implications. They have amazing memories for things that interest them. In some cases the special interests are associated with special skills at a high level, such as drawing, music, mathematical or calendrical calculations, or visuo-spatial abilities.

They tend to be physically clumsy except in the areas of special skill. Above all, Asperger emphasised their remarkable lack of commonsense in social situations and their ability to say and do socially embarrassing things. They are oblivious of or puzzled by other people's reactions to the social gaffes.

Most people with Asperger's syndrome are of average ability or above while a few are borderline or mildly retarded.

Variations in the clinical manifestations of the triad

Major problems of diagnosis arise because the clinical picture is so varied. In the past, because of Kanner's insistence that autism was a specific separate condition, there was a widespread belief that the possibility of autism should be rejected unless the perfect classic pattern was present. This view has its value in research work on Kanner's syndrome, but its application in clinical practice has led to the exclusion from appropriate education and other services of children and adults with autistic continuum conditions on the grounds that they were not really autistic.

The difficulty is that, although easy to recognise when present in typical Kanner's syndrome form, other manifestations, including Asperger's syndrome, are less familiar. In any case, there are no clear boundaries even to these named subgroups. There are far more children with bits and pieces of either or both than there are typical cases (Wing & Gould, 1979; Wing, 1988*a*). In many ways it makes more sense to look for the presence of the triad rather than to try to decide if the person concerned has a named syndrome. This is particularly true when the triad occurs together with severe mental retardation.

The variations in each of the elements of the triad will be described in turn so it will be possible to see how Kanner's and Asperger's syndromes merge into the continuum.

Social interaction

Impairment of social interaction can take the classic form of aloofness and indifference to other people. It can also be shown as an amiable, passive acceptance of social approaches, with little or no active initiation of interaction. The most difficult to recognise form is that of active but odd social approaches. The person concerned does initiate the approach, but it is one sided and dominated by the limited interests of the socially impaired person. Often anyone, friend or stranger, is approached with the same open, naive manner which gives the misleading impression of extrovert friendliness. Eye contact is not absent, but inappropriate, being disconcertingly hard and long at times. The problem in many people with the triad is not a positive rejection of social contact, but a lack of understanding of the rules of social interaction.

Communication

Communication problems can be shown in any of the following ways: absence of understanding and use of speech; monosyllabic utterances; mainly echolalic speech (immediate and delayed); some spontaneous utterances with many grammatical errors and problems over pronouns and other words where the meaning changes with time, place and person; at the top end of the scale, there can be a large vocabulary and good grammar, but speech is used in a repetitive way to talk on limited themes, and is pedantic and long winded in style, lacking the normal colloquialisms. Speech of this last kind can give the impression of good comprehension. However, the alert observer notices that, as soon as one tries to move on to another topic, or even introduces a variant of the favourite theme, the person concerned loses the thread and shuts off, or repeats what he has said before. There is a particular problem in comprehending any discussion of feelings, emotional preferences, or other people's ideas.

Imagination

Imaginative development is absent in many people with conditions in the autistic spectrum. In some, however, a kind of pretend play does develop, but it is narrow and limited in theme, and is not influenced by other children's ideas. Sometimes other people are used as aids in the 'play', for example, as helpers in building a network of roads and bridges, but there is no true sharing or joint development of imaginative themes. A few children and adults with these problems can create entire imaginary worlds, with many precise and pedantic details of physical features and the people who inhabit them, but the repetitive stereotyped quality is evident even here (see, for example, descriptions of young autistic adults in Bosch, 1970; Park, 1982).

Stereotyped activities

Repetitive stereotyped activities may also take many forms. At the simplest, they consist of, for example, rocking, teeth grinding, 'playing' with saliva, finger or object flicking. Somewhat more elaborate are spinning the wheels of toy cars, arranging objects in lines and patterns, or following rigid sequences of actions. The most complex are those involving words and abstract themes, such as asking repetitive questions, or learning and talking about railway timetables, the characteristics of British mammals, the movements of the planets, and so on. These may give an impression of high ability, but the concern is mostly with collecting facts and retelling them to anyone who will listen. No real discussion is possible. These circumscribed interests may, perhaps surprisingly, concern specific groups of people (for example the Royal Family), or even individuals, but again facts are collected, and there is little or no real involvement on the social and personal level.

Factors affecting the clinical picture

The ways in which the basic impairments are shown are affected by age, level of general intellectual ability and sex. In general, increasing maturation and higher levels of intelligence are associated with the more complex of the manifestations described above. Girls are affected much less often than boys, and tend to be more severely handicapped (Wing, 1981*b*) though can appear more superficially sociable than boys. There are some autistic girls of high ability and their apparent friendliness can make diagnosis particularly difficult.

The autistic spectrum can occur with any level of general intelligence, and with any other physical or mental handicap, including, though rather rarely, Down's syndrome. In the adolescents and adults with reasonably good speech, psychiatric illness, especially depression, may be super-imposed.

The autistic spectrum presents some remarkable contrasts. It includes the severely retarded, socially aloof and indifferent child who makes eye contact only in rare brief glances, who walks on tiptoe, and spends most time flapping, flicking pieces of string and spinning the wheels of a tricycle which is never ridden, and who runs away and climbs up to the roof of the house if given half a chance. It also includes the adolescent with overall average intelligence on IQ tests, but with a profile on the sub-tests showing that rote memory is far better than comprehension, who talks repetitively to friends and strangers about King Arthur and the Knights of the Round Table, while fixing them with a gaze as unwavering as the Ancient Mariner, who has the physical skills necessary for adequate self-care, but who has to be supervised to make sure clothes are changed, and who can become aggressive if pressurised to engage in the range of activities seemingly appropriate for their level of ability.

It is legitimate to ask if these conditions really are on the same continuum. A close relationship between them is very likely, first, because children may change from one picture to another as they grow older, second, because different manifestations can occur in different members of the same family (Burgoine & Wing, 1983; Bowman, 1988) and, third, because the principles of education and management are the same for all, although details of the practice must vary depending on the severity of the handicap and the level of unaffected skills.

Age of onset

Kanner and many later writers have insisted that 'true' autism always begins from birth or within the first 2 or 3 years of life. However, social impairment in babies and young children may not be recognised by parents who are not knowledgeable about child development. In the more able children particularly, behavioural abnormalities may not show until near or at school age, although all the typical impairments were present from early on. If someone is seen for the first time in adult life, there may be no-one to give the early history. Thus, the diagnosis may be missed because the details of the early history are missing. There are also a very few cases where the typical behaviour really does begin after 3 years of age, and it seems unreasonable to refuse to call such children autistic. Age of onset is of considerable interest, but should not be regarded as crucial when making a diagnosis.

Prevalence

Epidemiological studies (Lotter, 1966) have shown that the full picture of classic Kanner's syndrome occurs in about 2 children per 10000. Another 2–3 per 10000 have most but not all the classic features. A more recent study (Wing & Gould, 1979) of an area in London in which the prevalence of the whole autistic spectrum was examined gave the total rate of 21 per 10000 children aged under 15 years. This figure includes those of any level of intelligence on tests, from profoundly retarded to normal or even superior range, and with any other kind of handicap in addition to behaviour in the autistic spectrum. A study in Gothenburg in Sweden gave a similar prevalence (Gillberg *et al.*, 1986). The rate for the adult population is unknown, since no epidemiological study has been carried out. But, since follow up studies have shown that in most cases the autistic pattern lasts into adult life (Rutter, 1970) the adult prevalence is unlikely to be much lower than that found in childhood.

In the Camberwell study described above, about 78 % of those in the autistic spectrum were also severely mentally retarded. Conversely, approximately 49 % of all severely retarded children also had disorders in the autistic spectrum. A survey in 1980 of Darenth Park, an adult mental handicap hospital, which had gradually been reduced in numbers from a peak of over 2000 down to 890 at the time of the study, showed that one third of the 890 residents had autistic spectrum disorders, and that the most severe behaviour problems were found in this group (Wing, 1989). Thus the autistic conditions are of considerable importance in the field of mental retardation.

Autistic people of normal intelligence are fewer in number and present some different kinds of problems from those who are retarded, but they also need help to make use of their full potential and to compensate for their very real handicaps (Frith, 1991; Wing,1981*a*).

Education and care

Children who do not have the triad of social impairments, because they have inner thoughts and ideas are able to incorporate what they learn into an overall picture of the world and of the people in it. The general principles the child builds up can be applied, with appropriate modifications, in all kinds of situations.

People with autistic continuum conditions lack this skill. Some have no inner world of ideas at all. Those with higher ability have a kind of inner world, but this is limited in scope and is inflexible and cannot be adapted to new situations.

Education

The essence of education for children with autistic disorders is the provision of an external framework to give some order and structure to life so that they are better able to cope, at least within their familiar setting (Brown, 1975; Howlin, 1982; Howlin & Rutter, 1987; Wing, 1980).

Physical prompting and visual demonstration can help to compensate for problems of comprehension of speech. Teaching material has to be precise and specific to avoid misunderstanding and confusion.

Each individual needs help to develop any skills they may possess. The strong tendency to develop repetitive routines is a major problem, but this can be utilised to develop regular activities that are appropriate and useful, in schoolwork, domestic work, occupational skills or leisure.

Teachers need to have a detailed understanding of each child's pattern of skills and disabilities and an intuitive feel for what life must be like for them. This combination of intellectual understanding and emotional empathy is crucial for teaching skills and avoiding challenging behaviour (mostly due to the child's lack of comprehension, or interference with repetitive routines)

In contrast to sociable retarded children, those with autistic conditions do not learn from unstructured social play. Playtimes tend to be stressful for such children, who manage much better in a well organised class.

Organisation of the environment

For both children and adults with autistic disorders, appropriate organisation of the environment, with staff who understand the nature of the autistic continuum, is of the highest importance in improving the quality of life and diminishing the amount of challenging behaviour.

Behaviour modification has only a small part to play in helping people with the triad, especially those who are also severely mentally retarded. The impairments of particular kinds of psychological functions markedly affect their appreciation of rewards and disincentives. Their inability to understand events in any wider context means they have little ability to link cause and effect. Token economies, which rely upon the existence of some concept of future reward for an otherwise useless piece of plastic or a mark on a chart, are particularly inappropriate for those with no capacity to symbolise at even a primitive level. Even if behaviour modification techniques do work in the short term, while being applied with enthusiasm, it is difficult to carry them on over long periods of time. With no or only a limited inner world, there is no foundation on which to build a new and lasting pattern of behaviour.

The most effective way of helping is to provide the right kind of living environment, in the family home or in residential care. In residential homes, there should be sufficient personal space, inside and out, for the residents safely and easily to get away from other people when they wish to do so. It should also be possible for each resident to engage in repetitive behaviour, such as odd movements or noises, while on the premises, without annoying other residents or any neighbours. Some of those with the triad are oversensitive to noise and crowds, so a quiet location would be best for them.

Arranging which people should live in the same residence needs careful consideration. Some individuals with autistic disorders are able to live happily with those who are sociable without distress to either group. However, those who intensely dislike too close social contact would be better in a more specialised setting. People with severely challenging behaviour tend to affect adversely the quality of life of their co-residents and near neighbours, so can need separate provision. Experience with the Darenth Park closure has underlined the obvious point that different people have different needs and the needs of one group may conflict with those of another (Wing, 1989).

The programme for each day should be organised and explained to the residents in ways they can understand, such as a large picture timetable. There should be as little as possible time spent waiting around for the next event. Some spaces for the residents to engage in their own repetitive activities are necessary, but these should be planned and not happen just because the timetable is unplanned or disrupted. People with autistic disorders are much happier and more relaxed when they know from past experience what will happen next and how long it will last. It takes time for a routine to be established and learnt by the residents but progress can be seen in the gradual reduction of challenging behaviour, and in the diminishing urgency of motor stereotypies.

The content of the programme is equally important. There should be a range of activities that are within the capabilities of the residents and which they enjoy. One frequent cause of challenging behaviour is an attempt to push people with autistic disorders into engaging in activities that are beyond their level of ability. It is much better to find out by trial and error what types of occupation and leisure are enjoyed by which people and ensure they have access to the things they prefer. It is always worth trying an activity that has previously been refused after a lapse of time, as long as no pressure is brought to bear. Some may be willing to engage in constructive activities, including aspects of domestic work, but others will take part only in simple physical pursuits requiring no symbolic understanding, such as walking, swimming, car rides.

Plenty of organised, fairly vigorous physical activity has been shown to be helpful in reducing challenging behaviour and promoting relaxation (see, for example, the report on the Higashi school in Boston by Gould, Rigg & Bignell, 1991). This type of programme should also reduce the levels of tranquillising medication required. Those with epilepsy need careful medical supervision but should take part as much as possible.

The concepts of 'normalisation' and 'community care' should be modified when considering the organisation of services for people with autistic continuum disorders. For most such people, their needs are different from those of non-autistic, sociable mentally retarded individuals. While some people with autistic disorders can live together with others who do not have the same disabilities, it is necessary to have an adequate amount of separate residential provision to help those who need it. Some do not enjoy or benefit from living in a small house in an ordinary street, especially if the rooms are cramped and the garden small or non-existent. While living units for small numbers of people can more easily provide individualised care, such units do not have to be in small ordinary houses or flats. The National and Local Autistic Societies have set up specialised homes, some on small campuses, which do give their residents a lifestyle adapted to their needs.

Similarly, integration into the local community's education, occupation and leisure facilities presents major problems for many people with autistic disorders. Some separate arrangements are needed in these areas also, in order to ensure a good quality of life for the people concerned. This should not preclude some mixing for social and other purposes whenever possible, as long as an easy escape is available when the social pressures become too much.

Human beings, whether autistic or not, are notoriously resistant to being pushed into the same mould. No one system can suit everyone. A range of services, some separate and some mixed, is the best way of providing for all those in need.

Summary

Among the specific disabilities that can be associated with mental retardation is the triad of developmental impairments, due to biological causes, affecting reciprocal social interaction, communication and imagination. This triad is virtually always accompanied by a narrow, repetitive, stereotyped pattern of activities. The behavioural manifestations of the underlying impairments vary widely, but include typical Kanner's autism and Asperger's syndrome. The whole range is referred to as the 'autistic continuum' and is roughly equivalent to the 'pervasive developmental disorders'.

Two-thirds or more of those with autistic continuum disorders are also mentally retarded. Conversely, up to one-half of those with severe mental retardation have a disorder in the continuum. These individuals account for a large proportion of mentally retarded people with challenging behaviour.

People with the triad have certain special needs. Their challenging behaviour usually results from changes in the routine they have come to expect, interference with their stereotyped activities, pressure to perform beyond their level of ability, lack of comprehension of instructions arising from the communication problems, or too close proximity to other people or noisy, busy situations. They therefore require staff who understand the impairments and their consequences, a predictable, organised routine for each day, and a range of activities within their ability level. They also need personal space, both indoors and out. Some physical exercise each day has been found to be helpful in reducing challenging behaviour. While some can live with sociable mentally retarded people and join in the activities of the local community, others need special provision for accommodation, or education, occupation or leisure.

References

Akinsola, H. A. & Fryers, T. (1986). A comparison of patterns of disability in severely mentally handicapped children of different ethnic origins. *Psychological Medicine*, **16**, 127–33.

American Psychiatric Association (1987). *Diagnostic and Statistical Manual of Mental Disorders*: 3rd Edition Revised. Washington: APA.

Asperger, H. (1944). Die autistischen Psychopathen im Kindesalter. *Archiv für Psychiatrie und Nervenkrankheiten*, **117**, 76–136.

Baron-Cohen, S. (1989). The autistic child's theory of mind: a case of specific developmental delay. *Journal of Child Psychology and Psychiatry*, **30**, 285–97.

Bosch, G. (1970). *Infantile Autism*. New York: Springer-Verlag.

Bowman, E. P. (1988). Asperger's syndrome and autism: the case for a connection. *British Journal of Psychiatry*, **152**, 377–82.

Brown, W. (1975). *Practical Guidance for Those Who Work with Autistic Children*. London: National Autistic Society.

Bullova, M. ed. (1979). *Before Speech: The Beginning of Interpersonal Communication*. Cambridge: Cambridge University Press.

Burgoine, E. & Wing, L. (1983). Identical triplets with Asperger's Syndrome. *British Journal of Psychiatry*, **143**, 261-5.

Clarke, A. M. & Clarke, A. D. B. (1976). *Early Experience: Myth and Evidence*. London: Open Books.

Coleman, M. & Gillberg, C. (1987). *The Biology of the Autistic Syndromes*. New York: Praeger.

Damasio, A. R. & Maurer, R. G. (1978). A neurological model for childhood autism. *Archives of Neurology*, **35**, 777–86.

DeMyer. M. K. (1975). Research in infantile autism: a strategy and its results. *Biological Psychiatry*, **10**, 433–52.

DeMyer, M. (1979). *Parents and Children in Autism*. Washington: Winston.

Folstein, S. E. & Rutter, M. L. (1988). Autism: familial aggregation and genetic implications. *Journal of Autism and Developmental Disorders*, **18**, 3–30.

Frith, U. (1989). *Autism: Explaining the Enigma*. Oxford: Blackwell.

Frith, U. (Ed.) (1991). *Autism and Asperger Syndrome*. Cambridge: Cambridge University Press.

Gillberg, C. (1988). The neurobiology of infantile autism. *Journal of Child Psychology and Psychiatry*, **29**, 257–66.

Gillberg, C., Persson, E., Grufman, M. & Themner, U. (1986). Psychiatric disorders in mildly and severely mentally retarded urban children and adolescents: epidemiological aspects. *British Journal of Psychiatry*, **149**, 68–74.

Gillberg, C., Steffenburg, S. & Schaumann, H. (1991). Is autism more common now than ten years ago? *British Journal of Psychiatry*, **158**, 403–9.

Gillberg, I. & Gillberg, C. (1989). Asperger syndrome–some epidemiological considerations: A research note. *Journal of Child Psychology and Psychiatry*, **30**, 631–8.

Gould, J., Rigg, M. & Bignell, L. (1991). *The Higashi Experience*. London: National Autistic Society.

Howlin, P. (1982). The education and management of autistic, psychotic children. In J. K. Wing & L. Wing, eds. *Psychoses of Uncertain Aetiology*, pp. 246–250. Cambridge: Cambridge University Press.

Howlin, P. & Rutter, M. (1987). *Treatment of Autistic Children*. Chichester: Wiley.

Kanner, L. (1943). Autistic disturbances of affective contact. *Nervous Child*, **2**, 217–50.

Lane, H. (1977). *The Wild Boy of Aveyron*. London: Allen and Unwin.

Lotter, V. (1966). Epidemiology of autistic conditions in young children. I. Prevalence. *Social Psychiatry*, **1**, 124–37.

Lowe, M. (1975). Trends in the development of representational play in infants from one to three years–an observational study. *Journal of Child Psychology and Psychiatry*, **16**, 33–47.

Park, C. C. (1982). *The Siege*. Boston: Little, Brown.

Ricks, D. M. & Wing, L. (1975). Language, communication and the use of symbols in normal and autistic children. *Journal of Autism and Childhood Schizophrenia*, **3**, 191–221.

Rutter, M. (1970). Autistic children; infancy to adulthood. *Seminars in Psychiatry*, **2**, 435–50.

Sheridan, M. D. (1969). Playthings in the development of language. *Health Trends Quarterly Review*, **1**, 7–10.

Sheridan, M. D. (1977). *Spontaneous Play in Early Childhood from Birth to Six Years*. Windsor: NFER.

Schaffer, H. R. (1974). Early social behaviour and the study of reciprocity. *Bulletin of the British Psychological Society*, **27**, 209–16.

Schopler, E. & Mesibov, G. B., eds. (1987). *Neurobiological Issues in Autism*. New York: Plenum.

Trevarthen, C. (1974). Conversations with a two-month old. *New Scientist*. **62**, 230–5.

Wing, L. (1980). Autistic Children: *A Guide for Parents*. London: Constable.

Wing, L. (1981a). Asperger's syndrome: a clinical account. *Psychological Medicine*, **11**, 115–29.

Wing, L. (1981b). Sex ratios in early childhood autism and related conditions. *Psychiatry Research*, **5**, 129–37.

Wing, L. (1988a). The continuum of autistic characteristics. In E. Schopler & G. Mesibov, eds. *Diagnosis and Assessment in Autism*, pp. 91–110. New York: Plenum.

Wing, L. (Ed.) (1988b). *Aspects of Autism–Biological Research*. London: Gaskell.

Wing, L. (1989). *Hospital Closure and the Effects on the Residents*. Aldershot: Avebury.

Wing, L. & Gould, J. (1979). Severe impairments of social interaction and associated abnormalities in children: epidemiology and classification. *Journal of Autism and Developmental Disorders*, **9**, 11–29.

World Health Organization (1992). *International Classification of Diseases: Tenth Revision. Draft Research Diagnostic Criteria*. Geneva: WHO.

11

Challenging behaviour

GERALDINE HOLT

Introduction

The term challenging behaviour is used to describe behaviours 'of such an intensity, frequency or duration that the physical safety of the person or others is likely to be placed in serious jeopardy, or behaviour which is likely to seriously limit or delay access to and use of ordinary community facilities' (Emerson *et al.*, 1987).

Such behaviour is described as challenging because it is necessary for services to be creative and persistent in their efforts to work with the individuals involved. The term is used to emphasise the need for an appropriate service response and so has a different focus to terms such as maladaptive behaviour or difficult behaviour.

Challenging behaviour includes very aggressive behaviour towards the environment, others or the self. It challenges not only the resources of services but also that of families. It can lead to the breakdown of community placements (Intagliata & Willer, 1982) and puts the individual at risk of abuse by service providers (Rusch, Hall & Griffin, 1986).

Epidemiology

Studies of people with mental retardation have considered different samples, e.g. from hospital or the community, those with differing degrees of mental retardation, and have used differing definitions of what could be subsumed under the heading of challenging behaviour. This makes interpretation of the literature in this field problematic.

Surveys of people with severe mental retardation from the UK suggest that approximately 20 % of the child and adolescent population and 15 % of the adult population have some form of severe behaviour disorder (Wing, 1971; Kushlik & Cox, 1973). Lund (1989) reported that behaviour disorders are commoner in men and are associated with greater degrees of mental retardation and epilepsy.

Aetiology

The term challenging behaviour is descriptive; in itself its use does not help those working with individuals who show such behaviour to decide how to proceed. It is vital then to better understand why an individual shows such behaviour and what that behaviour exactly is before planning one's intervention. A number of theories have been proposed as to the origins of challenging behaviour. When considering an individual's behaviour one or more of these models may be assumed to be relevant in the origin of or the maintenance of such behaviour. Such assumptions can then be tested and provide a rationale for an individualised approach by the service to the person's needs. In order to ascertain what factors might be contributing to an individual's challenging behaviour a thorough assessment is required which includes taking a detailed history (not only of the behaviour, but of the individual's development, his relationships, his family, health, etc.) This may involve talking not only to the individual but also carers, etc., a physical examination, specialist investigations if appropriate e.g. EEG if epilepsy is suspected, a detailed assessment of the individual's skills and needs and behavioural observation.

Factors associated with challenging behaviour

(i) Pain or discomfort: Challenging behaviour may occur as a response to pain, particularly if an individual is unable to explain his discomfort of for example toothache, cystitis, otitis media etc.

(ii) Epilepsy: Gedye (1989 *a* and *a*) has proposed that self-injurious behaviour can result from frontal lobe seizure activity. Gualtieri (1989) suggests that, in people with challenging behaviour and epilepsy, good seizure control can reduce the challenging behaviour. He considers that paroxysmal self-injurious behaviour may be a 'seizure equivalent'.

(iii) Medication: Gualtieri (1989) states that sedative anticonvulsants (such as phenobarbitone, primidone, phenytoin and exthosuxamide) are associated with self-injurious behaviour in some individuals, as are xanthines (theophylline and caffeine) and neuroleptics (such as chlorpromazine and haloperidol).

It is important then that drugs are used correctly, that is only when they are providing demonstrably desirable effects and are used at the appropriate dosage level.

(iv) Psychiatric disorders: Psychiatric disorders (see Part II) lead to changes in behaviour. People with mental retardation may not be able to express their emotional distress verbally so that their change in behaviour may not be understood by others and appropriate help not offered, leading to an escalation of the behaviour and so a vicious circle starts.

 (v) Autism and autistic spectrum disorders: Challenging behaviour is more common in those people with mental retardation who are also socially impaired (Wing, 1971). Such people find it difficult to make links between their behaviour and what caused it.

(vi) Communication disorders: Frustration resulting from difficulties in communicating may result in challenging behaviour. An assessment by a speech therapist is invaluable in such cases.

(vii) Level of arousal: It has been suggested that for some people challenging behaviour serves to bring the level of arousal to its optimum level, increasing stimulation in those who are bored and decreasing it in those who are overaroused, by for example, enabling task avoidance.

(viii) Lesch–Nyhan syndrome: This is caused by an X-linked deficiency of the enzyme hypoxanthine quanine phosphoriboyl transferase. It is associated with mental retardation, athetosis and severe self-biting, particularly of the lips, tongue and fingers. One theory for this behaviour was that the increased levels of uric acid in the saliva acted as an irritant. However, treatment with allopurinol of young patients to reduce the uric acid level does not reduce the behaviour.

Cataldo and Harris (1982) suggest that the dopaminergic and serotoninergic systems (see later) may also be disturbed in this condition.

Possible mechanisms for the relationship between these associated factors and challenging behaviour

Biological Approach

A number of biological models have been advocated. The more important ones are discussed here.

(i) Endorphin model

It has been suggested that repeated self-injury and thus repeated stimulation of endorphin receptors may lead to a reduced reactivity of these receptors, so that greater injury is required to stimulate them. This has led to work in which the endorphin receptors have been blocked by Naltrexone (Herman *et al.*, 1987) or Naloxone (Sandman *et al.*, 1983) to remove the biological reinforcing consequences of the challenging behaviour and allow extinction to occur. Whilst these reports show some success, the numbers of people studied are small.

(ii) Serotonin model

Cataldo and Harris (1982) review the literature linking low serotonin levels in the CNS of animals to impulsive and aggressive behaviour. Certain syndromes which are associated with self-injurious behaviour are also sometimes accompanied by low serotonin levels, e.g. Down's syndrome, Lesch–Nyhan syndrome, autism, Cornelia de Lange syndrome. Gualtieri (1989) reports on a child with self-injurious behaviour who he successfully treated with L-tryptophan and fluoxetine.

(iii) Dopamine Model

Abnormalities of the dopaminergic system have been implicated in Lesch–Nyhan syndrome and also in Riley–Day syndrome, both conditions being associated with self-injurious behaviour. Patients with Riley–Day syndrome have abnormal sensory nerves and organs, nerve fibres and autonomic nerve plexuses. Their perception of pain and taste is reduced. Such patients have reduced levels of dopamine β-hydroxylase, the enzyme which converts dopamine to noradrenaline.

Learning Approach

In this model challenging behaviour is a learned response which is shaped and maintained by external contingencies which provide positive reinforcement or negative reinforcement (the termination of an aversive event, i.e. an escape or avoidance response). This model is further considered in Part IV.

Psychodynamic approach

Zuk (1960) separates self-injury from self-mutilation. He proposes that in the former the aggressive impulse is not directed at the self but rather against some frustrating event, object or person whereas in the latter the aggression is a means of punishing the self for transgressions. The aggression in either case may be directed consciously or unconsciously.

Anna Freud (1954) believed that self-injurious behaviour allowed the child to differentiate itself from the rest of the world.

Management

In considering how best to work with people with challenging behaviour one can approach the topic under three headings:

Where

There is a debate as to whether services to people with mental retardation and challenging behaviour should be provided in specialised units or via specialist teams working in main stream day care and residential facilities. Criticism has been made of the methodology of papers evaluating specialist units (Hoefkins & Allen, 1990) and yet many of the alternative models have not endured with time and are unable to cope if a placement breaks down. It would appear that, ideally, a variety of patterns of service of delivery should be available so that the most appropriate choice can be made to fit an individual's needs.

Who

By definition people with challenging behaviour require services to be responsive to their needs. The assessment required to try to better understand an individual's situation needs to be wide ranging, considering the various possible aetiological factors previously discussed. This necessitates the use of a multidisciplinary approach, with the assessments leading to a plan of action tailored to that individual's needs, which can then be evaluated. It is important that all those working with the individual are committed to the approach and are aware of the framework in which they are expected to work. This may require the setting up of specific staff training programmes (McDonnell, Dearden & Richens, 1991).

What

The interventions which are implemented will depend on an individual's needs, and may require the concomitant use of more than one approach. Behavioural strategies (see Part IV) are used increasingly alongside other approaches. Certainly in the UK aversive techniques are rarely used and emphasis is on techniques relying on positive reinforcement of desired behaviours.

Other psychotherapeutic techniques (see Part IV) may be helpful as may treatment of underlying psychiatric disorders and epilepsy.

Summary

Challenging behaviour is not a unitary phenomenon. The challenge provided to services is to undertake a thorough assessment of each individual with challenging behaviour to better understand what that behaviour is and what might be causing it. Only then can a planned intervention be made, allowing hypotheses to be tested and adapted accordingly.

References

Cataldo, M. F. & Harris, J. (1982). The biological basis for self injury in the mentally retarded. *Analysis and Intervention in Developmental Disabilities.* **2**, 21–40.

Emerson, E., Barrett, S., Bell, C., Cummings, R., McCool, C., Tooqood, A. & Mansell, J. (1987). Developing services for people with severe learning difficulties and challenging behaviours. University of Kent at Canterbury, Institute of Social and Applied Psychology.

Freud, A. (1954). Problems of infantile neurosis: a discussion. In *The Psychoanalytic Study of the Child vol. 9*. New York: International Universities Press.

Gedye, A. (1989*a*). Extreme self-injury attributed to frontal lobe seizures. *American Journal on Mental Retardation*, **94**, 20–26.

Gedye, A. (1989*b*). Episodic rage and aggression attributed to frontal lobe seizures. *Journal of Mental Deficiency Research.* **33**, 369–79.

Gualtieri, C. T. (1989). The differential diagnosis of self-injurious behaviour in mentally retarded people. *Psychopharmacology Bulletin.* **25**(3), 358–63.

Herman, B. H., Hammock, M. K., Arthur-Smith, A., Chatoor, I. & Zelnik, N. (1987). Naltrexone decreases self-injurious behaviour. *Annals of Neurology.* **22**, 550–2.

Hoefkins. A. & Allen, D. (1990). Evaluation of a special behaviour unit for people with mental handicap and challenging behaviour. *Journal of Mental Deficiency Research.* **34**, 213–28.

Intaqliata, J. & Willer, B. (1982). Reinstitutionalization of mentally retarded persons successfully placed into family-care and group homes. *American Journal of Mental Deficiency*, **87**, 34–39.

Kushlik, A. & Cox, G. R. (1973). The epidemiology of mental handicap. *Developmental Medicine and Child Neurology*, **15**, 748–759.

Lund, J. (1989). Measuring behaviour disorder in mental handicap. *British Journal of Psychiatry*, **155**, 379–83.

McDonnell, A., Dearden, B. & Richens, A. (1991). Staff training in the management of violence and aggression: Part 2. *Mental Handicap*, **19**, 109–12.

Rusch, R. G., Hall, J. C. & Griffin, H. C. (1986). Abuse provoking characteristics of institutionalized mentally retarded individuals. *American Journal of Mental Deficiency*, **90**(6), 618–24.

Sandman, C. A., Datta, P. C., Barron, J., Hochler, F. K., Williams, C. & Swanson, J. M. (1983). Naloxone attenuates self-abusive behaviour in developmentally disabled clients. *Applied Research in Mental Retardation*, **4**, 5–11.

Wing, L. (1971). Severly retarded children in a London area: prevalence and provision of services. *Psychological Medicine*, **1**, 405–15.

Zuk, G. H. (1960). Psychodynamic implications of self-injury in defective children and adults. *Journal of Clinical Psychology*, **16**, 58–60.

Part III
Special issues

12

The Fragile X syndrome

JEREMY TURK, RANDI J. HAGERMAN,
ANGELA BARNICOAT AND JOHN MCEVOY

Introduction

The Fragile X syndrome is the commonest inherited cause of mental
retardation. It occurs in up to one in every thousand individuals and
accounts for 10 % of people with learning difficulties (Webb *et al.*, 1986).
The syndrome's recognition has been a major advance in explaining the
preponderance of men over women with mental retardation. It also partly
explains the tendency for such special needs to run in families affecting
males more than females, so-called 'X-linked mental retardation'; due to
the assumption that the gene responsible must be on the X chromosome.
Various physical features are associated, but none of these is needed for
diagnosis and they all occur in other syndromes and normal individuals.
The important aspect for those working in services for people with mental
retardation is the associated psychological and behavioural features, the
so-called 'behavioural phenotype'. Aspects of this phenotype are often
early hints of the syndrome's presence. Subtle versions occur in otherwise
asymptomatic carriers. They focus attention on special needs common to
many with the condition and point the way to appropriate remedial
interventions.

The Fragile X syndrome therefore requires a working knowledge of all
fields contributing to the welfare of people with mental retardation.
Professionals must collaborate in order to provide comprehensive multidisciplinary services to such individuals and their families.

Epidemiology

Fragile X syndrome occurs in all races and cultures. Institutional and
school studies yield prevalence estimates between 0.19 to 0.92 per 1000

135

(Herbst & MIller, 1980; Blomquist *et al.*, 1983). Bundey, Webb, Thake and Todd (1985) found 8.9% of children with 'idiopathic' severe mental retardation to have fragile X. The calculated prevalence of Fragile X for all schoolchildren was 1 per 1000 (Webb *et al.*, 1986). A further study found 8% of mildly learning disabled children to have fragile X syndrome (Thake *et al.* 1987). Recently, concern has arisen over varying diagnostic rates for different geographical areas. Speculation persists as to whether this is due to true prevalence variations or to difficulties in standardising the complex chromosomal analysis.

Documentation of a non-pathological fragile site on the X chromosome producing false positive results (Sutherland & Baker, 1990) prompted review of the above community studies (Webb & Bundey, 1991). Four cases out of the original 29 raised sufficient doubt regarding diagnosis for them to be excluded from the fragile X cohort. Recalculation still gave a prevalence of 1 in 1039 compared with the previous figure of 1 in 952. Thus fragile X syndrome remains a common and underdiagnosed condition for which informed genetic counselling and individualised intervention programmes are available and necessary.

Genetics

The syndrome's genetics have proved difficult to unravel since its first report. The clinical phenotype was described in 1943 (Martin & Bell, 1943). The chromosomal anomaly was not documented for a further 26 years (Lubs, 1969). Only in 1977 were the phenotype and cytogenetic changes linked (Sutherland, 1977).

Fragile X syndrome derives its name from characteristic appearances of the X chromosome when chromosomes from cells cultured in folate depleted media are examined by light microscopy. The X chromosome appears to have a small lightly staining, ragged break near the long arm's tip (position Xq27.3). This appearance is only seen in a proportion of cells, usually between 5 and 50% in affected males. Diagnosis in females is more difficult with only 50% of obligate carriers demonstrating the fragile site (Sutherland, 1979).

Fragile X syndrome is inherited in an X linked fashion but has unusual features. Some men are shown by pedigree to have transmitted the mutation but are clinically and cytogenetically normal (Fryns & van den Berghe, 1982). They are known as normal transmitting (non-penetrant) males. Until recently they were only identified once they had had affected grandsons (since their X chromosome is passed only to their daughters who are all obligate carriers). Also, the proportion of a woman's offspring who are affected depends on her own clinical status (Sherman *et al.*, 1985). About one-third of obligate carriers have clinical symptoms. Clinically normal women have on average 40 % of their sons affected (as opposed to 50 % which would be expected). The shortfall is believed to consist of normal transmitting males. Symptomatic women have the expected 50 % of their sons affected and a greater proportion of their daughters have clinical symptoms.

Understanding of fragile X syndrome has been revolutionised by identification of gene FMR-1 (Verkerk *et al.*, 1991) and documentation of a mutation in the gene in most fragile X families (Oberle *et al.*, 1991; Yu *et al.*, 1991). FMR-1 has a section with recurrent CGG base triplets which code repeatedly for the amino acid arginine. In fragile X families there is increased length of this region. There is also aberrant gene methylation in affected males (methylation of specific sites is a feature of inactivated genes, but it is unusual to find an inactivated gene on the single X chromosome of a male). The insertion's size is variable with normal transmitting males having length increases of about 500 base pairs. Affected males have an increase of up to 5000 base pairs (Oberle *et al.*, 1991). The insertion size in females may relate to clinical severity but this has yet to be confirmed (Oberle *et al.*, 1991).

These advances have transformed advice given to individuals. Usually one can identify even clinically and cytogenetically normal heterozygous females. These women can be told of the high risk of affected offspring and counselled regarding prenatal testing. Conversely, many women at risk of being carriers can be reassured that they do not have the mutation and can have families without anxiety. Likewise, it is possible to detect males who are unaffected transmitting carriers but who may have affected grand-children (born to their daughters who will all be obligate carriers). Many males can also be reassured that they are not carriers of the mutation. Tracing of the mutation within a pedigree may indicate which family members are at highest risk. Previously the female line only was examined. Since many grandfathers of affected children are now known to be transmitting males the direction of family studies may be altered by tracing the mutation back through several generations.

There are still unanswered questions. About 10 % of pedigrees diagnosed cytogenetically do not show the above changes (Rousseau *et al.*, 1991). They may have a different mutation elsewhere in FMR-1, another gene responsible for the same clinical phenotype, or another nearby site on the X chromosome which also demonstrates fragility (Sutherland & Baker, 1990). Also the repetitive section length is not fixed in the normal population and it will be important to determine the normal range (Fu *et al.*, 1991). No new mutations have yet been documented by molecular studies but the mutation rate is predicted to be high (Sherman *et al.*, 1984). The shift from normal to pathological is thought to be gradual (Fu *et al.*, 1991). Finally, the protein coded for by FMR-1 has yet to be identified and the mechanisms of production of the clinical phenotype from the pathological change await elucidation.

Medical and physical aspects

Physical features associated with fragile X syndrome are often subtle or absent. However, their presence, while not diagnostic, may indicate the underlying pathology. The head may be longish with slightly enlarged circumference. Ears are often primitive and protruding. The nasal bridge may be long and flattened, the palate high arched, and the jaw large (macrognathia). Skin can be soft and velvety, and abnormal palmar and plantar dermatoglyphics are sometimes observed (Simko *et al.*, 1989). Testicular enlargement (macro-orchidism) is common in postpubertal males, but is too subtle to be useful diagnostically before then (Turner, Daniel & Frost, 1980). Physical features typical of males common among affected heterozygote females include prominent ears, long face, and hyperextensible finger joints.

Medical personnel should be alert to common physical anomalies. Orthopaedic problems can arise in association with connective tissue dysplasia. Flat feet occur often with pronation (inturning). A shoe insert improves uneven shoe wear and provides ankle support. Foot pain is almost never a problem. More aggressive treatment is rarely needed (Davids, Hagerman & Eilert, 1990). Joint dislocations are rare. They include recurrent patellar dislocation and congenital dislocation of the hip. Scoliosis is commoner and may require orthopaedic follow-up. Hernias are occasionally seen. They probably result from connective tissue laxity and require surgery (Hagerman, 1991).

Connective tissue problems probably also explain aortic dilatation, and mitral valve prolapse which occurs in approximately 50% of fragile X males (Sreeram *et al.*, 1989). A murmur or click heard on cardiac examination warrants a specialist cardiac opinion. Antibiotic prophylaxis against subacute bacterial endocarditis is recommended for individuals with significant mitral valve prolapse, especially if mitral valve regurgitation is present. However, cardiac problems are not life threatening and do not shorten life span. Heterozygous females can also experience mitral valve prolapse and may complain of palpitations or rarely chest pain.

Infant boys with fragile X often have hypotonia (floppiness) and motor milestone delay. Early interventions by occupational therapists and physiotherapists can help. Some individuals have difficulty tolerating certain food textures because of oral tactile sensitivities. Failure to thrive occurs occasionally when this problem is severe. Gastro-oesophageal reflux may aggravate failure to thrive. Reflux or recurrent vomiting appear to relate to a floppy gastro-oesophageal sphincter. Most children respond to positional changes, thickening of feeds and medication. Surgery may be indicated in severe cases.

Hearing and visual impairments are important and remediable. Recurrent secretory otitis media (glue ear) is a substantial problem for 60 % and produces fluctuating hearing loss which further impairs speech and language development (Hagerman, Altshul & McBogg, 1987). Treatment should be early and vigorous with grommet insertion if needed. Common eye problems include squint, short and long sightedness, nystagmus and ptosis (Maino *et al.*, 1990).

Epilepsy affects approximately 20 % of males. Seizures usually present in early childhood as staring spells, akinetic episodes, complex partial seizures or generalised tonic clonic episodes. They are usually infrequent and respond well to anticonvulsants, particularly carbamazepine (Wisniewski *et al.*, 1991). Musumeci *et al.* (1989) have reported characteristic rolandic spikes in EEG's of individuals with epilepsy. Central nervous system pathology is also suggested by nuclear magnetic resonance imaging (Reiss *et al.*, 1991). Posterior cerebellar vermis hypoplasia is the most striking finding and may be linked to sensory integration deficits.

Psychiatric and behavioural aspects

Various psychological and behavioural features have been proposed as being associated with fragile X syndrome since awareness grew that it was these aspects, rather than physical attributes, which were most characteristic (Thake *et al.*, 1985). Research has focused on:

1. psychological functioning
2. speech and language
3. autism and other social impairments
4. disorders of attention and concentration.

Psychological functioning
General intelligence

Intellectual functioning in males varies widely but is usually in the mild to moderate learning disability range (IQ 35–70). Up to 30% are severely or profoundly affected (Curfs *et al.*, 1989). Average or near average IQs have been reported (Daker, *et al.* 1981) though usually with specific cognitive delays (Goldfine *et al.* 1987). Some clinically affected fragile X positive males function in the borderline or low normal range, at least initially, often with normal early motor milestones (Golfine *et al.*, 1987). Some males who carry the fragile X gene are unaffected clinically (Froster-Iskenius *et al.*, 1986). If these higher functioning individuals do come to professional attention, it is usually due to associated behavioural disturbances.

Intellectual profile

An uneven intellectual profile is common with relative strengths in verbal skills and visual learning, and special needs with numeracy, visuospatial abilities and auditory learning (Theobald, Hay & Judge, 1987; Herbst *et al.*, 1981). Other studies have found no such difference (Chudley, 1984). Curfs *et al.*, (1989) found higher performance IQ than Verbal IQ particularly in higher functioning fragile X males. Average level of cognitive functioning must be considered in interpreting verbal performance discrepancies.

Children with fragile X syndrome seem to have particular difficulty with tasks involving sequential processing, or short-term memory in the recall or reproduction of items in serial or temporal order (for example, recalling a series of digits or object words). They also have substantial problems imitating a series of motor movements (Dykens, Hodapp & Leckman, 1987; Kemper, Hagerman & Altschul-Stark, 1988). Conversely, performance is relatively strong on tasks requiring simultaneous information processing (integrative, frequently spatial approaches to problem solving e.g. block design). With the exception of arithmetic, performance on achievement tests such as those tapping vocabulary or basic information are also relatively unimpaired. Other special needs include problems processing novel information as opposed to verbally based factual material (Reiss & Freund, 1990*a*). Added demands on short-term memory and the need for flexibility in problem solving accentuate these difficulties.

Males also have relative strengths in daily living skills, particularly domestic (cleaning, cooking) and personal (toileting, grooming) (Dykens *et al.* 1987).

Trajectory of intellectual development

Studies of the trajectory of intellectual development have reported varying findings. Lachiweicz *et al.* (1987) suggest that IQ scores decrease in early childhood. In contrast it has been proposed that following steady cognitive growth during childhood there is gradual plateauing in the rate at which new yet-to-be-learnt abilities are attained (Dykens *et al.*, 1989). This decline is reported to be most marked in early puberty and tends to affect individuals with higher initial intellectual levels more. Explanations as to the underlying cause and the age at which this decline commences are areas of debate. Both neurobiological and task-related factors have been implicated in this slowing of intellectual development (Hodapp *et al.*, 1990). The phenomenon may result from relatively greater weaknesses with abstract reasoning and symbolic language skills that are stressed in the cognitive testing of later childhood and adolescence (Hagerman *et al.*, 1989). The complexities of this issue are illustrated by a large multicentre study (Fisch *et al.*, 1991). 67% of males showed a decline in IQ but the decline was significant in only 45% of subjects. Significant decreases were observed irrespective of age at testing. The authors attributed the IQ decline to dynamic neurological processes of variable occurrence.

Females display substantial range and variation in cognitive functioning. Sherman *et al.* (1985) found borderline or below borderline IQ in approximately 35% of affected females. Loesch and Hay (1988) suggest that up to 85% of heterozygotes demonstrate cognitive deficits. Brainard, Schreiner and Hagerman (1991) emphasise the importance of differentiating between cytogenetically positive and negative women. Failure to do so is likely to produce an underestimate of the overall level of cognitive functioning of fragile X negative women. Fragile X women are seen as generally cognitively unimpaired and the authors advise against prediction of carrier cognitive status from WAIS-R subtest patterns.

A subtest profile of low scores on arithmetic, digit span and block design has been reported for fragile X females (Miezejeski *et al.*, 1986), though other researchers have not found this (Wolff *et al.*, 1988). Visual–motor coordination problems have also been reported (Hagerman & Smith, 1983). Freund and Reiss (1991) found relative weaknesses in short-term memory for non-verbal, sequential material and strengths on verbal short term memory for sequenced information in fragile X females.

It seems that cytogenetically negative female obligate carriers are relatively unaffected, though they may have a slight weakness in verbal short-term memory (Wolff *et al.*, 1988; Brainard *et al.*, 1991). For fragile X cytogenetically positive females there is the suggestion of a specific cognitive phenotype with weaknesses on arithmetic, digit span and block design subscales. Possible qualitative differences between the phenotypes of positive and negative carrier females prevent major conclusions on cognitive functioning. Many studies fail to discriminate between positive and negative females and between women and girls.

Neuropsychological studies of normal intelligence heterozygote females have shown significant frontal lobe deficits in cytogenetically expressing individuals. Features include perseveration, tangential speech, impulsivity, distractibility and difficulty with transitions (Mazzocco *et al.*, 1992). These disabilities may relate to schizotypal traits reported by Reiss *et al.* (1988) in mildly affected women.

Depression has been reported in over 70% of low-expressing fragile X positive women compared with 40% of control women who have developmentally delayed non-fragile X children (Sobesky, summarised in Mandel *et al.*, 1992). Depression is also common in heterozygous women negative for fragile X who do not have significant cognitive deficits. The relative contributions of the fragile X gene and environmental stressors are as yet unknown. The subtlest effect of the fragile X gene may involve personality changes including shyness and a predisposition to anxiety or depression.

Speech and Language

Speech and language development is almost always delayed and often displays multiple abnormalities. A characteristic pattern of talking has been described as 'jocular' (Hagerman, 1989), 'litany-like' to describe up and down swings of pitch (Turner *et al.*, 1980), and 'cluttered' due to rapid, disrhythmic and garbled pronunciation with poor topic maintenance and frequent tangential comments (Hanson, Jackson & Hagerman, 1986). Other features recall autistic disturbances. These include echolalia, palilalia and repetitiveness. This delayed, deviant repetitive language is distinct from that of individuals with Down's syndrome or autism suggesting that it is not due to either the level of adaptive functioning or autistic-like behaviours (Sudhalter *et al.*, 1990). Verbal perseveration is particularly common and is thought to be due to word retrieval problems and/or stalling behaviour while processing an utterance or searching for a word. It is also suggested that the more frequent self-repetition shown by people with fragile X may be assisting conversation pace and flow and confirming and maintaining conversational topic while minimising demands on expressive language abilities (Ferrier *et al.*, 1991). This is consistent with fragile X individuals having greater understanding of conversational conventions than autistic people, despite having problems in managing complexities of verbal dialogue.

Articulation errors compound the above. They probably arise from combinations of higher-level linguistic encoding difficulties, developmental dyspraxia and associated physical abnormalities including large jaw, high-arched palate and articulatory muscle/temporo-mandibular joint laxity. Female carriers may demonstrate these features (Hagerman, 1987).

Autism and other social impairments

Individuals experience a range of disabilities in social functioning, language and communication, and ritualistic tendencies reminiscent of autism. Some people with fragile X do have typical autism, but suggestions of a significant link between the two once intellectual level has been controlled for (Gillberg & Wahlstrom, 1985) have not been supported by recent research. Prevalence figures for fragile X in autistic populations range from 0% (Goldfine *et al.*, 1985) to 22.7% (Brown *et al.*, 1982). Reasons for this variation include samples being drawn from a variety of sources, variable assessment methods and diagnostic criteria and varying thresholds for cytogenetic diagnosis (Piven *et al.*, 1991). Recent studies (Payton *et al.*, 1989; Piven *et al.*, 1991) suggest that the prevalence of fragile X in people with autism is 2–3%. This means the syndrome is still an important association of autism and must be checked for in people diagnosed as such, even if it is not that common an association.

Assessing individuals with fragile X for autism has revealed rates of 7% (Bregman, Leckman & Ort, 1988) to 17.6% (Reiss & Freund, 1990*b*) with higher rates for the wider diagnostic category of pervasive developmental disorder, and for having met diagnostic criteria for autism previously. Thus while a minority of males with fragile X have autism, more do not, though many display certain autistic-like social impairments.

Comparison of fragile X populations with control groups matched on chronological age and developmental level again fails to demonstrate a consistently higher rate of autism in fragile X than in mental retardation generally. However a profile of characteristic social impairments is frequently observed which distinguishes fragile X populations from comparison groups (Borghraef *et al.*, 1987; Cohen et al., 1988; Einfeld, Molony & Hall, 1989, Cohen *et al.*, 1991*b*). Increased relational disturbance coexists with general sensory defensiveness which often manifests as an aversion to eye contact (Cohen *et al.*, 1989), and sometimes even the need to avert the face and body during greeting of others (Wolff *et al.*, 1989). It may also present as tactile defensiveness, hyperacusis or intolerance of crowded, bright and noisy environments for example shopping centres. Hand flapping is common. Hand biting sometimes occurs especially with excitement, anxiety or frustration. Cohen *et al.* (1991*a*) conclude that 'although the fragile X site has autism associated with it, the fragile X site is even more strongly associated with another readily recognisable behavioral phenotype: social avoidance'.

Less than 25% of clinically affected heterozygote females show hand flapping and hand biting but shyness and social anxiety occur in over 60% (Hagerman *et al.*, 1992). This study also reports hyperactivity as being milder than in affected boys.

There is now much evidence for a characteristic profile of social impairments, even in the absence of typical autism, which is of use diagnostically and therapeutically. Generalised sensory defensiveness coexists with social anxiety which is commoner than social indifference. Frequent speech and language abnormalities include immediate and delayed echolalia and repetitive speech. Stereotypic behaviour, in particular hand flapping and less often hand biting occur. Individuals may show excessive insistence on routine with magnified behavioural responses to changes in routine or the environment. For such individuals variety is far from being the spice of life.

Disorders of attention and concentration

Many families report members with fragile X as having substantial problems with concentration span, being restless, fidgety, impulsive, and overactive. Together these features are consistent with a diagnosis of 'nuclear hyperactivity' (Taylor, 1986) or attention deficit hyperactivity disorder (American Psychiatric Association, 1987) if they occur in multiple settings. These special needs have been less researched than social functioning but some authors claim them to be the most pervasive and troublesome of the associated disabilities (Fryns *et al.*, 1984; Hagerman, 1987). Recent work suggests that such features may be largely attributable to the level of learning disability (Einfeld, Hall & Levy, 1991).

Clinical observation would, however, support the view that poor concentration and attentional skills are indeed frequently associated in early childhood but often improve with age. However distractibility and impulsiveness can persist and interfere with development of social contacts and occupational abilities as well as maximisation of intellectual potential. Research is needed examining possible associations of components of 'attention deficit disorder' with the syndrome instead of looking for direct links with discrete diagnostic categories. Whether or not such associations are found it is still important to consider fragile X syndrome in those with features of hyperactivity owing to reports of hyperactive behaviour as the single presenting feature in non-retarded boys with fragile X syndrome (Hagerman, Kemper & Hudson, 1985).

Interventions: medical

Medication for behavioural difficulties associated with fragile X syndrome has focused on psychostimulant and related agents for features of hyperactivity. Methylphenidate, the most commonly prescribed stimulant, has been demonstrated to help approximately two-thirds of children with fragile X and associated attention deficit disorder, although side effects including mood lability, tantrums and anorexia with weight loss do occur (Hagerman, Murphy & Wittenberger, 1988; Aman *et al.*, 1991). Lower doses often avoid problems while maintaining benefits. Stimulants should always be used cautiously, but particularly so in preschool children due to the greater frequency of adverse reactions.

Interest in folic acid has fluctuated since anecdotal reports of its usefulness (Lejeune, 1982). Rogers and Simensen (1987) reported improvements in intellectual performance and behaviour on subjective parent and teacher ratings. Parental reports of clinical improvement were also found in a double-blind cross-over study (Hagerman et al., 1986). However another double-blind cross-over trial using higher doses found no significant effect (Fisch *et al.*, 1988).

A recent double-blind cross-over pilot study of two boys with fragile X syndrome and attention deficit disorders demonstrated behavioural improvement on 5 mg twice daily (Giannopoulou, Turk & Gath, 1991). A survey of the British Fragile X Society (Turk, unpublished manuscript) found two thirds of children who had received medication for behavioural problems to have been given folic acid. Of these, two-thirds had benefited, similar to the proportion said to improve on methylphenidate when prescribed for attentional deficits. Improvements associated with folic acid were reported by parents as usually being related to improved concentration with some evidence of diminished restlessness and defiance. Features associated with non-responsiveness included postpubertal status, inadequate dosage (5 mg or less daily) and deliberate misbehaviours.

It seems that folic acid may decrease features of attention deficit disorders in prepubertal fragile X children in a fashion qualitatively similar to methylphenidate. Few changes are noted in intellectual functioning, language ability or autistic features, or in postpubertal subjects. Many families find folic acid more acceptable than amphetamine derivatives owing to its relative safety, concerns over possible adverse reactions and addiction potential with stimulants, and the fact that folic acid is a naturally occurring dietary constituent. Significant side effects are usually not a problem. Thus folic acid can be tried in young children. Benefits are usually seen within four to six weeks.

Other potentially useful medications include clonidine, an antihypertensive, which can be beneficial for features of attention deficit hyperactivity disorder, particularly in younger children. Anecdotal reports claim a calming and organising effect but sedation is a major problem (Hagerman, 1991). Other medications have been reported anecdotally as helpful for aggression in fragile X men. These include carbamazepine, beta-blockers, lithium, buspirone, and fluoxetine. Properly controlled trials to evaluate their efficacy are lacking. Whenever possible, antipsychotic medications (neuroleptics) should be avoided owing to long-term effects on motor function.

While there is healthy concern for prescribing psychotropic medication to people with mental retardation there are many who have the potential to benefit from judicious use of such agents which may enhance their responsiveness to psychological interventions and improve family functioning. There is a need to shift from a view of psychotropic medication as an end in itself to a view of such agents as part of a multimodal intervention package including psychological, social and educational aspects.

Interventions: Psychological

Particularly in adolescence some individuals appear to become more aggressive. Under these circumstances environmental evaluation and functional analysis of challenging behaviour should be undertaken to search for possible antecedent or consequent events, or other situational factors, which may be causing or maintaining the disturbance, often through sensory overstimulation. Counselling or psychotherapy helps such individuals communicate frustrations, as does the teaching of coping strategies (Brown, Braden & Sobesky, 1991).

Interventions: educational

Educational goals should be determined individually owing to varying abilities. For more able boys, and fragile X positive girls, individualised or small group remediation to support regular classroom work may be sufficient. Most likely this will be necessary for mathematics (Hagerman, 1989). For children with lower cognitive abilities, all academic areas are affected with poor performance in mathematics particularly noticeable (Hagerman, 1987).

Children with fragile X with strengths in simultaneous processing will respond well to teaching strategies which stress the overall aim of a task before breaking it down into component parts. Making tasks concrete and using materials such as graphs models and pictures aid visualisation of what is to be learnt. Weakness in sequential processing may manifest as difficulty with word attack skills. Teaching strategies which emphasise the verbal or temporal, and rely on verbal cues and auditory memory, elicit poor performance. Many special educational schemes rely on presentation of materials in a step-by-step manner. This may be frustrating or anxiety provoking for fragile X children.

Much learning seems to be context specific (Hagerman, 1989). Many fragile X students struggle to generalise what they have learnt. Teaching situations which create familiar, concrete conditions with specially designed materials based on the child's interests are best. Abstract concepts associated with number may hold little meaning, yet simply designed board games can assist in counting and numeracy by involving the student directly and demonstrating the value of counting and number use (McEvoy & McConkey, 1986).

Microcomputers capitalise on strong visual skills and allow individually paced learning. Short-term memory strengths lend themselves to verbal labelling strategies (Freund & Reiss, 1991), verbal labelling strategies and verbal mediation interventions.

Summary

Much work has been undertaken to elicit the complex genetics, psychiatry, psychological functioning, and rehabilitation of individuals with fragile X syndrome. There is still a great deal to be learnt regarding the consequences of having a fragile X chromosome, the likelihoods of developing certain special needs and challenging behaviours, and the most appropriate remedial interventions. Awareness of the condition remains sparse despite its high prevalence. There is much to be gained, not only regarding the fragile X syndrome, but also for other biologically determined handicapping conditions, by adopting the multidisciplinary collaborative perspective.

References

Aman, M. G., Marks, R. E., Turbott, S. H., Wilsher, C. P. & Merry, S. N. (1991). Clinical effects of methylphenidate and thioridazine in intellectually subaverage children. *Journal of the American Academy of Child and Adolescent Psychiatry*, **30**, 246–56.

American Psychiatric Association (1987). DSM-III-R. Diagnostic and Statistical Manual of Mental Disorders (3rd edn., revised). Washington, DC: American Psychiatric Association.

Blomquist, H. K., Gustavson, K-H., Holmgren, G., Nordenson, I. & Palsson-Strae, U. (1983). Fragile X syndrome in mildly mentally retarded children in a northern Swedish county: a prevalence study. *Clinical Genetics*, **24**, 393–8.

Borghraef, M., Fryns, J. P., Dielkens, A., Pyck, K. & van den Berghe, H. (1987). Fragile (X) syndrome: a study of the psychological profile in 23 prepubertal patients. *Clinical Genetics*, **32**, 179–86.

Brainard, S. S., Schreiner, R. A. & Hagerman, R. J. (1991). Cognitive profiles of the carrier Fragile X woman. *American Journal of Medical Genetics*, **38**, 505–8.

Bregman, J. D., Leckman, J. F. & Ort, S. I. (1988). Fragile X syndrome: genetic predisposition to psychopathology. *Journal of Autism and Developmental Disorders*, **18**, 343–54.

Brown, J., Braden, M. & Sobesky, W. (1991). The treatment of behavioral and educational problems. In R. J. Hagerman & A. C. Silverman, eds. *Fragile X Syndrome: Diagnosis, Treatment and Research*, pp. 311–326, Baltimore, London: The Johns Hopkins University Press.

Brown, W. T., Jenkins, E. C., Friedman, E. *et al.* (1982). Autism is associated with the Fragile X syndrome. *Journal of Autism and Developmental Disorder*, **12**, 303–7.

Bundey, S., Webb, T. P., Thake, A. & Todd, J. (1985). A community study of severe mental retardation in the West Midlands and the importance of the Fragile X chromosome in its aetiology. *Journal of Medical Genetics*, **22**, 258–66.

Chudley, A. (1984). Behavior phenotype. In: *Conference Report; International Workshop on the Fragile X Syndrome & X-linked Mental Retardation* (Chudley, A. & Sutherland, G., eds.) *American Journal of Medical Genetics*, **17**, 45–53.

Cohen, I. L., Fisch, G. S., Sudhalter, V. *et al.* (1988). Social gaze, social avoidance, and repetitive behavior in Fragile X males: a controlled study. *American Journal of Mental Retardation*, **92**, 436–46.

Cohen, I. L., Vietze, P. M., Sudhalter, V., Jenkins, E. C. & Brown, W. T. (1989). Parent–Child dyadic gaze patterns in Fragile X males and in Non-fragile X males with autistic disorder. *Journal of Child Psychology and Psychiatry*, **30**, 845–56.

Cohen, I. L., Sudhalter, V., Pfadt, A., Jenkins, E. C., Brown, W. T. & Vietze, P. M. (1991*a*). Why are autism and the Fragile-X syndrome associated? Conceptual and methodological issues. *American Journal of Human Genetics*, **48**, 195–202.

Cohen, I. L., Vietze, P. M., Sudhalter, V., Jenkins, E. C. & Brown, W. T. (1991*b*). Effects of age and communication level on eye contact in Fragile X males and Non-fragile X autistic males. *American Journal of Genetics*, **38**, 498–502.

Curfs, L. M. G., Borghgraef, M., Wiegers, A., Schreppers-Tijdink, G. A. J. & Fryns, J. P. (1989). Strengths and Weaknesses in the cognitive profile of Fragile X patients. *Clinical Genetics*, **36**, 405–10.

Daker, M., Chidiac, P., Fear, L. & Berry, A. (1981). Fragile X in a normal male: a cautionary note. *Lancet*, **i**, 780.

Davids, J. R., Hagerman, R. J. & Eilert, R. E. (1990). The orthopaedist and Fragile X syndrome. *Journal of Bone and Joint Diseases*, **72**, 889–96.

Dykens, E. M., Hodapp, R. M. & Leckman, J. F. (1987). Strengths and weaknesses in the intellectual functioning of males with Fragile X syndrome. *American Journal of Mental Deficiency*, **92**, 234–6.

Dykens, E. M., Hodapp, R. M., Ort, S., Finucane, B., Shapiro, L. R. & Leckman, J. F. (1989). The trajectory of cognitive development in males with Fragile X syndrome. *Journal of the American Academy of Child and Adolescent Psychiatry*, **28**, 422–6.

Dykens, E., Leckman, J., Paul, R. & Watson, M. (1987). The Cognitive, Behavioural and adaptive functioning of Fragile X and Non-fragile X retarded men. Journal of Autism and Developmental Disorders, **18**, 41–52.

Einfeld, S., Hall, W. & Levy, F. (1991). Hyperactivity and the Fragile X Syndrome. *Journal of Abnormal Child Psychology*, **19**, 253–62.

Einfeld, S., Molony, H. & Hall, W. (1989). Autism is not associated with the fragile X syndrome. *American Journal of Medical Genetics*, **34**, 187–93.

Ferrier, L. J., Bashir, A. S., Meryash, D. L., Johnston, J. & Wolff, P. (1991). Conversational skills of individuals with Fragile-X syndrome: a comparison with autism and Down syndrome. *Developmental Medicine and Child Neurology*, **33**, 776–88.

Fisch, G. S., Arinami, T., Froster-Iskenius, U. *et al.* (1991). Relationship between age and IQ among Fragile X males: a multicenter study. *American Journal of Medical Genetics*, **38**, 481–7.

Fisch, G. S, Cohen, I. L., Gross, A. C., Jenkins, V., Jenkins, E. C. & Brown, W. T. (1988). Folic acid treatment of Fragile X males: a further study. *American Journal of Medical Genetics*, **30**, 393–9.

Freund, L. S. & Reiss, A. L. (1991). Cognitive profiles associated with the Fra(X) syndrome in males and females. *American Journal of Medical Genetics*, **38**, 542–7.

Froster-Iskenius, U., McGillivray, B. C., Dill, F. J., Hall, J. G. & Herbst, D. S. (1986). Normal male carriers in the Fra(x) form of X-linked mental retardation (Martin-Bell Syndrome). *American Journal of Medical Genetics*, **23**, 619–31.

Fryns, J. P., Jacobs, J., Kleczkowska, A. & van den Berghe, H. (1984). The psychological profile of the Fragile X syndrome. *Clinical Genetics*, **25**, 131–4.

Fryns, J. P. & van den Berghe, H. (1982). Transmission of fragile (X)(q27) from normal male(s). *Human Genetics*, **61**, 262–3.

Fu, Y-H., Kuhl, D. P. A., Pizzuti, A., *et al.* (1991). Variation of the CGG repeat at the Fragile X site results in genetic instability: resolution of the Sherman paradox. *Cell,* **67**, 1047–58.

Giannopoulou, I., Turk, J. & Gath, A. (1991). Folic acid as a treatment for hyperactivity in children with the Fragile X syndrome. *European Society for Child and Adolescent Psychiatry; Conference Abstracts.* Oxford: Pergamon Press.

Gillberg, C. & Wahlstrom, J. (1985). Chromosome abnormalities in infantile autism and other childhood psychoses: a population study of 66 cases. *Developmental Medicine and Child Neurology,* **27**, 293–304.

Goldfine, P. E., McPherson, D. M., Hardesty, V. A., Heath, G. A., Beauregard, L. J. & Baker, A. A. (1987). Fragile X chromosome associated with primary learning disability. *Journal of the American Academy of Child Psychiatry,* **26**, 589–92.

Goldfine, P. E., McPherson, P. M., Heath, A., Hardesty, V. A., Beauregard, L. J. & Gordon, B. (1985). Association of Fragile X syndrome with autism. *American Journal of Psychiatry,* **142**, 108–10.

Hagerman, R. J. (1987). Fragile X syndrome. *Current Problems in Pediatrics,* **17**(11), 627–74.

Hagerman, R. (1989). Behaviour and treatment of the Fragile X syndrome. In K. E. Davies, ed., *The Fragile X syndrome,* pp. 56–75. Oxford: Oxford University Press.

Hagerman, R. J. (1991) Medical follow-up and pharmacotherapy. In R. J. Hagerman & A. C. Silverman, eds., *Fragile X Syndrome: Diagnosis, Treatment and Research,* pp. 311–326. Baltimore, London: The Johns Hopkins University Press.

Hagerman, R. J., Altshul, D. & McBogg, P. (1987). Recurrent otitis media in boys with the Fragile X syndrome. *American Journal of Diseases in Children,* **141**, 184–7.

Hagerman, R. J., Jackson, C., Amiri, K., Cronister-Silverman, A. C., O'Connor, R. & Sobesky, W. (1992). Girls with Fragile X syndrome: physical and neurocognitive status and outcome. *Pediatrics,* **89**, 395–400.

Hagerman, R. J., Jackson, A. W., Levitas, A., *et al.* (1986). Oral folic acid versus placebo in the treatment of males with the fragile X syndrome. *American Journal of Medical Genetics,* **23**, 241–62.

Hagerman, R., Kemper, M. & Hudson, M. (1985). Learning Disabilities and attentional problems in boys with the Fragile X syndrome. *American Journal of Diseases of Children,* **139**, 674–8.

Hagerman, R. J., Murphy, M. A. & Wittenberger, M. D. (1988). A controlled trial of stimulant medication in children with the Fragile X syndrome. *American Journal of Medical Genetics,* **30**, 377–92.

Hagerman, R. J., Schreiner, R. A., Kemper, M. B., Wittenberger, M. D., Zahn, B. & Habicht, K. (1989). Longitudinal IQ changes in Fragile X males. *American Journal of Medical Genetics,* **33**, 513–8.

Hagerman, R. J. & Smith, A. C. M. (1983). The heterozygous female. In R. J. Hagerman & P. M. McBogg, eds., *The Fragile X Syndrome: Diagnosis, Biochemistry and Intervention,* pp. 83–94. Dillon, Colorado: Spectra Publishing.

Hanson, D. M., Jackson, A. W. & Hagerman, R. J. (1986). Speech disturbances (cluttering) in mildly impaired males with the Martin-Bell/Fragile X syndrome. *American Journal of Medical Genetics,* **23**, 195–206.

Herbst, D., Dunn, G., Dill, F., Kalousek, D. & Krywaniuk, L. (1981). Further delineation of X-linked mental retardation. *Human Genetics,* **58**, 366–72.

Herbst, D. S. & Miller, J. R. (1980). Nonspecific X-linked mental retardation II: the frequency in British Columbia. *American Journal of Medical Genetics*, 7, 461–9.

Hodapp, R. M., Dykens, E. M., Hagerman, R. J., Schreiner, R., Lachiewicz, A. M. & Leckman, J. F. (1990). Developmental implications of changing trajectories of IQ in males with Fragile X syndrome. *Journal of the American Academy of Child and Adolescent Psychiatry*, 29, 214–19.

Kemper, M. B., Hagerman, R. J. & Altshul-Stark, D. (1988). Cognitive profiles of boys with the Fragile X syndrome. *American Journal of Medical Genetics*, 30, 191–200.

Lachiewicz, A., Gullian, C., Spiridigliozzi, G. & Aylsworth, A., (1987). Declining IQs of young males with the Fragile X syndrome. *American Journal of Mental Retardation*, 92, 272–8.

Lejeune, J. (1982). Is the Fragile X syndrome amenable to treatment? *Lancet*, 1, (8266), 273–4.

Loesch, D. Z. & Hay, D. A. (1988). Clinical features and reproductive patterns in Fragile X female heterozygotes. *Journal of Medical Genetics*, 25, 407–14.

Lubs, H. A. (1969). A marker X chromosome. *American Journal of Human Genetics*, 21, 231–44.

McEvoy, J. & McConkey, R. (1986). Count me in: teaching basic counting and number skills. *Mental Handicap*, 14, 113–15.

Maino, D. M., Schlange, D., Maino, J. H. & Caden, B. (1990). Ocular anomalies in Fragile X syndrome. *Journal of the American Optometric Association*, 61, 316–23.

Mandel, J-L., Hagerman, R., Froster, U. *et al.* (1992). Conference Report: Fifth International Workshop on the Fragile X and X-linked Mental Retardation. *American Journal of Medical Genetics*, (*in press*).

Martin, J. P. & Bell, J. (1943). A pedigree of mental defect showing sex-linkage. *Journal of Neurology Neurosurgery and Psychiatry*, 6, 154–7.

Mazzocco, M., Hagerman, R., Cronister-Silverman, A. & Pennington, B. (1992). Specific frontal lobe deficits among women with the Fragile X gene. *Journal of the American Academy of Child and Adolescent Psychiatry*, (*in press*).

Miezejeski, C. M., Jenkins, E. C., Hill, A. L., Wisniewski, K., French, J. H. & Brown, W. T. (1986). A profile of cognitive deficit in females from Fragile X families. *Neuropsychologia*, 24, 405–9.

Musumeci, D. A., Ferri, R., Colognola, R. M., Neri, G., Sanfilippo, S. & Bergonzi, P. (1989). Prevalence of a novel epileptogenic EEG pattern in the Martin-Bell Syndrome. *American Journal of Medical Genetics*, 30, 207–12.

Oberle, I., Rousseau, F., Heitz, D. *et al.* (1991). Instability of a 550-base pair DNA segment and abnormal methylation in Fragile X syndrome. *Science*, 252, 1097–102.

Payton, J. B., Steele, M. W., Wenger, S. L. & Minshew, N. J. (1989). The Fragile X marker and autism in perspective. *Journal of the American Academy of Child and Adolescent Psychiatry*, 28, 417–21.

Piven, J., Gayle, J., Landa, R., Wzorek, M. A. & Folstein, S. (1991). The prevalence of Fragile X in a sample of autistic individuals diagnosed using a standardised interview. *Journal of the American Academy of Child and Adolescent Psychiatry*, 30, 825–30.

Reiss, A. L. & Freund, L. (1990a). Fragile X syndrome. *Biological Psychiatry*, 27, 223–40.

Reiss, A. L. & Freund, L. (1990b). Fragile X syndrome, DSM-III-R, and autism. *Journal of the American Academy of Child and Adolescent Psychiatry*, **29**, 885–91.

Reiss, A. L., Aylward, E., Freund, L. S., Joshi, P. K. & Bryan, R. N. (1991). Neuroanatomy of Fragile X syndrome: the posterior fossa. *Annals of Neurology*, **29**, 26–32.

Reiss, A. L., Hagerman, R. J., Vinogradov, S., Abrams. & King, R. J. (1988). Psychiatric disability in female carriers of the Fragile X chromosome. *Archives of General Psychiatry*, **45**, 25–30.

Rogers, R. C. & Simensen, R. J. (1987). Fragile X syndrome: a common etiology of mental retardation. *American Journal of Mental Deficiency*, **91**, 445–9.

Rousseau, F., Heitz, D., Biancalana, V. *et al.* (1991). Direct diagnosis by DNA analysis of the Fragile X syndrome of mental retardation. *New England Journal of Medicine*, **325**, 1673–81.

Sherman, S. L., Jacobs, P. A., Morton, N. E. *et al.* (1985). Further segregation analysis of the Fra(x) syndrome with special reference to transmitting males. *American Journal of Medical Genetics*, **69**, 389–99.

Sherman, S. L., Morton, N. E., Jacob, P. A. & Turner, G. (1984). The Marker (X) syndrome: a cytogenetic and genetic analysis. *Annals of Human Genetics*, **48**, 21–37.

Simko, A., Hornstein, L., Soukup, S. & Bagamery, N. (1989). Fragile X syndrome: recognition in young children. *Pediatrics*, **83**, 547–52.

Sreeram, N., Wren, C., Bhate, M., Robertson, P. & Hunter, S. (1989). Cardiac abnormalities in the Fragile X syndrome. *British Heart Journal*, **61**, 289–91.

Sudhalter, V., Cohen, I. L., Silverman, W. & Wolf-Schein, E. G. (1990). Conversational analysis of males with Fragile X, Down syndrome and autism: comparison of the emergence of deviant language. *American Journal of Mental Retardation*, **94**, 431–41.

Sutherland, G. R. (1977). Fragile sites on human chromosomes: demonstration of their dependence on the type of tissue culture medium. *Science*, **197**, 265–6.

Sutherland, G. R. (1979). Heritable fragile sites on human chromosomes. Detection of Fra(X)(q27) in males with X linked mental retardation and in their female relatives. *Human Genetics*, **53**, 23–7.

Sutherland, G. R. & Baker, E. (1990). The common Fragile site in Band q27 of the human X chromosome is not coincident with the Fragile X. *Clinical genetics*, **37**, 167–72.

Taylor, E. A. (1986). *The Overactive Child.* Oxford: Spastics International, Blackwell Scientific.

Thake, A., Todd, J., Bundey, S. & Webb, T. (1985). Is it possible to make a clinical diagnosis of the Fragile X syndrome in a boy? *Archives of Disease in Childhood*, **60**, 1001–7.

Thake, A., Todd, J., Webb, T. & Bundey, S. (1987). Children with the Fragile X chromosome at schools for the mildly mentally retarded. *Developmental Medicine and Child Neurology*, **29**, 711–19.

Theobald, T. M., Hay, D. A. & Judge, C. (1987). Individual variation and specific cognitive deficits in the Fragile X syndrome. *American Journal of Medical Genetics*, **28**, 1–11.

Turner, G., Daniel, A. & Frost, M. (1980). X-linked mental retardation, macro-orchidism, and the Xq27 Fragile site. *Journal of Pediatrics*, **96**, 837–41.

Verkerk, A. J. M. H., Pieretti, M., Sutcliffe, J. S. *et al.* (1991). Identification of a gene (FMR-1) containing a CGG repeat coincident with a breakpoint cluster region exhibiting length variation in Fragile X syndrome. *Cell*, **65**, 905–14.

Webb, T. & Bundey, S. (1991). Prevalence of Fragile X syndrome. *Journal of Medical Genetics*, **28**, 358.

Webb, T., Bundey, S., Thake, A. & Todd, J. (1986). The Frequency of the Fragile X chromosome among school children in Coventry. *Journal of Medical Genetics*, **23**, 396–9.

Wisniewski, K. E., Segan, S. M., Miezejeski, C. M., Sersen, E. A. & Rudelli, R. D. (1991). The Fra(X) syndrome: neurological, electrophysiological, and neuropathological abnormalities. *American Journal of Medical Genetics*, **38**, 476–80.

Wolff, P. H., Gardner, J., Lappen, J., Paccia, J. & Meryash, D. (1988). Variable expression of the fra(x) syndrome in heterozygous females of normal intelligence. *American Journal of Medical Genetics*, **30**, 213–25.

Wolff, P. H., Gardner, J., Paccia, J. & Lappen, J. (1989). The greeting behavior of Fragile X males. *American Journal of Mental Retardation*, **93**, 406–11.

Yu, S., Pritchard, M., Kremer, E. *et al.* (1991). Fragile X genotype characterised by an unstable region of DNA. *Science*, **252**, 1179–81.

13

Down's syndrome and Alzheimer's disease
ANTHONY J. HOLLAND

Introduction

The relationship between the inheritance of an extra chromosome 21 (trisomy 21) which results in Down's syndrome and an illness characteristically associated with old age, Alzheimer's disease, has stimulated considerable recent research (Oliver & Holland, 1986). However, the possibility of 'decline' in later life (Fraser & Mitchell, 1876) and the occurrence of Alzheimer-like neuropathology in people with Down's syndrome (Struwe, 1929) were first reported many years ago but its significance is only now being fully recognised for two main reasons. First, there has been a marked increase in the mean life expectancy of people with Down's syndrome and therefore identifying and meeting the mental health needs of older people with Down's syndrome has become increasingly important. It has been estimated that nearly 15 % of males and over 20 % of females with Down's syndrome are over 55 years of age (Fryers, 1986; McGrother & Marshall, 1990) (Fig. 13.1). Secondly, with the application of increasingly sophisticated molecular genetic techniques to the study of psychiatric disorders such associations as this are important clues as to the possible chromosomal location of 'candidate genes' which, in this case, may predispose to Alzheimer's disease.

As a result of previous cross-sectional studies and, more recently, longitudinal studies (Lai & Williams, 1989), it is now clear that people with Down's syndrome do develop dementia. It is therefore important to examine how the diagnosis can be reliably made and how good management practices can be applied to the care of people with Down's syndrome who are dementing. This chapter reviews the association between the two disorders and discusses the difficulties associated with the diagnosis of dementia in a group of people with a pre-existing learning disability.

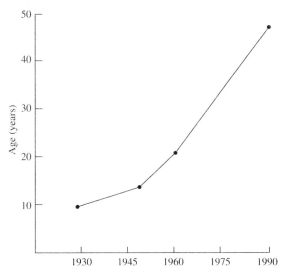

Fig. 13.1. Changes in mean life expectancy of people with Down's syndrome over time.

Neuropathological studies

Following the report of Struwe (1929), describing the presence of the classical neuropathological findings of Alzheimer's disease in the brains of older people with Down's syndrome, numerous subsequent studies have shown that nearly all people with Down's syndrome who die over the age of 35 years show Alzheimer-like neuropathology (Ball & Nuttall, 1980; Whalley, 1982; Wisniewski, Wisniewski & Wen, 1985). Malamud (1966) studied the brains of 251 people with Down's syndrome who had died. Twenty had been older than 37 at the time of death and all had Alzheimer-like neuropathology. The age of onset and extent of these changes appear unique to people with Down's syndrome and are not found in excess in other disorders associated with learning disability, suggesting that something specific about having Trisomy 21 gives rise to this increased risk of Alzheimer-like neuropathology.

More detailed studies have also reported that the Alzheimer-like changes are very similar to those changes found in people with Alzheimer's disease but who do not have Down's syndrome. For example, Yates *et al.* (1980) reported that the neurochemical findings were very similar and Anderton *et al.* (1982) reported that antibodies raised to neurofilaments cross-reacted with those found in Down's syndrome brains. Furthermore, in a study using electron microscopy to examine the brain of a person with Down's syndrome, O'Hara (1972) reported that the findings were identical to those found in the brains of people who had died from Alzheimer's disease but who had not had Down's syndrome. A more recent study of plaque formation in the brains of people with Down's syndrome has, however, suggested that there may be differences when the plaques in Down's syndrome are compared to those in people with Alzheimer's disease but without Down's syndrome (Allsop *et al.*, 1986).

Down's syndrome has proved to be a very useful model for the study of the development of Alzheimer-like neuropathology. Mann *et al.*, (1986) have studied the evolution of Alzheimer-like neuropathology by examining the brains of people with Down's syndrome who have died at different ages. They report that plaques appear with increasing frequency during the third decade and subsequently neurofibrillary tangles occur and by the fourth and fifth decade both were invariably present.

Although these neuropathological studies are very convincing, there have been a few reports of people with Down's syndrome dying age 30 years or older who do not have these classical changes (Whalley, 1982). It is also of some concern that the process whereby someone with Down's syndrome might come to postmortem could result in a preferential selection for 'deterioration' thus distorting the true picture. Thus, although probably nearly all people with Down's syndrome will develop significant neuropathological changes characteristic of Alzheimer's disease in middle age, a small percentage will be spared.

Genetic studies

The prime link between Down's syndrome and Alzheimer's disease has been the presence of the neuropathology. However, another association has been reported which has taken on a new significance in the light of the most recent genetic findings. Heston and Mastri (1977) in their family study of Alzheimer's disease not only found high rates of dementia in the first degree relatives of 125 probands who had died from Alzheimer's disease but they also reported finding a higher than expected rate of Down's syndrome births. They argued that this could not be accounted for by such effects as maternal age. However, a later study by Whalley (1982) in Edinburgh was unable to confirm these findings although a further American study by Heyman *et al.*, (1983) did report similar findings.

The most recent genetic findings are, however, of considerable importance. Over the past few years, with the development of new molecular genetic techniques, it has become possible to look for 'candidate genes' which might predispose to a particular psychiatric disorder. The above reported association between Down's syndrome and Alzheimer's disease gave rise to the hypothesis that the gene localised on chromosome 21 may be a candidate gene predisposing to Alzheimer's disease. In a space of a few months the gene coding for the amyloid precursor protein was localised on chromosome 21 (Goldgaber *et al.*, 1987) and a linkage was established between an anonymous DNA mark on chromosome 21 and Alzheimer's disease (St George-Hyslop *et al.*, 1987). Since then mutations in the amyloid gene has shown to segregate with affected individuals in early onset Alzheimer's disease (Goate *et al.*, 1991; Murrell *et al.*, 1991).

Amyloid is found in the neural plaques of people with Alzheimer's disease, however, it has remained unclear as to whether amyloid deposition is a primary or secondary phenomenon. In the case of people with Down's syndrome they have a 50% increase in mean levels of serum amyloid as would be expected from a gene dosage effect (Rumble *et al.*, 1989) and therefore there is a possibility that amyloid deposition in the brain is a primary factor in the aetiology of Alzheimer's disease in Down's syndrome. Mann *et al.* (1989) reported finding defuse cerebral deposition of amyloid as an early feature in people with Down's syndrome followed by aggregation with an unidentified oligosaccaride into plaques and then a neuronal response.

Clinical studies

Following the early neuropathological observations regarding the relationship between Down's syndrome and Alzheimer's disease, there followed numerous single case reports and later more detailed studies of the possible clinical relevance of these neuropathological observations. Early reports described clinical findings similar to those observed in people without Down's syndrome but who had Alzheimer's dementia. For example, Jervis (1948) reported personality changes and Rollin (1946) described worsened toilet habits, loss of speech and changes in behaviour. Later studies reported clear evidence of change in behaviour with increasing age as well as loss of speech and skills (Verhaart & Jelgersma, 1952; Haberland, 1969; Crapper *et al.*, 1975). Examples of people with Down's syndrome who apparently had no evidence of dementia prior to death yet had clear evidence of significant Alzheimer-like neuropathology were also reported. Unlike in the early studies of Alzheimer's disease in the general population where a link was established between the extent of the pathology and the extent of dementia (Blessed *et al.*, 1968), this association is less clear in Down's syndrome.

These earlier studies were unable to establish the prevalence rate for dementia in people with Down's syndrome. The problem was to be able to distinguish between the absence of skills and cognitive abilities owing to the fact that the person had Down's syndrome and resultant cognitive impairments, from a loss of skills and ability consequent upon the onset of a new disorder, Alzheimer's disease. In addition, many of the earlier studies were of people in institutional settings. In these settings, relatively low demands were placed upon those with Down's syndrome and any loss of ability may not have been immediately apparent. However, there have now been a number of both cross-sectional and longitudinal studies which have been able to identify more clearly the clinical features of dementia and to establish prevalence rates. Thase *et al.* (1982) reported that 60% of people with Down's syndrome over the age of 45 were totally disorientated compared to 30% of matched controls. In addition, they reported increasing decline with age in digit span scores and rates of apraxia and the results of memory tests were poorer in older Down's syndrome subjects compared to controls. They concluded in a subsequent paper that rates of clinical dementia were as high as 50% in the older Down's syndrome population. Other studies using standardised assessments such as Adaptive Behaviour Scales have reported conflicting results. For example, Fenner, Hewitt and Torpy, 1987 found little evidence of loss of skills in ageing people with Down's syndrome and Silverstein *et al.*, 1986 using the Clinical Development Evaluation form to study 413 people with Down's syndrome compared with a non-Down's syndrome control group, found little difference. However, they expressed concern about the use of this particular method of study.

Lai and Williams (1989) studied 96 people with Down's syndrome over the age of 35 for a period of three years. They found evidence of cognitive decline, loss of skills and changes in behaviour sufficient to meet the diagnosis of dementia in 8% of those between the ages of 35 and 49, and 75% of those over the age of 60. Haxby (1989) used a battery of neuropsychological tests and demonstrated a range of cognitive abnormalities in those with Down's syndrome with the clinical features of dementia, in contrast to more specific deficits in those with Down's syndrome without dementia. In this latter group there was, however, evidence of impairment of the ability to form new long term memories and as well as impaired ability on visuospatial construction tests when they

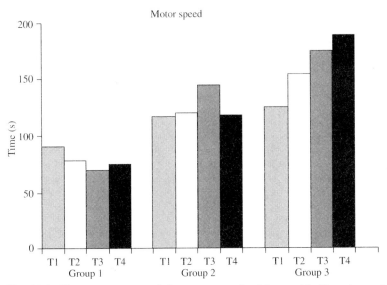

Fig. 13.2. The mean scores of three groups of subjects with Down's syndrome divided according to age: Group 1 age 30–39; Group 2 age 40–49; and Group 3 age 50+. The histograms give the results at 6 monthly intervals (total of four occasions) on test-motor speed (Fig. 13.2) and orientation (Fig. 13.3). The older group score lower in tests of orientation and are slower in tests of motor speed than the younger group and show evidence of deterioration over time.

were compared to a younger group of people with Down's syndrome. It therefore remains unclear whether evidence of specific, as opposed to generalised, cognitive impairments are indicative of very early dementia, although this would seem likely.

Crayton *et al.* (1991) have carried out an extensive longitudinal study of a cohort of older people with Down's syndrome. The results of this study are still in the process of being analysed, but there is definite evidence of loss of ability in the older group of people with Down's syndrome (50 years and above) compared to a younger group (30–39). An example of this is shown in Figs. 13.2 and 13.3.

In Fig. 13.2 there is clear evidence of decreasing motor skill as tested using card sorting test. In Fig. 13.3 there is loss of orientation using a standard battery of questions.

Further evidence of the clinical significance of Alzheimer-like neuropathology in Down's syndrome has come from scanning and neurophysiological studies. Schapiro *et al.*, 1989 reported evidence of cerebral

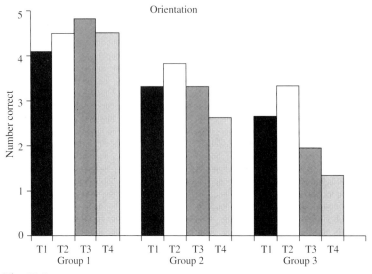

Fig. 13.3.

atrophy in those people with Down's syndrome who met the diagnostic criteria for dementia. Unlike many people with developmental learning disabilities, epilepsy is not common in childhood but increases with age and rates of up to 30% have been reported in those people with Down's syndrome over 30 years of age (Veall, 1974). This may be a reflection of the developing Alzheimer neuropathology. Both EEG and auditory evoked potential studies have reported changes with age (Tangye, 1979; Blackwood *et al.*, 1988).

Diagnosis and management

It is clear that dementia occurs in a significant proportion of people with Down's syndrome over the age of 30. It is important that this is appropriately diagnosed and that other disorders which may mimic dementia are identified. For example, hypothyroidism occurs in as many as 30% of people, Down's syndrome (Dinani & Carpenter, 1990) and sensory impairments also occur later in life, for example, cataract formation and hearing loss. These disorders may mimic dementia and are themselves potentially treatable. Depression may also occur either by itself or in conjunction with the early features of dementia (Birt, Loveland & Lewis, 1992).

Dementia is defined as an 'organic psychosis of a chronic or progressive nature, which if untreated is usually irreversible and terminal'. As is the case with organic psychotic conditions there is 'impairment of orientation,

Table 13.1. *Diagnostic criteria for dementia in people with learning disabilities*

A. Evidence of deterioration in short- and long-term memory. This includes a deterioration in the ability to learn new information, and an inability to remember personal information. It needs to be established that the ability previously existed but has been lost by, for example, using standard tests of memory repeated at 6 monthly intervals or by reliable information from informants (e.g. previously able to remember date or place of birth but now cannot).

B. At least one of the following (in each case evidence of loss of ability is required either through informants or by the repeated use of standardised tests or assessment schedules):
    1. Evidence of a deterioration in the ability to think and reason. A slowing of mental processes or a deterioration in the ability to describe one's thoughts, feelings and experiences.
    2. Evidence of the development of disturbance of higher cortical function such as aphasias (disorder of language due to brain dysfunction), apraxias (inabilty to carry out motor activities despite intact comprehension and motor function) and agnosias (failure to recognise or identify objects despite intact sensory function).
    3. Evidence of previously acquired complex living skills. For example, the ability to prepare drinks or meals, to play a particular game or to carry out tasks such as shopping.
    4. Evidence of personality change. For example, alteration or accentuation of previous pre-morbid traits.

C. The loss of cognitive abilities are of sufficient severity to interfer with social or occupational functioning.

D. State of consciousness not clouded (i.e. does not meet the criteria for delirium or intoxication).

At least G and either E or F:

E. Evidence from the history, physical examination or on investigation of specific organic factor that is judged to be aetiologically related to the disturbance. For example, the recent onset of seizures suggestive of the development of an organic brian disorder, evidence of celebral atrophy on CAT brain scan.

F. In the absence of such evidence, an organic factor necessary for developemnt of the syndrome can be presumed if conditions other than organic mental disorder have been reasonably excluded and if the observed changes represent cognitive changes in a variety of areas.

G. Such factors as sensory impairments or thyroid disorder can be shown to be absent or, if present, not to be the sole explanation for the observed change.

memory, comprehension, calculation, learning capacity and judgement' (World Health Organisation, ICD 9). DSM IIIR (American Psychiatric Association, 1987) diagnostic criteria requires evidence for the presence of a number of cognitive impairments of a sufficient severity to interfere with

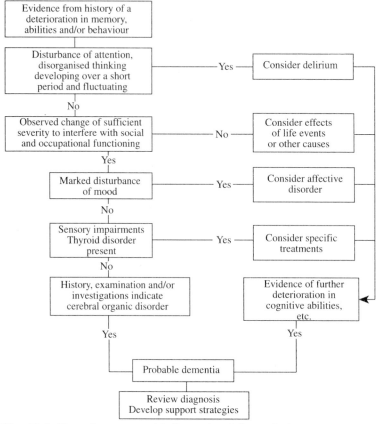

Fig. 13.4. Flow diagram to aid diagnosis of dementia in people with Down's syndrome

'social or occupational functioning'. Deterioration of memory is essential to the diagnosis and there should also be evidence of at least one of the following: impaired thinking, impaired judgment, disturbance of other higher cortical functions (e.g. dyspraxias, dysphasia etc) and personality change. In addition, evidence for an organic rather than functional cause is also required. In the case of Down's syndrome the dilemma is to separate cognitive impairment due to the preexisting learning disability from that secondary to the onset of a dementing disorder. For this reason, some of the criteria in DSM IIIR are not in their present form applicable and a suggested modification is given in Table 13.1.

Figure 13.4 gives a proposed flowchart to aid in the diagnosis of dementia in people with Down's syndrome. It is based upon DSM-IIIR diagnostic criteria which takes into account the difficulties of diagnosing dementia in a group of people with preexisting learning disabilities. The main emphasis is to be able to demonstrate evidence of change over time. If a person with Down's syndrome presents with the absence of a particular skill, for example, the ability to dress him or herself unaided it should not be assumed that this is consequent upon the presence of Down's syndrome but should be established whether such skill had in the past been acquired and has now been lost.

As yet, there is no specific treatment which can prevent the neuronal cell death characteristic of Alzheimer's disease and therefore arrest the progress of the disorder. The focus of continuing support following the diagnosis is one of management rather than of definitive treatment. This management is based upon a sound knowledge regarding the nature and likely course of Alzheimer's disease. This disorder is progressive and therefore the needs and types of intervention are likely to change over time. Alzheimer's disease in the general population has been described as having three stages (Sjorgren, 1950). Early in the course of the disorder the predominate features may be that of anxiety or depression related to the developing memory loss. Later, in the second stage, more obvious disabilities emerge such as disorientation, and speech and more complex skills become affected. In the third stage motor signs also become apparent and dyspraxias are obvious. Epilepsy, incontinence and abnormal mental experiences may also occur. Management has therefore to be based on a continuing assessment which helps to identify the changing level of ability.

A knowledge of the nature of Alzheimer's disease and its likely course is needed in order to keep care givers informed and to be able to offer advice and support. Families may have to make a difficult decision about where their relative, who is now dementing, should be cared for. People with Down's syndrome may continue to live at home with now elderly parents and if this issue is not addressed, a crisis can occur when one of the parents dies. The management of people with Down's syndrome/Alzheimer's disease does not end with the establishment of the diagnosis. It is essential that other medical problems such as infections or anaemias are treated and that there is a regular review of sensory impairments and thyroid disorder. The extent of disability in Alzheimer's disease is not simply a function of the progression of the disorder but is likely to be an interaction between environmental factors which either mitigate against success or help compensate for the disability. Management should therefore include an examination of the relevant environmental problems which may for example contribute to confusion. These includes such things as lighting at night, as well as a clear marking of individual rooms, the toilet etc.

Studies of psychological interventions in people within the general population who have Alzheimer's disease have also shown that specific help with maintaining skills such as dressing and feeding oneself can be beneficial. Such an approach tries to match what is known about the person's strengths and weaknesses to what is known about the task, and use positive rather than negative reinforcement. It does not presume that skills can necessarily be relearned, but rather that those skills which have not already been lost can be maintained (see Woods, 1987). Disorientation is one major effect of Alzheimer's disease and there has been considerable literature on reality orientation programmes as a means of reducing this type of disability. In essence, this requires that staff are aware of the nature of the disability consequent upon Alzheimer's disease and help compensate for this in their day-to-day interactions with the person concerned. This includes reminders about who is working that day, where they are, and what the day and month and time of year is. Specific strategies may also help the person continue to find their way around. This includes changes in the environment as well as prompting.

Summary

The observed association between Alzheimer's disease and Down's syndrome has led to significant progress in research. For example, the localisation of the amyloid gene on chromosome 21 and the relevance of mutations in that gene in the case of specific families with early onset Alzheimer's disease has been an important step forward. In the case of a population of people with Down's syndrome the aetiology of Alzheimer's disease is likely to be the same and the problem of aetiological heterogeneity which complicates studies in the general population is less likely to be a confounding factor. It may be, for example, that the increased expression of the amyloid protein due to the presence of three copies of the amyloid gene may be of aetiological significance. However, this is very speculative.

The increased risk for not only developing the Alzheimer-like neuro-pathology but also the clinical syndrome of dementia in people with Down's syndrome has now been well established but is also clear that not all people with Down's syndrome develop dementia in old age. Further studies are required to establish what factors might influence the age at which dementia becomes manifest and to investigate the precise re-lationship between the extent and localisation of the neuropathology and the extent of cognitive decline.

Observed apparent deterioration in cognitive and living skills of older people with Down's syndrome requires an explanation. If Alzheimer's disease is suspected, information on previous abilities and the exclusion of other causes which may mimic dementia is essential. The diagnosis of dementia will depend on being able to demonstrate the presence of increasing memory disturbance and a progressive loss of other higher cortical functions. It seems likely that the cognitive and other changes which do occur are similar to those found in people without Down's syndrome who have developed Alzheimer's disease. However, in the case of a person with Down's syndrome the extent of the preexisting learning disability and other circumstances may influence the point at which deterioration is first noticed. In the absence of any specific treatment, the diagnosis of Alzheimer's disease requires the development of management strategies which can modify the impact of the developing impairments.

Acknowledgements

My thanks to Ms Robbie Patterson for her considerable help in the preparation of the chapter and to Dr C. Oliver, Ms L. Crayton and Ms J. Bradbury for permission to report the preliminary data of their study. This study has been supported by The Wellcome Trust.

References

Allsop, D., Kidd, M., Landon, M. & Tomlinson, A. (1986). Isolated senile plaque cores in Alzheimer's disease and Down's syndrome show differences in morphology. *Journal of Neurology, Neurosurgery and Psychiatry*, **49**, 886–92.

American Psychiatric Association (1987). *Diagnostic and statistical Manual of Mental Disorders*, 3rd edn revised. Washington, D.C.

American Psychiatric Association (1980). *Diagnostic and Statistical Manual of Mental Disorders DSM-III*, 3rd edn. Washington DC: Division of Public Affairs, APA.

Anderton, B. H., Breinburg, D. Downes, M. J. *et al.*. (1982). Monoclonal antibodies show that neurofibrillary tangles and neurofilaments share antigenic determinants. *Nature*, **298**, 84–6.

Ball, M. J. & Nuttall, K. (1980) Neurofibrillary tangles, granulovasculolar degeneration and neuron loss in Down's Syndrome: quantitative comparison with Alzheimer dementia. *Annals of Neurology*, **17**: 278–82.

Birt, D. B., Loveland, K. A. & Lewis, K. R. (1992). Depression and the onset of dementia in adults with mental retardation. *American Journal on Mental Retardation*, **96**, 502–11.

Blackwood, D. H. R., St Clair, D. M., Muir, W. J., Oliver, C. J. & Dickens, P. (1988). The development of Alzheimer's disease in Down's syndrome assessed by auditory event-related potentials. *Journal of Mental Deficiency Research*, **3**, 233–9.

Blessed, G., Tomlinson, B. & Roth, M. (1968). The association between quantitative measures and degenerative changes in the cerebral grey matter of elderly patients. *British Journal of Psychiatry*, **114**, 797–811.

Crapper, D. R., Dalton, A. L., Skopitz, M., Eng. P., Scott, J. H. & Hachinski, V. (1975). Alzheimer's degeneration in Down's Syndrome. *Archives of Neurology*, **32**, 618.

Crayton, L., Bradbury, J., Oliver, C. & Holland A. J. (1991). *Seminar on Down's Syndrome and Alzheimer's Disease.* London: Institute of Psychiatry.

Devenny, D. A., Hill, A. L., Patxot, O., Silverman, W. P. & Wisniewski, K. E. (1992). Ageing in higher functioning adults with Down's Syndrome: an interim report in a logitudinal study. *Journal of Intellectual Disability Research*, **36**, 241-250.

Dinani, S. & Carpenter, S. (1990). Down's syndrome and thyroid disorder. *Journal of Mental Deficiency Research*, **34**, 187–93.

Fenner, M. E., Hewitt, K. E. & Torpy, B. M. (1987). Down's syndrome: intellectual and behavioural functioning during adulthood. *Journal of Mental Deficiency Research*, **31**, 214–49.

Fraser, J. & Mitchell, A. (1876). Kalmuc idiocy: report of a case with autopsy with notes on 62 cases. *Journal of Mental Science*, **22**, 161.

Fryers, T. (1986). Survival in Down's Syndrome. *Journal of Mental Deficiency Research*, **30**, 101-110.

Goate, A., Chartier-Harlin, M. C., Mullan, M. *et al.* (1991). Segregation of a missence mutation in the amyloid precursor protein gene with familial Alzheimer's disease. *Nature*, **349**, 704–706.

Goldgaber, D., Lerman, M. I., MacBride, O. W., Saffioti, U. & Gajdusecek, D. C. (1987). Characterisation and chromosomal localisation of a cDNA encoding brain amyloid of Alzheimer's Disease. *Science*, **235**, 877–80.

Haberland, C. (1969). Alzheimer's disease in Down's Syndrome: cliniconeurological observations. *Acta Neurologica Belgica*, **69**, 369–80.

Haxby, J. V. (1989). Neuropsycyhological evaluation of adults with Down's syndrome: patterns of selective impairment in non-demented old adults. *Journal of Mental Deficiency Research*, **33**, 193–210.

Heston, L. L. & Mastri, A. R. (1977). The genetics of Alzheimer's disease: association hematologic malignancy and Down's Syndrome. *Archives of General Psychiatry*, **34**, 976–81.

Heyman, A. Wilkinson, W. E., Hurwitz, B. J. *et al.* (1983) Alzheimer's disease: genetic aspects and associated clinical disorder. *Annals of Neurology*: **14**, 507–16.

Jervis, G. A. (1948). Early senile dementia mongoloid idiocy. *American Journal of Psychiatry*, **105**, 102-106.

Lai, F. & Williams, R. S. (1989). A prospective study of Alzheimer's disease in Down's syndrome. *Archives of Neurology*, **46**, 849–53.

McGrother, C. W. & Marshall, B. (1990). Recent trends in incidents, morbidity and survivial in Down's Syndrome. *Journal of Mental Deficiency Research*, **34**, 49–57.

Malamud, N. (1966). The neuropathology of mental retardation. In I. Phillips, ed. *Prevention and Treatment of Mental Retardation*, pp. 24–32, New York: Basic Books.

Mann, D. M. A., Yates, P. O., Marcyniuk, B. & Ravindra, C. R. (1986). The topography of plaques and tangles in Down's Syndrome patients with different ages. *Neuropathology and Applied Neurobiology*, **12**, 447–57.

Mann, D. M. A., Brown, A. M. T., Prinja, D. *et al.* (1989). An analysis of the morphology of the senile plaques in Down's syndrome patients of different ages using immunocytochemical and lecithin histochemical methods. *Neuropathology and Applied Neurobiology*, **15**, 317–29.

Murrell, J., Farlow, M., Ghetti, B. & Benson, M. D. (1991). A mutation in the amyloid precursor protein associated with hereditary Alzheimer's disease. *Science*, **254**, 97–9.

O'Hara, P. T. (1972). Electron microscopical study of the brain in Down's Syndrome. *Brain*, **95**, 681–684.

Oliver, C. & Holland, A. J. (1986). Down's syndrome and Alzheimer's disease: a review. *Psychological Medicine*, **16**, 307–22.

Rollin, H. R. (1946). Personality on mongolism with reference to incidents of catatonic psychosis. *American Journal of Deficiency*, 219–33.

Rumble, B., Retallack, R., Hilbich, C. *et al.* (1989). Amyloid A4 protein and its precursor in Down's syndrome and Alzheimer's disease. *New England Journal of Medicine*, **320**, 1446-52.

Schapiro, M. B., Luxenberg, J. S., Kaye, J. A., Haxby, J. V., Friedland, R. P. & Rapoport, S. L. (1989). Serial quantative CT analysis of brain morphometrics in adults with Down's syndrome with different ages. *Neurology*, **39**, 1349-53.

Silverstein, A. B., Herbs, D., Nasuta, R. & White, J. F. (1986). Effects of age on the adaptive behaviour of institutionalised individuals with Down syndrome. *American Journal of Mental Deficiency*, **90**, 659–62.

St. George-Hyslop, P. H., Tanzi, R. E., Polinsky, R. J., Haines, J. L., Nee, L., Watkins, P. C. *et al.* (1987). The genetic defect causing familiar Alzheimer disease maps on chromosome 21. *Science*, **235**, 885–9.

Sjogren, T., Sjogren, H. & Lindgren, A. G. H. (1952). Morbus Alzheimer and Morbus Pick: a genetic, clinical and pathoanatomical study. *Acta Psychiatrica et Neurologia Scandinavica*; Suppl. 82.

Struwe, F. (1929). Histopathologische Untersuchungen über Entstehung und Wesen der senilen Plaques. *Zeitschrift für die gesamte Neurologie and Psychiatric*, **122**, 291.

Tangye, S. R. (1979). The EEG and incidence of epilepsy in Down's Syndrome. *Journal of Mental Deficiency Research*, **33**, 17–24.

Thase, M. E., Liss, L., Smeltzer, D. & Maloon, J. (1982). Clinical evaluation of dementia in Down's Syndrome: a preliminary report. *Journal of Mental Deficiency Research*, **36**, 239–44.

Veall, R. M. (1974). The prevalence of epilepsy among mongols related to age. *Journal of Mental Deficiency Research*, **19**, 99–106.

Verhaart, W. J. C. & Jelgersma, H. C. (1952). Early senile dementia in mongolian idiocy. Description of a case. *Folia Psychiatrica Neerlandica*, **55**, 453–9.

Whalley, L. J. (1982). The dementia of Down's Syndrome and its relevance to the aetiological studies of Alzheimer's disease. *Annals of the New York Academy of Sciences*, **396**, 39–53.

Wisniewski, K. E., Wisniewski, H. M. & Wen, G. Y. (1985). Occurrence of neuropathological changes and dementia of Alzheimer's disease in Down's Syndrome. *Annals of Neurology*, **17**, 278–82.

Woods, R. (1987). Psychological management of dementia. In *Dementia*, ed. B. Pitt, pp. 281–95, Edinburgh: Churchill Livingstone.

Yates, C. M., Simpson, J., Maloney, A. F. J., Gordon, A. & Reid, A. H. (1980). Alzheimer-like cholinergic deficiency in Down's Syndrome. *Lancet*, **ii**, 979.

14

Sexuality: towards a more balanced view

HILARY BROWN & VICKY TURK

Introduction

Recent attitudes towards issues of sexuality facing people with learning disabilities have tended to be split between those advocating greater rights to sexual expression and relationships, and those urging caution and protectiveness. The importance of this debate has grown as services find it increasingly necessary to face up to the reality of sexual abuse and the problems of inappropriate sexual behaviour.

Parents have always been more cautious and protective about advocating sexual rights (Brown, 1987); anxious that sexual expression might lead to rejection or exploitation. They realise that stating people's rights, in isolation from responsibilities, is naive and simplistic. Their experiences of talking to staff have tended to perpetuate polarisation rather than create common understandings, in that staff are often unwilling to acknowledge the tenuous acceptance which is extended to them and to their adult sons or daughters by members of the public.

Paid workers, in facing up to issues of abuse and abusing, are taking on board an agenda which parents have been anxious to address. Indeed, a positive outcome of being more realistic and balanced in considerations of sexuality is that real partnership may now be possible. Separate groupings are forming around sexuality issues, in which self-advocacy, parents' lobbies and professional expertise are developed separately but then brought together, (People First 1991; Ryan, 1992; Boniface, 1992). These would seem to offer the best hope of empowerment and protection for people with learning disabilities in facing sexual issues.

There is no reason to suppose that sexual abuse is a new phenomenon. There is evidence of a sexual subculture in hospitals which flourished despite segregated wards and little privacy. Such activities went on unsupervised and therefore uncommented upon. When people came to leave hospitals, their sexual experiences were largely ignored. In some cases people who had had long-standing relationships were moved out without being kept in touch. Other experiences, such as parenthood, which was often the trigger for admission, were also lost in the system so those aspects of people's lives which did not fit in to the prevailing attitudes about learning disability were 'edited out' of official discharge records.

There is also no reason to think that abuse within the community was not always a reality. Increased awareness of child sexual abuse and concern about its effects has alerted professionals to look for abuse where before it was hidden. This growing awareness of child sexual abuse crashed through the naïvete of discussing sexual behaviour and relationships without attending to issues of power and social context. Sinason (1989), when considering the sexual abuse of adults with learning disabilities, coined the phrase 'thinking the unthinkable' to convey the sense of not being able to see something until you know what you might be looking for.

The sexual issues which face people with learning disabilities are inevitably tied into public mood and awareness about sexuality in general. There is always an added layer, a question mark as to whether people with learning disabilities are included or excluded from such a picture. This is expressed in different terms. Some workers will, for example, suppose that people with severe learning disabilities are not 'attractive' enough to be the victim's of abuse , while others will espouse views about sexual rights but stop short of advocating 'real' relationships, such as marriage or parenthood. Homosexual behaviour may be tolerated or even encouraged, but there is ambivalence about whether such behaviour might lead on to a sexual identity. One rarely hears service users being described as gay or lesbian even if they are known to seek out same sex partners.

Thus while the argument in favour of community based services has been partly won, we would suggest that the argument about sexual integration has not. Giami (1987) hypothesised that:

sexuality constitutes a central theme which enables one to discover, within the practices of coping with disabled people, the elements of their personal and social behaviours which are tolerated, encouraged or checked, and, therefore to outline the limits of their social integration.

Services, despite the 'metaphor' (Felce, 1992, unpublished data) of normality, have not been organised on the basis of 'ordinary' gender roles, nor have they facilitated the development of sexual relationships and opportunities. A feature of staffed housing services is their studious asexuality, sometimes disguised as gender neutrality and slipped into service rhetoric under the guise of an equality which does not exist in service hierarchies or in the social networks and hence potential role models of service users and their families. As Jan Burns (1992) comments:

This sanitised version of independent living often ignores sex roles and the division of domestic labour. This is not through any societal metaplan which hopes to do away with sex roles, but is part of a covert, protective, avoidance of the fact that society does not really wish these people to be fully independent because it fears the consequences in terms of procreation. Hence people are trained up to the position of semiindependence, like adolescents just before they leave their parental home, however these individuals are never really expected to leave home, but to remain in a state of suspended adolescence.

Hence sexuality continues to challenge the values on which our services and clinical interventions are based. It is not coincidental that in services where people have been most unequivocally helped to articulate their sexual needs and aspirations, they have also been given words to complain about abuse and to begin to discriminate for themselves between wanted and unwanted sex. Unfortunately this is no easy task. For someone with learning disabilities and a lifetime of mixed messages about sexuality, but with the prevailing attitudes of asexuality and sexual taboo, to assert a positive and wanted relationship is perhaps the hardest challenge of all. It is no wonder that issues concerning consent become so difficult to unravel in potential sexual abuse cases involving two people with learning disabilities when considering whether the sexual activity was wanted.

The sanitised version of independent living, coupled with an overzealous and poorly informed interpretation of normalisation, has also led to services becoming blinkered to sexual offending by some people with learning disabilities. To name and document this has been seen as excessively risky in terms of reactivating people's prejudices and myths of people with learning disabilities as oversexualised and disinhibited. Consequently people with difficult sexual behaviour have received no specialised services and their victims no recognition or support.

Sexual abuse is a widespread phenomena both for children and for adult women and men in our society (Russell, 1986). Amongst the general population, experience of sexual abuse is a critical predisposing factor towards later referral for medical and psychological intervention (Jacobson & Richardson, 1987; Nibert, Cooper & Crossmaker, 1989; Rose, Peabody & Stratigeas, 1991). There is no reason to suppose that this is not so for people with learning disabilities. While it is tempting to see each issue as personal, 'clinical' and self contained, we believe that practitioners need to approach such referrals with a wide perspective, as well as awareness of the

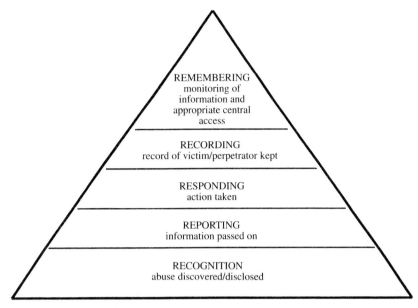

Fig. 14.1. Filtering out cases of sexual abuse

specific issues, in order to (1) prevent sexual distress and abuse, (2) support people with learning disabilities who have been abused and (3) manage risks around people with learning disabilities whose abusive sexual behaviour places them at risk of abusing others.

The remainder of the information contained within this chapter is derived primarily from a three-year research programme on the Sexual Abuse of Adults with Learning Disabilities funded by the Joseph Rowntree Foundation and carried out at the University of Kent at Canterbury. The detailed aspects of the methodology and results can be found elsewhere (Turk & Brown, 1993). The initial findings from this project support our argument–that it is necessary to confront 'cosy' notions of sexual behaviour. They indicate that people with learning disabilities are at significant risk of not only sexual abuse but also of abusing others.

Finding out about sexual abuse

A feature of sexual abuse is often the secrecy surrounding and maintaining it. Any incidence or prevalence studies are restricted to discovered, disclosed or suspected sexual abuse. Reported sexual abuse represents the tip of an iceberg. This has been well documented and discussed in the child sexual abuse literature (James, 1988; Vizard, 1989). Retrospective studies asking adults if they have been abused as children demonstrate the extent of underreporting (Russell, 1986; Finkelhor *et al.*, 1990). For people with learning disabilities with poor communication skills and a reduced capacity to recall and articulate incidents, this method is more difficult (Hard & Plumb, 1987).

Figure 14.1 shows the 'iceberg' in terms of the levels of potential filtering out at an organisation level of cases of sexual abuse involving adults with learning disabilities.

This pyramid can be used to consider how different amounts of sexual abuse will be reported depending on the level of enquiry and methodology used, for example who is asked, when, about what and in what circumstances and settings.

Service competencies

These five 'R's' shown in Figure 14.1 can also be used as a guide to those agencies involved in working out new contractual relationships to ensure that each stage of the process is clearly allocated within the system and that channels of communication are kept open.

Many services fail to recognise signs which might be indicative of sexual abuse or to question whether relationships between service users are in the interests of both people. Guidance on consent is sparse in most agency policies and often limited to a superficial view of the legal situation in which people with severe learning disabilities are deemed not able to give consent. Issues of power are not analysed nor are structures put in place to ensure discussion of difficult decisions. Failure to recognise the problems are often compounded by lack of procedures for reporting and is indicative of the unwelcome nature of such information within and across agencies.

It can also be seen from this diagram that increases in reported incidence can be a measure of good practice rather than escalating trends in actual abuse.

Another limitation of previous studies is a failure to distinguish adequately between single abusive incidents and long-term ongoing abuse. The former cases are more likely to be discovered or disclosed than the latter, where greater attention is paid to the maintenance of secrecy. This leads to confused messages about recognition. Workers are often asked to look for changes in behaviour when sexual abuse may have been ongoing. The symptoms of long term abuse may have been discounted over a long period of time. There is a two way cause and effect relationship between abuse and disability. Abuse may cause disabilities as well as increase a child's or adult's risk or vulnerability to sexual abuse (Buchanan & Oliver, 1977; Glaser and Bentovim, 1979; Groce, 1988; Mullins, 1986; Sandgrund, Gainies & Green, 1974). Clinicians working psychodynamically suggest that the trauma of sexual abuse can also lead to an acquired or exaggerated learning disability (Sinason, 1986).

Where services are not able to respond appropriately to sexual abuse, the likelihood of abusive incidents being recorded is reduced. Recording presents its own ethical problems, as information is usually incomplete and often uncorroborated. Without good records services cannot remember what has happened to the person(s) concerned. They cannot alert themselves to the possibility of repeated abuse by an alleged perpetrator, nor can they monitor service decisions and provision in the light of sexual abuse, assign resources to fund treatment and safe houses, or question service models, staffing practices or training needs.

Defining sexual abuse

Definitions used in the study described depended on services firstly defining sexual acts accurately and then approaching the issue of consent critically (for a fuller account see Brown & Turk 1992). Most of the reported incidents (67%) included penetration, or attempted penetration, implying that less tangible forms of sexual abuse had not been picked up or not regarded as serious enough to report.

We followed the usually accepted convention, dividing non-contact abuse from contact abuse, but adding within the contact abuse category a separate heading for masturbation of victim or perpetrator. Sexual abuse was defined as including acts performed by the perpetrator, by both the victim and the perpetrator and sometimes those where the perpetrator forces the victim to do things to him. Table 14.1 gives further details of the acts considered as abusive.

While grouping these acts is helpful to improve consistency, seriousness cannot be implied automatically. For example, a sexual act, which falls short of penetrative intercourse, but which is perpetrated by someone known and trusted, can have more devastating effects than a more brutal act committed by a stranger (Russell, 1986).

The key issues in assessing consent are twofold: whether the person *did*, and whether the person *could* give their consent. In deciding the latter, a judgment has to be made as to whether the person had the ability to consent to sexual relationships in general and/or was able to do so without undue pressure in this particular situation. Such ability need not be

Table 14.1.

Non-contact abuse	Looking, photography, indecent exposure, harassment, serious teasing or innuendo, pornography
Contact abuse	*Touch*, e.g. of breast, genitals, anus, mouth *Masturbation* of either or both persons *Penetration or attempted penetration* of vagina, anus, mouth with or by penis, fingers, other objects

conceived of as a permanent quality of the person but is to do with an assessment of their ability to make decisions at that time. For some people, the severity of their learning disability may mean that there is little chance of their being able to make such judgments in the foreseeable future and services should plan on that basis. For others, it is possible that good sex education may change their status, or that otherwise autonomous individuals may have temporary periods of not being able to give consent, for example, because of a depressive illness . This judgment is independent of whether the other person was deliberately exploiting their ignorance or inadvertently abusing it, as might be the case if the perpetrator were another service user. In peer abuse it is sometimes unclear which party is abusing, and which is being abused, and given a definition which stresses non-consent it is possible that neither party is able to consent to the acts they are involved in.

Consent should be given freely. Factors which pressurise the person unduly and preclude any real choice are referred to as barriers to consent (Sgroi, 1988). These include:

– the presence of a parental, or familial relationship between the persons involved;
– the presence of a custodial or caretaking relationship between the persons involved ;
– the use of a weapon, threat of injury, or use of force by the first person;
– the presence of a power imbalance between them which precludes consent by the weaker person.

In short, authority, coercion and inequality (often involving men) negate the validity of consent given by an otherwise autonomous person (usually a woman). In order to determine if either of these are present, one needs to analyse differences in power between the two parties.

Inequality is often vaguely defined but nevertheless an important issue, particularly in cases of the abuse of one service user by another when judgments about the mutuality of the relationship have to be made. There is a parallel issue in the field of child sexual abuse where peer abuse has been investigated. De Jong (1989) seeks to discriminate experimentation from exploitation in sexual interaction between siblings and cousins, by assessing the power differential in terms of age difference (and by implication developmental stage) and coercion, with documented physical injury and penetrative acts being seen as further indicators of abuse. The author suggests asking six questions which could be translated into services for people with learning disabilities. These relate to:

- age (and by implication cognitive and developmental) difference;
- touching being more indicative of exploration as opposed to penetrative sexual acts being more likely to signify abuse;
- motivation of the participants;
- consensual/coercive nature of the act(s);
- if there is a third party or evidence of prearrangement/exploitation;
- the putative victim's emotional response, discriminating guilt from strong reactions including anger, fear, sadness, etc.

Where adults involved in sexual activity have a mild or moderate learning disability, workers might intervene only if there were considerable evidence of an abusive or exploitative relationship. Where either party is, by virtue of their severe learning disability, deemed not to be able to give consent, workers should satisfy themselves that the activity is mutual and the consent valid, because, in effect, they are looking for evidence to challenge the blanket assumption of incapacity to consent contained in the legislation.

The consent issue is subtly different in abusive relationships which are ongoing as opposed to abusive acts which consist of an isolated incident, mirroring recent debate about 'date rape' and marital rape. In ongoing relationships, there is the issue of whether, if consent is given on some occasions, it can be withheld on others. It is our experience that service workers are reticent about intervening in established relationships, even where there is concern about violence or abusive sexual behaviour. Such non-intervention mirrors ambivalence within generic agencies in the face of domestic violence. Burns (1992) comments that women with learning disabilities are often themselves ambivalent about what to put up with in their relationships but cautions against services taking a purist approach.

What can be learned from the University of Kent study?

This study is based on a large-scale survey of the incidence of new cases of sexual abuse of adults with learning disabilities (aged 18 years or more) which occurred within a two-year time period in one large Regional Health Authority. All the main statutory providers of services for adults with learning disabilities were approached and all but one social service department participated. A standard questionnaire was filled in by service managers or clinicians for each case/incident reported which fitted the definitions and parameters of the survey (Brown & Turk, 1992; Turk & Brown, 1993). Questionnaires were filled in by individuals with different amounts of experience and knowledge of sexual abuse. Results reflect this variation in that the number of valid forms returned by different agencies ranged from 0–16 (once invalid cases and double counts had been considered). This wide discrepancy cannot be accounted for by the different population sizes of the districts covered or by the numbers of people with learning disabilities living in these areas. Some of the smallest districts had the greatest numbers of returned questionnaires.

138 completed questionnaires were returned to the project. Twelve questionnaires were excluded as they did not meet the project's criterion – most usually these concerned people who were children at the time of abuse suggesting that workers with adults are also dealing with disclosure of sexual abuse sustained by people in childhood. This may demand particular skills and understanding by service workers. A further 14 questionnaires represented double counts and the data was transferred onto a single form hence retaining seven returns, resulting in a total of 119 valid forms.

The region has a total population in excess of 3.6 million. These results suggest an average of 60 new cases reported each year. If the figures are extrapolated to cover the population of England and Wales (50.7 million), then an expected incidence of approximately 830 new cases would be found (940 cases when including Scotland and Northern Ireland).

The 119 cases of alleged sexual abuse were categorised as to the probability of the sexual abuse having occurred, using criteria devised for this purpose (Brown & Turk, 1992). The results are given in Table 14.2.

84 of the cases (over 70% of sample) were proven or had sufficient evidence to suggest the sexual abuse was highly likely to have occurred. In 25 cases (21%) there was continued concern, in the absence of substantive evidence. Half of these cases involved a suspected family member as the perpetrator. A further 10 cases contained information that made it questionable whether the act alleged actually constituted sexual abuse or

Table 14.2. *Probability that sexual abuse had occurred*

	N	%
Proven/highly probable	41	34.5
Highly suspected	43	36.1
Possible abuse: Ongoing concern	25	21.0
Too difficult/insufficient information to classify	10	8.4
Total	119	100.0

where the questionnaire responses were insufficiently detailed to allow categorisation to be made. The 84 proven/highly suspected cases were used as the basis for the detailed analyses which follow.

Who is at risk?

Of the victims 61 were women (73%) and 23 men (27%), which is almost identical to the whole sample of 119 (74% and 26% respectively). The high incidence of women as victims is consistent with previous studies (Allington, 1992; Sobsey & Varnhagen, 1989; Hard & Plumb, 1987).

The average age of the victims was 31 years (range 18–61), although the largest percentage of reported cases was in the age range 21–30 years. This heightened vulnerability to abuse during early adulthood has parallels in the general population. (Schneider, 1992). For some individuals, the sexual abuse was long-standing, originating in childhood. For others, the recorded incident was the first known. The average age at which the current abuse first occurred was 29 years (range 5–60).

People across the whole range of ability are at risk. 16 people (19.6%) have severe or profound learning disability (IQ 35 or less), 33 (40.2%) have severe/moderate to moderate learning disability (IQ 36–50). The remaining 33 (40.2%) had mild or borderline learning disability (IQ 51–80). Hence 60% of the sample are legally unable to consent to sexual intercourse as they have severe mental impairment.

Almost 70% of the sample had a secondary handicap, 21 of the 84 had two or more such disabilities. The most frequently reported difficulty was communication (41%), followed by psychiatric/behavioral problems (24%) and epilepsy (15%). Approximately 11% had medical problems, 10% a physical handicap and 10% a sensory handicap. Each of these additional handicaps might be considered a risk factor in that they signal to a potential perpetrator that the person is vulnerable and less likely to: a)

Table 14.3. *Who Raised the Issue?*

	N	%
Client	57	67.9
Residential staff	12	14.2
Day centre	6	7.1
Family member	3	3.6
Professional	2	2.4
Other/unknown	4	4.8
Total	84	100.0

be able to tell others about what has been done to them, b) be believed if they are able to disclose the abuse.

Of the 84 victims 54 lived in managed properties, i.e. not the parental home, representing a greater risk in terms of contact with other service users and contact with multiple carers. The majority were in staffed housing (30) with smaller numbers living in hostels (12) hospitals (6) and other facilities (e.g. landladies, unstaffed housing). 26 of the remaining victims (31%) lived with their family at the time of the reported abuse.

Details of the person who initially reported the sexual abuse or their suspicions are presented in Table 14.3.

The person with learning disabilities was the most likely source of the disclosure: they reported the alleged sexual abuse in over two thirds of cases. Professional/careworkers reporting of abuse was low (less than 25%). This information raises concern about the likelihood of sexual abuse being detected and reported where the client with learning disabilities has insufficient language to initiate the disclosure process.

Details were coded of any information given on the form that could be considered as direct or indirect evidence in support of the allegation/ suspicion of sexual abuse. A lot of the evidence recorded was vaguely worded, ambiguous or highly circumstantial.

Forensic evidence of physical or sexual abuse was only recorded on 30 occasions. Within the group reported as having behavioural changes only a few of these were of a sexual nature, more being due to the onset of anxieties or phobias or to an increase in disruptive, distress or aggressive behaviours.

All three types of abuse described earlier could (and often did) occur, although on many forms people only recorded what they considered to be the most serious incident. Using this overlaying categorisation (i.e. where people can be classified into any or all of the three categories), non-contact

Table 14.4. *Type of evidence available*

	N
Victims verbal disclosure	69
Perpetrator's Confession	12
Behavioural/psychosomatic Change	62
Forensic Evidence of Non-specific abuse	30
Witness	17
Circumstantial witness	24
Circumstantial evidence	64
Background history	59

N = Number of occurrences in total sample of proven/highly suspected cases. Obviously each case had differing amounts of evidence.

abuse was reported in 23 % of cases and contact abuse in 95 % of cases. The contact abuse involved touch in 87 % of cases, masturbation in 31 % of cases and penetration/attempted penetration in 67 % of cases. Hence, similar to previous research, a very high percentage of the cases involved very serious assaults.

The majority of the sexual abuse took place in the victim's or perpetrator's main home (48 % and 10 % respectively). With 12 victims (14 %) the abuse took place in their day/leisure facility. In 10 cases (12 %) the abuse occurred in a public place, e.g. park, bus station. The remaining incidents occurred either on transport or in multiple, unspecified locations (16 %). Thus, in common with the rest of the population, people with learning disabilities are most at risk in the places where they live and work, not in public spaces.

Who is abusing?

Having established that the whole range of people with learning disabilities are at risk of serious sexual assault, it is important to look at who is doing the abusing and how people with learning disabilities can best be protected. It is also important to take note of the proportion of perpetrators who also have a learning disability since services have a specific responsibility to them as service users in their own right.

In over 97 % of the reported cases the perpetrator was a man. This was the same for the whole sample as well as for the 84 proven/highly suspected cases. The breakdown is as follows:

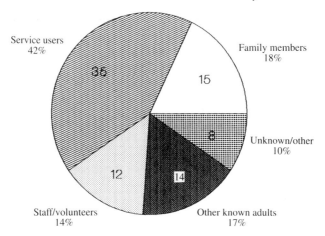

**Figures include multiple perpetrators,
e.g. 35 victims assaulted by 23 persons
who have a learning disability.**

Fig. 14.2. Relationship of perpetrator to each victim of sexual abuse

78   cases men perpetrators
 4   cases more than one man perpetrated the abuse
 1   case family group including men and women
 1   case woman perpetrator

This concurs with previous studies. Many of the cases reported involved one perpetrator offending against several people with learning disabilities, sometimes both men and women. 10 perpetrators accounted for 28 of the 84 cases of abuse. In a further 6 cases the alleged perpetrator was known to have offended before but outside the timescale of the current survey. Only just over half the cases (46) had a single perpetrator.

The perpetrator was known and familiar to the victim in the majority of cases (71 victims, 87%), emphasising the fact that stranger danger is not a major concern. In 7 cases (8%) there was very minimum contact prior to the alleged abuse, e.g. 2 visits, which in some ways could be seen to have 'set- up' the abusive situation. In only 4 cases (5%) was the perpetrator a total stranger. This is consistent with previous research, (Hard & Plumb, 1987; Sobsey & Varnhagen, 1989).

Fig. 14.2 shows a breakdown of the relationship between the perpetrator and the alleged victim.

It can be seen that other people with learning disabilities formed the largest group of reported offenders. For 35 victims (42%) the perpetrator also had a learning disability. Family members accounted for 15 cases, staff/volunteers for 12, and other known and trusted non-handicapped people, e.g. family friends, for a further 14 cases. These figures include multiple perpetrators. For example, although there were 35 victims with a learning disabled offender, this represented only 23 separate perpetrators. The 15 victims assaulted by family members were all single perpetrators, i.e. 15 family members as perpetrators.

The prevalence of cases where the abuser had assaulted more than one victim is significant in terms of alerting professionals to look for other victims with learning disabilities (both men and women) if the perpetrator has access to them. Similarly in the case of intrafamilial abuse, siblings or other family members need to be considered as potential victims, both to protect the individuals concerned, and also to secure evidence against the alleged perpetrator.

The high percentage of offenders with learning disabilities is probably not an accurate picture of the overall sex offender population. People with learning disabilities are more likely to commit their offences in public and/or to be detected compared to their non-handicapped peers, hence skewing the statistics. There is some evidence that abuse by close family members is less likely to be disclosed (Hard & Plumb, 1987). In this study, many suspected cases of incest or family abuse could not be acted on due to lack of evidence or information. It is unknown whether people with learning disabilities are more or less susceptible to offending behaviour. Factors associated with poor cognitive ability (such as impaired impulse control and poor understanding of consequences), coupled with social and environmental factors (such as inadequate sex education, institutionalisation, social isolation) may increase susceptibility. Biological and/or genetic abnormalities, e.g. under-developed genitalia, restricted social roles, staff supervision and mobility difficulties may render individuals less susceptible (Caparulo, 1988; Griffiths, Hingsburger & Christian, 1985; Schilling & Schinke, 1988). Further research is needed in this area.

The identification of 23 offenders in only a two-year time period is a source of concern given the lack of specialist treatment programmes currently available to help sex offenders with learning disabilities. Another recently published report confirms this concern (Jupp, 1991).

Very few of the cases identified in the University of Kent survey came to court or to a formal disciplinary hearing. No action was taken against the alleged perpetrator in almost half of the reported cases. Although a prosecution or staff disciplinary took place in 15 (18.5%) cases, at the time of the survey only 7 had been successful (4 prosecutions and 3 disciplinary hearings). Service competency in collecting evidence so as to secure successful prosecution, where appropriate, needs development.

Summary

The variation and patchiness of the figures themselves indicate that services are not consistently able to recognise and report cases of sexual abuse, while the amount of sexual abuse which is perpetrated by one service user on another is indicative of a 'hands off' approach to relationships and activities which should be subject to thoughtful scrutiny. Parents and carers, who have often been characterised in the past as overprotective, have been voicing justifiable fears about the degree of supervision and intervention which services are competent to deliver. The polarisation which has tended to occur, whereby service workers have advocated sexual rights, and parents have seemingly 'blocked' their progress, will need to be rethought. Rights and protection must be the twin goals of future sex education programmes.

We have to learn to deal with sexual issues in a way which is as sensitive as it is open. Explicitly addressing difficult sexual issues could backfire if it is not done in a context of empowerment and support for positive options. Anne Finger (1992) asserts that

While the story of rape and sexual abuse of disabled people must be told and while we must find ways to end it, the current focus on sexual exploitation of disabled people can itself become oppressive.

She warns against inadvertently conveying to people with disabilities an expectation that their sexuality will be realised through their sexual victimisation.

What is needed is a strong message that people with learning disabilities have a sexual identity and are valued as sexual people. To make this a reality, they must be supported in reaching out for positive options while being actively protected from abuse and from abusing against others. The only option which is not open to services is to sweep sexuality back under the carpet. The challenge is for them to find ways of intervening more consistently in support of valued sexual lifestyles for people with learning disabilities.

References

Allington, C. L. J. (1992). Sexual abuse within services for people with learning disabilities: staffs' perceptions, understandings of and contact with the problems of sexual abuse. *Mental Handicap*, **20**, 59–63.

Boniface, V. (1992). Voice: pressure group for parents of people with learning disabilities who have been sexually abused. PO Box 238, Derby DE1 9JN.

Brown, H. (1987). Working with parents. In A. Craft, ed. *Mental Handicap and Sexuality – Issues and Perspectives*. Tunbridge Wells: Costello.

Brown, H. & Turk, V. (1992). Defining sexual abuse as it affects adults with learning disabilities. *Mental Handicap*, **20**, 44–55.

Buchanan, A. & Oliver, J. E. (1977). Abuse and neglect as a cause of mental retardation: a study of 140 children admitted to subnormality hospitals in Wiltshire. *British Journal of Psychiatry*, **131**, 458–67.

Burns, J. (1992). Invisible women: women who have learning disabilities. *The Psychologist*, (*in press*).

Caparulo, F. (1988) *A Comprehensive Evaluation of an intellectually Disabled Sex Offender*. Vermont: Safer Society.

DeJong, A. (1989). Sexual interactions among siblings and cousins: experimentation or exploitation? *Child Abuse and Neglect*, **13**, 271–9.

Felce, D. (1992). Designing quality in residential services. Unpublished paper given to the RSM Forum, Mental Retardation, 26th June.

Finger, A. (1992). Forbidden fruit. *New Internationalist*, **233**, 8–11.

Finkelhor, D., Hotaling, G., Lewis, I. A. & Smith, C. (1990). Sexual abuse in a national survey of adult men and women: prevalence, characteristics and risk factors. *Child Abuse and Neglect*, **14**, 19–28.

Giami, A. (1987). Coping with the sexuality of the disabled: a comparison of the physically disabled and the mentally retarded. *International Journal of Rehabilitation Research*, **10**, 41–8.

Glaser, D. & Bentovim, A. (1979). Abuse and risk to handicapped and chronically ill children. *Child Abuse and Neglect*, **3**, 565–75.

Griffiths, D., Hingsburger, D. & Christian, R. (1985). Treating developmentally handicapped sexual offenders: the York behaviour management services treatment program. *Psychiatric Aspects in Mental Retardation Reviews*, **4**, 49–52.

Groce, N. E. (1988). Special groups at risk of abuse: the disabled. In: M. B. Straus, ed. *Abuse and Victimization Across the Lifespan*. New York: Johns Hopkins University Press.

Hard, S. & Plumb, W. (1987). Sexual abuse of persons with developmental disabilities: a case study. Unpublished manuscript.

Jacobson, A. & Richardson, B. (1987). Assault experiences of 100 psychiatric inpatients: evidence for the need for routine enquiry. *American Journal of Psychiatry*, **144**, 908–13.

James, S. K. (1988). Sexual Abuse of the Handicapped. Paper presented at Deaf/Blind/Multi-handicapped Conference. Austin, Texas.

Jupp, K. (1991). *Seeking the Answers for Those People with Learning Disabilities who Sexually Offend*. Cheshire: Opened Eye Publications.

Mullins, J. B. (1986). The relationship between child abuse and handicapping conditions. *Journal of School Health*, **56**, 134–6.

Nibert, D., Cooper, S. & Crossmaker, M. (1989). Assaults against residents of a psychiatric institution. Residents' history of abuse. *Journal of Interpersonal Violence*, **4**, 342–9.

People First (1991). Statement on Sexuality. People First, Instrument House, 207–215 Kings Cross Road, London WC1X 9DB

Rose, S., Peabody, C. & Stratigeas, B. (1991). Undetected abuse among intensive case management clients. *Hospital and Community Psychiatry*, **42**, 499–503.

Russell, D. E. H. (1986). *The Secret Trauma: Incest in the Lives of Girls and Women.* New York: Basic Books.

Ryan, M. (1992). Whose body is it anyway? *Community Care*, May Inside supplement, 3–4.

Sandgrund, A., Gainies, R. W. & Green, A. H. (1974). Child abuse and mental retardation : a problem of cause and effect. *American Journal of Mental Deficiency*, **79**, 327–30.

Schilling, R. F. & Schinke, S. P. (1988). Mentally retarded sex offenders: fact, fiction, and treatment. *Journal of Social Work and Human Sexuality*, 7, 33–48.

Schneider, B. (1992). Put up and shut up: workplace sexual assaults. *Gender and Society*, **5**, 533–49.

Sgroi, S. M. (1988). *Vulnerable Populations: Sexual Abuse Treatment for Children, Adult Survivors, Offenders and Persons with Mental Retardation,* vol. 2. Toronto: Lexicon Books.

Sinason, V. (1986). Secondary mental handicap and its relationship to Trauma. *Psychoanalytic Psychotherapy*, **2**, 131–54.

Sinason, V. (1989). Uncovering abuse in psychotherapeutic settings. In H. Brown & A. Craft eds. *Thinking the Unthinkable: papers on sexual abuse and people with learning difficulties.* London: FPA.

Sobsey, D. & Varnhagen, C. (1989). Sexual abuse and exploitation of people with disabilities: toward prevention and treatment. In M. C. Sapo & L. Gougen, eds. *Special Education across Canada.* Vancouver: Centre for Human Development and Research.

Turk, V. & Brown, H. (1992). Sexual abuse and adults with learning disabilities. Preliminary Communication of Survey Results. *Mental Handicap*, **20**, 56–8.

Turk, V. & Brown, H. (1993). The sexual abuse of adults with learning disabilities: results of a two year incidence survey. Mental Handicap Research. **6**, 193–216.

Vizard, E. (1989). *Incidence and Prevalence of Child Sexual Abuse in the Consequences of Child Sexual Abuse.* Occasional Paper, No.3, London: Association for Child Psychology and Psychiatry.

Part IV
Treatment methods

15

Pharmacotherapy in mental retardation

HENRY F. CRABBE

Introduction

Perhaps nothing is more controversial in the field of mental retardation than the use of psychotropic medication (Aman & Singh, 1988). 'The epidemic of neuroleptic overuse among people with mental retardation is one of those tragic experiments that nature, or history, will sometimes play, (Gualtieri, 1991). The advent of phenothiazines four decades ago in the medical marketplace heralded a hopeful pharmacological agent for treatment of individuals with psychotic illness. Unfortunately, psychiatrists construed the severe regression, withdrawal, self-injury and aggression of individuals with mental retardation to be representative of an underlying psychotic process. More recently, it has been thought that the prevalence of schizophrenia and other psychotic illnesses has been overreported and that people with mental retardation suffer from the full spectrum of psychiatric illness including affective and anxiety disorders (Sovner & Hurley, 1983; Menolascino & Stark, 1984). Thus, Gualtieri recounts this long-term tranquillisation of many persons with mental retardation displaying disruptive behaviour during which time the potential for long-term adverse side effects was over looked. Consequently, the emerging literature of neuropharmacology in mental retardation focuses on the potential use of alternative psychotropic agents.

Psychopharmacology in mental retardation, however, is currently more art than science. Even our familiar tool of diagnostic nomenclature can fail the physician in delineating a specific intervention. Is a self-injurious patient manic or depressed or psychotic, or does he suffer from cerebral impairment which contributes to failure in modulating arousal? Why does one patient respond to lithium, another to a beta blocker, or yet another to an anticonvulsant? Such are the dilemmas of the clinician who undertakes the challenging task of treating persons with mental retardation. The skilful physician is required to tap into his knowledge base of neuroscience, behavioural psychology and social matrix in which the patient finds himself to generate viable treatment strategies, but sometimes even seasoned clinical judgement is inadequate, and through trail and error, new treatment hypotheses are formulated. Despite the aforementioned limitations, our fledgling understanding of neuropharmacology is allowing us to consider an expanded armamentarium of chemotherapeutic agents to address the neurobehavioural disorders of persons with mental retardation.

Antipsychotic medication

The use of antipsychotic medication for the behavioural disorders of individuals with mental retardation has been controversial. A number of review articles (Lipman et al, 1978; Aman, 1983; Aman & Singh, 1983), has indicated that the vast majority of studies demonstrating the efficacy of antipsychotic medication of people with mental retardation has been methodologically flawed. Indeed, Schroeder (1988) states that 'most of the research on neuroleptics in developmental disabilities before 1980 can be safely ignored'.

Recent prospective studies on the use of antipsychotic medication with an adequate experimental design have been sparse. Singh and Aman (1981) conducted a placebo-controlled, double-blind, crossover study of thioridazine on 19 individuals with mental retardation. Their study concluded that the active drug conditions significantly reduced hyperactively, bizarre behaviours, and stereotypies without adverse effect on cognition. White and Aman (1985) studied eight people with severe mental retardation in a double-blind, placebo-controlled trial of pimozide. Target symptoms of irritability, hyperactivity, and noncompliance improved in response to active drug treatment.

Aman and Singh (1986) have reported after reviewing the literature that antipsychotic medication may have selective effects in suppressing stereotypic behaviour. They speculate that low dose antipsychotic drug therapy may indirectly promote adaptive behaviour by eliminating stereotypic mannerisms. Aman, White and Field (1984), in a placebo-controlled, crossover trial, found chlorpromazine (2.0–3.5 mg/kg) to significantly suppress stereotypic behaviour in six people with profound mental retardation. However, the moderate doses of chlorpromazine administered caused noticeable drowsiness in all patients and interfered with performance on an operant lever-pulling task. Aman *et al.* (1989) in a second study, utilising low-dose haloperidol (.025-.05 mg/kg) in 20 people with mental retardation in a double-blind, placebo-controlled, crossover trial, concluded that individuals with high levels of stereotyped behaviour tended to show a significantly more favourable response to haloperidol than those with low levels of stereotypy.

Given the paucity of well-designed clinical research on the role of antipsychotic medication, why is it so frequently prescribed in people with mental retardation? Reasons include its ability to suppress disruptive behaviour by its tranquillising effects. Such pharmacological intervention is, however, not treatment, but chemical restraint. Adverse effects in habilitative programming due to sedative and central anticholinergic properties may escape recognition by clinical staff. A second reason is the lack of experience or education by physicians and psychiatrists in the psychopharmacology of the developmental disabilities. Some clinicians consider antipsychotic drug therapy to be the 'buckshot' approach in treating a broad range of disruptive behavioural symptoms. Alternative pharmacological agents may offer a more favourable side effect profile as well as selectivity and specificity in targeting neurobehavioural disorders in people with mental retardation.

Interest has developed in recent years regarding the phenomenon of 'supersensivitity psychosis' (Chouinard & Jones, 1980) and the neuroleptic withdrawal syndrome described by Gualtieri as 'tardive akathesia' (Gualtieri & Schroeder, 1986). Discontinuation of long-term treatment with antipsychotic medication may lead to florid psychosis with schizophrenic patients or the emergence of disruptive behavioural symptoms in individuals with mental retardation. What ensues is a restoration of the original (or higher than original) dose and the fallacious assumption that the client might require indefinite antipsychotic pharmacotherapy. This reiterative cycle of increasing and decreasing medication leads to a 'yo yo effect' which may prolong the length of exposure to drug therapy.

Tardive akathesia is now accepted as a side effect of long-term neuroleptic therapy (i.e. greater that 6 months) or as the medication is tapered off and discontinued (Barnes & Braude, 1985; Gualtieri & Sovner, 1989). Tardive akathesia is a neuroleptic withdrawal syndrome believed by investigators in the field to be a variant of tardive dyskinesia. Unlike acute akathesia, tardive akathesia may be masked by increasing the antipsychotic drug dosage. Tardive akathesia may develop with either the high potency or low potency antipsychotic drugs.

Tardive akathesia is also frequently associated with the classical abnormal involuntary movements of tardive dyskinesia. Gualtieri (1991) estimated the prevalence of tardive akathesia to be 14% in institutional settings. The clinical manifestations of acute akathesia are identical to those of tardive akathesia. Thus tardive akathesia is characterised by motor restlessness, anxiety, increase of severity and frequency of maladaptive behaviour, and sleep disturbance. Frequently clients often lose 20–30 pounds of weight when antipsychotic drug therapy is tapered and discontinued.

No clear guidelines for the management of tardive akathesia have been established. Yassa *et al.* (1988) provided anecdotal data from two case studies on the utility of the beta blocker propranolol in this disorder. Gualtieri and Sovner (1989) recommended clonazepam as a possible strategy, although supporting literature exists only for its use in the treatment of acute akathesia (Kutcher *et al.*, 1989). None the less, benzodiazepines have frequently been suggested as a passive measure in the clinical management of tardive dyskinesia (Baldessarini *et al.*, 1980; Jeste & Wyatt, 1982).

Thaker *et al.* (1990), in a review of benzodiazepines treatment trials in the management of tardive dyskinesia, reported that 83% of patients exhibited some antidyskinetic response. This group of investigators also conducted a double-blind, placebo controlled, randomised crossover trial in 19 patients with tardive dyskinesia using clonazepam. The treatment trial produced a 37.1% overall reduction in dyskinesia scores. They speculate that the GABAmimetric action of clonazepam was responsible for the favourable effort since a reduction in nigral GABA-medicated neuronal transmission has been postulated to play pathophysiological role in tardive dyskinesia. Consequently, in tardive akathesia, selection of a benzodiazepine may be a viable option in selected cases.

The author has treated several cases of tardive akathesia successfully with low dosage of bromocriptine (less than 10 mg.). Bromocripine is a dopamine agonist which preferentially stimulates presynaptic auto-receptors thereby decreasing dopamine synthesis and release (Jeste & Wyatt, 1982). The underlying and unproven assumption is that dopaminergic hypersensitivity plays a role in the pathophysiology of tardive dyskinesia and tardive akathesia. The literature on low dose bromocriptine in the treatment of tardive dyskinesia has yielded mixed results (Jeste *et al.*, 1983; Lenox et al., 1985). Sitland-Marken *et al.* (1990) in a review of the literature on the use of bromocriptine in the management of tardive dyskinesia suggested that an optimal response occurs at doses of 7.5 mg per day or less. Currently, there exists only one publication in the literature of the effect of bromocriptine on tardive akathesia (Sachdev & Chee, 1990).

Psychopharmacology experts in mental retardation recommend that neuroleptic reduction be achieved in small doses over a period of months to years. This way, dramatic rebound exacerbations of maladaptive behaviour may be prevented. Unfortunately, studies have not been carried out to validate dose reduction with respect to prevention of tardive akathisia. Nor has the addition of a psychoactive agent such as a beta blocker, benzodiazepine, or bromocriptine, when a behavioural neuroleptic withdrawal syndrome occurs, been clinically substantiated in controlled studies. In some cases, the neuroleptic dosage may have to be increased.

If long-term dopamine antagonism by neuroleptics sensitises dopaminergic neurons, then sustained exposure to dopaminergic agonists could desensitise them and return the postsynaptic neuron to a more normal state. This concept has not been systematically studied with respect to tardive akathisia. High dose bromocriptine has been tried by Liberman *et al.* (1989) in the treatment of tardive dyskinesia with modest success. The use of amantadine and a neuroleptic has produced improvement in several cases with tardive dyskinesia (Allen, 1982). Dopamine agonists alone are generally ineffective and may worsen tardive dyskinesia. Ankenman (1989) reported favourable results in preventing severe tardive dyskinesia in a number of patients with mental retardation and with the concurrent prescription of neuroleptics and amantadine followed by very slow reduction of the neuroleptic. The protracted reduction may have altered the expression of tardive dyskinesia. This approach certainly warrants further investigation.

Unlike dopamine agonists, buspirone is not reported to exacerbate psychosis. It ameliorated acute akathisia in three patients in doses of 10–15 mg per day (D'Mello, McNeil & Harris, 1989). Whether buspirone is useful for tardive dyskinesia or tardive akathisia remains to be proven.

Given the controversies in the medical literature surrounding the use of antipsychotic agents, what are the appropriate and practical guidelines for the clinician? It is strongly recommended that antipsychotic medication is not the first line treatment of behavioural disorders unless the individual clearly demonstrates psychotic features. However, it is difficult, if not impossible, to make a definite diagnosis of schizophrenia in patients with IQs below 45 (Sovner & Hurley, 1983).

Behavioural techniques are clearly the main treatment modality for the disruptive behavioural disorders of individuals with mental retardation. Diagnostic assessment should exclude any psychiatric or medical cases for behaviour. For example, episodic hyperactivity and aggression may suggest mania, in which case the use of lithium might be a valuable treatment option.

Lithium

Clinical variants of affective disorder

In recent years, affective disorders have been frequently recognised in adults with mental retardation (Sovner & Hurley, 1983; Hasan & Mooney, 1979; Rivinus & Harmatz, 1979). Rigorous behavioural observations rather than standard psychiatric interviews have been the basics of diagnostic formulation (Sovner, 1988*a*, *b*) in this population. Psychiatric history and course of affective symptomatology have also been critical diagnostic determinants.

In a double-blind, placebo-controlled trial of lithium, Rivinus and Harmatz (1979) measured such variables as increased vocalisation, motor activity, aggressiveness, sleeplessness and decreased appetite as indicative of mania. Sovner (1986) proposed 'distortion-free' diagnostic behavioural criteria for major depression and mania. Such efforts in clarifying diagnostic criteria for people with mental retardation are critical in assessing the efficacy of drug and behavioural therapies.

Use of lithium in behaviour disorders

Some investigators have contended that lithium may have specific anti-aggressive properties even in the absence of an affective disorder (Sheard *et al.*, 1976; Tupin *et al.*, 1973). Sovner and Hurley (1981) argue that chronic hyperactivity is not suggestive of an affective disorder but episodic hyperactivity with a biphasic course is. Most writers seem to agree that not all symptomatology responsive to lithium is attributable to an affective disorder. Current knowledge cannot resolve this argument. However, it is conceivable that chronic vs. episodic hyperactivity may represent different phases of a spectrum of an underlying lithium-responsive neuro-behavioural disorder. Research evidence indicates that agents that deplete brain serotonin tend to cause an increase in aggression and self-destructive behaviour (Sheard, 1983, 1984; Crawley, Sutton & Pickar, 1985). Lithium may be efficacious in hyperactivity, aggression and self-injury behaviour by its ability to increase serotonin metabolism and release (Sheard, 1984; Gerbin, Oleshansky & Gershon, 1978). The symptomatic expressions of hyperactivity, aggression and self-injury may be due to multiple and diverse organic and psychological aetiologies. Consequently, only a subset of the behavioural disorders of people with mental retardation might be lithium responsive.

Use of lithium in persons with mental retardation

Review articles by Sovner and Hurley (1981) and Lapierre and Reesal (1986) address the use of lithium in chronic behaviour disorders in people with mental retardation. Tu and Smith (1983) have reported that 43 % of institutionalised clients with mental retardation displayed hyperactivity, aggression and self-injurious behaviour requiring clinical management. Recent publications of case reports (Amin & Yeragani, 1987), open clinical trials (Micev & Lynch, 1974) and double-blind controlled studies (Craft *et al.*, 1987) documented lithium responsiveness in these aberrant behaviours.

Existing literature supports the use of lithium in a wide range of behavioural disorders across a spectrum of psychiatric conditions. A smaller literature supports its use for hyperactivity, aggression and self-injurious behaviour in people with mental retardation. Clearly, more controlled studies are needed to establish efficacy and correlates of lithium responsiveness. An important consideration in prescribing lithium is the lack of any major effect on sedation, cognition, memory or reaction time (Platt *et al.*, 1984). Given potential short-term and long-term side effects of antipsychotic medication, a trial of lithium when non-pharmacological therapies have been ineffective in addressing hyperactivity, aggression and self-injurious behaviours is warranted (Jefferson *et al.*, 1987). In support of this notion, Wickham and Reed (1987) concluded that 'the effective use of lithium to control aggression should result in an improved quality of life for patients with reduced need for tranquillising medication, (and) better social integration into the community'.

Carbamazepine

Considerable attention has been given to the role of carbamazepine in treating recurrent bipolar affective disorder (Post & Uhde, 1987). Of clients with bipolar affective disorder 20–30 % are either treatment failures or suffer severe adverse effects from lithium, warranting discontinuation of the drug (Ayd, 1986). In this subpopulation of clients, carbamazepine is the most viable alternative treatment. Post and Uhde (1987) have indicated that the following correlates may predict a favourable response to carbamazepine: increased mania severity, increased dysphoria, rapid cycling and lack of positive family history for mania. None the less, the literature shows that 40 % of lithium non-responsive patients failed to respond to a trial of carbamazepine (Post, Kramlinger & Uhde, 1987) but may respond to a combination with lithium. In people with mental retardation, caution should be exercised when using this pharmacological strategy to avoid any potential neurotoxic side effects.

The use of carbamazepine for aggression and behavioural disorders (Patterson, 1987), psychosis (Luchins, 1983) and borderline personality disorder (Gardner & Cowdry, 1986) have also been reported.

Sovner (1988b) recommended carbamazepine as a therapeutic option for people with mental retardation suffering from affective disorders. Several reports (Singer, Benson & Rudnick, 1986) supported its efficacy in the treatment of bipolar disorder and depression in this population. A small literature also exists documenting the therapeutic effects of carbamazepine on behavioural disorders in people with mental retardation. Sovner (1988b) reported a case of a 27 year old severely retarded woman with organic personality disorder manifested by chronic irritability, self-injurious behaviour and hyposomnia. Treatment response, as measured by the frequency of four-point restraints, decreased on a trial of carbamazepine. Rapport *et al.* (1983) described the successful treatment of aggression in an adolescent with mental retardation who responded favourably to a combination of carbamazepine and behaviour therapy. Buck and Harvey (1986) reported on the case of a 23 year old man with mild mental retardation with frequent temper outbursts and who failed to respond to 17 different psychotropic medications. The client responded successfully to a trial of carbamazepine for a period of five months. After that time lithium was added due to a relapse of symptoms. During a follow-up period of eight months, the client's behavioural symptoms were still in substantial remission. He was able to participate regularly in a sheltered workshop and a community placement was planned. Crabbe and Rosenfield (1986) reported on a young man with severe mental retardation who had a diagnosis of organic affective disorder and displayed temper tantrums, impulsive behaviour, aggressiveness and property damage, and had complete remission of symptoms on a trial of carbamazepine. Reid, Naylor and Kay (1981) performed a double-blind, placebo-controlled crossover trial in 12 adults with profound mental retardation. Overactivity responded to carbamazepine. They concluded that there was no relationship between response to carbamazepine and the presence or absence of epilepsy.

Conclusions which may be drawn are that carbamazepine is a useful alternative treatment for lithium-refractory bipolar patients and can also be considered as pharmacotherapeutic agent in motor overactivity, aggression and behavioural disorders in clients not responding to behavioural therapy. Finally, carbamazepine is a particularly attractive choice in clients with epilepsy and affective illness or behaviour disorders.

Sodium valporate (Valporic acid)

Sodium valporate is another anticonvulsant that has received increasing attention in the psychiatric literature for affective disorders. McElroy *et al.* (1992) in a recent review of the treatment of bipolar disorder, reported a 63 % response rate in uncontrolled studies and a 62 % response rate in 5 placebo-controlled studies. Sovner (1989) published five case studies in which sodium valporate was used to treat patients with mental retardation and affective illness.

Kastner *et al.* (1990), reported on the use of sodium valporate to treat affective problems in three children with mental retardation. Target symptoms that were effectively treated included hyperactivity, emotional lability, sleep disturbance, aggression and self-injury. Sodium valporate may be particularly useful in patients who are refractory to treatment with either lithium or carbamazepine.

Beta blockers

Aggressive behaviour has been associated with varied manifestations of cerebral dysfunction including mental retardation, dementia, head trauma, strokes, encephalitis, Wilson's disease and Huntington's chorea (Stewart, Mounts & Clark, 1987). Despite the multiplicity of pathophysiological processes in these neurologically impaired individuals, beta blockers have been reported to play a role in ameliorating these uncontrollable rage outbursts. Sorgi, Ratey and Polakoff (1987) proposed that 'impulsive aggression may result when external stimulation from hyperactive autonomic receptors is conducted afferently into the CNS, thereby overwhelming fragile cognitive process'. They speculate that the mechanism of action of the beta blockers is by attenuating the responsiveness of peripheral adrenergic receptors. Thus, beta blockers may act like a braking mechanism which modulates the intensity of the feedback of somatic arousal transmitted to the brain. The hypothesis seems plausible given that the beta blockers attenuate aggressive states across a wide variety of CNS lesions and are not disease specific.

Single case studies (Polakoff, Sorgi & Ratey, 1986) and case series reports (Mattes, 1985) documents the efficacy of the beta blockers in uncontrolled rage outbursts in patients who have acute chronic organic brain syndromes. Silver and Yudofsky (1985) and Jenkins and Maruta (1987) have reviewed the literature. Of the 74 clients reviewed in these reports, 64 (86 %) improved on beta blockers with respect to aggressive and violent behaviour. Of the clients, 15 % had mental retardation and only 35% received antipsychotic medication in addition to the beta blockers.

Williams *et al.* (1982) in the largest retrospective case series, reported on 30 patients, aged 7 to 35, with uncontrolled rage outbursts and organic brain dysfunction. Twenty five patients were diagnosed to have conduct disorder, unsocialised, aggressive type, three with intermittent explosive disorder and two with pervasive developmental disorders. Of the patients, 75% were assessed to have moderate to marked improvement in rage outbursts after treatment with propranolol in the dose range of 50 to 1600 mg daily. Variables of age, sex, IQ, neurological or psychiatric diagnosis, EEG, inpatient vs. outpatient status did not correlate with outcome in terms of control of rage outbursts. Furthermore, all patients treated with propranolol had been unresponsive to previous pharmacological and psychotherapeutic interventions. Ratey *et al.* (1986) performed a prospective, consecutive case, clinical trial in four different institutions on the use of propranolol for the treatment of self-injurious and aggressive behaviours in individuals with severe and profound mental retardation. Fourteen of the 19 clients in this study continued to receive a maintenance dose of antipsychotic medication. The dose range of propranolol was 40 to 240 mg with mean dosage of 120 mg per day. The authors report a marked improvement in all clients, moderate improvement in five, and little or no improvement in three. In four clients antipsychotic medication was successfully discontinued, and eight patients had their daily antipsychotic medication dosage reduced. Symptoms of self-injury were also reduced in addition to aggressive behaviours. Although some of the clients improved immediately on propranolol, they stressed the conclusions of other investigators that clinical improvement may take weeks.

Ratey *et al.* (1987) performed another consecutive case, prospective study of eight autistic adults (five with mental retardation) in three hospital settings. All clients improved favourably with respect to aggressive and self-injurious behaviours. Of seven out of the eight clients on antipsychotic drugs, five had this medication reduced and, in one case, it was discontinued. It is uncertain, however, whether the improvement of communication skills was related to the decrease in antipsychotic medication or to the addition of beta blockers. Again, clinical improvement was gradual and progressive and, in some cases, was not seen for 12 weeks.

Kuperman and Stewart (1987) conducted a prospective, open trail study of propranolol on 16 clients with aggressive outbursts, aged 4 to 24, including 8 patients with mild to severe mental retardation. Ten out of the 16 clients were reported to be responders with ratings of moderate to much improvement, including 6 out of 8 clients with mental retardation.

Aggression is a multidimensional and complex phenomenon. Any treatment strategy should take into consideration any biological, psychological, social and environmental determinants. The optional treatment approach for aggressive states is behaviour therapy. Pending a thorough medical, neurological and psychiatric assessment, a pharmacotherapeutic intervention may be indicated in selected individuals. Conventional psychotropic medication may interfere with cognitive abilities and carries the long-term risk of tardive dyskinesia. In the absence of an affective disorder, beta blockers may be the treatment of choice in individuals with episodic behavioural disorders and concurrent cerebral dysfunction. Clients with observable signs of autonomic arousal, such as persistent tachycardia, may be particularly suited for this treatment approach.

Antidepressant Medication

Parsons, May and Menolascino (1984) stated that:

most cases of depression in individuals with mental retardation go unnoticed, or undiagnosed for a variety of reasons. Symptoms of depression are too often regarded as intrinsic elements of retardation or as typical of institutional behavior. Depressive symptoms may also appear to be secondary to more obvious problems. Finally, the non-disruptive nature of depression symptoms lessens the likelihood that institutional staff will view the behavior as a problem.

Sovner and Hurley (1983) stressed that the presence of mental retardation may modify the clinical manifestations of affective illness and make its detection difficult. Individuals with mental retardation manifest behavioural disturbances which might be 'depressive equivalents' and are at risk of being inappropriately treated with antipsychotic medication if careful diagnostic assessment is not available.

Sovner (1986) modified the DSM-III criteria by using purely behavioural descriptions to establish the diagnosis of major depression. Focusing on biological features such as appetite, sleep and energy level, diagnostic precision can be enhanced. For example, self-injury in the context of weight loss and early morning wakening is pathognomonic for the diagnosis of major depression. A family history of affective illness and alcoholism also places individuals at a higher risk for the development of depression.

The psychiatrist can make a rational decision to prescribe antidepressant medication only following a detailed diagnostic assessment which should include longitudinal behavioural observations and symptoms that correspond to Sovner's modified DSM-III criteria (Sovner, 1986).

Since depression has been infrequently diagnosed in people with mental retardation, the literature on pharmacological treatment consists primarily of descriptive case studies. Pirodsky *et al.* (1985) pointed out that 'individuals with mental retardation are likely candidates for depression as are those with normal intelligence, under the assumption that one's neurobiochemical profile is to some degree independent of one's cognitive ability'.

Cole and Hardy (1985) stated that depressive equivalents in people with mental retardation and non-verbal communication might include non-compliance, withdrawal, behavioural regression, aggression, self-injury, screaming, crying, as well as changes in appetite, weight and sleep. The presence of one symptom dose not clinch the diagnosis. Each behaviour needs to be considered in relationship to the entire symptom constellation which characterises the clinical picture.

Szymanski and Biederman (1984) reported on the use of antidepressant medication in the successful treatment of three individuals with Down's syndrome. Depressive symptoms in these clients include social withdrawal, deterioration of self-hygiene, crying spells, weight loss, irritability, sleep disturbance, oppositional behaviour, incontinence, and somatic complaints. The only client with mild mental retardation was able to provide self-report of dysphoric mood, guilty feelings and low self-esteem. Crabbe and Rosenfield (1986) reported a case study on a young woman with cerebral palsy and mild mental retardation. She displayed depression, suicide gestures (swallowing ammonia), self-injurious behaviour (face scratching), assaultive behaviour, rejection sensitivity, and craving for sweets. She was diagnosed as having a major depressive disorder and also had an abnormal dexamethasone suppression test. She was first taken off thioridazine with significant improvement of her motor coordination ability. She was then placed on imipramine with a dramatic improvement of her mood, assaultiveness and self-injurious behaviour, and was able to be transferred to a community training home. This case example illustrates the inappropriate use of antipsychotic medication for behaviour control and how diagnostic assessment and appropriate pharmacological intervention can improve psychosocial functioning.

A new class of antidepressants, the selective serotonin reputake inhibitors, has received much attention in the psychiatric literature. In general, their side effect profile is more benign than the older tricyclic antidepressants. Research literature has forged some tentative links between decrease CNS serotonergic activity and impulsive and aggressive behaviour (Sheard, 1983,1984; Crawley, Sutton & Pickar, 1985). Since this new class of antidepressants enhances serotonergic neurotransmission, there have been several case reports on its use to treat self-injurious and aggressive behaviour in persons with mental retardation. Markowitz (1992) treated 21 persons with severe and profound mental retardation and self-injury using 20–40 mg of fluoxetine. He reported marked improvement in 13 patients, moderate in 4, mild in 2 and no improvement in 2 patients. Bass and Beltis (1991) described the use of fluoxetine (40 mg daily) to treat a 17 year old man with severe mental retardation and self-injurious behaviour. Treatment diminished the self-injury by 45–55% for over a two-year observation period. King (1991) also reported on the use of fluoxetine to treat a 19 year old man with self-injurious behaviour. A clinically significant response was achieved, but a tolerance effect developed after 60–70 days warranting discontinuation of the drug. Selective serotonin reuptake inhibitors may be of use to a subset of clients with aggressive and self-injurious behaviour, but further study is warranted. One caveat is that fluoxetine may cause akathisia and overstimulation in some patients and could contribute to clinical deterioration (Rothschild & Locke, 1991).

Summary

The psychopharmacology of mental retardation is in its neonatal stage as is also our understanding of the human brain. Wherever possible, specific psychiatric disorders should be identified followed by appropriate pharmacological intervention. Indeed, these clients may be more vulnerable to mental illness than the population at large and conventional psychiatric treatment can enhance the quality of their lives. Neurobehavioural disorders involving hyperactivity, aggression and self-injury are more enigmatic. At times, the application of intelligent differential diagnosis can guide the clinician. Further research into the neuroscience underlying these behavioural syndromes may be the key to unlock this treatment challenge. Until that time, rational hypothesis testing is the most reasonable clinical strategy. Clearly, innovative pharmacotherapy may minimise clients' exposure to both short-term and long-term adverse effects associated with the 'conventional' use of antipsychotic agents.

References

Allen, R. M. (1982). Palliative treatment of tardive dyskinesia with combination of amantadine-neuroleptic administration. *Biological Psychiatry*, **17**, 719–27.

Aman, M. G. (1983). Psychoactive drugs in mental retardation. In J. L. Matson

& F. Andrisak, eds. *Treatment Issues and Innovations in Mental Retardation*. New York: Plenum.

Aman, M. G. & Singh, N. N. (1983). Pharmacological intervention. In J. L. Matson, J. A. Mulick & N. Y. Elmsford, eds., *Handbook of Mental Retardation*. Pergamon.

Aman, M. G. & Singh, N. N. (1986). A critical appraisal of recent drug research in mental retardation: the coldwater studies. *Journal of Mental Deficiency Research* **30**, 203–16.

Aman, M. G. & Singh, N. N. (1988). (eds) *Psychopharmacology of the Developmental Disabilities*. New York: Springer-Verlag.

Aman, M. G. & Teehan, C. J. *et al.* (1989). Haloperidol treatment with chronically medicated residents: dose effects on clinical behavior and reinforcement contingencies. *American Journal on Mental Retardation*, **93**, 452–60.

Aman, M. G., White, A. J. & Field, C. J. (1984). Chlorpromazine effects on stereotypic and conditioned behavior – a pilot study. *Journal of Mental Deficiency Research*, **28**, 253–60.

Amin, P. & Yeragani, V. K. (1987). Control of aggression and self-mutilation behavior in a mentally retarded patient with lithium. *Canadian Journal of Psychiatry*, **32**, 162–3.

Ankenman, R. (1989). The combination of amantadine and neuroleptics plus time may cure tardive dyskinesia. *Journal of Neuropsychiatry*, **1**, 96–7.

Ayd, F. J. (ed.) (1986). Carbamazepine therapy for manic depressive illness: an update. *International Drug Therapy News*, **21**, 9–12.

Baldessarini, R. J. & Cole, J. O. et al (1980). Tardive dyskinesia. *Task Force Report* No 18. Washington, DC: American Psychiatric Association.

Barnes, T. R. E. & Braude, W. M. (1985). Akathisia variants and tardive dyskinesia. *Archives of General Psychiatry*, **42**, 874–8.

Bass, J. N. & Beltis, J. (1991). Therapeutic effect of fluoxetine on naltrexone-resultant self-injurious behavior in an adolescent with mental retardation. *Journal of Child and Adolescent Psychopharmacology*, **1**, 331–40.

Buck, O. D. & Harvey, P. (1986). Combined carbamazepine and lithium therapy for violent behavior. *American Journal of Psychiatry*, **143**, 1487.

Chouinard, G. & Jones, B. D. (1980). Neuroleptic-induced supersensitivity psychosis: clinical and pharmacologic characteristics. *American Journal of Psychiatry*, **137**, 16–21.

Cole, J. O. & Hardy, P. M. (1985). Organic states. In A. F. Achatzberg (ed.). *Common Treatment Problems in Depression*. Washington, DC, American Psychiatric Press.

Crabbe, H. F. & Rosenfield, W. D. (1986). Treatment of the dually diagnosed mentally retarded: a model for rational intervention. In *Proceedings of the 94th Annual Convention of the American Psychological Association*. Washington, DC.

Craft, M. & Ismail, I. A. *et al.* (1987). Lithium in the treatment of aggression in mentally handicapped patients: a double blind trial. *British Journal of Psychiatry*, **150**, 685–9.

Crawley, J. N., Sutton, M. E. & Pickar, D. (1985). Animal models of self-destructive behavior and suicide. *Psychiatric Clinics of North America*, **8**, 299–310.

D'Mello, D. A., McNeil, J. A. & Harris, W. (1989). Buspirone suppression of neuroleptic-induced akathisia: multiple case reports. Journal of Clinical Psychopharmacology, **9**, 151–2.

Gardner, D. L. & Cowdry, R. W. (1986). Positive effects of carbamazepine on behavioral dyscontrol in borderline personality disorder. *American Journal of Psychiatry*, **143**, 519–22.

Gerbin, L., Oleshansky, M. & Gershon, S. (1978). Clinical use and mode of action of lithium. In M. A. Lipton, A. DiMascino & K. F. Kilam, eds. *Psychopharmacology: A Generation of progress*. New York Press.

Gualtieri, C. T. & Schroeder, S. R. *et al.* (1986). Tardive dyskinesia in young mentally retarded individuals. *Archives of General Psychiatry*, **43**, 335–40.

Gualtieri, C. T. & Sovner, R. (1989). Akathisia variants and tardive akathisia. *Psychiatric Aspects of Mental Retardation Reviews*, **8**, 83–8.

Gualtieri, C. T. (1991). A System for Prevention and Control. In J. J. Ratey, ed., *Mental Retardation: Developing Pharmacotherapies* pp. 35–49. Washington, DC: American Psychiatric Press.

Hasan, M. K. & Mooney, R. P. (1979). Three cases of manic-depressive illness in mentally retarded adults. *American Journal of Psychiatry*, **136**, 1069–71.

Jefferson, J. W. & Greist, J. H. *et al.* (1987). Mental Retardation. In J. W. Jefferson & J. H. Greist *et al.* eds. *Lithium Encyclopedia for Clinical Practice*. Washington, DC: American Psychiatric Press.

Jenkins, S. C. & Maruta, T. (1987). Therapeutic use of propranolol for intermittent explosive disorder. Mayo Clinical Proceedings, **62**, 204–14.

Jeste, D. V. & Cutler, N. R. *et al.* (1983). Low-dose apomorphine and bromocriptine in neuroleptic-induced movement disorders. *Biological Psychiatry*, **18**, 1085–91.

Jeste, D. V. & Wyatt, R. J. (1982). *Understanding and Treating Tardive Dyskinesia*. New York, Guildford Press.

Kastner, T., Freidman, D. L., Plummer, A. T., Ruiz, M. Q. & Henning, D. (1990). Valproic acid for the treatment of children with mental retardation and mood symptomatology. *Paediatrics*, **86**, 467–72.

King, B. H. (1991). Fluoxetine reduced self-injurious behavior in an adolescent with mental retardation. *Journal of Child and Adolescent Psychopharmacology* 1, 321–9.

Kuperman, S. & Stewart, M. A. (1987). Use of propranolol to decrease aggressive outbursts in younger patients. *Psychosomatics*, **38**, 315–9.

Kutcher, S. & Williamson, P. *et al.* (1989). Successful clonazepam treatment of neuroleptic-induced akathisia in older adolescents and young adults: a double-blind, placebo-controlled study. *Journal of Clinical Psychopharmacology*, **9**, 403–6.

Lapierre, Y. D. & Reesal, R. (1986). Pharmacologic management of aggressivity and self-mutilation in the mentally retarded. *Psychiatric Clinics of North America*, **9**, 745–54.

Lenox, R. H. & Weaver, L. A. *et al.* (1985). Tardive dyskinesia: clinical and neuroendocrine response to low dose bromocriptine. *Journal of Clinical Psychopharmacology*, **5**, 286–92.

Liberman, J. A., Alvir, J., Mukherjee, S. & Kane, J. M. (1989). Treatment of tardive dyskinesia with bromocriptine: a test of the receptor modification strategy. *Archives of General Psychiatry*, **47**, 908–13.

Lipman, R. S., DiMascio, A. *et al.* (1978). Psychotropic drugs and mentally retarded children in psychopharmacology: In M. A. Lipton, A. DiMascio & K. L. Killam, eds. *A Generation of Progress*. New York: Raven Press.

Luchins, D. J. (1983). Carbamazepine for the violent psychiatric patient. *Lancet*, **2**, 766.

Markowitz, P. I. (1992). Effect of fluoxetine on self-injurious behavior in the developmentally disabled; a preliminary study. *Journal of Clinical Psychopharmacology*, **12**, 27–31.

Mattes, J. A. (1985). Metoprolol for intermittent explosive disorder. *American Journal of Psychiatry*, **142**, 1108–9.

McElroy, S. L., Keck, P. E., Pope, H. G. & Hudson, J. I. (1992). Valproate in the treatment of bipolar disorder: literature review and clinical guidelines. *Journal of Clinical Psychopharmacology*, **12**, 42S-52S.

Menolascino, F. J. & Stark, J. A. (1984). (eds): *Handbook of Mental Illness in the Mentally Retarded*. New York: Plenum Press.

Micev, V. & Lynch D. M. (1974). Effect of lithium on disturbed, severely mentally retarded patients. *British Journal of Psychiatry*, **124**, 110.

Parsons, J. A., May, J. G. & Menolascino, F. J. (1984). The nature and incidence of mental illness in mentally retarded individuals. In F. J. Menolascino & J. A. Stark eds. *Handbook of Mental Illness in the Mentally Retarded*. New York: Plenum Press.

Patterson, J. F. (1987). Carbamazepine for assaultive patients with organic brain disease. *Psychosomatics*, **28**, 579–81.

Pirodsky, D. M., Gibbs, J. W. & Hesse, R. A. *et al.* (1985). Use of the dexamethasone suppression test to detect depressive disorders of mentally retarded individuals. *American Journal of Mental Deficiency*, **90**, 245–52.

Platt, J., Campbell, M. & Green, W. et al. (1984). Cognitive effects of lithium carbonate and haloperidol in treatment-resistant aggressive children. *Archives of General Psychiatry*, **41**, 657–62.

Polakoff, S. A., Sorgi, P. J. & Ratey, J. J. (1986). The treatment of aggressive and impulsive behavior with nadolol. *Journal of Clinical Psychopharmacology*, **6**, 125.

Post, R. M. & Uhde, T. W. (1987). Clinical approaches to treatment-resistant bipolar illness. In R. E. Hales & A. J. Frances, eds. *Psychiatric Update: American Psychiatric Association Annual Review*, vol. 6. Washington, DC: American Psychiatric Press.

Post, R. M., Kramlinger, K. G. & Uhde, T. W. (1987). Carbamazepine–lithium combination: clinical efficacy and side-effects. *International Drug Therapy News*, **22**, 5–8.

Rapport, M. D., Sonis, W. A., Fialkov, M. J., *et al.* (1983). Carbamazepine and behavior therapy for aggressive behavior. *Behaviour Modification*, **7**, 255–65.

Ratey, J. J., Mikkelsen, E. J. & Smith, G. B. *et al.* (1986). Beta-blockers in the severely and profoundly retarded. *Journal of Clinical Psychopharmacology*, **6**, 103–7.

Ratey, J. J., Mikkelsen, E. J. & Sorgi, P. et al. (1987). Autism: the treatment of aggressive behaviors. *Journal of Clinical Psychopharmacology*, **7**, 35–41.

Reid, A. H., Naylor, G. J. & Kay, D. S. G. (1981). A double-blind, placebo controlled, crossover study of carbamazepine in overactive, severely mentally handicapped patients. *Psychological Medicine*, **11**, 109–13.

Rivinus, T. M. & Harmatz, J. S. (1979). Diagnosis and treatment of affective disorder in the retarded: five case studies. *American Journal of Psychiatry* **136**, 551–4.

Rothschild, A. J. & Locke, C. A. (1991). Re-exposure to fluoxetine after serious suicide attempts by three patients. *Journal of Clinical Psychiatry*, **52**, 491–3.

Sachdev, P. & Chee, K. (1990). Pharmacological characterisation of tardive akathisia. *Biological Psychiatry*, **28**, 809–18.

Schroeder, S. R. (1988). Neuroleptic medications for persons with

developmental disabilities. In M. G. Aman & N. N. Singh, eds.
Psychopharmacology of the Developmental Disabilities. New York:
Springer-Verlag.

Sheard, M. H. (1983). Aggressive behavior: effects of neural modulation by
serotonin. In E. C. Simmel, M. E. Hahn & J. K. Walter, eds. *Aggression,
Genetic and Neural Aspects.* Hillsdale, NJ: Lawrence Erlbaum Associates
Press.

Sheard, M. H. (1984). Clinical pharmacology of aggressive behavior. *Clinical
Neuropharmacology,* **7**, 173–83.

Sheard, M. H., Marini, J. L., Bridges, C. I. *et al.* (1976). The effect of lithium on
impulsive aggressive behavior in man. *American Journal of Psychiatry,* **133**,
1409–13.

Silver, J. & Yudofsky, S. C. (1985). Propranolol for aggression: literature and
clinical guidelines. *International Drug Therapy News,* **20**, 9–12.

Singer, S. F., Benson, D. F. & Rudnick, F. D. (1986). Undetected affective
disorder in the developmentally retarded. *American Journal of Psychiatry,*
143–265.

Singh, N. N. & Aman, M. G. (1981). Effects of thioridazine dosage on the
behavior of severely retarded persons. *American Journal of Mental
Deficiency,* **85**, 580–7.

Sitland-Marken, P. A., Wells, B. G., Froemming, J. H., Chung-Chou, C. &
Brown, C. S. (1990). Psychiatric applications of bromocriptine therapy.
Journal of Clinical Psychiatry, **51**, 68–82.

Sorgi, P., Ratey, J. & Polakoff, S. (1987). Dr. Sorgi and associates reply (ltr to
ed). *American Journal of Psychiatry,* **144**, 539.

Sovner, R. (1986). Limiting factors in the use of DSM-III criteria with mentally
ill/mentally retarded persons. *Psychopharmacology Bulletin,* **22**, 1055–9.

Sovner, R. (1988*a*). Behavioral psychopharmacology: a new psychiatric
subspecialty. In J. A. Stark and F. J. Menolascino *et al.* eds. *Mental
Retardation and Mental Health: Classification, Diagnosis, Treatment,
Services.* New York: Springer-Verlag.

Sovner, R. (1988*b*). Anticonvulsant drug therapy of neuropsychiatric disorders
in mentally retarded persons. In S. L. McElroy, H. G. Pope & N. J. Clifton,
eds. *Use of Anticonvulsants in Psychiatry: Recent Advances.* Oxford Health
Care.

Sovner, R. (1989). The use of valproate in the treatment of mentally retarded
persons with typical and atypical bipolar disorder. *Journal of Clinical
Psychiatry,* **50**, (Suppl 3), 40–3.

Sovner, R. & Hurley, A. (1981). The management of chronic behavior disorders
in mentally retarded adults with lithium carbonate. *Journal of Nervous
Mental Disorders,* **169**, 191–5.

Sovner, R. & Hurley, A. D. (1983). Schizophrenia. *Psychiatric Aspects of Mental
Retardation Review,* **2**, 25–8.

Sovner, R. & Hurley, A. D. (1983). Do the mentally retarded suffer from
affective illness? *Archives in General Psychiatry,* **40**, 61–7.

Stewart, J. T., Mounts, M. L. & Clark, R. L. (1987). Aggressive behavior in
Huntington's disease: treatment with propranolol. *Journal of Clinical
Psychiatry,* **48**, 106–8.

Szymanski, L. S. & Biederman, J. (1984). Depression and anorexia nervosa of
persons with Down Syndrome. *American Journal of Mental Deficiency,* **89**,
246–51.

Thaker, G. K., Nguyer, J. A., Stauss, M. E., Jacobson, R. Kaup, B. A. &

Tamminga, C. A. (1990). Clonazepam treatment of tardive dyskinesia: a practical GABA mimetic strategy. *American Journal of Psychiatry*, **147**, 445–51.

Tu, J. & Smith, T. (1983). The Eastern Ontario survey: a study of drug-treated psychiatric problems in the mentally handicapped. *Canadian Journal of Psychiatry*.

Tupin, J. P., Smith, D. B., Clanon, T. L. *et al.* (1973). The long-term use of lithium in aggressive prisoners. *Comparative Psychiatry*, **14**, 311–17.

White, T. J. & Aman, M. G. (1985). Pimozide treatment in disruptive severely retarded patients. *Australian and New Zealand Journal of Psychiatry*, **19**, 92–4.

Wickham, E. A. & Reed, J. V. (1987). Lithium for the control of aggression and self-mutilating behavior. *International Clinical Psychopharmacology*, **2**, 181–90.

Williams, D. T., Mehl, R. Yudofsky, S. *et al.* (1982). The effect of propranolol on uncontrolled rage outbursts in children and adolescents with organic brain dysfunction. *Journal of American Academy of Child Psychiatry*, **21**, 129–35.

Yassa, R., Iskandar, H. *et al.* (1988). Propranolol in the treatment of tardive akathisia: a report of two cases. *Journal of Clinical Psychopharmacology*, **8**, 283–5.

16

Use of behavioural therapies to enhance personal competency: a multimodal diagnostic and intervention model

WILLIAM I. GARDNER AND
JANICE L. GRAEBER

Introduction

Within the past decade, the behaviour therapies and their applications to treatment of behavioural and emotional disorders presented by persons with mental retardation have undergone notable changes. As noted by Gardner and Cole (1990), these changes involve: (a) a decline in the number of clinical and research reports describing or evaluating the effects of various punishment procedures on aberrant behaviours; (b) an increased emphasis on use of behavioural diagnostics as a basis for developing client-specific treatment procedures; (c) the expansion of the unimodal behavioural operant learning model to include other psychological as well as biological and socioenvironmental contributors to aberrant behaviours; and (d) adoption of a skill deficit perspective with a habilitative treatment focus of teaching social/coping skills as replacements for aberrant responding. A collateral of the latter trend has been an increased emphasis on teaching skills of self-management as alternatives to the external management procedures that have dominated behavioural interventions (Gardner, 1988; Gardner & Cole, 1989).

This chapter describes a contemporary multimodal behavioural diagnostic and intervention model that reflects these and related trends. Following description of this model, applications to behavioural and emotional disorders presented by persons with mental retardation are described to illustrate its competency enhancement features.

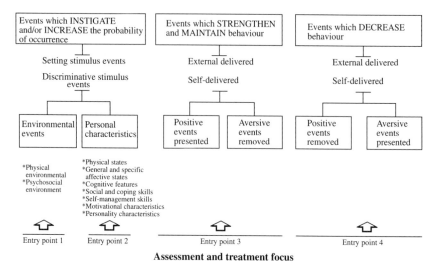

Fig. 16.1. Multimodal behavioural diagnostic and intervention model

Multimodal behavioural model

Functional diagnosis

A major assumption of the multimodal behavioural model is that behaviour, regardless of its aberrant nature, is functional (Gardner & Moffatt, 1990). The role of diagnosis is to identify factors which instigate and maintain aberrant symptoms. All behaviours, even those identified as maladaptive, reflect contemporary psychological and physical features of the person as those interact in a physical and social environmental context. What the person does, gains meaning only in relation to the combined effects of these multiple influences (Lowry & Sovner, 1991).

In identifying factors influencing specific symptoms, it is valuable to recognise that different aberrant behaviours such as aggression, pica, stereotypy, or self-injury may be initiated and strengthened by highly similar conditions (Oliver & Head, 1990). In illustration, when scheduled environmental stimulation is not provided regularly, John may begin to tap his face repetitively, Katherine may seek out and ingest small inedible objects, Steven may move across the room and push Becky out of a chair onto the floor, and Susan may begin to body rock at a rapid pace. These varying reactions to a similar state of stimulus deprivation reflect the unique learning histories of each individual. Each of these different aberrant behaviours in turn may be strengthened and thus maintained by the social and sensory feedback produced by each.

It also is useful to recognize that similar symptoms may reflect highly dissimilar influences (Matson & Gardner, 1991). In illustration, self-injurious behaviours (SIBs) such as head banging and face slapping may serve a variety of person-specific functions. SIBs may be functional in that they produce desired social attention and/or sensory feedback (Barrett *et al.*, 1989; Durand, 1986), or similar SIBs may remove unwanted demands (Repp, Felce & Barton, 1988). In a third instance, the SIBs may serve to modulate the emotional distress associated with depression and mania (Lowry & Sovner, in press). As a second example, a child with moderate mental retardation may present frequent toilet accidents as a clinical problem. This excessively occurring behaviour may be influenced in its occurrence and chronicity by any one or a combination of the following: (a) deficit or poorly developed toileting skills, (b) physical problems, (c) high anxiety level, (d) seizure activity, (e) negativism, (f) limited motivation to use his toileting skills, or (g) an attention-getting act. It is apparent that the treatment offered would be derived from diagnostic hypotheses about person-specific contributing influences.

The multimodal behavioural model, presented in Fig. 16.1, guides the clinician to determine the individually unique meaning of specific symptoms. Assessment focuses on identifying the multiple physical, psychological, and environmental variables contributing to the instigation of aberrant behavioural and emotional symptoms as well as those influencing the acquisition and persistent recurrence of these problem symptoms. Assessment includes evaluation of the interpersonal/environmental context of the person's difficulties as well as the person's unique physical and psychological structure and dynamics.

The model reflects a biopsychosocial perspective in that variables of a biological, psychological, and socioenvironmental nature and their interactions are considered (Gardner & Graeber, 1990). This functional diagnostic exercise represents a three-step process of (a) gathering information about variables that may contribute to the instigation, acquisition and persistent occurrence of symptoms, (b) developing client-specific hypotheses about specific contributing factors following analysis and interpretation of these assessment data, and (c) with this conceptual and empirical base, developing client-specific intervention procedures consistent with these hypotheses. In most instances of chronic behavioural and emotional disorders, multiple hypotheses about contributing factors may result in prescription of multiple person-specific intervention approaches.

Focus of assessment

External environmental variables

Initially, assessment involves identifying preceding interpersonal and other potential influences of the psychosocial and physical environments that may instigate the target symptoms. These events producing aberrant behaviours are person specific and can best be identified through systematic and objective observation of an individual in those particular situations in which target symptoms occur. These events may be reduction in staff attention, presentation of task demands, social disapproval, peer taunting, or removal of previously available positive consequences. Interviews with clients, staff, family, and peers, review of case records, and exposure to analogue conditions represent other means of gathering diagnostic information. In the most recently developed of these, the analogue assessment, the client is exposed either in a controlled or *in situ* setting to conditions assumed to set the occasion for and/or strengthen the target aberrant behaviours. Based on the client's differential reactions to these events, an individualised intervention programme is designed and evaluated (Mace *et al.*, 1986; Repp *et al.*, 1988).

Client characteristics

Client characteristics which may influence the occurrence of aberrant behaviours (Gardner & Cole, 1990; Lowry & Sovner, 1991) include physical/sensory factors such as fatigue, seizure activity, drug effects, chronic pain, hearing impairment, neurological impairment, premenstrual discomfort (Gedye, 1989; Kastner *et al.*, 1990; Sovner & Hurley, 1986), affective states such as anger, major depression, generalised anxiety, chronic sadness (Benson, 1986; Dosen, 1984; Fahs, 1989; Sovner & Hurley, 1990), and cognitive variables such as provocative covert verbal ruminations and paranoid ideation (Gardner *et al.*, 1983). A deficit or absence of skills such as social communication, anger management, self-management, and related problem-solving and coping skills may increase the vulnerability of the person to engage in maladaptive behaviours under conditions of provocation (Carr & Durand, 1985*a*; Durand, 1990; Gardner & Cole, 1989). Additional client characteristics that may contribute to aberrant responding include trait or personality variables and motivational characteristics. For example, a person with profound mental retardation, may have a generalised low threshold of tolerating changes and thus prone to aggressive outbursts under frequent unplanned disruptions in his daily routine (Gardner, 1988). Motivational variables include events that serve as positive reinforcers (e.g. adult approval, peer acceptance, exerting control over others, aggravating others), and the variety and relative effects of aversive events that influence the person's behaviour (e.g. rejection by peers, difficult task demands, adult reprimand) (Bailey & Pyles, 1989).

In summary, some personal characteristics such as excessive negative emotional arousal or generalised irritability may, by their presence, increase the likelihood of aberrant behaviours in those inclined to behave in a maladaptive manner. Other client variables, such as anger management or social communication skills and motivation to please others, by their absence or low strength, may render the person more vulnerable to aberrant responding under conditions of provocation.

Setting events: combining external and internal influences

It is highly unusual for a specific behaviour always to be produced by any specific stimulus condition. In illustration, a person may behave aggressively when taunted by a peer on one occasion but not on another. In most instances, a stimulus complex sets the occasion for aberrant behaviours. This stimulus complex frequently involves combined sources of internal and external stimulation. Gardner *et al.* (1986) describe an expanded behavioural assessment model that includes assessment of setting events in addition to the typical immediately preceding stimulus events–behaviour–consequences. These setting events are defined as those circumstances that influence which specific stimulus–response relationships would occur out of all those currently comprising a person's behavioural repertoire. These setting events may consist of (a) physiological conditions such as sleep deprivation, presence/absence of drugs, abnormal neurological activity producing overarousal and irritability, and discomfort associated with menses, (b) durational events such as presence of a specific staff member or work requirements in a vocational training programme setting, and (c) behavioural histories that represent temporally distant stimulus–response interactions wholly separate in space and time from current stimulus conditions such as an argument with mother prior to arriving at school. The effects of setting events may either facilitate or inhibit the occurrence of current stimulus-response functions.

Setting events are not constant across persons and thus must be individually defined and identified (Gardner *et al.*, 1986). This assessment provides a more complete and functionally meaningful description of the combination of physiological, durational, temporally historical, and temporally immediate events that influence aberrant behaviours (Gardner *et al.*, 1986; Schroeder, 1990).

Consequences of aberrant behaviour

Some recurring aberrant symptoms may be strengthened through positive reinforcement (Mace *et al.*, 1986; Martin & Foxx, 1973). Aberrant behaviours also may result in the reduction or termination of sources of aversiveness such as taunting from peers, unwanted task demands from caregiver, or high arousal level (Carr & Newsom, 1985; Durand, 1990). These maladaptive behaviours become functional in producing these desired positive or negative reinforcement consequences.

Focus of intervention

Functional diagnostics emphasise that the aberrant behaviours are not the primary focus of intervention; rather, the targets of intervention are the presumed physical, psychological, or socioenvironmental factors causing or contributing to their occurrence. Mere suppression of aberrant behaviours through punishment contingencies, as historically has been a major focus of behaviour therapy (modification), serves no viable role in this approach (Gardner, 1988). Instead, the primary objective of diagnostically based interventions is that of increasing the skill competency of the person. This competency enhancement entails an active programme of teaching and supporting the client to use more personally satisfying modes of relating to his/her physical and psychosocial environments.

Biopsychosocial perspective

A biopsychosocial perspective discourages the all too common practices of 'behaviourising' mental disorders that reflect major influences of biochemical or other physical and neurological variables or 'medicalising' aberrant symptoms that reflect the primary effects of previous experiences and current psychosocial influences. Biological interventions are disorder based (Sovner & Hurley, 1984; Sovner, 1986) and behavioural and other psychosocial interventions are based on a diagnostic view of the current influences of a psychological or socioenvironmental nature that result in the symptoms (Gardner & Moffatt, 1990).

To illustrate, a biologically based psychiatric condition, such as schizophrenia, or a bipolar disorder may result in changes in cognitive functions, affective states, emotional regulation, and behaviours. These changing psychological and physical characteristics may result in new behavioural or emotional symptoms or may influence the occurrence or increased severity of problems that predated the current psychiatric episode. These symptoms, in turn, create changes in the manner in which the social environment responds to and interacts with the person and his/her problem behaviours. These experiences with the social environment may in a reciprocal manner reinforce the problem behaviours, intensify the emotional arousal, or influence the person's perceptions of the social feedback. Intervention to be most effective must be sensitive to these reciprocal interrelationships and provide attention to these influences within the context of the biopsychosocial perspective.

Treatment vs. management

Optimal interventions are those that result in changes in the individual that are of a greater than transitory nature. These treatments interventions may be psychosocial or biological in nature. Other interventions may address physical and psychosocial conditions that, while not producing enduring change in the individual, do serve to remove or reduce the conditions that contribute to the instigation of behavioural symptoms. These latter interventions serve to manage behavioural symptoms but, in isolation, do not result in enduring changes in those physical or psychological variables that produce or contribute significantly to the occurrence or durability of the aberrant symptoms. Upon termination of the management procedures and exposure of the person to the original conditions influencing the aberrant behaviours, these symptoms recur (Gardner & Cole, 1987).

Psychological treatment results in reduction in the frequency, duration, and/or intensity of excessive aberrant behaviours, through enhancing personal competency by teaching such skills as communicating one's preferences, interacting with peers in a socially appropriate manner or expressing anger through appropriate verbal or other coping means (Benson, 1986; Durand, 1990; McNally & Ascher, 1987). The major objective of treatment is that of producing behaviour change that will persist across time and situations.

In summary, the treatment programme seeks to change the person's responsiveness to external and internal physical and psychological conditions that instigate and/or increase the likelihood of problem behaviours through teaching new socially appropriate emotional and behavioural skills that will replace the inappropriate acts (Cole, Gardner & Karan, 1985). For example, an adolescent with severe mental retardation involving agitated/disruptive outbursts, would be taught not merely to 'control his temper' but also to identify and express his emotions in a more acceptable manner.

Interventions may also involve behaviour management. These management approaches are designed to (a) eliminate or minimise specific stimulus conditions likely to instigate aberrant behaviours, (b) present or emphasise specific stimulus conditions that increase the likelihood of prosocial functional alternative behaviours, (c) present or emphasise specific stimulus conditions that inhibit the occurrence of aberrant responding, and (d) minimise the duration and intensity of problem behaviours following their occurrence. These management procedures are supportive of treatment interventions, but differ critically in function in that these do not produce durable changes in behaviour strength (Gardner & Cole, 1987).

Similarly, biomedical treatment results in more than transitory reduction or removal of those conditions that contribute to the aberrant symptoms. Use of neuroleptic medication during the acute phase of a schizophrenic disorder during which the person behaves in a violent manner provides an illustration. Following reduction and even termination of the drug therapy, the aggressive symptoms may not recur due to the successful treatment of the biochemical abnormality presumed to underlie the schizophrenic disorder.

Biomedical intervention may also serve a management function relative to specific behavioural or emotional symptoms or clusters of symptoms. Drugs such as lithium or carbamazepine may reduce aggression and irritability or generalised restlessness in a person with profound mental retardation by raising the person's threshold to aggressive responding (Thompson, 1988). On termination of the drug, aggressive acts and irritability may return to the preintervention level as the inclination to aggression in the absence of the medication had not been reduced. Combining the drug intervention with a behaviour therapy programme designed to teach the person to cope both with the factors producing the anxiety as well as to the specific factors instigating the aggression, does offer promise of an enduring treatment effect following withdrawal of the medication.

Finally, internal (e.g. excessive anxiety, repetitive thinking about a disturbing experience) or external (e.g. presence of a peer, excessive noise) stimulus conditions may produce aberrant behaviours that actively compete with the performance of previously learned coping behaviours. Behaviour therapy approaches would seek to reduce the inhibiting or interfering functions of specific stimulus conditions. In selected instances, behaviour therapy would be combined with medical therapy to insure reduction of organically based anxiety or other affective states (Lowry & Sovner, 1991).

Staging of intervention focus

As the specific factors influencing problem behaviours and emotions vary in their relative potency as well as in the ease or difficulty with which change in these factors may be accomplished, a staging of intervention becomes the rule. This indicates that the primary focus of intervention at any given time may vary depending upon the nature and relative importance of the current factors presumed to contribute to the person's difficulties. Harry, an adult with profound mental retardation, illustrates this staging process. His increased self-injurious episodes correlate with an acute ear infection. Initial primary intervention will focus on reducing/removing the abnormal physical conditions presumed to contribute to the SIBs. After this is accomplished, the primary intervention focus may shift to teaching Harry to communicate his physical discomfort in ways other than through face slapping and head banging. As this goal of teaching alternative modes of communication is accomplished, the primary intervention focus may shift to the social environment to insure that Harry is prompted and reinforced for using his newly acquired communication skills in expressing his needs.

Enhancing personal competency

As emphasised, functional diagnosis directs treatment at those person-specific factors that are presumed to contribute to the instigation and recurrence of aberrant symptoms. To insure durability of intervention gains, an integrated biopsychosical treatment plan is designed to change those biological and psychological features of the person to the extent that these treatment effects are maintained following treatment withdrawal. In view of the widespread skill deficits that contribute to aberrant responding in those with mental retardation, an educative or habilitative approach guides the behaviour therapy component of this treatment plan. As new skills are acquired, the personal competency of the person in coping with conditions previously producing aberrant behaviours is enhanced. Illustrations are provided of use of various behaviour therapy procedures in treatment of a range of behavioural and emotional symptoms.

Teaching alternative communicative skills

In an initial demonstration of decreasing aggressive behaviours when an alternative non aggressive behaviour is strengthened, Carr, Newsom, and Binkoff (1980) taught a severely handicapped adolescent a non-aggressive tapping response, as a means of escaping from an aversive demand situation. Previously observed high rates of aggressive behaviours reduced significantly whenever this alternative behaviour became functional. In a follow-up demonstration of this procedure of teaching a functionally equivalent, but appropriate, means of escape from aversive conditions, Carr and Durand (1985*a*, *b*) initially exposed children with both developmental disabilities and chronic problems of self-injury, stereotypy, aggression, and related agitated/disruptive behaviours to an instructional programme that varied in task difficulty and in the level of teacher attention. Both low levels of teacher attention and high levels of task difficulty were demonstrated to be discriminative for aberrant behaviours. Of interest were the findings that (a) the specific conditions that served to instigate misbehaviour differed across children, and (b) similar aberrant behaviours of a specific child could be escape motivated under certain conditions and reinforcement motivated under others.

Based on these individualised diagnostic data, children were provided training in functional communication designed to teach each child those communicative phrases that served to alter the stimulus conditions that controlled their problem behaviours (e.g. deprivation of adult social attention or difficulty of task demands). Children who were more likely to exhibit aggression under low levels of adult attention were taught to solicit praise through a relevant communicative response. Similarly, children who demonstrated an increased likelihood of aberrant responding under difficult task demands were taught to solicit assistance by simply saying 'I don't understand'. Following training and consistent use of these communicative phrases, disruptive behaviours reduced to low levels. Thus, the newly acquired communicative behaviours were functionally equivalent to the aberrant behaviours in expressing individual concerns.

Teaching anger management skills

Benson in Chapter 17 reports in detail the success of anger management training in reducing aggressive and related disruptive behaviours in clients with mental retardation and various psychiatric disorders.

Teaching skills of self-management

Stereotyped behaviours

Morrow and Presswood (1984) demonstrated the clinical usefulness of a self-management treatment package in reducing three stereotyped behaviours of a 15-year-old adolescent with multiple physical and psychological difficulties. This student, institutionalised for three years, had (a) a profound bilateral, sensorineural hearing loss, (b) a psychiatric diagnosis of schizophrenia and was described as frequently being out of contact with reality, and (c) a prorated Wechsler Intelligence Scale for Children–Revised IQ of 10.

Treatment occurred in the student's classroom, located in a state residential treatment centre for mentally ill and behaviourally disordered children and youth. Although enrolled in a token economy programme at the time of initiation of the self-management treatment programme (tokens awarded every 30 minutes for being in the assigned area and completing academic assignments), staff reported no positive effects of the token system. Target behaviours consisted of (a) jaw and ear flapping with the palm of the hand, (b) hand contortions consisting of sudden closing and opening of the fist and inappropriate movement of the fist around the mouth, and (c) inappropriate shrieking noises when a response was not requested.

The adolescent was taught to self-monitor the occurrence of his behaviours during a predetermined time interval and to self-record on a grid the occurrence or nonoccurrence of the three target behaviours. During training, a timer was set to ring after a predetermined time interval. If the target behaviour (e.g. jaw and ear flapping) had not occurred during the interval, an apparatus on the desk displayed a happy face and he was prompted to sign 'I did not flap my ear or jaw' and record a plus (+) on a grid card located on his desk. The timer was reset and the adolescent was prompted to resume his assigned work, a match-to-sample vocabulary task. If a target behaviour did occur before the timer rang, an unhappy face would be displayed and the adolescent would be prompted to sign 'I did flap my ear or jaw' and record a minus (-) on the card. Training was continued until he was able to set the timer and correctly self-assess his target behaviours. No external reinforcement was provided. At the end of each daily session, the grid card was collected without feedback.

Jaw and ear flapping reduced from a mean of 18.6 occurrences per 30 minutes during baseline to 0 in 8 days following treatment. The target did not occur during the remaining 33 days of data collection. Hand contortions showed a similar immediate reduction (mean of 12.4 per minute to 4 or fewer within 6 days and then to 0 episodes for the remaining days). Inappropriate noises also showed an immediate and significant reduction (83.4 episodes per 30 minutes during baseline to 17.2 following treatment initiation), although this behaviour was not eliminated until an additional procedure of contingent exercise was introduced. To evaluate generalisation of these treatment effects, probes were conducted for each of the three target behaviours in four school-related environments during the entire 5.5 hour school day on 3 different days. All probes revealed zero instances of the target behaviours, indicating generalisation effects across time and settings.

These results are interesting in that the self-management procedures represented the only intervention used. Morrow and Presswood (1984) speculated that the rapid and marked changes in the student's behaviour resulted in more social interactions and approval from peers and adults. Additionally, the inclusion of self-monitoring, self-evaluation, and self-recording may also have prompted a self-reinforcement reaction. Advantages of these procedures include its (a) ease of implementation by caregivers, (b) cost-effectiveness, as no backup reinforcers were required, and (c) flexibility of application to a number of ongoing classroom instructional activities.

Multiple agitated/disruptive behaviours

In a series of three studies, Gardner and colleagues (Cole *et al.*, 1985; Gardner, Clees & Cole, 1983; Gardner *et al.*, 1983) evaluated the effects of a treatment package that included multiple self-management procedures. Subjects in the studies were adults with mild to moderate levels of mental retardation who displayed chronic problems that had not responded to a variety of psychological, psychiatric, and behavioural procedures. The programme rationale and procedures were based on the authors' clinical experiences with clients who presented such chronic difficulties as verbal and physical aggression, temper outbursts, inappropriate expression of anger, and other states of heightened negative emotional arousal that suggested that these clients often acted impulsively in response to sources of provocation. The clients provided minimal if any indication that they engaged in the self-management activities of self-observation, self-evaluation, self-instruction, or self-consequation, or that such skills were in their repertoires.

In the initial study, Gardner *et al.* (1983) evaluated the effects of a self-management package on the high rate disruptive verbal behaviours (e.g. teasing and taunting, swearing, name calling, threatening, yelling) of two adults with moderate mental retardation who attended a vocational training programme. In the absence of frequent staff intervention, the disruptive verbal behaviours typically escalated into acts of physical aggression. Both clients had been enrolled in a vocational training programme prior to the study but were irregular in attendance and erratic in work production, and demonstrated highly disruptive social behaviours.

Both had experienced lengthy suspensions from work because of staff difficulties in managing their behaviours.

During initial baseline conditions, clients received frequent social praise and monetary reinforcers. Reinforcement was contingent on such appropriate work and social behaviours as displaying positive affect, being on task, working quietly, ignoring provocative behaviours of peers, and fulfilling staff requests. Following baseline, self-management training was provided, initially in a training room and later in the work setting for *in situ* rehearsal.

During a 1-day training session, each client was initially taught to:

1. Self-monitor (discriminate the occurrence of such behaviours as yelling/not yelling, teasing/not teasing, and singing loudly/working quietly). Following trainer modelling and appropriate client labelling of the behaviours, the client was guided to self-monitor his/her own role-played behaviours.
2. Self-evaluate his/her own actions. Appropriate behaviours were labelled by the trainer as 'good adult worker' behaviour and undesirable behaviours were labelled 'not adult worker' behaviour. Numerous problem situations were described and modelled, the client prompted to role play appropriate and inappropriate responses to each and to self-evaluate these actions. In addition, each client was provided a laminated 6×8.5 inch card displayed at the work station. A coloured photograph of the client smiling was attached to one side and was labelled as 'good adult worker', while the flip side, with a photograph of the client frowning, was labelled as 'not adult worker' behaviour.

    Several opportunities for role playing various behaviours were provided with the client intermittently labelling his/her own behaviour (self-monitoring) and, using the display card, assessing it is 'good adult worker' behaviour or 'not adult worker' behaviour (self-evaluation). Finally, each client was prompted to rehearse several prosocial alternatives to inappropriate behaviours, using self-instruction when appropriate.
3. Self-consequate his/her own behaviour (i.e. to self-deliver a reinforcer or to self-punish with a brief timeout and response cost contingent on self-evaluation of behaviour). The trainer, removing a coin from a container placed on the client's work table, clipped it to the good adult worker side of the display card. The card was flipped several times to emphasise that 'good adult worker' behaviour earned money, while 'not adult worker' behaviour did not.

Finally, each client was provided a timer, taught to set it independently for a designated period of time, and informed, 'Whenever you decide to be a 'good adult worker' until the bell rings, you'll earn a coin'. The trainer initially modelled setting the timer and differentially consequating behaviours. When appropriate behaviour was engaged in throughout the time interval, the client was prompted to (a) self-monitor, (b) self-evaluate, and (c) self-reinforce by taking a coin from the card. In contrast, inappropriate behaviour was followed by immediate flipping of the display card to the 'not adult worker' picture and stopping the timer. Inappropriate behaviour thus was followed by a self-initiated timeout (i.e. temporary loss of opportunity to work and earn money) and a response cost (i.e. loss of minutes accumulated prior to occurrence of the inappropriate behaviour). The client was prompted to rehearse, with the trainer, alternative appropriate behaviours and, when the client decided that he/she was ready to begin working again, to flip over the card to the 'good adult worker' picture, reset the timer, and begin working. Each client then rehearsed engaging in and labelling the entire behaviour-consequence contingency.

On resuming work in the workshop, clients were provided additional training to insure generalisation to this setting. Whenever inappropriate behaviour occurred, the trainer prompted the client through the above-described sequence, corrected errors and labelled and praised appropriate responses. Because *in situ* events such as a threatening gesture from a peer frequently preceded inappropriate behaviour, these peer interactions served as a basis for rehearsal of alternative self-managed behaviours. Whenever possible, the peer(s) who provoked the client participated with the client in rehearsal of more appropriate behaviours. During the initial self-management phase, the trainer continued to verbally prompt the client upon hesitation (e.g., to set the timer) or error (e.g., failing to attach a coin to the display card) in the behaviour sequence. Staff also intervened at the end of each successfully completed work interval and upon every occurrence of inappropriate behaviour. The client was prompted to self-monitor, self-evaluate, and self-consequate and to rehearse appropriate alternative behaviours following inappropriate ones. Trainer intervention was faded gradually as each client demonstrated independence in the various self-management activities.

An immediate and significant reduction in the disruptive verbalisations was obtained for both clients. Treatment gains were maintained during a fading phase and at 6-month follow-up.

In a second investigation of this treatment package, Gardner *et al.* (1983) assessed its effects in a vocational training setting on the high rate disruptive vocalisations (verbal ruminations and non-speech sounds) of a man who had moderate mental retardation. These behaviours seemed to be self-stimulatory in nature and unrelated to current external stimulation. Although not directed toward others initially, the content, frequency, and volume of these verbal behaviours resulted in agitated/disruptive reactions from peers that required staff intervention. In addition, potential con-current changes in behaviours (talking to others, stereotypic/motor movements, and production rate) not selected as specific targets of intervention were evaluated.

Disruptive vocalisations showed an immediate effect upon introduction of treatment (97.5% to near-zero occurrence following 3 weeks of treatment). The near-zero level was maintained through fading and at 6- and 12-month follow-up. Similar therapeutic effects were obtained for collateral behaviours not targeted for intervention. Stereotyped behaviours were virtually eliminated, production rate increased, and appropriate talking to others improved.

In the third study in this series, Cole *et al.* (1985) evaluated the effects of the treatment programme on the high rate disruptive behaviours of six adults functioning in the mild to moderate range of mental retardation. All clients displayed chronic and severe behavioural/emotional difficulties. Although each had been provided a range of psychiatric and psychological treatment, none had demonstrated desired progress. In fact, for all subjects, clinically significant conduct difficulties had resulted in dismissal from, or precluded placement in, community vocational rehabilitation pro-grammes.

Disruptive verbal and physical behaviours specific to each person served as treatment targets. In addition to the training programme described previously, clients in this study were provided more detailed self-instructional training. Video and audio tapes of specific provocative situations (e.g. peer taunting, staff corrective feedback) were presented. The trainer modeled appropriate self-verbalisations in the presence of these provocative cues (e.g. 'Jerry's teasing me, but I won't yell. I'm a good adult worker, I'll ignore him'). Later, the client was prompted to use these statements to self-direct his/her appropriate behaviour. During client rehearsal, the duration and intensity of the stimulated provocation was gradually increased and the client was encouraged to speak more and more softly, with the ultimate goal of subvocal self-talk under actual provo-cation. Following individual training, each client resumed working in the vocational training setting with the programme materials placed at his/her work station. In addition to the *in situ* training procedures previously described, each client was frequently encouraged to self-instruct and rehearse appropriate coping responses.

The intervention package produced immediate and clinically significant reductions in severe conduct difficulties in all six clients. Nine-month follow-up under different work conditions revealed continued maintenance of treatment gains.

Teaching alternatives to phobias

Numerous studies have demonstrated the usefulness of behaviour therapy procedures in teaching persons with mental retardation to cope with events and activities that previously had produced debilitating anxiety and phobic reactions (McNally & Ascher, 1987). As one illustration, Burgio, Willis and Burgio (1986) described the successful use of operant-based treatment procedures in treating a 21 year old male with severe mental retardation who had become increasingly fearful of stairs. The client displayed severe avoidance responses when approaching stairs and frequently refused to use them. Fear and avoidance responses were more likely to occur when there were many versus few steps.

Treatment consisted of therapist modelling, contingent praise, and edible reinforcement. At the beginning of a trial, the therapist instructed the client to watch him/her, and with the edible reinforcer in hand, walked up the stairs while holding onto the railing. A second therapist then instructed the client to go up (down) the stairs, remembering to use the railing. In early sessions, praise and attention were administered contingent upon each step climbed. Later, approximately 1 praise per 4 stairs was administered. If the client completed all stairs unassisted, praise and an edible reinforcer were delivered. Edibles were never given for stair use that was assisted.

During the last sessions of treatment, the schedule of reinforcement decreased. During the final three sessions, no edibles were provided. When the client was reliably using the stairs in the assessment settings, inpatient staff and family members were instructed to prompt and reward him with praise. In both inpatient and home settings, prompts and praise were faded so that the client would use the stairs in response to natural opportunities.

At the end of therapy, the client was consistently ascending and descending the stairs in both settings with staff employing only intermittent contingent praise. Staff and family members reported that the effect generalised to non-treatment setting within the hospital and to the home. Pretreatment emotional responses such as crying and trembling were no longer occurring in any setting, and the client was soon returned to the community where anecdotal reports suggest that he was experiencing no difficulty in stair climbing 2 years after termination of therapy.

Summary

The use of functional diagnosis based on a multimodal biopsychosocial perspective provides the basis for integrating a variety of treatment and management approaches into a comprehensive intervention plan for a person with mental retardation and behaviour disorders. This diagnostic integration of medical and psychosocial interventions reduces the common practice of 'behaviourising' symptoms that reflect biologically based disorders and 'medicalising' aberrant symptoms that reflect the primary effects of previous experiences and current psychosocial influences. Deriving interventions from client-specific diagnostic information also results in programme approaches designed to teach those competency skills useful to a client in coping with external and internal conditions that influence aberrant responding.

References

Bailey, J. S. & Pyles, D. A. (1989). Behavioral diagnostics. In E. Cipani (ed.) *The Treatment of Severe Behavior Disorders*, pp. 85–107. Washington, DC: American Association on Mental Retardation.

Barrett, R. P., Feinstein, C. & Hole, W. T. (1989). Effects of naloxone and naltrexone on self-injury: a double blind, placebo-controlled analysis. *American Journal of Mental Retardation*, **93**, 645–51.

Benson, B. A. (1986). Anger management training. *Psychiatric Aspects of Mental Retardation Reviews*, **5**, 51–5.

Benson, B. A., Rice, C. J. & Miranti, S. V. (1986). Effects of anger management training with mentally retarded adults in group treatment. *Journal of Counselling and Clinical Psychology*, **54**, 727–9.

Black, L., Cullen, C., Dickens, P. & Turnbull, J. (1988). Anger control. *British Journal of Hospital Medicine*, **22**, 325–9.

Burgio, L. D., Willis, K. & Burgio, K. L. (1986). Operantly based treatment procedures for stair avoidance by a severely mentally retarded adult. *American Journal of Mental Deficiency*, **91**, 308–11.

Carr, E. G., & Durand, V. M. (1985a). Reducing behavior problems through functional communication training. *Journal of Applied Behavior Analysis*, **18**, 111–26.

Carr, E. G. & Durand, V. M. (1985b). The social-communicative basis of severe behavior problems in children. In S. Reiss & R. P. Bootzin, eds. *Theoretical Issues in Behavior Therapy*, pp. 219–254. New York: Academic Press.

Carr, E. G. & Newsom, C. D. (1985). Demand-related tantrums: conceptualization and treatment. *Behavior Modification*, **9**, 403–26.

Carr, E. G., Newsom, C. D. & Binkoff, J. A. (1980). Escape as a factor in the aggressive behavior of two retarded children. *Journal of Applied Behavior Analysis*, **13**, 101–17.

Cole, C. L., Gardner, W. I. & Karan, O. C. (1985). Self-management training of mentally retarded adults presenting severe conduct difficulties. *Applied Research in Mental Retardation*, **6**, 337–47.

Dosen, A. (1984). Depressive conditions in mentally handicapped children. *Acta Paedopsychiatrica*, **50**, 29–40.

Durand, V. M. (1986). Self-injurious behavior as intentional communication. In K. D. Gadow, ed. *Advances in Learning and Behavioral Disabilities*, vol. 5, pp. 143–157, Greenwich, CT: JAI Press.

Durand, V. M. (1990). *Severe Behavior Problems*. New York: Guilford Publications.

Fahs, J. J. (1989). Anxiety disorders. In *American Psychiatric Association, Treatment of Psychiatric Disorders*, vol. 1, pp. 14–19. Washington, DC.

Gardner, W. I. (1988). Behavior therapies: past, present, and future. In J. A. Stark, F. J. Menolascino, M. H. Albarelli & V. C. Gray, eds. *Mental Retardation and Mental Health: Classification, Diagnosis, Treatment, Services*, pp. 161–172. New York: Springer-Verlag.

Gardner, W. I. (1991). Effects of psychological welfarism on durability of behavior disorders in those with mental retardation. *Psychology in Mental Retardation and Developmental Disabilities*, **16**, 2–5.

Gardner, W. I., Clees, T. J. & Cole, C. L. (1983). Self-management of disruptive verbal ruminations by a mentally retarded adult. *Applied Research in Mental Retardation*, **4**, 41–58.

Gardner, W. I. & Cole, C. L. (1987). Behavior treatment, behavior management, and behavior control. *Behavioral Residential Treatment*, **2**, 37–53.

Gardner, W. I. & Cole, C. L. (1989). Self-management approaches. In E. Cipani, ed. *The Treatment of Severe Behavior Disorders*, pp. 19–35. Washington, DC: American Association on Mental Retardation.

Gardner, W. I. & Cole, C. L. (1990). Aggression and related conduct difficulties. In J. L. Matson, ed. *Handbook of Behavior Modification with the Mentally Retarded* (2nd ed., pp. 225–251). New York: Plenum.

Gardner, W. I., Cole, C. L., Berry, D. L. & Nowinski, J. M. (1983). Reduction of disruptive behaviors in mentally retarded adults: a self-management approach. *Behavior Modification*, **7**, 76–96.

Gardner, W. I., Cole, C. L., Davidson, D. P. & Karan, O. C. (1986). Reducing aggression in individuals with developmental disabilities: an expanded stimulus control, assessment, and intervention model. *Education and Training of the Mentally Retarded*, **21**, 3–12.

Gardner, W. I. & Graeber, J. L. (1990). Persons with mental retardation and severe behavior disorders: a multimodal diagnostic and treatment model. *NADD Newsletter*, **7**(3), 1–4.

Gardner, W. I. & Moffatt, C. W. (1990). Aggressive behavior: definition, assessment, treatment. *International Review of Psychiatry*, **2**, 91–100.

Gedye, A. (1989). Episodic rage and aggression attributed to frontal lobe seizure. *Journal of Mental Deficiency Research*, **33**, 369–79.

Kastner, T., Friedman, D. L., O'Brien, D. R. & Pond, W. S. (1990). Health care and mental illness in persons with mental retardation. *The Habilitative Mental Healthcare Newsletter*, **9**, 17–24.

Lowry, M. & Sovner, R. (1991). The functional significance of problem behavior: a key to effective treatment. *The Habilitative Mental Healthcare Newsletter*, **10**, 59–63.

Lowry, M. & Sovner, R. (in press). Severe behavior problems associated with rapid cycling bipolar disorder in two adults with profound mental retardation. *Journal of Mental Deficiency Research*.

Mace, F. C., Page, T. J., Ivancic, M. T. & O'Brien, S. (1986). Analysis of environmental determinants of aggression and disruption in mentally retarded children. *Applied Research in Mental Retardation*, **7**, 203–21.

Martin, P. L. & Foxx, R. M. (1973). Victim control of aggression of an institutionalized retardate. *Journal of Behavior Therapy and Experimental Psychiatry*, **4**, 161–5.

Matson, J. L. & Gardner, W. I. (1991). Behavioral learning theory and current applications to severe behavior problems in persons with mental retardation. *Clinical Psychology Review*, **11**, 175–83.

McNally, R. J. & Ascher, L. M. (1987). Anxiety disorders in mentally retarded people. In L. Michelson & L. M. Ascher (eds.) *Anxiety and Other Disorders*, pp. 379–394. New York: Guilford Press.

Morrow, L. W. & Presswood, S. (1984). The effects of a self-control technique on eliminating three stereotypic behaviors in a multiply-handicapped institutionalized adolescent. *Behavior Disorders*, **9**, 247–53.

Oliver, C. & Head, D. (1990). Self-injurious behavior in people with learning disabilities: determinants and interventions. *International Review of Psychiatry*, **2**, 101–16.

Repp, A. C., Felce, D. & Barton, L. E. (1988). Basing the treatment of stereotypic and self-injurious behaviors on hypotheses of their causes. *Journal of Applied Behavior Analysis*, **21**, 281–9.

Schroeder, S. R. (ed.) (1990). *Ecobehavioral Analysis and Developmental Disabilities*. New York: Springer-Verlag.

Sovner, R. (1986). Limiting factors in the use of DSM-III criteria with mentally ill/mentally retarded people. *Psychopharmacological Bulletin*, **22**, 1055–9.

Sovner, R. & Hurley, A. (1984). The role of the medical model in psychiatry. *Psychiatric Aspects of Mental Retardation Reviews*, **3**, 45–8.

Sovner, R. & Hurley, A. (1986). Managing aggressive behavior: a psychiatric approach. *Psychiatric Aspects of Mental Retardation Reviews*, **5**, 16–21.

Sovner, R. & Hurley, A. (1990). Affective disorder update. *Habilitative Mental Healthcare Newsletter*, **9**, 103–8.

Thompson, T. (1988). Prevention and early treatment of behavior disorders of children and youth with retardation and autism. In J. A. Stark, F. J. Menolascino, M. H. Albarelli & V. C. Gray (eds.), *Mental Retardation and Mental Health: Classification, Diagnosis, Treatment, Services*, pp. 98–105. New York: Springer-Verlag.

17

Anger management training: a self-control programme for persons with mild mental retardation

BETSEY A. BENSON

Introduction

In the United States, the process of community integration of persons with mental retardation has proceeded steadily since the 1970s, resulting in the closure of many large institutions and the transfer of persons to smaller homes in the community (Lakin *et al.*, 1982). The integration process has heightened the need for methods of dealing with aggressive and disruptive behaviour as there is less tolerance for it in the community and less staff capability in dealing with it in the new settings (Jacobson & Schwartz, 1983; Thiel, 1981). Anger outbursts and aggressive behaviour are among the most frequent reasons that persons with mental retardation are referred for outpatient mental health services (Benson, 1985).

Methods of dealing with the aggressive behaviour of persons with mental retardation have relied, for the most part, on drug treatments or behaviour management of the aggressive behaviour through punishment procedures (Gardner & Cole, 1984). Although punishment techniques have been found effective in suppressing maladaptive behaviours, limitations have been noted in the generalisation of control from one setting to another and ethical issues have been raised about the use of aversive techniques (Harris & Ersner-Hershfield, 1978). Self-control procedures in which the individual self-manages behaviour offers an alternative to externally controlled management techniques. Self-control training offers the potential for greater transfer of training from one situation to another and, in addition, reduces staff time in implementing behavioural programmes.

The Anger Management Training (AMT) Programme (Benson, 1992) described in this chapter is one method for instructing individuals in self-control techniques and can be accompanied by other individual or group interventions to manage problem behaviours. The following sections describe the theoretical basis for the programme, the components of the training, research on its effectiveness, and needed future developments.

Model of anger arousal

The AMT Programme was developed for persons with mental retardation and was based on the work of Raymond Novaco with non-retarded adults (Novaco, 1975; 1978). Novaco's cognitive–behavioural model of anger arousal includes four components: the external events; an internal, cognitive labelling process; the emotional arousal of anger; and the behavioural reaction. The external events are viewed as affecting the individual experience of anger indirectly through a cognitive filtering or labelling process. It is at this point that events are appraised and may be identified as threatening to the individual. Events viewed as threatening or as provocations may be reacted to with the emotional arousal that is called 'anger'. The anger experience may culminate in a variety of behavioural reactions, including aggression or withdrawal.

Intervention programmes for nonretarded children and adults

The anger control programme Novaco developed was based on this model of anger arousal and included relaxation training, self-instructional training and problem-solving skills (Novaco, 1978). Research reports indicated that the training was effective with a variety of nonretarded adults including a depressed man, probation counsellors, and persons with general anger control problems (Novaco, 1977; 1980; 1975, respectively).

Programmes to improve self-control skills have also been developed for non-retarded children. Camp *et al.* (1977) worked with aggressive boys using the 'think aloud' programme to reduce impulsive responding. Self-instructional training and problem solving of impersonal and interpersonal problems was included in individual training of 6–8 year old aggressive boys with positive results.

Saylor, Benson and Einhaus (1985) reported a study completed with emotionally disturbed boys in an inpatient setting. A cognitive–behavioural intervention was designed to reduce aggressive behaviour and included relaxation, adaptive self-statements, and role playing of problem situations. In comparison to a placebo control condition, the treated boys showed improvement in self-reported anger, but teacher and staff ratings did not indicate significant group differences.

226

Cognitive–behavioural treatments for aggressive behaviour in non-retarded children and adults have yielded promising results. In most cases, a combination of treatment techniques has been used, making it difficult to determine which components are responsible for the positive effects, if any, that were achieved.

Anger management training programme components

The AMT Programme (Benson, 1992) was modified from interventions developed for nonretarded children and adults with adaptations to meet the developmental level of the adult with mental retardation while taking into account his/her work and living environments. The programme is designed for a group therapy format, although it has been used in individual training. In a group format, the programme includes 15 weekly sessions, each lasting 90 minutes. The groups generally include 6–8 participants and two group leaders. An outline of the session topics is included in Table 17.1.

Appropriate group members include persons functioning in the mild to moderate range of mental retardation who are verbal and recognise that anger outbursts and aggressive behaviour are creating problems for themselves. Prospective group members are first screened during an individual interview. Persons who are hallucinating, who do not respond to the interview questions, or who have difficulty completing a self-report anger inventory are not accepted into the group, but may be seen in individual anger management training, if appropriate. Although many person with anger control problems tend to place the blame on others for their difficulties ('I wouldn't have hit her with my cane if she hadn't changed the time of the meeting'), they frequently state that they are not satisfied with the current situation. Taking responsibility for the problem behaviours is not required for the person to be accepted into the training program.

The group sessions follow a consistent pattern each week. The session begins with a review of the previous session and the homework assignment. This is followed by the introduction of the major topic of the session by the group leaders. It may include a minilecture or a demonstration. Group members then practice the skill and receive feedback from the group leaders and other group members. Reviewing a videotape of role playing may be part of the feedback. A homework assignment is then given for the next week.

There are four components of the AMT Programme: identification of

Table 17.1. *Anger management training session outline*

Session	Topic
1	Introduction and rationale, identification of emotions
2	Identification of emotions and introduction to relaxation training
3	Relaxation training
4	Relaxation training with role playing I
5	Relaxation training with role playing II
6	Introduction to self-instructional training
7	Self-instructional training with role playing I
8	Self-instructional training with role playing II
9	Self-instructional training with role playing III
10	Self-instructional training silently
11	Introduction to problem solving
12	Problem-solving skills I
13	Problem-solving skills II
14	Problem-solving and preparation for termination
15	Review and termination

feelings; relaxation training; self-instructional training; and problem-solving skills. The identification of feelings phase was included in the training because it has been found that persons with mental retardation may have difficulty identifying emotions (Maurer & Newbrough, 1987). Identification of feelings is an important prerequisite skill for anger management because individuals are asked to use self-control techniques when they are angry, and preferably when they are first becoming angry. The recognition of one's angry feelings is necessary for that to occur.

Identification of feelings

The identification of feelings phase of the training includes discussion of basically three feeling states: happy, sad, and angry. Group members are asked to think of situations or events in which they have experienced the feelings (What things make you feel happy?) and to identify the feelings they might have if certain events occurred (How would you feel if your best friend moved away?) (Ludwig & Hingsburger, 1989). Daily monitoring of moods is introduced and group members are given the homework assignment to complete a mood check form daily. Discussion in subsequent weekly meetings includes reviewing the completed homework assignment and drawing attention to the connections between the feelings experienced and events. Group members sometimes add notes about events or relabel the faces to provide a broader array of feelings, from sad to disappointed, for example.

It seems important to discuss other feelings in addition to anger because for some individuals, sad feelings are associated with aggressive behaviour and because discussing other feelings places anger in the context of other emotions. It is emphasised that anger is a natural feeling that everyone has at times and that it is not anger that causes problems, but the things people do when they are angry that may get them into trouble at work or at home.

Relaxation training

The second phase of the programme is relaxation training. Group members are taught a tension-release method of relaxation (Bernstein & Borkovec, 1973) with ten muscle groups. Group leaders model the exercises and physically guide the group members, if necessary. After several sessions of group practice, individual members are given an audio cassette tape of the exercises to practise at home. In later sessions, relaxation training is practised during role playing of anger-arousing situations. Individuals are encouraged to notice if they experience tension in a particular part of the body when upset. Group members sometimes report that they notice tension in their stomach, their neck and shoulders, or their forehead. These bodily signs of tension can function as cues to use the self-control techniques. Group members are encouraged to 'Get the signals' that their body is sending them and try to relax.

There are many methods of achieving relaxation. The tension-release method was chosen for the AMT Programme because of the ease of training and the ability of the group leader to verify that the exercise is being completed as requested. In addition, tension is a natural ac-companiment of anger. To ask group members to tense muscles allows them to do what is already happening to them when they become upset. At a later stage, the tense muscles can serve as a signal to use the relaxation skills.

Some individuals find the sensations associated with the muscle tension relaxation to be unpleasant, or, due to physical handicaps, have difficulty completing some portion of the exercises. Adaptations can be made to the standard routine (Cautela & Grodin, 1979) or alternative methods of relaxation may be used. One individual in AMT preferred to imagine a favourite song when he became upset, for example.

Self-instructional training

The next phase of the programme includes training in self-instructions. This component focuses on increasing coping self-statements during problem situations. Group members are taught a discrimination between coping statements and 'trouble statements' and practise coping statements during role playing of problem situations. The practice progresses in a stepwise fashion from the group leader repeating the coping statements out loud, another group member repeating the statements, the group member repeating out loud, and then the group member saying the statements silently during role playing of problem situations. Group members are encouraged to choose their own coping statements. Some of the statements chosen include, 'Take it easy', 'Be cool', 'Stay calm', and 'Relax'.

When training in self-instructions begins, group members are usually not aware of the types of self-statements that they customarily use. As practice continues with the coping statements, however, individuals sometimes report noticing that they have been thinking trouble statements in situations in which they have become upset.

In Novaco's anger control training, situations are divided into four steps, two preparatory stages, the incident, and the aftermath (Novaco, 1975). Individuals repeat different self-statements for each stage. This model was too difficult for many of the adults with mental retardation who were seen for anger management training, although it could prove useful for some. The preparatory stages are most helpful when one can anticipate a stressful event.

Problem-solving skills

The final phase of the AMT programme is training in problem-solving skills. This is perhaps the most difficult section of the training because the focus becomes more abstract and therefore more difficult for many persons. A four-step problem- solving process is introduced, similar to that used by Camp *et al.* (1977). The steps include: What is the problem? What potential solutions are there? Choose a solution and follow a plan. How did I do?

In the first step of problem solving, defining the problem, group members are asked to define the problem in objective, concrete terms from both person's point of view. Perspective taking is often difficult for persons with mental retardation (Leahy, Balla & Zigler, 1982). Role playing can sometimes be helpful in improving group members' ability to look at a problem from more than one point of view. To start out the discussion on defining a problem, group leaders may role play a problem situation and then ask group members to define the problem.

When discussing the solutions to a problem, group leaders encourage 'brain storming' to generate multiple problem solutions without evaluating them at first. Persons with anger management problems often have difficulty generating multiple solutions to problems. The group leaders contribute more suggestions initially until the group members become more proficient in problem solving. When choosing a solution, group members are asked to anticipate the consequences of each of the alternatives that were listed in step 2. Many group members are aware that aggressive behaviour results in negative consequences. Once a solution is selected, group members practise performing it in the group. It cannot be assumed that individuals know how to put the solution into effect. The verbal and nonverbal aspects of the interaction are addressed, what the person says as well as how he/she says it. The last step is 'How did I do'? This step is designed as a 'looking back' stage in which one reviews the outcome and determines if the problem was solved satisfactorily. It is also a point at which to avoid the trouble statements that were dealt with in the self-instructions phase of the programme. Individuals are encouraged to give themselves a 'pat on the back' if the situation turned out well and to try again if it did not turn out as expected.

The group leaders demonstrate each phase of the problem-solving process and group members practise solving problems during role playing of anger-arousing situations. Individuals who have difficulty with the four-step process of analysing situations may benefit from practising several 'If ... then' guides for behaviour. They can practise what to do if a particular situation occurs. For example, 'if another worker keeps bothering me by talking to me while I am supposed to be working, then I will tell the supervisor'. The individual would practise what to say to the supervisor and how to say it.

Research and future developments

The AMT programme was evaluated in a research study in which four groups were compared, a relaxation training group, a self-instructions group, a problem-solving group, and a combined anger management condition (Benson, Rice, & Miranti, 1986). The results suggested that each component of the programme, as well as the combined programme can have therapeutic effects on adults with mental retardation.

Additional research is necessary to establish the effectiveness of the programme, to identify the contribution of the individual components of the training to the programme's success, and to identify subject variables that predict a positive response to the training. Longer term follow-up of programme participants is also indicated to inform about the durability of behaviour changes and also to examine if improvement continues beyond the training phase.

Research of a more basic nature is also needed. A substantial body of research has been conducted on social-cognitive factors in the functioning of non-retarded, aggressive children (e.g. Dodge, 1980; Dodge & Newman, 1981; Dodge & Somberg, 1987). The studies have found that aggressive boys display a hostile, attributional bias when interpreting ambiguous events involving peers. The bias is thought to influence the aggressive boys' responding and to reinforce a cycle of aggressive behaviour. Research conducted with adults with mental retardation is needed to determine if similar processes are operating with aggressive individuals. If so, there are implications for intervention programmes. One would want to address the interpretation bias and include specific training in perspective taking and empathy, for example. The findings from this type of basic research could be useful in prevention efforts as well.

Summary

The application of cognitive–behavioural techniques to the psychological treatment of persons with mental retardation is in its infancy. However, this approach to treatment holds out the promise of remediating problems while at the same time increasing personal control. As adjuncts to other interventions or as treatments in their own right, the field of mental retardation is bound to hear more about cognitive therapies in the future.

References

Benson, B. A. (1985). Behavior disorders and mental retardation: Associations with age, sex, and level of functioning in an outpatient clinic sample. *Applied Research in Mental Retardation*, **6**, 79–85.

Benson, B. A. (1992). *Teaching Anger Management to Persons with Mental Retardation*. Worthington, OH: International Diagnostic Systems.

Benson, B. A., Rice, C. J. & Miranti, S. V. (1986). Effects of anger management training with mentally retarded adults in group treatment. *Journal of Consulting and Clinical Psychology*, **54**, 728–9.

Bernstein, D. & Borkovec, T. (1973). *Progressive Relaxation Training: A Manual for the Helping Professions*. Champaign, IL: Research Press.

Camp, B. W., Blom, G. E., Herbert, F. & Van Doorninck, W. (1977). 'Think aloud': A program for developing self-control in young aggressive boys. *Journal of Abnormal Child Psychology*, **5**, 157–69.

Cautela, J. R. & Grodin, J. (1979). *Relaxation: A Comprehensive Manual for Adults, Children, and Children with Special Needs*. Champaign, IL: Research Press.

Dodge, K. A. (1980). Social cognition and children's aggressive behavior. *Child Development*, **51**, 162–70.

Dodge, K. A. & Newman, J. P. (1981). Biased decision making processes in aggressive boys. *Journal of Abnormal Psychology*, **90**, 375–9.

Dodge, K. A. & Somberg, D. R. (1987). Hostile attributional biases among aggressive boys are exacerbated under conditions of threats to the self. *Child Development*, **58**, 213–24.

Gardner, W. I. & Cole C. L. (1984). Aggression and related conduct difficulties in the mentally retarded: a multicomponent behavior mode. In S. E. Breuning, J. L. Matson & R. P. Barrett, eds. *Advances in Mental Retardation and Developmental Disabilities*, vol. 2, pp. 41–84). Greenwich, CT: JAI Press.

Harris, S. L. & Ersner-Hershfield, T. (1978). Behavioral suppression of seriously disruptive behavior in psychotic and retarded patients: a review of punishment and its alternatives. *Psychological Bulletin*, **85**, 1352–75.

Jacobson, J. W. & Schwartz, A. A. (1983). Personal and service characteristics affecting group home placement success: a prospective analysis. *Mental Retardation*, **21**, 1–7.

Lakin, K. C., Krantz, G. C., Bruininks, R. H., Clumpner, J. L. & Hill, B. K. (1982). One hundred years of data on populations of public residential facilities for mentally retarded people. *American Journal of Mental Deficiency*, **87**, 1–8.

Leahy, R. L., Balla, D. & Zigler, E. (1982). Role taking, self-image, and imitativeness of mentally retarded and nonretarded individuals. *American Journal of Mental Deficiency*, **86**, 372–9.

Ludwig, S. & Hingsburger, D. (1989). Preparation for counseling and psychotherapy: Teaching about feelings. *Psychiatric Aspects of Mental Retardation Reviews*, **8**(1).

Maurer, H. & Newbrough, J. R. (1987). Facial expressions of mentally retarded and nonretarded children: I. Recognition by mentally retarded and nonretarded adults. *American Journal of Mental Deficiency*, **91**, 505–10.

Novaco, R. W. (1975). *Anger Control: The Development and Evaluation of an Experimental Treatment*. Lexington, MA: Lexington Books.

Novaco, R. W. (1977). Stress inoculation: a cognitive therapy for anger and its application to a case of depression. *Journal of Consulting and Clinical Psychology*, **45**, 600–8.

Novaco, R. W. (1978). Anger and coping with stress. In J. P. Foreyt & D. P. Rathjen eds. *Cognitive Behavior Therapy*, pp. 135–173. New York, NY: Academic Press.

Novaco, R. W. (1980). Training of probation counselors for anger problems. *Journal of Counseling Psychology*, **27**, 385–390.

Saylor, C. F., Benson, B. A. & Einhaus, L. (1985). Evaluation of an anger management program for aggressive boys in residential treatment. *Journal of Child and Adolescent Psychotherapy*, **2**, 5–15.

Thiel, G. W. (1981). Relationship of IQ, adaptive behavior, age, and environmental demand to community-placement success of mentally retarded adults. *American Journal of Mental Deficiency*, **86**, 208–11.

18

Individual, group and family psychotherapy

SHEILA HOLLINS, VALERIE SINASON AND
SOPHIE THOMPSON

Introduction

There are 300 000 children and adults in the UK with an organically caused mental retardation/learning disability that severely affects their ability to have an independent life. In addition there are over one million children and adults with a mild mental retardation that is not caused by brain damage or chromosomal abnormality. This group are potentially able to live full independent or relatively independent lives but many have their potential eroded by environmental trauma, poverty and abuse (physical, emotional or sexual) which takes a severe emotional toll on functioning. What happens when some of these children or adults want or need help with the emotional burden their disability or environment can create?

Despite the encouraging rise in advocacy groups and the long standing involvement of art and music therapists (Heal, 1989; Cantle (formerly Buckley), 1989) and other professionals, there is still too little psychodynamic treatment offered. All too often, the emotional distress is ascribed to the disability rather than to the emotional state of the individual. Psychoanalytically informed treatment whether individual (Sinason, 1990) group treatment (Hollins & Evered, 1990) or family (Thompson 1986) is still rare. Indeed, for some, any treatment is.

Oliver, Murphy & Corbett (1987) looked at one category of emotional disturbance in children and adults with handicaps in their area. They found that of 596 self-injuring children and adults only 12 were receiving psychological treatment and one received psychoanalytic psychotherapy.

Individual psychoanalytic psychotherapy

It was in 1904 that Freud suggested 'a certain measure of natural intelligence' was a prerequisite for analysis. However, the work of the Tavistock Clinic Mental Handicap Workshop (Stokes, 1987; Sinason, 1986; Stokes & Sinason, 1992) has pinpointed the need for 'emotional' rather than cognitive intelligence. Stern's (1985) work on the inter-subjective state supports this. Severely mentally retarded children and adults (Sinason, 1986; 1992) are able to understand the meaning of time and the therapeutic task and make good use of it.

In the work at the Tavistock Clinic and at St George's Hospital, London with children and adults who are emotionally troubled and have mild, severe or profound mental and multiple handicaps we have come to several major conclusions. First, there is no level of retardation which makes someone ineligible for psychoanalytic treatment. Such therapy relies on emotional understanding, not on cognitive skills. Secondly, no mentally disabled person is disabled throughout. There will be areas of intact functioning as well as areas that can not work. What is needed is flexible provision that offers expectancy and support for the highest and lowest levels of functioning in each person.

Technical issues

The technical issues in therapy with clients having mental retardation are few.

1. Even more than other patients, those with organic or environmental handicaps require the emotional and physical attention of the therapist. They are so used to the mirror of their caretakers' eyes registering withdrawal, hurt, pity or hate that inattention, however momentary, is actively destructive.
2. Visual contact is needed for adult patients with severe and profound mental retardation in the same way as it is for children. Only a few adults with a very mild handicap can manage the usual lack of facial contact that lying on a couch involves.
3. It is no good commenting on lack of integration or disintegration if the client has no integration to begin with.
4. Where clients are functioning at an infantile level (partly due to actual deficit and partly emotional) the therapist has the function of being an auxiliary brain, someone who aids the development of thinking. This might involve filling in missing words or sentences. It only becomes

collusion if it continues long after the client would be capable of giving it up.

5. Curiosity and anger, the two most internally and externally attacked functions require extra notice. When D, aged 17, an abused multiply handicapped adolescent looked under my chair – 'You are really interested in what's under my chair:' was a necessary first step that might eventually lead to voicing more symbolic, perverse or sadistic wishes. 'You want to see what's under me' or 'you want to be where my bottom is', if said precipitously, would destroy the first attempts at infantile geography.

There has to be a transitional interpretation space where the deepest-level meaning is held by the therapist until it is safe to mention.

6. Unless an angry attack is actually dangerous, we have found it helpful to acknowledge anger in a tone that shows it is allowed to be angry. Unlike conduct-disordered delinquent non-handicapped patients who need a firm voice in such instances, retarded clients need something more facilitating.

7. Negative transference interpretations similarly can be taken in when they are said in a facilitating tone of voice. Otherwise they are experienced as direct complaints from the therapists.

8. With profoundly handicapped patients, wondering aloud at what you observe and appropriately verbalising your counter-transference is a major source for therapeutic change.

9. The levels of loss over sexuality, attachment and handicap means skilled supervision and support are needed.

Group-analytic therapy

Several authors have described initial explorations in group work with people with mental retardation (Hollins & Evered, 1990; Pantlin, 1985). Few have sustained their efforts over many years, and it has fallen to new therapists to enthuse and to write in each generation. Working with groups is challenging, but the experience of therapists both at St George's Hospital, London, and at the Tavistock Clinic, over the last decade has shown the lasting value of group interventions. In common with some other interventions with this client group, new approaches have sometimes been left to beginners, or to inadequately trained or supervised professionals. Working with people who, by definition, have more complex needs than average, demands more highly trained staff, not less. The ideal therapist is one who has become proficient and confident in the techniques of group therapy before beginning to apply them to people with mental retardation. Skilled supervision from a group analyst who is familiar with the particular demands of this client group is advisable.

Setting up a group

In a small catchment area, it is probable that most members of a group of six or eight people with mental retardation will know each other already through special schooling, clubs or social services. A 'stranger' group is thus unlikely. However, the same time and place boundaries which are traditional in an adult 'stranger' group are appropriate. The content of group discussions will reflect this ongoing social contact within the group. Confidentiality must be stressed repeatedly, but is not too difficult a concept for members to understand. It is likely to be more problematic for parents and other carers, who may be accustomed to knowing all the intimate details of an individual's life, and who sometimes resent the secrecy which the group may come to represent.

Some members may rely on their carer's support to enable them to attend regularly. It behoves the therapist to address the needs of any carers in advance to avoid the possibility that they might undermine the group after it has started. One approach is to arrange an intermediary who will liaise with any other stakeholders in the therapy, including the handicapped person when it comes to practical matters. A shortage of skilled workers may lead to this advice being ignored, and to the therapist also taking on the role of care manager, social worker or psychiatrist. The impartiality of the therapist is thus threatened, and the use of transference and counter-transference in the group compromised.

Open versus closed groups

Commitment to the group cannot be assumed in advance since it is only through membership of the group that members will understand what the group has to offer. In one group, one woman was convinced that the reason for her attendance was in some way linked to her social workers' application for her to move to a group home. The repetition of the word 'group' was very confusing for her. In the end she remained a member of the outpatient group long after she had both moved to and left the group home.

New leaders may be tempted to limit the planned duration of the group from the start. This may stem from their apprehension about being bored, or a fear that the group will encourage dependence, or a reluctance to consider the possibility of handing the group onto another therapist in the event of personal commitment waning. Some of these factors arise from the counter-transference, and the later discussion in this chapter about maternal preoccupation will shed some light on the therapist's behaviour.

Whatever the feelings in the counter-transference, the therapist's punctuality and reliability is of paramount importance, in building self esteem and a sense of being in control for each member. The group will learn from each other and, given enough time, will not only come to terms with their own real limitations, but also recognise their own unique talents. Such a process of 'joining' and 'travelling' as a group cannot be rushed, and open groups may be favoured mainly for this reason. For a realistic chance of growth and change membership of two or three years is recommended.

Although working in groups with art, music and drama is also recognised as therapeutic, our practice involves the use of spoken language even with people for whom verbalising language is very difficult. Focused be-reavement work in a group allows a combination of a traditional group-analytic approach with a more action orientated educational and guided mourning approach (Hollins & Evered, 1990). Stories told in pictures, which use colour and mime to enhance communication about feelings of grief, can be used both individually and in groups. Two therapists are an advisable minimum, with Davies (1992) recommending three therapists, thus allowing one to represent each of mother, father and the self.

Getting started

Early contributions are usually addressed to one of the therapists who are firmly placed in parental roles. Therapists are objects of much curiosity, and may find a greater measure of self disclosure is achieved than is customary in a group. Therapists are frequently more active in the beginning sessions, helping to make connections for members, and to ensure understanding. The group may seek an inordinate amount of reassurance, before they eventually settle down to the work of the group. Breaks at holiday times are useful experiences of separation and loss which will test the viability of the group, and take considerable time to recover from.

Learning to value the hesitant contribution of a fellow group member will pay dividends for each party in later life. The sense of solidarity which emerges in a successful group puts group-analytic therapy ahead of individual psychoanalytic psychotherapy for those people in whom it is indicated.

The three secrets described by Hollins and Grimer (1988) of dependence and handicap, sexuality and mortality are central. The experiences of loss associated with these themes are painful to share.

Assessment

The main requirement is an ability to stay with the group. The main exclusions are aggressive acting out behaviour, and psychosis. Neurotic and developmental difficulties are ideally suited to a group approach. Research at St George's and the Tavistock Clinic, indicates that long-term groups are more effective than shorter-term ones.

Family therapy

Most people with mental retardation live in 'family' groups, be those nuclear families, hostels, institutions, or group homes. This social and emotional context, and its influence on their development cannot be ignored when trying to provide therapy. Changing the environment with them and their 'family' participating together can be more powerful and helpful for all concerned than focusing on the individual alone.

Family therapy theories and techniques can usefully inform work with families where there is a member with mental retardation. There are some specific patterns and difficulties that these families may experience.

Ideas from family therapy

The theme of recurrent loss (Bicknell, 1983; Hollins, 1985) needs to be negotiated by each family with a member with mental retardation. Initially the loss of the 'perfect child' that did not arrive but then also the ongoing losses of failure to achieve developmental milestones, to enter normal schooling, to attain adulthood and social and sexual relationship, and often the loss of the freedom and pleasure of having grown up children who leave home. At each stage of the family life cycle more losses may need to be negotiated, as well as the usual critical periods for any family.

If the family can work through the stages of grief (from denial through the emotional phase of sadness and anger, thence to some acceptance) then it will be able to move on in a healthy way to the next stage of family life. If, however, the grieving is incomplete, then a family may get 'stuck', for example, at the stage of denial and will shop around for a cure for their disabled child; or at the stage of anger and will punish each other or the professionals or the world at large; or at sadness and become chronically sad and increasingly isolated. Then with each new loss along the way the family may become troubled and their maladaptive responses become more entrenched.

What may also frequently occur and can compound the above difficulties is the roles assigned to family members. In every family, members are unconsciously and consciously assigned roles, e.g. the dependable one, or the naughty one. This is part of normal family life and only becomes a problem if the roles are too tightly held and cannot be shed from time to time, eg. it would be healthy for the dependable one to be irresponsible occasionally. Hence if the person with mental retardation is assigned the role of 'the stupid one' in all areas of functioning, then any potential he may have is simply ignored. Another role for the person with learning disabilities may be that he is 'special'. He may be seen as the family 'pet' or the reason for the family to stay together or a foil for parental difficulties. Sometimes siblings carry the burden of having to be 'special' or particularly successful. Gath (1973) showed that of the siblings of children with Down's syndrome the eldest sister was particularly vulnerable to problems at school.

Finally, mother may be caught in the role as the only one who can manage the disabled person.

In working with families, these issues of loss, the stage of the family life cycle, and how they have managed, as well as the roles assigned to various family members can be explored. It is also worth remembering that people with mental retardation may well have an 'emotional intelligence' (Stokes & Sinason, 1992) that those with higher IQs may lack. In Carl Jung's (1970) scheme of four functions, thinking and feeling are put on one axis, and sensation and intuition on another. When people are not 'busy' with their thinking function they may be better able to use their other functions instead. Many people with mental retardation are better cued into current important emotional issues, whilst other family members are getting lost in rationalisations and intellectualisations.

Assessment of families

As with any family meeting, it is critical to engage the interest of family members (including key professionals who are part of their network) so that it is possible for all members to come and participate in what may be a traumatic but also potentially a fruitful experience. If any key people are absent, it is very difficult to make any accurate assessment of how the family functions, its strengths, its patterns of responses and its real difficulties. It may be that individuals feel too anxious, too worried about blame, too frightened to face what seems insurmountable, and hence a lot of work may need to be done before the family even meets together in one place.

Once together, the problems can be discussed, paying attention to possible losses for the family and the individuals within it, the roles assigned to members, the life cycle stage of the family. Particular attention needs to be paid to non-verbal information and the process of the interview, how the family communicates (verbally and non-verbally), the atmosphere, the alliances within the family and sub systems (parental subsystems, sibling subsystem, etc.) and the therapist's own experience of being with the family.

As well as focusing on the difficulties, assessment also needs to be made of the families coping resources:

their energy and morale
problem-solving skills
social networks
practical resources
general beliefs, e.g. religious beliefs
specific beliefs
capacity to grieve
strength of the marital bond

The literature published regarding families where there is someone with mental retardation is not very helpful, as it is often based on maternal self-reports and rarely looks at relationships or the family as a whole. However, as a brief summary, some important findings include:

(i) larger families seem to cope better. (Black, 1982).
(ii) One study (Farber, 1960) found that handicap is tolerated less well in boys and
(iii) the good marriage may be strengthened, but the strain on a weak marriage may be too great. (Black, 1982). Hence the importance of trying to assess the marital bond.

Berger and Fowles (1980) looked at families with young handicapped children and suggested four common maladaptive patterns:

1. Freezing the family at an early stage of development
2. Placing child in a role so as to deter parental conflict

3. Cross-generational alliance between handicapped child and grand-parents
4. Overinvolvement of one parent.

Freezing the family at an early stage of development seems a particularly common pattern in clinical practice. It can seem as if the alliance between mother and handicapped child is like a prolonged and pathological maternal preoccupation, with the father left on the periphery and unable to help the family move on to a more healthy triangular relationship. In normal development such physical and emotional closeness between mother and child lasts only a few months and then father helps the child with his 'otherness' to loosen this close bond and learn about other relationships. However, if the child is handicapped, the mother, father and child have their own 'reasons' for staying at this early stage, allowing the family to become stuck and unable to move on. Mother may well feel very protective of her disabled child and hold on tightly. Father may feel so wounded in his creativity that any further masculine assertive efforts may feel too risky. The child must surely sense that something terrible is wrong with him and hang onto his mother for protection and care.

One of the thrusts of therapy with a family like this is to help the family to grieve together, with each others support, for what has happened to them as a family. Another is to empower father to help the child leave his mother's protection and to mature and dare to grow up. Often it feels in therapy as if it is up to the therapist to promote this fathering principle. Frequently the professionals mirror inside themselves the family dilemma, with their 'maternal concerns' – 'poor lad he cannot help it, he needs help' in tension with their 'paternal' views – 'he must be made to grow up and behave appropriately'.

If the biological parents have died or are unavailable, the functional 'family' unit in the hostel or institution may also have difficulties in resolving 'maternal and paternal' views in providing a healthy environment in which an individual can grow and develop.

However, despite the enormous challenge which disability may pose within a family, some families do cope and seem better off for their struggle. Perhaps what we need to find out is what these coping families are doing and try to apply some of their strategies to those families who are still struggling.

Family therapy techniques can be extremely useful in helping to understand and deal with the problems that may present during the life of a family where someone has mental retardation. Different family members bring different experiences and strengths to the pool of coping resources that the family can build up as a unit. Family members often want to help but feel too troubled, or despairing or simply do not know what to do.

Family therapy and systemic thinking helps to lift the burden of the responsibility for growth for the individual to a group, the family group including the professionals. Families working as a unit, using their own shared troubles and strengths may be able to negotiate problems that are too much for an individual. Bloom (1969):

People are much greater and much stronger than we imagine, and when unexpected tragedy comes...we see them so often grow to a stature that is far beyond anything we imagined. We must remember that people are capable of greatness, of courage, but not in isolation...They need the conditions of a solidly linked human unit in which everyone is prepared to bear the burden of others.

Summary

Individual, group and family therapy all have a valuable place in the repertoire of mental health workers in the field of mental retardation. These treatments can be offered on their own or in conjunction with other interventions. It is seldom appropriate for more than one psycho-dynamically focused therapy to be offered to the same individual at any one time. Any worker proposing to make any significant change to a treatment or living programme must inform the therapist to maximise all therapeutic opportunities. Different therapeutic approaches are not in competition – resources are too scarce for that!

References

Berger & Fowles (1980). Family Intervention Project: A family network model for servicing young handicapped children. *Young Children*, **51**, 22–32.

Bicknell, D. J. (1983). The psychopathology of handicap. *British Journal of Medical Psychology*, **56**, 161–78.

Black, D. (1982). Handicap and family therapy. In A. Bentovim, G. Gorrell-Barnes, A. Cooklin, eds. *Family Therapy: Complementary Frameworks of Theory and Practice*. London: Academic Press.

Bloom, B. L. (1969). Psychotherapy and the community mental health movement. *International Psychiatric Clinics*, **6**, 235–48.

Buckley, A. (1989). Unconscious Imagery. In D. Brandon, ed. *Mutual Respect: Therapeutic Approaches to Working with People who have Learning Difficulties*. Good Impressions Pub. Ltd.

Davies, H. (1992). Group therapy. Paper presented at Centre for Studies in Mental Handicap Symposium, Glasgow.

Farber, A. (1959). Effects of a severely mentally retarded child on family integration. *Monographs of the Society for Research in Child Development*, **21** (1), Serial 75.

Gath, A. (1973). The school age siblings of mongol children. *British Journal of Psychiatry*, **123**, 161–7.

Heal, M. (1989). In tune with the mind. In D. Brandon, ed. *Mutual Respect: Therapeutic Approaches to Working with People who have Learning Difficulties*. Good Impressions Pub. Ltd.

Hollins, S. (1985). Families and Handicap. In I. Craft, J. Bicknell and S. Hollins, eds. *Mental Handicap: The Multidisciplinary Approach*, pp 140–146. London: Bailliere Tindall.

Hollins, S. & Grimer, (1988). *Going Somewhere: Pastoral Care for People with Learning disability*. London: Society for Promoting Christian Knowledge.

Hollins, S. & Evered, C. (1990). *Group Process and Content: The Challenge of Mental Handicap Group Analysis*, 23(1), 55–67

Hollins, S. & Sireling, L. (1990). When Mum Died. The Sovereign Series, St George's Mental Health Library, Department of Mental Health Sciences, St George's Hospital Medical School, London.

Hollins, S. & Sireling, L. (1991). When Dad Died. *Working through Loss with People who have Learning Disabilities. A Professional Learning Resource*. Windsor: NFER-Nelson.

Jung, C. (1970). *Mysterium Coniunctionis: An Inquiry into the Separation and Synthesis of Psychic Opposites in Alchemy. collected works, vol 14, 2nd edn.* Routledge & Kegan Paul.

Oliver, C. Murphy, G. H. & Corbett, J. A. (1987). Self-injurious behaviour in people with mental handicap: a total population study. *Journal of Mental Deficiency Research*, **31**, 147–62.

Pantlin, A. W. (1985). Group-analytic psychotherapy with mentally handicapped patients. *Group Analysis*, **XVIII**/1, 44–53.

Sinason, V. (1986). Secondary mental handicap and its relationship to trauma. *Psychoanalytical Psychology*, **2**, 131–54.

Sinason, V. (1988). Dolls and bears: from symbolic equation to symbol. *British Journal of Psychotherapy*, **4**, 4.

Sinason, V. (1990). Individual psychoanalytical psychotherapy with severely and profoundly handicapped patients. In A. Dosen, A. Van Gennep, G. Zwanniken, eds. *Treatment of Mental Illness and Behavioural Disorder in the Mentally Retarded*, pp. 71–80. The Netherlands: Logon.

Sinason, V. (1992). *Mental Handicap the Human Condition: New Approaches from the Tavistock*. London: Free Association Books.

Stern, D. N. (1985). *The Interpersonal World of the Infant, A view from Psychoanalysis and Developmental Psychology*. USA: Basic Books.

Stokes, J. (1987). Insights from psychotherapy. Paper presented at Royal Society of Medicine International Symposium on Mental Handicap. The Mental Handicap Workshop. London: Tavistock Clinic.

Stokes, J. & Sinason, V. (1992). Secondary mental handicap as a defence. In A. Waitman, ed. '*Psychotherapy and Mental Handicap*' pp. 46–59. Conboy Hills: Sage Publications.

Thompson, S. (1986). Families and mental handicap. Unpublished Dissertation. Institute of Family Therapy, London.

19

A modality for treating aggressive behaviours and sexual disorders in people with mental retardation

DIANE COX-LINDENBAUM AND
LOUIS LINDENBAUM

Introduction

Aggression and sexual offences are two of the most difficult disorders exhibited by persons with mental retardation. Sovner and Hurley (1983, 1986) stated that aggressive behaviour and 'deviant' sexual behaviour posed a threat to other clients and staff and frequently jeopardised that person's placement in the community. Gardner and Cole (1984) concur with regard to chronic aggression leading to possible institutionalisation and dismissal or exclusion from community-based vocational, educational and rehabilitation programmes.

Sovner and Hurley (1983) emphasised the importance of determining whether the behaviour is 'deviant', needing clinical treatment or whether the person with mental retardation simply needs education about his/her sexuality and sexually appropriate behaviour. Meyers (1991), suggested that there is no sexual behaviour or misbehaviour specific to persons with mental retardation.

Since aggressive behaviour and sexual disorders in people with mental retardation may result from a variety of environmental, psychological and physical factors, the treatment must be eclectic and based on a model with various components interfacing with one another to ensure a consistent therapeutic approach.

The Social Sexual Group Treatment Programme

The Social Sexual Group Treatment Programme is currently being utilised in both institutional settings and in community outpatient centres for people with mental health problems and mental retardation. It was initially developed as a result of the authors' work during the deinstitutionalisation

244

process in New York State in the middle to late 1970s. Among the population with mental retardation at that time, were a small percentage who had been referred by the Department of Mental Health and Mental Retardation as individuals who had 'sexual problems'. The assumption on the part of professionals at that time was that these people had no opportunity for sexual activity and that their acting out was merely sexual misconduct that manifested itself due to lack of knowledge and opportunity.

In fact what actually occurred at that time was that there were a few repeat sex offenders with mental retardation who had been processed through the Community Sex Education Programme and who had not been able to discontinue, modify or decrease the sexually acting out behaviours. This occurred regardless of the sex education programme, opportunities for sexual relationships or periodic sex counselling, indicating the need for a more specialised treatment programme.

The development of the Social Sexual Programme focused on group treatment and was based upon Groth's (1983) premise, that it is the primary treatment of choice for the sex offender who is isolated from his peers and whose major problem behaviours occur in the area of interpersonal peer relationships. Group therapy implies individual responsibility among its members for progress of all individuals.

Treatment assumptions

The goal of treatment is to reduce the risk of the sex offender repeating his offence (Groth, 1983). The assumptions underlying the Social Sexual Treatment Programme are:

1. Each person is born with basic needs that do not change with age: the need to love and be loved and feel worthwhile to yourself and others. Responsible behaviour means meeting one's needs without depriving others of meeting theirs. Irresponsible behaviour is meeting one's needs while depriving others of meeting theirs. Involvement with at least one other person who is successful in meeting his/her needs is the foundation for successful treatment (Glasser, 1960).
2. Sexual assault is a multidetermined act resulting from the interaction of both internal psychological determinants and external factors.
3. Sexual assault is the result of early deprivation in the failure to receive consistent love, support and discipline and a consequence of early neglect, maltreatment and sexual abuse.

4. Sexual assault is the acting out of some unresolved developmental issue and as a symptom is an indicator of psychological distress. Although self-defeative and self-perpetuating, it does defend against anxiety, expresses a conflict and gratifies an impulse.
5. Sexual assault is an interpersonal act involving both sexuality and aggression and as such it is the sexual expression of aggression whereby non-sexual needs, motives and issues are sexually expressed.
6. For treatment to be successful there needs to be changes in the offender's internal psychological state as well as the external environment.

Treatment goals

The task of the Social Sexual Treatment Programme is to assist the sex offender in achieving the following goals (Groth, 1983).

1. To recognise and acknowledge that he does have a problem through an understanding of his symptoms.
2. To accept responsibility for his actions.
3. To reevaluate his attitudes and values towards sexuality and aggression.
4. To realise that sexual assaultiveness is repetitive/compulsive behaviour over which he must gain control.

The offender must not only realise he has a problem but also do something about it by developing more effective ways of dealing with his problems and the stresses of life. There needs to be an attitudinal change by appreciating the inappropriateness of sexual aggression on both the victim and himself before a behavioural change can occur. The offender has to view his problems as chronic with the need for lifelong treatment since the problem can be treated, not cured, controlled, not eliminated (Groth, 1983).

Other goals with which the group leaders in the Social Sexual Treatment Programme assist the clients are: (1) to assess, describe and accept personal, intellectual, emotional and behavioural strengths and weakness; (2) to define realistic personal goals; (3) to develop and implement action strategies to reach personal goals; (4) to experiment in the group setting with alternative behavioural strategies available in pursuit of personal objectives; (5) to appropriately communicate personal needs and feelings to others; (6) to seek help when feeling overcome rather than acting out feelings of frustration, anger and helplessness; (7) to accept responsibility for own behaviour rather than making excuses or placing blame outside oneself; (8) to gain control over situations in these areas which are possible and accept limitations in those areas where control is not possible at the time; (9) to accept obstacles and setbacks as real events to be overcome as opposed to making them excuses for quitting.

The Social Sexual Group Treatment Programme has always been viewed as part of a more comprehensive treatment approach for sex offenders with a mental retardation. That is, the treatment methods are eclectic with group therapy supplemented by individual therapy, behaviour techniques and psychiatric intervention.

The Social Sexual Group Treatment Programme addresses the cognitive limitations, perceptual distortions and personality deficits of the sex offenders with mental retardation as part of the treatment model.

Philosophy and paradigms

In the realm of human sexuality, whether in counselling or education, the primary goal is the preparation of people to cope with their internal sexual pressures and self-image in order to deal with the social and environmental impact of sexuality that impinges upon them day after day. At the heart of meeting the needs of the human growth and self-actualisation is the need to learn problem solving. However, before becoming competent problem solvers, individuals need to feel 'in control' and 'responsible'.

Specialists who treat sex offenders reject the word 'cure', drawing a parallel between sex offenders and persons who have long term addictive patterns of behaviour. Wolfe (1981) suggests the word 'control' and not 'cure' referring to the effects of treatment.

The Social Sexual Treatment Group approach is intended to meet the special needs of the sex offender with mental retardation by enabling the person to increase his own sense of power by taking responsibility for his behaviour while integrating newly learned skills through cognitive restructuring and relearning. Cognitive therapy increases the client's knowledge about himself and helps the person manage his emotions while psychotherapy helps the client to integrate that knowledge and utilise it experientially through the group therapy process.

Assumptions that all acting out sexually assaultive behaviours are merely 'self-indulgent, erotic behaviours' must be denied and therapists must try to work in a holistic treatment approach by allowing the clients the opportunity to enrich their life and meet their basic needs through involvement and responsibility.

The two paradigms utilised in the Social Sexual Group Treatment Programme are 'Mastery of Affect – Growth Cycle' and 'You Can't Think If You Can't Feel' (Hurtson, 1975).

The Growth Cycle consists of the following components: anxiety, depression, anger, crying and joy. Conflict initially generates anxiety which then leads to depression if the person can get beyond the anxiety and acknowledge the issue/conflict. With full acceptance of the work necessary to change and the ambivalence connected to it, anger becomes the paramount feeling. Assisting the person through the anger in the therapeutic process results in the crying stage which according to this paradigm is not part of depression but rather tears that may lead to the feeling of joy in resolving an issue/conflict in the person's life. There may be a subcycle between any two stages related to another issue/conflict connected to the first which may need to be dealt with before further work can be done on the major issue/conflict. The subcycle has the same components as the Growth Cycle. To master the affect is the process by which feelings are not tolerable are rendered tolerable by experience.

The second paradigm of not being able to think if you cannot feel is connected to the Mastery of Affect paradigm. In this paradigm the objective of the therapy process is to assist the person to talk about his feelings, to think about his feelings rather than repress them or act out. Any action that is taken is then fully understood with regard to either positive impact or harmful effects. Since the goal of the Social Sexual Treatment Programme is to assist the sex offender to control his assaultive/aggressive behaviours then it is imperative that he process his feelings by thinking about and understanding them before taking any action which may lead to harm for himself and/or others.

Methodology and criteria for admission

Following a comprehensive social sexual assessment, clients are placed in a group consisting of 8–10 members representing both sexes. This initial larger group size is to allow for a consistent drop out rate. Members should have similarities in chronological age, functioning levels and treatment needs. Group meetings should be scheduled weekly for one hour with strict time keeping. The group should meet in a setting conductive to therapeutic interchange which ensures privacy and confidentiality. There should be two therapists, preferably a male and a female.

Criteria for admission to the group are:

1. Client should be able to participate in the group process and be able to tolerate one hour sessions.
2. Client has a pattern of high anxiety related to a stressful situation. This may be manifested in loud, aggressive verbalisation, explosive/aggressive behaviour, disconnected thought process, perseverative behaviour, self-abuse, persisting psychosomatic complaints, repetitive movements.
3. Client should have a potential for developing alternative coping mechanisms.
4. Fair to good ability to communicate verbally.
5. Fair to good attention and concentration.
6. Deficits in social/personal interactive skills.
7. Conflicts in male/female and/or male/male relationships.
8. Inappropriate sexual behaviour and/or fear or anxiety during social/sexual interactions.
9. Low self-esteem as manifested in poor personal appearance, un-assertiveness, and lack of consideration for the rights of others.
10. Destructive or self-defeating social interactions which lead to social isolation and/or interpersonal rejection by others.

The process of group – Getting started – The contract

The primary goal of the Social Sexual Group Treatment Programme is to enable its members to take responsibility for their behaviour. The leader begins by noting that they will all be meeting together to explore issues which have proven to be problems or obstacles to success with the intent of resolving them. Before they can start looking at such issues, however, it is necessary to establish the 'group rules' that will ensure that the meetings are safe and useful for all concerned. The leader then invites the group to reflect on past, similar experiences each has had and identify types of problems they have encountered which prevented effective working. As concerns are raised, each is examined/discussed to clarify and subsequently to determine what guidelines the group wants to establish in order to avoid the problem. Over time, the leader encourages the group going further into emotional areas – what is frightening and hurtful – and support the group in establishing boundaries that provide security.

Typical concerns to be addressed include: physical violence; absence; lateness; anticipating toilet needs and refreshment needs; leaving in the middle of group; handling strong feelings; emotional withdrawal within the group; emotional violence; sleeping, writing/reading in group; and so on. Also, expressions of strong feelings – is it okay? If so, how? Acting out versus verbalising feelings.

It is the leader's responsibility to ensure that his and the group's needs for safety are met. He will maintain every boundary established and ensure all limits or guidelines are agreed to by everyone (leader included).

The initial process is typically lengthy, sometimes taking a few sessions, for the members are naive communicators and tend to mishear, argue and resist, often acting on authority issues or simply testing the leader. The leader's role is to facilitate the process by ensuring (1) each speaker is heard and responded to before moving on; (2) the topic is adhered to and kept clear; (3) no 'dirty dynamics', such as name calling, intrude; (4) each speaker speaks for himself and to the topic and (5) that consensus is achieved fully and only after everyone is clear with no railroading or expediencies allowed since such decisions would not have any binding power. In addition, the leader prevents any emotional work on personal or interpersonal issues until the group is ready, i.e. only after 'contract' is fully negotiated.

There are only a few imposed limits – no physical violence to person or property. It must be clear from the outset that such limits are non-negotiable. The group seeks to have a clear understanding of the reasons for the limits, and might work with anyone anticipating problems in honouring the limits.

Once boundaries are determined, the group moves on to discuss its specific goals. In much the same vein as determining guidelines, the group members raise the kinds of things they would like to get out of group. Keeping in mind behaviours related to sexual issues and aggression which brought them to the group, the leader facilitates the group to work on goals related to these issues. The task here is to ensure clarity in each member's mind about what is okay and what is not okay to raise and to talk about. Again, full consensus is required.

The final step to be addressed is how the group wants to go about pursuing the goals. Procedures such as speaking one at a time, holding back on an issue if someone is already working, giving feedback, talking about blaming others versus dealing with self, would be discussed. The leader here works to keep encounter, projecting, failing to checkout assumptions, and so on, out of group.

Once the contract is clear and established, the group can begin with personal issues. The entire contracting process may well take two, three or even four weeks. The leader must be careful to prevent his anxieties about 'getting stuff done' from short-circuiting the process.

There is a two-fold purpose for this concentration on contracting at the beginning. The first has been noted – safety. The procedure outlined gives each member the opportunity to establish his own boundaries so as to protect his own territory from anticipated hurt and anxieties stemming from unknown dragons are reduced. This state of safety remains so long as the leader consistently maintains the agreed-upon limits.

The second purpose is to minimise initial risk-taking by keeping the focus off personal issues and on more 'distant' ones. Moreover, through the negotiating process, the leader is teaching effective group member skills such as thinking, listening, responding, deferring gratifications, etc. By the time the group begins dealing with personal issues, the chances of accidents through bad dynamics is to some degree reduced.

The Treatment Programme

The Social Sexual Group Treatment Programme is one part of a total treatment process which may also include individual therapy and psycho-pharmacological intervention. Clinical intervention is based on cognitive modules derived from the initial assessment. The cognitive modules are not classroom instruction but rather the presentation of didactic material and the integration of this information through an interpersonal dynamic process.

The 'Social Sexual Evaluation Profile' (Perroncel, 1989) was used during the initial assessment to assist in identifying the psychological deficits and strengths of the client. It showed that many clients had poor social skills, lack of knowledge about sexuality and poor judgment and these deficits provide the content for the cognitive modules utilised in treatment. In addition, we found that the offender lacks the capability for bonding with peers. The group process should enable development of social skills and fostering of intimate relationships. The structure of these didactic exercises sets the foundation on which to build the experiential process. Through sharing amongst the group members, the bonding process occurs allowing each client to identify stressors and patterns of self-destructive behaviours, to explore some responsible alternative behaviours and to connect and be intimate with peers in a socially appropriate manner.

Treatment focuses on the developmental life cycle of the person with mental retardation who has learned to use sex and violence dysfunctionally as an expression of his inner conflicts and stress. The programme examines his disability as a source of his alienation from society and one of the sources for his feeling of rage.

It is the authors' clinical assumption that sexually violent behaviours are complex and require a multifaceted treatment approach. These behaviours represent underlying psychological differences and are manifested in impaired social–sexual relationships. The most prevalent issue of sex offenders whether having mental retardation or not, is the visible absence of close, emotionally intimate relationships. The goal of the group process is for the client to make a connection with his peers and bond with other group members.

Treatment consists of three stages:

Stage I: Feeling identification, relaxation training and anger management.
  Stage II: Cognitive restructuring and social skills training.
  Stage III: Transition planning.

In Stage I the module begins with Feeling Identification. The appropriate labelling of feelings are essential to the understanding and identification of the antecedents of sexually aggressive behaviour. In the sex offender with mental retardation the focus is the identification and exploration of feelings of rage and shame associated with their cognitive disability. The exploration of these feelings are the experiential part of the programme. Group members share the defence mechanism of denial of their disability and any pain associated with it.

Relaxation training enables the clients to identify emotional and physical stressors and to develop techniques to reduce stress through an experiential group process.

Anger management training utilises modified version of Benson's (Benson, Rice & Miranti, 1986). This enables clients to overcome their denial and identify their anger and rage related to their disability, cognitive limitations, family dysfunction, own victimisation, restrictive placement and sense of powerlessness. Through assertiveness training, understanding one's own feelings and self destructive behaviour, the client learns to control his emotions and find more appropriate, responsible ways of expressing these feelings.

Cognitive restructuring, Stage II helps clients explore their own self destructive cycles and their perceptual distortions through self-examination. This phase addresses their emerging sense of depression and loss, their alienation and rejection of peers as an expression of their own self hate. It aims to increase awareness and promote acceptance of responsibility for one's own sexual behaviour.

Social skills training addresses the client's fear and anxiety with peer interaction and sexual identity. Goals are to develop communication skills, enhance interpersonal relationships with peers and assertiveness training.

Stage III involves transition planning. During this stage of treatment the client identifies coping strategies, recognises safety cues, recognises and overcomes distortions, accepts dependency issues and utilises supportive peer interactions in a positive way. The ability to accept one's dual diagnosis and commitment to manage it though the participation in the treatment process becomes the focus of the programme with regard to aftercare. Prevention of relapse is an integral part of the transitional planning process.

Summary

Sexual assault is complex and multidetermined. A multidisciplinary approach and interagency cooperation is needed to address this problem. Treating aggressive behaviours and sexual disorders in people with mental retardation involves a variety of psychodynamic, behavioural, cognitive and pharmacological elements including a wide range of educational and training components.

The Social Sexual Group Programme is a crucial component for the multidisciplinary approach to treatment of sexual disorders. The group leaders must be well trained and feel comfortable with their own feelings in relation to the clients who manifest explosive, aggressive and sexually assaultive behaviours.

Treating sex offenders with mental retardation poses a major challenge to the therapist, the client and the community. The responsibility on the part of the therapist is building a therapeutic alliance with and among the group members and the issues involved in the treatment are unique.

The treatment takes into account their cognitive limitations and incorporates it in addressing the underlying emotional issues and consequent dysfunctional sexual acting out behaviours.

The Social Sexual Group Treatment Programme teaches the clients to be responsible for their own behaviour, for what they have done, for restitution and for changing their own behaviour. The person learns that the therapists and other group members care and that help is available which develops a feeling of self-worth for the individual for perhaps the first time in his life.

References

Benson, B. A., Rice, C. J. & Miranti, S. V. (1986). Effects of anger management training with mentally retarded adults in group treatment. *Journal of Consulting and Clinical Psychology*, **154**, 728–9.

Glasser, W. (1960). *Mental Health or Mental Illness?* New York: Harper & Row.

Gardner, W. I. & Cole, C. L. (1984). Aggression and related conduct difficulties in the mentally retarded: a multicomponent behaviour model. In Breuning, S. E., Matson, J. L., Barrett, R. P., eds. *Advances in Mental Retardation and Developmental Disabilities: A Research Annual*, pp. 41–84. Greenwich, CT: JAI Press.

Groth, A. N. (1983). Treatment of the sex offender in a correctional institution. In J. G. Greer & I. R. Stuart, eds. *Sexual Aggression: Current Perspectives on Treatment*. New York: Van Nostrand Reinhold.

Hurston, R. (1975). Psychotherapy seminar. The Centre for Alternative Education. Boston, Massachusetts.

Meyers, B. (1991). Treatment of sexual offenses by persons with developmental disabilities. *American Journal on Mental Retardation*, **95**, 563–9.

Perroncel, C. C. (1989). *The Social Sexual Evaluation Profile*. Connecticut: Torrington.

Rivinus, T. M. (1980). Psychopharmacology and the mentally retarded Patient. In L. S. Szymanski & P. B. Tanguay, eds. *Emotional Disorders of Mentally Retarded Persons*, pp. 195–221. Baltimore: University Park Press.

Sovner, R. & Hurley, A. D. (1983). Treatment of sexual deviation in mentally retarded persons. *Psychiatric Aspects of Mental Retardation*, **2**, 4.

Sovner, R. & Hurley, A. D. (1986). Managing aggressive behaviour: a psychiatric approach. *Psychiatric Aspects of Mental Retardation Reviews*, **5**, 4.

Szymanski, L. S. & Rosejsky, Q. B. (1980). Group psychotherapy with retarded persons. In L. S. Symanski & P. B. Tanguay, eds. *Emotional Disorders of Mentally Retarded Persons*, pp. 173–194. Baltimore: University Park Press.

Wolfe, R. (1981). Taped site-interview. In F. H. Knopp, ed. *Retraining Adult Sex Offenders: Methods and Models*. Vermont: Orwell.

20

The phenomena of playing within the process of sandplay therapy

NEHAMA T. BAUM

Introduction

This focuses on the use of play therapy and sandplay therapy in the psychotherapeutic treatment of children and adults with mental retardation and severe emotional or psychiatric disorders. The phenomena of playing, during the making of a sand picture within the process of sandplay therapy, is explored. An explanation of the methods of non-directive play therapy and sandplay therapy is made to demonstrate, that in spite of different theoretical frameworks, these two modalities have a lot in common and can become intertwined during the therapeutic process.

More and more psychotherapists who work with people with mental retardation realise that doing therapy with this population differs very little from doing therapy with 'normal' people.

Hellendoorn (1990) suggested that play therapy might be particularly suitable for people with mental retardation because 'play provides them with a relatively free and safe environment to express experiences and problems'. Baum (1990) demonstrated the effectiveness of sandplay therapy, a Jungian-based psychotherapeutic modality, in the treatment of people with developmental handicaps and mental illness. One might conclude that through these modalities, the stories of the rich inner life of children and adults with mental retardation can be told and their deep therapeutic process can be clearly noticed.

Play therapy

Children naturally use play as a tool for learning and expression. The acquisition of cognitive, interpersonal and social skills are all naturally played out by children. Children also realise naturally that through play they have the opportunity to act out situations and express feelings, problems and life issues.

It was a natural development for therapeutic modalities to utilise the child's natural affinity for play. It was not surprising that therapists have started also to use play therapy with children and adults with retardation. In a somewhat reductionist way, it was assumed that since people with retardation have mental abilities comparable to younger children, play therapy would be suitable to their 'child-like' mental age. In spite of this attitude, this acceptance of the commonality and suitability of play therapy for this population opened the door to therapeutic interventions with children and adults with retardation even in programmes which were behavioural in philosophy.

Play therapy has developed along two main directions. In directive play therapy the therapist is the director and instructor of the therapeutic process. He/she guides the client, assuming responsibility for the process itself and provides ongoing interpretations of the out-played issues.

Non-directive play therapy implies that the therapist does not control the therapeutic process. He/she leaves the total responsibility for the process and its direction to the client. Thus, instead of being the instructor of the client he/she becomes the companion in the unfolding of the client's path.

Axline (1969) explains the foundation of non-directive play therapy. Her modality is based on Rogerian humanistic therapeutic principles which put the client at the centre of the therapeutic process (Rogers, 1951). Within the framework of Rogerian therapy, it is believed that in each individual there seems to be a force which continuously strives for self-actualisation and fulfilment. Non-directive play therapy is based on these principles. It puts trust in the process of change which occurs through the provision of a safe play environment. In it, a person can allow him/herself to act out through play any emotions, external life situations or inner conflicts.

Sandplay therapy

The principle, which entrusts the client with the responsibility for the therapeutic process and the resulting change, is shared by other therapeutic disciplines. One might be cautioned that the statement that the therapist is not the one who carries the responsibility for change, but rather that this responsibility lies with the client, might sound to be similar to some behavioural approaches. In such approaches the client is called to behaviourally comply, as part of his/her responsibility, with external demands for behavioural change. That is, the locus of control for change is maintained externally and the therapist continues to be the one who is in charge of the therapeutic process and the only responsibility the client carries is the responsibility to comply.

Sandplay therapy is a non-directive form of playing. Playing in the sand gives permission for the imaginative freedom to be expressed in the process of creation. This imaginative freedom contains all the positive and negative; all the external successes and failures and the internal feelings about them; all conscious life experiences and all unconscious psyche issues. Sandplay therapy is a 'pathway to the psyche' as the client is able to play in a 'free and protected space' (Kalff, 1980).

Upon entering a sandplay therapy room, one gets a somewhat different impression from that of a regular play therapy room. It has hundreds and hundreds of various figurines (toys) placed on shelves. In the room there are also two sandtrays which become the stage for the unfolding inner dramas a client might express. The trays have very specific dimensions ($19\frac{1}{2}'' \times 28\frac{1}{2}'' \times 3$) which allow the therapist to observe the tray at a glance. The toys represent every possible figurine to allow for the creation of most inner and external life situations. The therapist is a companion to, rather than a controller of, the therapy process. This gives the client the opportunity to be whom ever he/she wants to be, and to do whatever he/she wants to do within the boundaries of this 'free and protected space'.

This space becomes the container for the individual. It is free in that a person can create anything he/she, consciously or unconsciously, needs to express. It is protected because its physical dimensions and the concreteness of the figurines provide the safe container within which the person's fantasy can be held. Thus the freedom to unload onto either the dry or wet sandtrays any conscious or unconscious aspect of life is grounded by the safe and limited physical reality of the tray and the figurines.

Weinrib (1983) says that, by arranging the figurines in the tray in the course of making a picture, and by having the possibility of looking at the tray at a glance without moving the eyes, the person relates to the tray as a container which has the effect of 'focusing and then reflecting back the (person's) inner vision'. In addition to this effect of the tray, the concrete, three-dimensional realistic figurines give form to still unconscious inner images. Thus, in this safe space, i.e. the tray, healing of the inner psychological and emotional wound can occur. Whatever place the individual reaches through this process, the psyche is touched and healing takes place.

Weinrib spoke about people with normal intellectual functioning. Can we assume that these processes will also evolve in therapy with people with developmental handicaps (mental retardation)? Many professionals have debated the notion of the suitability of such in-depth analytical psychodynamic therapy for the population of people with developmental handicaps, stating the seemingly qualitative psychological differences between them and non-retarded persons.

Similar theoretical questions have been raised about this population (Baum, 1990) with regard to: (a) the evolvement and the constellation of the Self; (b) the course of development of ego-consciousness; (c) the effect intellectual deficiencies have on insight; and (d) the question of whether people with retardation have the ability to express themselves in the symbolic language of the unconscious or whether all their expressions are merely a reproduction of concrete elements of external events.

Although in both play and sandplay therapy the individual 'plays' with toys, sandplay therapy differs in a few aspects from play therapy. In play therapy, the child uses the toys as partners to his/her play. It is with these partners that he/she elaborates upon life situations and expresses his/her inner world, i.e. feelings and issues. Sandplay therapy, however, specifically addresses the symbolic value of the process. It perceives the figurines not only as partner-toys, but also primarily as manifestations of a person's inner reality.

If we assume that all of us, regardless of our intellectual ability, have an unconscious within which exist parts of ourselves on both the personal and archetypal-collective levels, then we have to accept that similar to people with a normal level of intelligence, persons with retardation also exist on both personal and collective levels, manifesting their archetypal images in a symbolic language. This symbolic language appears in dreams. It also appears in their sand pictures. The difference between the symbolic expression in dreams and in sandplay pictures is that in the latter, these symbols are incarnated in the manageable size and shape of the figurines, rather than the more abstract images of dreams.

It seems that the person who is engaged in creating the picture knows that the figurines may be the representations of such deep inner images and not just the expressions of concrete reality. This, according to Dundas (1990), occurs regardless of 'whether the individual understands the significance of the symbols'. She adds that by using the sandtray 'he seems to feel liberated – as the more painful, angry and confusing parts of himself surface – and at last in touch with what had been locked inside'.

With people with developmental handicaps who are deficient in their verbal abilities frequently, these inner images cannot come to consciousness in a more traditional way. Verbal language is the instrument of thought and when impoverished, the person is limited in his/her ability to explore, elaborate and reflect upon inner conscious and unconscious images and issues. Sandplay therapy bypasses this need. It enables the disabled person to experience these inner images, give them concrete form and eventually find a way to heal.

Kalff (1980) views the therapeutic process of sandplay as a natural process which occurs on the matriarchal level. She states that playing in the tray while creating sand pictures, transfers onto the tray 'unused parts of themselves or repressed parts, or personal images from the past, or archetypal images' (Bradway, 1991).

Projections of parts of oneself onto the sandtray during the making of a picture is not the sole property of people with normal ability. Similarly, people who are even extremely limited, experience the manifestation of their Self and benefit from the resulting strengthening of their ego-consciousness through the playing and the making of pictures in this matriarchal 'free and protected space.'

Kate, a 20 year old woman is a person with dual diagnosis (mental retardation and mental health problems). She is non-verbal and exper-iences physical difficulties owing to her rare handicapping condition. In one of her sandplay therapy sessions she picked up a cat, which she used most frequently in her play, and a roadrunner. In her play, the roadrunner was pushing the cat and forcefully squashing it into the sand. While playing this part, Kate made stress noises that were a quieter version of the screaming she usually made when she expressed her distress. She continued to act out the conflict and this time, the cat hit the roadrunner back. After playing a while, it seemed as if some reconciliation had emerged. The two figurines became 'friends'. They were moving together in the sand with the roadrunner carrying the cat on its back. Concurrently, the hitting and the yelling ceased. At the end of her play, Kate placed both figurines in a horizontal position in the sand. She appeared content, flapping her hands in a very happy gesture. With the aid of her communication book she explained that both the cat and the roadrunner 'are lying down to rest'.

She was able to feel what Bradway (1986) calls 'transformative and healing powers' that were evoked during this experience.

Understanding sand pictures

There are a few ways by which one may approach and analyse the process of sandplay therapy.

1. Sandplay pictures may be looked upon as a report of events.

Reporting of events that happened in an actual external reality may occur when the person needs to hang onto a concrete reality. At such a time the sand picture becomes the visual documentation of such an event. As in play therapy, a picture like this is a playing/acting-out of a difficult situation. Through such play the person comes to terms with, and finds solutions to the occurrences. (Fig. 20.1)

Jay, a 14 year old boy who presented psychotic-like ideation and severe abusive behaviour, experienced tremendous anxiety in, what he perceived, were conflict situations. In this picture, he visually documented an incident in which he met three boys and felt that they were going to attack him. He was sure one of the boys, whom he felt was a 'bully', would bring his friends and beat him up. In the actual incident, he ran away and felt very humiliated because of it. 'I hate it. I hate it that I ran away.'

After some discussion, we concluded that the only way to resolve his feelings would be to accept that he would need to encounter his fear and not run away but face the boy. He then created a picture depicting the confrontation. For the two boys, he chose adult male figurines and put them in threatening positions. As in past pictures, he identified with the little boy figurine. In playing out the situation, he used the little boy figurine, which represented himself, to knock down the two threatening boys.

This description illustrates the play therapy part of the process. However, the choice of the other figurines and some other features in the unfolding of the picture suggest the existence of an additional, symbolic aspect to the process. Similar to dreams, the choice to create certain events in the tray and the selection of specific figurines indicate the expression of a deeper unconscious symbolic level of the process.

Jay told me that he met the boys on the stairs to the subway. However, in the picture he used a bridge instead of the stairs. This seemed to be a conscious choice since when talking about the picture he referred to it as a bridge rather than stairs. It was interesting to notice that after placing the two boys beside the bridge he looked for 'a man that will help me'. He placed this man at the centre of the bridge, and only afterwards did he put himself in the picture. It seemed as if he needed to make sure that the

Fig. 20.1.

emerging centralising mature force within him will take his place to provide the necessary protection and assistance.

Moreover, after knocking the two boys with the figurine that represented himself, he rearranged the picture to show it to his mother (who used to join us in the latter part of the sessions). When he again acted out the knocking down of the two boys he did not use the little boy. This time he used the man from the bridge, thus expressing his acknowledgement of this emerging part of himself.

One might look at such a threat as a documentation of the concrete attack. However, on the symbolic level, another message is projected. Jay put two boys in the picture. In the external reality, he met three boys and was really afraid of only one of them. Two is a symbol of the opposites. For Jay, the holding together of the opposites, his abusing manners and his fear of confrontation, was a life issue. In this picture he was able not only to contain the opposites with the assistance of the man, but also to struggle with them and symbolically manage his abusive side in order to face his fear.

Furthermore, Jay used an extremely powerful archetypal image in the picture. Bradway (1986) mentions that in sand scenes which include the transcendence of opposites, the bridge is often used as the connector of the opposing parts of one's psyche as presented in the tray. Or, as mentioned by Dundas (1990), 'symbolically, a bridge is laid between fantasy and reality. In fact, a bridge is one of the most frequently used sandtray miniatures once a person starts reaching out to life. As a transition and communication tool, the bridge is often a connection to life itself'.

2. Sandplay pictures may be looked at and analysed from a developmental point of view.

From her experience Kalff (1980) realised that children's sand pictures correspond with their stage of ego development. She identified three developmental stages in the process of sandplay, which coincide with Neumann's (1973) stages of ego development.

Kalff's stages of development are: (a) an undifferentiated stage which she calls 'the animal, vegetative stage'; (b) a conflictual stage which she calls 'the fighting stage'; and, (c) a constellation stage which she calls 'the adaptation to the collective stage'. Although these are developmental stages, they might appear at various times in the therapy, in both children's and adults' processes.

(a) The animal-vegetative stage: In this stage the ego expresses itself mainly in pictures in which animals and vegetation are paramount. Bradway (1981) mentions that in this stage, the child usually uses wild or pre-historic animals These animals differ from domesticated animals in that they are a representation of the instinctual, still undifferentiated primary level of a child's development and inner reality.

Murray was born with Down's Syndrome and was given up by his natural parents at birth. He spent the first 7 years of his life in an institutional type setting. He learned to be extremely violent and started to demonstrate autistic-like behaviours. In the institution he was neglected physically, medically, and psychologically, which subsequently led to the loss of his sight in one eye. When Murray was 7 years old, he was placed in a professional foster home. He was not toilet-trained. He had very little receptive language and almost no expressive language. Through the enriched and supportive home environment of the foster placement and through his additional enrolment at the Muki Baum Children Day Treatment Centre, he started a play therapy process.

In light of the severe retardation in his development, Murray did not know how to play with toys. Initially, the animals were used as sticks or inanimate objects. It took Murray approximately two years to discover dramatic play, which continued to be mostly full of aggressive confrontations. However, the animals ceased to be solely used as hitting objects and were given identities and used as participants. Murray used specific animals, identifying them as significant others in his life. The big elephant

Fig. 20.2.

was always used as the daddy, the giraffe was mommy and the small elephant represented himself.

As Murray's play became more complex, it was felt that he could start sandplay therapy. In the beginning, he continued to play on the floor with toys using the sandtray as a dumping ground for the toys he no longer needed. Murray gradually realised that he could also use the sandtray as a stage for his play.

Murray started to intentionally create dramas in the sandtray, leaving them as pictures at the end of his play. Murray did not know how to tell the story of his pictures, but the dramas spoke for themselves. (Fig. 20.2).

This picture was made by Murray after three years of sandplay therapy. The big elephant (daddy) is standing big and strong beside his son. The little elephant is in an enclosed, fenced area. It seems as if the little elephant maybe needs to be protected from the destruction outside, which is represented by the gun and the wrestlers. The big, strong daddy elephant is capable of coping with these destructive forces, but the son elephant needs to be protected.

In sand pictures, much like in dreams, everyone and everything represents parts of ourselves. Therefore, one might ask about the aggression Murray existentially 'knows' is within himself. The fence around the little elephant (himself) can be interpreted additionally as a positive sign of the evolvement of inner boundaries, which eventually will be able to contain the violence. The emergence of such boundaries signifies

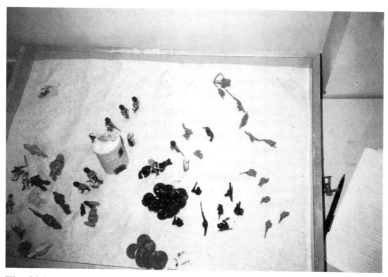

Fig. 20.3.

a strengthening of the ego which is the centring and guiding force of consciousness. The almost central placement of the little fenced elephant further supports this observation.

(b) The fighting stage: This is the stage of battle of conflictual confrontation. The child emerges from the undifferentiated matriarchal domain and moves into what Neumann calls the active fighting stage at the beginning of the patriarchal domain. Kalff mentions that although battles appear again and again in sand pictures at different ages, they are most significant in puberty. At this time the personality is already strengthened to such a degree, that battles with external forces can be taken on and as a result, the accomplishment of separation can occur. Puberty, and consequently, adolescence is the age of breaking and destroying the Old so that the New can be born. Fighting scenes in which everything is destroyed symbolically represent this evolution. Normally, after sufficient repetitions, the individual is able to emerge victorious from the fight and move on to the next phase.

For people with mental retardation who also have a deep emotional disturbance, the length of this phase is clearly affected by the level of fixation in the battle. This by itself is indicative of the disturbance. Figures 20.3 and 20.4 were made by Albert, an 11 year old boy with schizophrenia who was fixated on again and again creating the fight–death sequence.

Brian is a 24 year old man with Down's Syndrome and emotional

Fig. 20.4.

difficulties in the area of sexuality and sexual conduct. He experiences confusion in regard to sexual roles and gender identity. He acts out this confusion in an antisocial fashion, directing his misconduct at children and adults from both sexes.

In therapy, Brian used to create his pictures quickly with little care or attention. His process was characterised by an ongoing focus on the masculine with a complete elimination of the feminine. He used only male figurines, generally wrestlers, creating battle scenes full of conflict and confrontation. His images were always the battle of good against evil without the emergence of a clear winner. He would come into the room to make his picture and would immediately try to leave the session.

The session in which Brian made these pictures (Figs. 20.5, 20.6, 20.7) was the first one in which he allowed himself to play a series of events in the tray.

In the scene (Fig. 20.5), Brian set up the stage for battle. He identified the six wrestlers, whom he placed in the four corners, as heroes who were going to slay the monster. During the evolvement of the play, the six heroes moved from the corners to the middle and surrounded the 'prehistoric beast' which was placed at the centre of the tray (Fig. 20.6).

The battle was fierce. The central prehistoric beast was able to knock down the six heroes and move to join the other eight beasts surrounding the heroes. Here the heroes soon found themselves surrounded by eight other beasts, and realised that they were in a radically changed situation.

Fig. 20.5.

Fig. 20.6.

Where they previously stood a good chance of slaying the beast and winning the battle, they now had to fight for their own lives. However, the concept of good over evil, prevailed. After a long process, the heroes were able to stand up again. They were then successful in attacking, conquering and eventually killing the nine threatening beasts (Fig. 20.7).

Fig. 20.7.

The analysis of these three pictures might be contextual, that is, story-oriented. 'Good', represented by the heroes is fighting Evil, represented by the beasts. This analysis emphasises the course of the playing which occurred during the process. As such, it is not only a good example of an in-depth play therapy process, but also a manifestation of the way by which the fighting stage might come to a resolution.

Another way to understand these pictures is on the symbolic level. The tray here is a clear manifestation of the universe and the battle is anchored at a primary, fundamental, instinctual level. One gets a numinous sense, while looking at the pictures. The evolvement of the process starts with the movement from the quaternity (the heroes in the four corners). It then proceeds to the circle at the centre (the six heroes surrounding the prehistoric beast), over to the larger circle of the eight beasts surrounding the heroes and finally to the circular resolution of heroes who have successfully 'slain the dragons'. Symbolised by the circle, this is a movement to wholeness, to actualisation and to achievement. For Brian, it marked a movement from a split, in which the female was completely eliminated, to the risk-taking of inclusion of this rejected part of himself.

It is interesting to note that, in his next session, in spite of creating another battle scene, Brian included a woman figurine in the form of a female wrestler. In the story of this picture, the woman was able to 'beat up' a ninja fighter and then join her mate in another corner of the tray,

Fig. 20.8.

where they then kissed. This kiss symbolically represented the emergence to awareness of the feminine aspect in Brian's inner life. Moreover, it marked the beginning of the mending of the split and the repossessing of a rejected part of himself. For Brian, who had experienced such great difficulty in his gender identity, this was an important first manifestation of clarifying who he was.

(c) Adaptation to the collective stage: A successful resolution to the fighting stage is the surfacing of a wish to be admitted to the environment as a person, thus, becoming a member of the collective.

Figs. 20.8 and 20.9 are two more of Jay's pictures in which the manifestation of this stage can be observed.

In Fig. 20.8, Jay was on the verge of transition between the fighting stage and the adaptation to the collective stage. On the left side of the picture one can still see an army in an offensive position. However, the right side, which symbolises connectedness to external reality, depicts peaceful, working villagers, their children and their domestic animals. The villagers do not seem to be bothered by the show of force of the army. They continue to live their lives and do their work. Among the villagers one can recognise three groups: the first one is a group of workers taking care of their farming chores and their animals; the second group are elders, who symbolise the possession of wisdom which exists in all of us; the last group is comprised of children within whom playfulness, expressed as the eternal child inside all of us, is maintained. This is a picture of a multigenerational community wherein a peaceful life flows despite seemingly external disturbances.

The fact that Jay placed these two groups – the army and the villagers – in one picture suggests a transformative transition: the movement from left to right as exhibited by a searching-for-contact army moving towards the working villagers focused on their work and life, symbolising the transition from conflict to a stable establishment. This is a distinct sign of change when the fighter has the potential to be transformed into a peace-loving villager who invests his/her energies in working the fields (earth) to bring about new life and growth.

At the centre of the picture Jay placed a police woman. She is the order-keeping force who is able to keep the peace, mediate between the two sides, and create a bridge through which this transformation can occur.

Fig. 20.9 was made a few weeks later. Jay created a scene in which he describes the event of being brought to a sleepover summer camp by his mother. In the picture, he is saying goodbye to his family and his dog before entering the camp area. Behind the fence some children are involved in camp sports and activities. Jay, after separating from his family, is going to enter the camp and join them in their activities. Here, the transition from one realm to the other, is even more noticeable. In order to join his peer group, Jay has to become differentiated from his family. Only through separation can he acquire the key to the peer collective. He is doing it with some difficulty, but with the acceptance of this necessary step.

When elaborating upon this stage, Dundas (1990) speaks about the appearance of cars and trucks in the pictures. She says that they symbolise the movement of transition and adaptation to the collective.

Bradway (1981) mentions that fences also appear very frequently at this stage. She sees the use of fences as coinciding with the children's emerging ability to both confront and be confronted by the outer forces of reality. The fences then symbolise the strengthening of the boundaries of ego-consciousness, and the ability to eventually find a harmonious balance between the pull of outer forces and the push of inner demands. In his picture, Jay is separating from the realm of the family and moving to the domain of a peer collective, within which he will be able to continue with the process of his transformation.

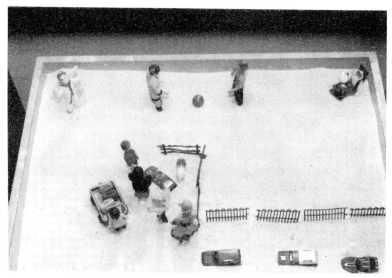

Fig. 20.9.

*3. Sandplay pictures may be looked at and analysed on a symbolic-
archetypal level.*

A central aspect of Jungian psychology is the existence of a deeper level of
the unconscious, which Jung terms the collective unconscious. From this
level, archetypal images surface to enter the personal aspects of a person's
psyche. These archetypes are the in-potentia, collective, symbolic entities
to be filled with personal content by each human being. Originating in the
collective unconscious, these archetypes are universal in nature and exist
across cultures and beyond personal differences.

Through the analysis of sand pictures, one gets a strong impression of
the universality of the symbols coming from the unconscious of people
with developmental handicaps. They are similar to the symbols which
appear in the dreams, art and sand pictures of people without handicaps.
An analysis of these universal symbols will bring into awareness the
personal expressions and manifestations of these archetypes. Through
becoming increasingly conscious of these personal manifestations of the
more universal aspects of the psyche, change and growth can occur.

Summary

The process of making a sand picture entails a choice made by the person
to use a tray with either wet or dry sand as well as to select the specific
figurines needed. The person then arranges his/her inner picture in the

sand, which then gives physical form to inner conscious and unconscious occurrences.

Children and adults engage in a play therapy process through which their inner dramas evolve. The end result is not of a singular product, but rather a sequence of pictures that mark the various evolving and unfolding stages of this therapeutic process.

Sandplay therapy differs from a regular play therapy in that it provides the client with a physical space which sets the stage for the expression of these inner stories. This physical stage, combined with the understanding and acceptance of the non-directive and unjudged process by the therapist, forms the 'free and protected space'. Within this 'free and protected' space, a person can safely experience the freedom to play out and express inner issues, needs or complexes. Simultaneously, he/she is protected by the clear boundaries of this space which provide the physical and psychological grounding for the psyche and the containment of the fantasy. The harmonious balance of this freedom and this protection activate the inner process and enable change and growth.

References

Axline, V. M. (1969). *Play Therapy*. Canada: Random House of Canada Limited.

Baum, N. T. (1990). Therapy for people with dual diagnosis: treating the behaviours or the whole person? In A. Dosen, A. Van Gennepe, & G. J. Zwanikken, eds. *Treatment of Mental Illness and Behavioural Disorder in the Mentally Retarded*, pp. 143–156, Leiden, the Netherlands: Logon Publications.

Bradway, K. (1981). Developmental stages in children's sand worlds. In Sisa Sternback, ed. *Sandplay Studies: Origins, Theory and Practice*, pp. 93–100, Boston: Sigo Press.

Bradway, K. (1986). What makes it work? In M. A. Mattoon, ed. *Proceedings of the Tenth International Congress for Analytical Psychology*, Berlin, pp. 409–414, Zurich: Daimon Verlag.

Bradway, K. (1991). Transference and countertransference in sandplay therapy. *Journal of Sandplay Therapy*, 1(1), 25–43.

Dundas, E. T. (1990). *Symbols Come Alive in the Sand*. Boston: Coventure Ltd.

Friedman H. S. & Mitchell R. R. (1991). Dora Maria Kalff: Connections between life and work. *Journal of Sandplay Therapy*, 1(1), 17–23.

Hellendoorn, J. (1990). Indications and goals for play therapy with the mentally retarded. In A. Dosen, A. Van Gennepe, & G. J. Zwanikken, eds. *Treatment of Mental Illness and Behavioural Disorder in the Mentally Retarded*, pp. 179–187. Leiden, the Netherlands: Logon Publications.

Kalff, D. N. (1980). *Sandplay: A Psychotherapeutic Approach to the Psyche*. California: Sigo Press.

Kalff, D. N. (1986). Introduction to sandplay therapy. CH-Zollikon. Reprinted: (1991). *Journal of Sandplay Therapy*, 1(1), 7–15.

Neumann, E. (1973). *The Child.* New York: G. P. Putnam & Sons.
Rogers, C. R. (1951). *Client-Centred Therapy: Its Current Practice Implications and Theory.* Boston: Houghton Miffin Co.
Von Franz, M. L. (1991). *Dreams.* Boston & London: Shambhala Publications, Inc.
Weinrib, E. L. (1983). *Images of the Self: The Sandplay Therapy Process.* Boston: Sigo Press.

Part V

Service systems

21

Psychiatric services in mental retardation generic or specialised provision?

KENNETH DAY

Introduction

The phasing out and closure of large hospitals for people with mental retardation during the last decade has highlighted the special needs of those patients with psychiatric problems. The widely held view that many of these problems were a direct consequence of institutional care and would quickly disappear with changes in service delivery patterns has increasingly shown to be false. Concerns about the consequences of deinstitution-alisation programmes in the absence of planned alternative facilities have been voiced in many countries. Service providers now face the following questions. What type of services are needed? Can provision be sat-isfactorily made in the generic mental health services? Are specialist psychiatric services required, and if so, what form should they take? The answers will be explored in this chapter, primarily in relation to the data available on adult services, but the arguments apply equally to services for children and adolescents.

Provision in generic mental health services

Proponents of generic service provision argue from normalisation prin-ciples that people with mental retardation should be catered for within ordinary mental health services as part of a general policy of integration. It is also argued that specialised services lead to stigmatisation, labelling and negative professional attitudes (Blunden & Allen, 1987, Newman & Emerson, 1991) and that people with mental retardation would receive a superior service within mainstream services (DHSS, 1979). Until recently these views have remained essentially theoretical but it is now possible to examine them in practice. The overwhelming conclusion is that provision within ordinary mental health services, whether by default or design, cannot satisfactorily meet the treatment and care needs of people with mental retardation and psychiatric and behaviour problems.

Normalisation principles have also been advanced as an argument that people with mental retardation who offend should be dealt with in the penal system. This is to misunderstand normalisation philosophy, however, for as Jackson (1983) aptly points out, recognition of the human worth of a mentally retarded individual does not logically require that he receives identical treatment to that accorded to a non-retarded citizen.

Generic provision by default

There is a substantial literature from the United States of America describing the problems associated with attempts to treat people with mental retardation with psychiatric and behaviour problems in the mental health system (Parkhurst, 1984; Houston, 1984; Marcos, Gil & Vazquez, 1986; Gold *et al.*, 1989). Marcos *et al.* (1986) reported dually diagnosed people in New York City regularly having to spend two days or more, and sometimes up to two weeks, in hospital emergency departments whilst a suitable placement was found. A national survey by the New York Office of Mental Retardation and Developmental Abilities in 1986 concluded that services for the dually diagnosed in the USA were deficient in availability, accessibility and adequacy (Jacobson & Ackerman, 1988). Similar concerns have been expressed about offenders with mental retardation who in the absence of appropriate forensic services frequently enter the Criminal Justice System (Menolascino, 1974; Jackson, 1983; French, 1983) and who in some States remain subject to the death penalty for murder (Conley, Luckasson & Bouthilet, 1992; Calnen & Blackman, 1992).

The response has been a growth of specialised services for the psychiatrically disordered (Houston, 1984; Landsberg, Fletcher & Maxwell, 1987; Reiss 1988; Fletcher 1988; Gold *et al.*, 1989) and for mentally retarded offenders (Santamour & Watson, 1982; Denkowski, Denkowski & Mabli, 1983).

Generic services by design

Attempts to cater for psychiatrically disordered people with mental retardation within ordinary mental health services in Sweden and Denmark have proved unsuccessful (Day, 1992). This is highly significant in two countries so strongly committed to the principles of normalisation and with such well-resourced and good-quality services. Parallel experiences have been reported in the USA (Menolascino personal communication). Inappropriateness of setting, lack of staff knowledge and expertise and particularly a lack of psychiatric input are the main problems. Health districts in England and Wales which have deliberately opted not to provide specialist services have similarly found it impossible to cope and necessary to seek 'out of district' and sometimes expensive specialist hospital placements (O'Brien, 1990). In the light of experience, the Welsh Office has recently revised its original strategy for services for people with mental retardation in Wales, which embodied the generic approach to mental health provision (Welsh Office, 1983) and it is now proposed to develop specialist psychiatric services (All Wales Advisory Panel, 1991).

Specialised psychiatric services

The case for specialised services

The case for specialised psychiatric services for people with mental re-tardation has been well documented (Day 1984, 1988a; Gold *et al.*, 1989; Marcos *et al.*, 1986; Houston 1984; Newman & Emerson, 1991). Special expertise and experience is required for the accurate diagnosis of mental illness in the face of atypical presentation, communication difficulties and absence of subjective complaints (Reid, 1972; Hucker *et al.*, 1979, Wright, 1982; Sovner, 1986; Menolascino, Gilson & Levitas, 1986). Highly specialised assessment and treatment techniques are required in the management of behaviour disorders – many unique to this population, which account for approximately half of the problems presented (Day, Hamilton & Smith, 1988). Counselling, psychotherapy and other thera-peutic interventions have to be modified to take account of intellectual limitations (Levitas & Gilson, 1989). Drug therapy is complicated by a high frequency of side effects and unusual responses (Snaith, James & Winokur 1979). Underlying dependency levels and coexisting physical disabilities, including epilepsy, have to be taken account of in treatment, rehabilitation and aftercare (Day, 1984).

People with mental retardation are disadvantaged and vulnerable in generic treatment settings: they do not on the whole mix well with other mentally disordered patients, the pace of ward life is usually too fast for them and it is difficult to gear therapeutic interventions to meet their needs (Day, 1984; Gold *et al.*, 1989). Assessment and treatment takes longer and rehabilitation is slower than in the non-handicapped (Marcos *et al.*, 1986).

Because of the small numbers involved, there is little opportunity for staff of all disciplines to gain the necessary experience, knowledge and skills. Specialised services, on the other hand, provide a focus for action, bring the benefits of cumulative experience, increase staff competence and skills development, ensure 'ownership' of the task in hand and increase the probability of effective and successful treatment (Clements, 1987). They also facilitate the establishment of a cadre of experts to carry out teaching and research: the substantial research effort in this field over the past decade has emanated entirely from clinicians and others working in specialist services.

Suggested disadvantages of specialised services include isolation, stigmatisation of service users and problems of transfer to community services (Newman & Emerson, 1991) but these result from inadequate conceptualisation and organisation rather than inherent defects in the system (Clements, 1987). Small, poorly resourced and undersupported services are likely to be isolated and the staff demoralised but this is certainly not the case in well established and well run services where morale is high and staff are keen to work with previously unpopular groups (Day, 1983). In the vast majority of cases, stigmatisation and 'labelling' of service users, which it is argued makes them unacceptable within mainstream mental retardation services, has already occurred prior to entry to specialised services as a consequence of the nature of the problems they present (Newman & Emerson 1991). Difficulties in returning people from specialised to community services is essentially a function of the complexity and chronicity of many of the illnesses and disorders presented. An individual with a complex psychiatric or behavioural problem managed successfully in a highly specialised setting cannot necessarily be expected to maintain improvements in an ordinary community setting. Whilst the ultimate goal of specialised services is to improve an individual to the point where he/she can successfully return to mainstream services it is increasingly apparent that many will continue to require specialised care for much, if not all, of their lives (Reid *et al.*, 1984). Specialised rehabilitation and continuing care facilities feature in many of the specialist services being developed (Day, 1984, Fletcher 1988, Menolascino 1989).

Service trends

Specialist psychiatric services are increasingly the preferred option in many countries (Day 1988*a*; Houston, 1984; Landsberg *et al.*, 1987; Zarfas, 1988; Dosen, 1988; Jenssen & Morch 1990). In the United Kingdom mental handicap has been a psychiatric specialty for 150 years

(Day & Jancar, 1991). Psychiatrically and behaviourally disordered people with mental retardation, including offenders, are cared for within the mental retardation services and specialist facilities have been established. A SPECIAL HOSPITAL service for offenders with mental retardation was introduced in 1920 (Parker, 1985) and more recently, medium secure units (Royal College of Psychiatrists 1980). The continuing need for specialist psychiatric services was called into question in the early 1970s with the advent of Care in the Community policies (Godber, 1973). During the ensuing debate the Royal College of Psychiatrists argued strongly for specialised services and specialist psychiatrists (Royal College of Psychiatrists, 1974, 1978, 1983, 1986). An indepth review of the service needs of this group of patients was carried out by a study team of the Department of Health (DoH, 1989) which underpinned a recent major policy statement by the Minister of State for Health in which the long term need for specialist mental health provision and doctors specialising in the psychiatry of mental handicap was reaffirmed (Dorrell, 1991).

Components of a specialist psychiatric service

A specialist psychiatric service for people with mental retardation should be fully comprehensive and provide for the following groups:

— acute and chronic mental illness
— severe mental retardation with behaviour problems
— mild mental retardation with maladjustment, emotional problems and social inadequacy
— offenders with mental retardation
— people with brain damage, epilepsy and associated behaviour problems
— elderly people with mental retardation and psychogeriatric problems

A full range of services are required including diagnostic and treatment services in the community, acute and longer term inpatient assessment and treatment facilities, rehabilitation, aftercare and continuing care (Landsberg *et al.*, 1987, Day, 1984; Fletcher, 1988, Department of Health, 1989, Menolascino, 1989).

Inpatient provision should include a sufficient number of treatment settings to enable the provision of specialised programmes for the spectrum of problems presented and to take account of the range of intellectual levels as well as age and sex. Mixing diagnostic groups is counter-productive, makes it difficult to develop specific treatment programmes and should be avoided (Day 1983, 1988*a*).

Specialist treatment units are needed for more serious and dangerous offenders. For those not requiring residential treatment, a network of services in the community for rehabilitation and aftercare is needed (Day, 1988*b*, 1990).

People with mental retardation and psychiatric or behaviour problems, including offenders, rarely fit well into mainstream community facilities, usually requiring a different style of approach with more support and supervision. Specialist rehabilitation and continuing care facilities include specialist support teams, residential, vocational training and recreational services, day treatment facilities and employment (Day, 1984; Fletcher, 1988; Menolascino, 1989).

Skilled professionals required include psychiatrists, nurses, social workers, clinical psychologists, vocational trainers, occupational therapists and educationalists. Comprehensive staff training programmes are essential.

Models of service delivery

How the different elements described above are best provided remains a matter of discussion and debate. A variety of service models have been developed. They can be broadly divided into i) unit based services and ii) community based services.

Unit-based services

Specialist units are the main focus for treatment and management in unit based services. Outpatient, domiciliary treatment and support and other outreach services are also provided by unit based staff (Day, 1983, Bouras & Drummond, 1989, Murphy *et al.*, 1991) but this aspect of the work has been generally under-reported and overlooked in discussions about the relative merits and demerits of this service model. Day (1988*a*) has proposed a comprehensive national model for the United Kingdom comprising subregional services based upon specialist units and incorporating three levels of secure provision for offenders (Table 21.1).

The advantages of specialist units have been delineated by a number of workers (Day 1983; 1984; 1988*b*; Department of Health, 1989; Blunden & Allen, 1987; Newman & Emerson, 1991). Specialist units are cost efficient; able to provide intensive therapeutic programmes; can cope with high levels of disturbed and violent behaviour; physical features can be tailored to match patient needs, e.g. provision of security, seclusion facilities; and staff expertise will be high. Specialist units provide intensive support to

Table 21.1. *Organisation of psychiatric services for people with mental retardation in the United Kingdom*

Level	Facility	Role	Number of places
National	Special hospital	High security	5/million population[1]
Regional	Medium secure units	Medium security offenders and severely behaviourally disturbed short to medium term	10/million population[2]
Subregional	Specialist psychiatric unit	Acute mental illness	30
		Chronic mental illness	30
		Offenders	30*
		Behaviour Disorders	40
		Rehabilitation	10
			140/500000 population[3]
		Rehabilitation unit	20/500000 population
		Day hospital	30/500000 population
District	Specialist clinical teams		
	Specialist community based services for rehabilitation and continuing care including day and residential facilities		

[1] Existing provision
[2] Oxford Regional Health Authority, 1976
[3] Day, 1983
* Some modification may be required according to the demographic features of the population served; for example, there is likely to be a greater need for offender beds in socially deprived urban areas than in rural areas.
Source: Day, 1983, 1988.

care staff which is essential in view of the stressful nature of the work and the vulnerability of many of the patients (Rusch, Hall & Griffin, 1986). They provide a resource centre for community-based staff and facilities.

A number of potential disadvantages of specialist units have been raised (Keene & James, 1986, Blunden & Allen, 1987; Maher & Russell, 1988; Newman & Emerson, 1991). It is suggested that specialist units, particularly those providing a regional or subregional service, are remote from patients' homes making visiting, rehabilitation and long-term clinical follow-up difficult; that admission will lead to labelling and stigmatisation of service users; that specialist units will become marginalised and the staff professionally isolated and demoralised with high turnover and burn-out; that patient throughput will be difficult to maintain leading to silting up, stagnation and the danger of a return to institutional patterns of care; that the presence of a specialist unit will encourage the ready referral of even mild cases and discourage the development of local competence and services; and that the substantial resources locked in such units cannot be easily redirected, thereby stifling community developments (Clements, 1987).

Whilst distance can be an impediment to relatives visiting and sometimes creates problems for rehabilitation, such disadvantages have to be balanced against the very substantial advantages of care and treatment in a high quality specialist setting with a high level of staff skill and expertise. It is often a positive advantage for offenders to be managed away from their own locality. Fears of marginalisation, isolation and demoralisation are not borne out by the examples of well-organised and established units with good resources and active therapeutic regimes (Day, 1983). The question of stigmatisation and labelling has already been considered. Other perceived disadvantages are not inherent in the service model and should not occur where a specialist unit is part of a comprehensive service which includes community-based facilities and has good relationships with other service agencies and is adequately resourced.

Specialist treatment units vary in size, nature and setting. Comprehensive campus based units are strongly favoured by the author on the grounds of therapeutic and economic viability; enabling provision of a full range of treatment settings, an economic use of specialist staff, a high level of care staff support and providing asylum for those who require it. The critical catchment population is 500 000. A typical example established within the grounds of a mental handicap hospital has been described by Day (1983; 1984). The unit currently provides a total of 135 beds for a catchment population of approximately 600 000 with some regional commitment for offenders. It has 14 separate treatment settings for the management, care and rehabilitation of mildly and severely mentally retarded adults and adolescents with acute and chronic mental illness and severe behaviour disorders and a special three stage treatment programme for mentally retarded offenders (Day, 1988*b*, 1990). Unit staff provide a domiciliary service to the whole catchment area and work closely with local statutory, voluntary and private agencies. Planned expansions include a medium secure unit and a specialist head injury unit on site and specialist respite care, aftercare and continuing care facilities in the community.

Much smaller units of 10 to 30 beds have been established in many services, located either within the grounds of mental handicap or mental illness hospitals (Gold *et al.*, 1989; Murphy *et al.*, 1991, Houston, 1984; Hoefkens & Allen 1990; Krishnamurti, 1990) or in association with psychiatric departments in general or teaching hospitals (Bouras & Drummond, 1989, Nolan, 1992) or based in the community (Galligan, 1990). The emphasis in these units is on short duration of stay, and admissions are usually restricted to moderately and mildly mentally retarded people with mental illness and behaviour problems although some also provide assessment and treatment services for mentally retarded offenders (Murphy *et al.*, 1991) and severely mentally retarded people presenting severe behaviour problems (Fidura, Lindsey & Walker, 1987; Gold *et al.*, 1989).

Small locally based treatment units, whilst having the advantage of closeness to the community served, suffer a number of serious disadvantages. They cannot cope with severely disturbed patients or serious offenders and require back-up from more specialised facilities. Their limited range of treatment settings restricts the types of patients admitted and leads to inappropriate mixing of patient groups. The small number of patients presenting similar problems resident in the unit at any one time makes it difficult to develop appropriate and viable therapeutic regimes either on an individual basis, e.g. token economy regimes for the behaviourally disturbed, or a group basis, e.g. management programmes for offenders. There are also problems of medical cover, staff support, emergency back-up in the event of serious problems and the provision of an adequate range of occupational and recreational facilities.

Specialist units for the treatment and management of mentally retarded offenders under conditions of security have been established particularly in the United Kingdom and the USA (Day, 1988*b*; 1990; Mayor *et al.*, 1990; Smith, 1988; Santamour & Watson, 1982; Denkowski *et al.*, 1984;

Sandford, Elzinga & Grainger, 1987). In the United Kingdom there is a well-established three level approach to inpatient provision for mentally disordered offenders (Royal College of Psychiatrists, 1980). The majority of mentally retarded offenders are provided for by local services; those convicted of serious offences who require a high degree of security are treated in Special Hospitals (three in England and Wales and one in Scotland) jointly run by the Department of Health and the Home Office; and Regional Medium Secure Units are being established to cater for those patients requiring intermediate levels of security (Isweran & Brener, 1990).

Community-based models

Proponents of the community-based service model argue from normalisation principles that patients should be treated as far as possible in their own homes supported by specialist community teams or failing that in small intensively staffed specialist group homes (Newman & Emerson, 1991; Blunden & Allen, 1987; Menolascino, 1989). These views have been particularly developed in relation to severely mentally retarded people presenting severe behaviour disorders, it being generally conceded that some specialist treatment facilities will be required for the acutely mentally ill and for offenders. It is argued that behaviour therapy units have not been successful (Keene & James, 1986), that it is difficult to maintain management programmes and treatment gains on return to the community (Newman & Emerson, 1991), that it makes most sense to attempt to effect behavioural change in the patient's normal environment (Allin, 1988) as admission to a specialist unit will only remove them from factors which may have been maintaining their behaviour and will be of little benefit if they are to return to the same unaltered environment after a period of treatment (Carr & Durrand, 1985; McBrien, 1987), and that the congregate grouping of people displaying severely disturbed behaviour is anti-therapeutic, creates a chaotic environment, impairs the development of systematic and consistent approaches to treatment and provides inappropriate models of behaviour for patients (Blunden & Allen, 1987; Newman & Emerson, 1991).

Specialist teams, variously known as 'challenging behaviour teams', 'intensive support teams' and 'special development teams' have been established in many areas to develop and provide specialist services, advise and support staff in local services or provide 'trouble-shooting services', primarily in relation to severe behaviour disorders in severely mentally retarded people (Blunden & Allen, 1987; DoH, 1989; Emerson *et al.*, 1987, 1989, Harris, 1991; Allin, 1988). Some teams have an associated small specialist residential facility (Harris, 1991). Specialist teams, it is suggested, overcome many of the perceived problems of specialist units, provide a more responsive and flexible service and foster the development of local competence and tolerance. The specialist team model is based on the hypothesis that there is a substantial functional element in the origins and maintenance of behaviour problems in mentally retarded people which requires a behavioural approach to management and care (Baumeister, 1989). However, the growing body of research evidence pointing to the importance of neuropathological factors (Lund 1985; Reid *et al.*, 1984), underlying mental illness (Reid, 1972; Hucker *et al.*, 1979; Reiss 1990) and disorder specific neurobiological mechanisms (Coyle, 1988; Hunt & Cohen 1988, Berg & Gosse, 1990) in causation, together with the limited success of behavioural approaches, are cogent reasons why the care and treatment of mentally retarded people exhibiting severe behaviour problems should remain the responsibility of specialist psychiatric services.

Community-based service models usually comprise a small acute inpatient treatment unit and a range of community provision including small specialist group homes, regular group homes and day provision supported by specialist teams (Menolascino 1989; Fletcher, 1990). They have difficulty coping with severely disturbed patients and those with special needs and the need for a 'fall-back' facility is acknowledged (Blunden & Allen, 1987). Intensive professional input into the home setting in the facilities in England and Wales visited by O'Brien (1990) did not obviate the need for hospital admission and often led to crisis situations and the need for precipitate recourse to 'out of district' placements as opposed to planned admission to a psychiatric treatment unit.

Evaluation of service models

Service developments in all countries are currently being critically influenced by ideology. Rigorous evaluative research by independent researchers is essential to provide a sound scientific basis for future provision. Comparative evaluations between different service models is required as well as evaluation of individual services. Issues of efficacy, comprehensiveness, sustainability and cost effectiveness must be addressed and the views of consumers, including parents and professionals as well as patients, sought. Disadvantages inherent in a service system must be clearly distinguished from those consequent upon under resourcing or poor organisation and operation (Clements, 1987). Too often under-resourced existing services have been unfairly, and unproductively, compared with new highly resourced demonstration projects.

Staff training

It is essential that psychiatrists, nurses and other professionals working in specialised psychiatric services for mentally retarded people are properly trained. Lack of appropriately trained and experienced professionals, particularly a paucity of interested psychiatrists, has proved a major barrier to the development of specialised services in many countries (Dosen 1988, Zarfas, 1988, Parmenter, 1988). The United Kingdom has well established training programmes in mental handicap psychiatry which could serve as a model (Day & Jancar, 1991).

Since 1972, when all postgraduate medical education in the United Kingdom underwent a major revision, a doctor wishing to specialise in the field of mental handicap psychiatry must first undertake a 3–4 years general psychiatric training in a scheme approved by the Royal College of Psychiatrists (Table 21.2). This includes a 3–6 months full-time clinical placement in a psychiatric service for the mentally retarded and a course of academic lectures on the topic (RCPsych, 1985). The specialist qualifying examination (MRCPsych) taken at the end of training includes questions on mental handicap psychiatry and candidates may be clinically examined in the subject (RCPsych, 1987). General psychiatric training is followed by a further 3–4 year period of full-time specialist training in the psychiatry of mental handicap undertaken in a training scheme approved by the Joint Committee on Higher Psychiatric Training (JCHPT, 1990). The required academic and clinical components are summarised in Table 21.2.

Currently there are 200 Consultant Psychiatrists in mental handicap working in the United Kingdom and 70 Senior Registrars undergoing specialist training. The first Chair in the Psychiatry of Mental Handicap was established in 1980 and there are now seven Chairs throughout the country with academic posts at Senior Lecturer level in all University Departments (Day & Jancar, 1991). Medical students receive an average of eleven hours lectures and 'hands on' experience in mental retardation during their undergraduate training (Hollins & Bradley, 1987) and the topic is beginning to be introduced into the training and continuing medical education of General Practitioners (Bicknell, 1985).

Nurses working in the field of mental retardation have received specialist training leading to specialist qualifications in the United Kingdom since 1919 (Day & Jancar 1991). Over the years, the content of training programmes has tended to reflect service philosophy and there has been an unfortunate shift in emphasis recently from medical and psychiatric aspects of care towards social care. This trend is now reversing and nurses

Table 21.2. *Training of consultant psychiatrists in mental retardation in the United Kingdom*

General psychiatric training

Senior house officer and Registrar grades

3–4 years in training scheme approved by the Royal College of Psychiatrists

Rotational, including experience in all the major psychiatric specialties

3–6 months clinical placement and academic lectures in mental handicap

MRCPsych by examination on completion

Specialist training in the psychiatry of mental handicap

Senior Registrar grade

3–4 years in a training scheme approved by the joint Committee in Higher Psychiatric Training

Focus on psychiatric and behavioural aspects and family psychiatry

Clinical experience must cover full range of treatment interventions & settings, children and adults, forensic aspects, special experience, e.g. clinical genetics, management and administration

Academic programme must include seminars, journal clubs, research & teaching experience, national and international conferences, visits to other units

Eligible for Consultant post on successful completion

working in psychiatric services for the mentally retarded are increasingly obtaining training and qualifications in both mental handicap and psychiatric nursing. Social workers and clinical psychologists also receive academic lectures and practical placements in the subject during training (Day, 1988).

Summary

Psychiatric disorder is a common complication of mental retardation. Proper provision for this group of patients is an essential component of a comprehensive mental retardation service and of crucial importance to successful community care for the majority. Arguments in favour of provision within the generic mental health services are essentially ideological, a misinterpretation of normalisation philosophy and are failing in practice. There are sound arguments in favour of specialist psychiatric services which are increasingly the preferred option in most countries. Specialisms are a legitimate response to special needs: the aim being to improve service provision to a particular client group and a major feature of medicine, psychiatry and every other disciplines. Specialised psychiatric services for mentally retarded people are not in conflict with the principles of normalisation. Most services for mentally retarded people are, in fact, specialised.

References

All Wales Advisory Panel on the Development of Services for People with Mental Handicaps (1991). Challenges and responses: a report on services in support of adults with mental handicaps with exceptionally challenging behaviours, mental illnesses or who offend.

Allin, R. B. (1988). Intensive home based treatment interventions with mentally retarded/emotionally disturbed individuals and their families. In: J. A. Stark, F. J. Menolascino, M. H. Albarelli & V. C. Gray, eds. *Mental Retardation and Mental Health: Classification, Diagnosis, Treatment, Services*, pp. 265–280. New York: Springer-Verlag,

Baumeister, A. A. (1989). Etiologies of self-injurious and destructive behaviour. *Proceedings of the Consensus Conference on the Treatment of Severe Behaviour Problems and Developmental Disabilities*. Bethesda: National Institute of Health.

Berg, J. M. & Gosse, G. C. (1990). Specific mental retardation disorders and problem behaviours. *International Review of Psychiatry*, **2**, 53–60.

Bicknell, J. (1985). Educational Programmes for General Practitioners and Clinical Assistants in the Mental Handicap Service. *Bulletin of the Royal College of Psychiatrists*, **8**, 154–5.

Blunden, R. & Allen, D. (1987). Facing the challenge: an ordinary life for people with learning difficulties and challenging behaviour. *Kings Fund Project Paper No. 74*, London: Kings Fund Centre.

Bouras, N. & Drummond, C. (1989). Community psychiatric service in mental handicap. *Health Trends*, **21**, 72.

Calnen, T. & Blackman, L. S. (1992). Capital punishment and offenders with mental retardation: response to penvry brief. *American Journal of Mental Retardation*, **96**, 557–64.

Carr, E. G. & Durrand, V. M. (1985). The social-communicative basis of severe behaviour problems in children. In: S. Reiss & R. R. Bootzin, eds. *Theoretical Issues in Behaviour Therapy*. New York: Academic Press.

Clements, J. (1987). Units and teams: challenges in common. Quoted in Newman and Emmerson (1991). Specialised treatment units for people with challenging behaviours. *Mental Handicap*, **19**, 113-19.

Conley, R. W., Luckasson, R. & Bouthilet, G. N. (1992). The Criminal Justice System and *Mental Retardation*. Baltimore: Paul Brooks Publishing Company.

Coyle, J. T. (1988.) Psychiatry, neuroscience and the double disabilities. In J. A. Stark, F. J. Menolascino, M. H. Albarelli & V. C. Gray, eds. *Mental Retardation and Mental Health: Classification, Diagnosis, Treatment, Services*, pp. 81–89. New York: Springer-Verlag.

Day, K. (1983). A hospital based psychiatric unit for mentally handicapped adults. *Mental Handicap*, **11**, 137–40.

Day, K. (1984). Service provision for mentally handicapped people with psychiatric problems. In *Care in the Community, Keeping it Local*. Report of MIND's 1983 Annual Conference.

Day, K. (1988*a*). Services for psychiatrically disordered mentally handicapped adults – a UK perspective. *Australia and New Zealand Journal of Developmental Disabilities*, **14**, 19–25.

Day, K. (1988*b*). A hospital based treatment programme for male mentally handicapped offenders. *British Journal of Psychiatry*, **153**, 635–44.

Day, K., Hamilton, J. & Smith, P. (1988). *Behaviour Problems in Mental Handicap: An Annotated Bibliography* 1970–1985. London: Gaskell Press.

Day, K. (1990). Treatment of antisocial behaviour. In A. Dosen, A. Van Gennep & G. J. Zwanikken, eds. *Treatment of Mental Illness and Behavioural Disorder in the Mentally Retarded*. Leiden: Logon Publications.

Day, K. & Jancar, J. (1991). Mental handicap and the Royal Medico-Psychological Association: a historical association 1841–1991. In G. E. Berrios & H. Freeman, eds. *150 Years of British Psychiatry 1841–1991*. London: Gaskell Press.

Day, K. (1992). Mental health care for the mentally handicapped in four European countries: the argument for specialised services. *Italian Journal of Intellective Impairment*, **5**, 3–11

Denkowski, G. C., Denkowski, K. M. & Mabli, J. (1983). A fifty state survey on the current status of residential treatment programmes for mentally retarded offenders. *Mental Retardation*, **21**, 197–203.

Department of Health and Social Security (1979). Report of the Committee of Enquiry into Mental Handicap Nursing and Care (The Jay Report). *Cmnd. 7468*, London: HMSO.

Department of Health (1989). Needs and responses: Services for adults with mental handicap who are mentally ill, who have behaviour problems or who offend: report of a Department of Health Study Team. Stanmore, Middlesex: Department of Health Leaflets Unit.

Dorrell, S. (1991). Statement on services for people with learning disabilities by the Minister of State, 25th June 1991.

Dosen, A. (1988). Community care for people with mental retardation in The Netherlands. *Australia and New Zealand Journal of Developmental Disabilities*, **14**, 15–18.

Emerson, E., Toogood, A., Mansell, J., Barrett, S., Bell, C., Cummings, R. & McCool, C. (1987). Challenging behaviour and community services: 1. Introduction and overview. *Mental Handicap*, **15**, 166–9.

Emerson, E., Cummings, R., Hughes, H., Toogood, S., McCool, C. & Barrett, S. (1989). Challenging behaviour and community services: 6. Evaluation and overview. Mental *Handicap*, **17**, 104–7.

Fidura, J. G., Lindsey, E. R. & Walker, G. R. (1987). A special behaviour unit for treatment of behaviour problems of persons who are mentally retarded. *Mental Retardation*, **25**, 107–11.

Fletcher, R. J. (1988). A county systems model: comprehensive services for the dually diagnosed. In J. A. Stark, F. J. Menolascino, M. H. Albarelli and V. C. Gray, eds. *Mental Retardation and Mental Health: Classification, Diagnosis, Treatment, Services*, pp. 254–64. New York: Springer-Verlag.

French, S. (1983). The mentally retarded offender and pseudo-retarded offender: a clinical/legal dilemma. *Federal Probation*, **47**, 55.

Galligan, B. (1990). Serving people who are dually diagnosed: a programme evaluation. *Mental Retardation*, **28**, 353–358.

Godber, G. (1973). The responsibilities and role of the doctor concerned with the care of the mentally handicapped. *British Journal of Psychiatry*, **123**, 617–20.

Gold, I. M., Wolfson, E. S., Lester, C. M., Ratey, J. J. & Chmielinskih, E.

(1989). Developing a unit for mentally retarded mentally ill patients on the grounds of a state hospital. *Hospital and Community Psychiatry*, **40**, 836–40.

Harris, J. (ed.) (1991). Service responses to people with learning difficulties and challenging behaviour. *BIMH Seminar Papers No. 1.* British Institute of Mental Handicap, Kidderminster, Worcester.

Hoefkens, A. & Allen, D. (1990). Evaluation of a special behaviour unit for people with mental handicaps and challenging behaviour. *Journal of Mental Deficiency Research*, **34**, 213–28.

Hollins, S. & Bradley, E. (1987). Mental handicap in context: medical undergraduate education. *Bulletin of the Royal College of Psychiatrists*, **11**, 389–91.

Houston, H. (1984). A plan designed to deliver services to the multiply handicapped. In F. J. Menolascino and J. A. Stark, eds. *Handbook of Mental Illness in the Mentally Retarded.* New York: Plenum.

Hucker, S. J., Day, K. A., George, S. & Roth, M. (1979). Psychosis in mentally handicapped adults. In F. E. James and R. P. Snaith, eds. *Psychiatric Illness and Mental Handicap.* pp. 27–35. London: Gaskell Press.

Hunt, R. D. & Cohen, D. J. (1988). Attentional and neurochemical components of mental retardation: New methods and old problems. In J. A. Stark, F. J. Menolascino, M. H. Albarelli and V. C. Gray, eds. *Mental Retardation and Mental Health: Classification, Diagnosis, Treatment, Services*, pp. 90–97. New York: Springer-Verlag.

Isweran, M. S. & Brener, N. (1990). Psychiatric disorders in mentally retarded patients and their treatment in a medium secure unit. In A. Dosen, A. Van Gennep, G. J. Zwanikken, eds. *Treatment of Mental Illness and Behaviour Disorder in the Mentally Retarded.* Leiden: Logon Publications.

Jackson, R. (1983). Mental retardation and criminal justice: some issues and problems. *Mental Subnormality*, **29**, 7–12.

Jacobson, J. W. & Ackerman, L. J. (1988). An appraisal of services for people with mental retardation and psychiatric impairments. *Mental Retardation*, **26**, 377–80.

Joint Committee on Higher Psychiatric Training (1990). Requirements of specialist training. In *Mental Handicap Psychiatry*, pp. 44–47, **66**, 71–72.

Jenssen, T. & Morch, W. T. (1990). *Tidsskr Nor Laegeforen.* **110**, 1721–7. (Summary in English in: *Mental Retardation.* (1990). Medline Current Awareness Topics Search. British Library Document Supply Centre, Boston Spa, West Yorkshire.

Keene, N. & James, H. (1986). Who needs hospital care? *Mental Handicap*, **14**, 101–3.

Krishnamurti, D. (1990). Evaluation of a special behaviour unit for people with mental handicaps and challenging behaviour: a riposte. *Journal of Mental Deficiency Research*, **34**, 229–31.

Landsberg, G., Fletcher, R. & Maxwell, T. (1987). Developing a comprehensive community care system for the mentally ill mentally retarded. *Community Mental Health Journal*, **23**, 131–4.

Levitas, A. & Gilson, S. F. (1989). Psychodynamic psychotherapy with mildly and moderately retarded patients. In R. J. Fletcher and F. J. Menolascino, eds. *Mental Retardation and Mental Illness.* Massachusetts: Lexington Books.

Lund, J. (1985). The prevalence of psychiatric disorder in mentally retarded adults. *Acta Psychiatrica Scandinavica*, **72**, 563–70.

Maher, J. & Russell, O. (1988). Serving people with very challenging behaviour. In D. D. Towell (Ed.), *An Ordinary Life in Practice: Developing Comprehensive Community Based Services for People with Learning Disabilities.* London: Kings Fund.

Marcos, L. R., Gil, R. M. & Vazquez, K. M. (1986). Who will treat the psychiatrically disturbed developmentally disabled patients? A health care nightmare. *Hospital and Community Psychiatry*, **37**, 171–4.

Mayor, J., Bhate, M., Frith, H., Graham, A., Knox, P. & Tyrer, S. (1990). Facilities for mentally impaired patients: three years experience of a semi-secure unit. *Psychiatric Bulletin*, **14**, 333–5.

Menolascino, F. J. (1974). The mentally retarded offender. *Mental Retardation*, **12**, 7–11.

Menolascino, F. J., Gilson, S. F. & Levitas, A. (1986). Issues in the treatment of mentally retarded patients in the community mental health system. *Community Mental Health Journal*, **22**, 314–27.

Menolascino, F. J. (1989). Model services for treatment/management of the mentally retarded mentally ill. *Community Mental Health Journal*, **25**, 145–55.

Murphy, G., Holland, A., Fowler, P. & Reep, J. (1991). MIETS: a service option for people with mild mental handicaps and challenging behaviour or psychiatric problems. 1. Philosophy, Service and Service Users. *Mental Handicap Research*, **4**, 41–66.

McBrien, J. (1987). The Haytor Unit: specialised day care for adults with severe mental handicaps and behaviour problems. *Mental Handicap*, **15**, 77–80.

Newman, I. & Emerson, E. (1991). Specialised treatment units for people with challenging behaviours. *Mental Handicap*, **19**, 113–9.

Nolan, M. E. (1992). Generic services for people with a mental handicap. *Psychiatric Bulletin*, **16**, 212–3.

O'Brien, G. (1990). Current patterns of service provision for the psychiatric needs of mentally handicapped people: visiting centres in England and Wales. *Psychiatric Bulletin*, **14**, 3–7.

Oxford Regional Health Authority (1976) A survey of the need for secure psychiatric facilities in the Oxford region. Department of Psychiatry, University of Oxford.

Parker, E. (1985). The development of secure provision. In L. Gostin, ed. *Secure Provision*, pp. 15–65. London and New York: Tavistock Publications.

Parkhurst, R. (1984). Need assessment and service planning for mentally retarded mentally ill persons. In F. J. Menolascino and J. A. Stark, eds. *Handbook of Mental Illness in the Mentally Retarded.* New York: Plenum.

Parmenter, T. R. (1988). Analysis of Australian mental health services for people with mental retardation. *Australia and New Zealand Journal of Developmental Disabilities*, **14**, 9–13.

Reid, A. H. (1972). Psychosis in adult mental defectives. *British Journal of Psychiatry*, **120**, 205–12.

Reid, A. H., Ballinger, B. R., Heather, B. B. & Melvin, S. T. (1984). The natural history of behavioural symptoms among severely and profoundly mentally retarded patients. *British Journal of Psychiatry*, **145**, 289–93.

Reiss, S. (1988). A university based demonstration programme on outpatient mental health services for mentally retarded people. In J. A. Stark, F. J. Menolascino, M. H. Albarelli and V. C. Gray, eds. *Mental Retardation and Mental Health: Classification, Diagnosis, Treatment, Services*, pp. 249–253. New York: Springer-Verlag.

Reiss, S. (1990). The prevalence of dual diagnosis in community based day programmes in the Chicago metropolitan area. *American Journal of Mental Retardation*, **94**, 578–85.

Royal College of Psychiatrists (1974). Mental Deficiency Section: Memorandum on the responsibilities and role of the Consultant Psychiatrist in Mental Handicap. *British Journal of Psychiatry Supplement, News and Notes. May* 5.

Royal College of Psychiatrists (1978). Mental handicap. *Bulletin of the Royal College of Psychiatrists. April*. 56–61.

Royal College of Psychiatrists (1980). Secure facilities for psychiatric patients: a comprehensive policy.

Royal College of Psychiatrists (1983). Mental handicap services–the future. *Bulletin of the Royal College of Psychiatrists*, **7**, 131–4.

Royal College of Psychiatrists (1985). Registrar training in mental handicap. *Bulletin of the Royal College of Psychiatrists*, **9**, 206.

Royal College of Psychiatrists (1986). Psychiatric services for mentally handicapped adults and young people. *Bulletin of the Royal College of Psychiatrists*, **10**, 321–2.

Royal College of Psychiatrists (1987). General information and regulations for the MRCPsych. examination.

Rusch, R. G., Hall, J. C. & Griffin, H. C. (1986). Abuse provoking characteristics of institutionalised mentally retarded individuals. *American Journal of Mental Deficiency*, **90**, 618–24.

Santamour, M. B. & Watson, P. S. (1982). *The Retarded Offender*. New York: Praeger Publications.

Sandford, D. A., Elzinga, R. H. & Grainger, W. (1987). Evaluation of a residential behavioural programme for behaviourally disturbed mentally retarded young adults. *American Journal of Mental Deficiency*, **91**, 431–4.

Smith, J. (1988). An open forensic unit for borderline mentally impaired offenders. *Bulletin of the Royal College of Psychiatrists*, **12**, 13–15.

Snaith, R. P., James, F. E. & Winokur, B. (1979). The drug treatment of mental illness and epilepsy in the mentally handicapped patient. In F. E. James and R. P. Snaith, eds. *Psychiatric Illness and Mental Handicap*. London: Gaskell Press.

Sovner, R. (1986). Limiting factors in the use of DSM III criteria with mentally ill/mentally retarded persons. *Psychopharmacology Bulletin*, **22**, 1055–9.

Welsh Office (1983). All Wales Strategy for the Development of Services for Mentally Handicapped People, Welsh Office, Cathays Park, Cardiff.

Wright, E. C. (1982). The presentation of mental illness in mentally retarded adults. *British Journal of Psychiatry*, **141**, 496–502.

Zarfas, D. E. (1988). Mental health systems for people with mental retardation: a Canadian perspective. *Australia and New Zealand Journal of Developmental Disabilities*, **14**, 3–7.

22

Community psychiatric services for people with mental retardation

NICK BOURAS, DAVID BROOKS,
KATIE DRUMMOND

Introduction

In recent years there has been a profound change in the role and working practice of psychiatric services for people with mental retardation. This has been characterised by the development of flexible and innovative schemes, aiming to meet individual need. Psychiatrists have been able to participate in this challenge by focusing on the diagnosis, treatment and prevention of mental illness, as opposed to the traditional role of seeking the aetiology of mental retardation and concern with general health care and the administration of residential facilities.

In the early 1970s, the focus of care in the UK moved from institutions to integration in the local community. This change was reinforced by the development of a critique of the social process which causes devaluation and exclusion of certain social groups. This movement initially called 'normalisation' and later 'social role valorisation', influenced a radical reappraisal of planning and organisation of services for people with mental retardation. On the introduction of the National Health Service in Britain in 1948, it had been decided that the Health Service should manage the long-stay institutions, although it was recognised at that time that much of this care was more social than health. In the last decade, with resettlement into community, the NHS is progressively transferring its role for residential and social care back to the local authorities and focusing its own activity on the health needs of this client group (Caring for People, 1989). This approach, however, fails to recognise the complex interaction between health and social needs. Over the last decade with the gradual reduction of the inpatient population in long-stay hospitals and the development of alternative community services, there has been a tendency for the National Health Service to focus predominantly on health needs of the clients, though still offering residential facilities either in institutions or in the community.

An applied psychiatric service

In a geographical area of SE London with a population of 320 000 the development of residential and specialist services began in 1982. It is estimated that in this area there are about 1000 people with severe and 4000 with a mild mental retardation. Service planning contained two elements: first to resettle the people moving out from long-stay institutions in 'ordinary housing' in the community and secondly, to support those already living in the community either with their families or in residential facilities such as group homes or hostels.

Community multidisciplinary teams were formed to facilitate the development of the residential service and through the mechanism of individual planning and case management, to access a variety of social, health and vocational opportunities to meet individual needs. There were no clear plans for services to be provided for people with mental retardation and mental health needs, although this service had been offered in the past as part of the institutional care.

A new Community Specialist Psychiatric Service (CSPS) for people with mental retardation was developed as part of the generic psychiatric service (Bouras & Drummond, 1990). The CSPS in mental retardation is fully integrated with the generic mental health service and has the great advantage of accessing existing expertise and facilities while providing specialist input. A close working relationship also exists with the community teams and other community agencies.

The functions of the CSPS have been clinical and consultative. The clinical role involves psychiatric assessment and treatment of adults with mental illness, management of behavioural problems, work with offenders including the interface with the judiciary system and the treatment of epilepsy that has psychological implications. The latter involves close collaborative work with other medical disciplines. The consultative role includes regular consultation and support to multidisciplinary community teams, social services, voluntary and private organisations, day centres, service managers relatives and care staff. Participation in training initiatives, in particular skills transfer to care staff, and the generation of ideas for improving and developing the service are also important parts of this role.

All referrals receive a detailed assessment, and are presented and discussed at the weekly community clinical meeting, where a therapeutic intervention plan is formulated. The main treatment interventions in operation are: home-based intervention, out-patient care and admission to a psychiatric unit.

Home-based intervention

The intervention occurs in the clients' normal living environment and is seen as the preferred option, as it focuses on the environment, where the identified behaviour is occurring and directly involves the people with whom the client interacts and who are important agents for producing and maintaining change.

A detailed assessment is made and a treatment plan constructed. Then the intensive intervention phase occurs, which identifies specific goals relating to symptoms or function. When changes are seen to have been established, gradual reduction of input occurs and the supportive phase starts. Finally, the regular specialist involvement is withdrawn and progress is reviewed at intervals. The treatment plan is devised to meet the needs of a particular client and is unique, flexible and responsive to changing needs.

Outpatient care

Clients may attend outpatient clinics for client-centred work such as assessment, pharmacotherapy, counselling or psychotherapy. Long-term monitoring is also provided.

Admission

Admission may be needed occasionally, when a more complex and detailed assessment is required, or the intervention cannot be carried out in the normal living environment. Inpatient beds are available for this purpose in a designated general psychiatric ward. The role of the community nurses is vital in liaising with the ward staff and community agencies, while working directly with the client to implement a treatment plan. In all forms of intervention the existing resources and skills from community agencies, generic psychiatric and other services, may be used.

Service evaluation

This new service has been monitored and evaluated in three areas:

1. New referrals to the psychiatric service
2. Care staff related issues in community supported houses and
3. Adolescents with mental retardation and their families.

New referrals

All referrals to the CSPS since the development of the service, ($n = 356$ over 10 years), have been assessed and information has been recorded on a specially devised form, 'The assessment and information rating profile'. This semistructured assessment procedure covers areas such as: social and demographic characteristics, family information, medical history, level of mental retardation, skills assessment, behavioural problems, psychiatric assessment, a problem-oriented list and clinical management decision.

The aims of this monitoring evaluation were to identify the characteristics of the people with mental retardation referred to the specialist psychiatric service, the type of their problems and their service needs.

Although the largest single group of people (49%) were living at home with their family, 25% were living in residential facilities run by social services and private and voluntary organisations, 15% were living in staff supported houses for people recently resettled from institutions and 11% were living independently. Most of the people (57.6%) fell in the category of mild mental retardation, 27.4% moderate and 15% had severe mental retardation.

A psychiatric diagnosis, based on clinical criteria of DSM III-R, was made in 42.6% of the people referred. Behaviour problems were present in 187 (52.5%) people. The most frequent behavioural problem was aggression towards others (33.3%). Self-injurious behaviour was more common in women while delinquent and socially inappropriate behaviour rated more for men. Only 35 (11%) of the referrals were admitted to a psychiatric unit. Of those clients admitted, 40% suffered from schizophrenic or paranoid psychosis and 17% from depression. In addition, physical aggression was present in 50% of the admitted clients, comparing with 30% among the non-admitted.

Care staff-related issues in community supported houses

One area of particular change, in terms of service delivery for people with mental retardation, has been the development of community residential homes. People with mental retardation have limited abilities in processing information and responding appropriately to demanding situations, yet they need training and support to master certain skills to achieve and maintain an optimal level of functioning. Hence, the nature of the living environment is critical in affecting outcomes (Richardson, 1981). The crucial area of interaction is between the residents and staff.

Staff who are committed and supported are likely to be a positive and powerful factor in achieving an optimal level of functioning. Staff behaviour and attitude may be modified by their knowledge, training and skills as well as by work practices, which are determined by the organisation. It is recognised that working with this client group may be stressful and lead to burnout (Freudenberger & Richelson, 1980). Burnout has important implications for clients, staff and the service organisation. Quantifying this syndrome and finding associated factors may generate interventions that could be developed to reduce its prevalence.

The aims of this evaluation were, first, to describe and measure the impact of 'ordinary' housing staff and clients and, secondly, to identify the important interactions affecting staff and their work practice. Data were collected for 79 adults with mental retardation living in 23 staff supported houses and 39 senior members of staff. The level of burnout found was similar to that reported in studies of general nurses working in a hospital setting. The only variable which was found to be related to burnout was 'thinking about leaving the job' ($F = 2.9$, $p < 0.05$). This suggests that burnout may be the end stage in a process which leads to staff resignation.

Consideration of clients' factors revealed only one statistically significant positive correlation between the frequency of behaviour problems and a measure of organisational complexity called 'hierarchy of authority'. This was the result of additional input provided to the clients and staff by professionals, including the specialist psychiatric service. As a result, the senior members of staff could not take management decisions without regular discussion with specialists and line managers.

Adolescents with mental retardation and their families

Important issues in the development of community services are particularly well illustrated as children and adolescents with mental retardation mature and family needs change. The transition period from childhood to adulthood has been shown to coincide with major life cycle changes (Wikler, 1986). Recent research discards a simple cause and effect relationship between the development of the child with mental retardation and the family.

It is necessary to examine adolescent and family characteristics in order to assess the burden of care and stress in these families, their coping mechanisms and the various factors more directly related to the transition to adulthood. The multidimensional assessment focused on clinical and service interventions, effectiveness of current service provision and future service needs; taking into consideration the psychosocial dimensions of a health care system.

Pupils ($n = 59$), attending special schools, aged from 13 to 19 were assessed as well as their mothers. Adolescents with severe mental retardation were shown to be more behaviourally disturbed and to have mothers who were more stressed, more negative in their attitude to their offspring and perception of psychosocial family effects. Maternal stress, attitudes, perceived social support and behaviour problems were positively correlated with specific psychosocial family effects, such as pressure of care, extra time demands and less time for siblings.

There was evidence of significant unmet needs in a variety of areas. More difficulties were evident in the families with a member having severe mental retardation during the transitional stage from child to adult services. These issues were not reflected in the service planning. For example, only 29 % of stressed mothers received the required support services (respite care, social work). Interventions must continue through the transitional period from child to adult services. The nature of the agency to coordinate this provision should be considered in the context of the changing structure of primary care and community care legislation in Britain.

Summary

Good quality health and psychiatric care services are essential for the successful maintenance of people with mental retardation in the community. The Health Service will have to make appropriate provision for certain groups of people with mental retardation, such as those with psychiatric disorders, serious medical problems, the elderly and offenders (SETRHA, 1993). The interface between mental health and mental retardation services requires further clarification (Mansell, 1993). Both must feel well equipped and take their share of responsibility in meeting the needs of people with mental retardation and psychiatric problems. Areas of continuing debate in the development of community services for people with mental retardation include the long-term viability of integrating people with mental retardation and challenging behaviour as well as specialist psychiatric vs. generic services. This chapter has highlighted some of the challenges that community psychiatric services for people with mental retardation face. They must focus not only on the diagnosis and treatment of the individual client, but also on: the provision of clinical services, multidisciplinary working relationships, staffing issues, liaison with other medical services such as primary care physicians (Bouras & Drummond, 1992), the promotion of preventative services for children and their families and effective transition to adult services. Staff characteristics and organisational practices, rather than client factors, were found to be the most important aspects for staff well being in supported houses. Issues of individual planning, consent to treatment, medication, risk policies, and legal issues are all new areas for consideration. The training implications for care staff, medical students, general practitioners and psychiatrists are considerable and will increase with the expansion of services.

The advancement of diagnostic and treatment procedures is at the core of psychiatric practice in mental retardation. The application of biological techniques in such areas as molecular genetics and neuroimaging will undoubtedly improve the ability to effectively diagnose and treat people with mental retardation and psychiatric disorders. Services will also be affected and the need will remain for continued documentation and analysis of the utilisation of new services, to facilitate its objectives and management. This is a necessary contribution to the process of evaluation of quality of care.

References

Bouras, N. & Drummond, C. (1990). Diagnostic and Treatment Issues for Adults in Community Care. In A. Dose, A. Van Gennep & G. J. Zwanilcken, eds. *Treatment of Mental Illness and Behavioural Disorder in the Mentally Retarded*. Leiden: Logon.

Bouras, N. & Drummond, C. (1992): Behaviour and psychiatric disorders of people with mental handicaps living in the community. *Journal of Intellectual Disability Research*, **36**, 349–57.

Caring for People: Community care in the next decade and beyond (1989). *HMSO, CM 849*, London.

Freudenberger, H. & Richelson, G. (1980). *Burnout,*. London: Arrow Books.

Mansell, J. L. (1993). *Services for People with Learning Disabilities and Challenging Behaviour or Mental Health Needs*. London: HMSO.

Richardson, S. A. (1981). Living environments. In H. C. Haywood & J. R. Newbrough, eds. *An Ecological Perspective in Living Environments for Developmentally Disabled Persons*. Baltimore: University Press.

SETRHA (1993). The mental health needs of people with learning disabilities: Report of a working group. South East Thames Regional Health Authority: Bexhill, Kent.

Wikler, L. M. (1986). Periodic stresses of families of older mentally retarded children. *American Journal of Mental Deficiency*, **90**, 703–6.

23

Integrated employment and vocational services for youth and adults with disabilities in the United States

JOHN R. JOHNSON AND FRANK R. RUSCH

Introduction

Over the past decade individuals with disabilities have benefited from dramatic changes in employment opportunities and vocational services in the United States (Rusch, Chadsey-Rusch & Johnson, 1991; Rusch et al., 1992). Such changes have resulted in 'integrated employment' of thousands of persons experiencing many types and degrees of disability. 'Integrated employment' refers to a person with a disability working in a local business or industrial setting.

This approach represents a sharp divergence from placement in traditional workshop settings that characterised 'vocational services' and/or 'community services' during the 1960s and 1970s. Employers in a multitude of occupations have employed individuals with disabilities, offering not only a job in natural employment settings but opportunities for socialisation and interaction with non-disabled coworkers. Many Americans experiencing diverse disabilities have realised dramatic gains in the number of hours worked, wages earned, type of jobs performed, skills learned, and general access to and participation in integrated community-based services and activities. Such gains may be attributed to what has come to be referred to as 'supported employment'. This chapter provides a review of the history, development, implementation, and vocational outcomes associated with the supported employment initiative in the United States.

Problems with traditional adult vocational services and outcomes

The rate of unemployment among individuals with disabilities in the US is approximately 60–80 % (Kiernan & Bruininks, 1986). In spite of

300

significant attitudinal changes in American society, Rusch *et al.* (1992) noted that 'Traditional views of persons with severe handicaps continue to pose enormous challenges to contemporary educational and rehabilitation practices'.

One area undergoing major change is the structure of rehabilitation and employment services provided to adults with disabilities. Presently, a large portion of fiscal resources continue to support segregated 'sheltered workshop' and 'day activity' programmes for adults (Braddock, 1987; Buckley & Bellamy, 1984; McGaughey *et al.*, 1991). These programmes offer a range of adult services including vocational training, assessment and evaluation, activities of daily living, and sheltered employment provided in facilities designated solely for persons with disabilities (Nelson, 1971). Vocational services are designed to prepare individuals for competitive or supported employment under the assumption that 'One reason why individuals cannot work is that they are not ready to meet work requirements of competitive employment' (Nelson, 1971). The assumptions and implications of the 'work readiness' concept are fundamental to the structure and delivery of segregated adult services. These services are arranged hierarchically, with the adult day activity programme at the lowest level. Participants in this programme experience the most severe disabilities. Services focus on habilitation and may include physical therapy, occupational therapy, building work tolerance, and activities of daily living. Work emphasis is prevocational in nature, and it is usually assumed that individuals at this programme level are incapable of competitive employment.

The next level, referred to as 'work activity', usually involves the participation of individuals who experience more moderate disabilities. While greater emphasis is placed on 'work readiness' as individuals demonstrate greater skill and productivity on benchwork tasks (e.g. assembly, packing, sorting), the emphasis continues to be on developing work habits, work conditioning, and work tolerance. The term 'work adjustment' has been used to describe many of the activities at this level.

The next level of service involves sheltered employment. Nelson (1971) described three types of sheltered employment that continue in some fashion today. Transitional employment is focused on upgrading productivity and possibly movement to competitive employment. Extended and sheltered employment involve long-term employment in segregated facilities for individuals with disabilities. Work is generally subcontracted from outside businesses and industries, which transport materials and supplies to the facility where work is completed. Such work usually involves benchwork activities completed at piecerate wages (e.g. wage determined on the basis of number of units assembled) by persons with disabilities. Transitional, extended, and sheltered employment have been referred to as 'regular workshop programmes' in US Department of Labor studies on sheltered workshops (US Department of Labor, 1979).

Numerous national studies of sheltered workshops in the US (General Accounting Office, 1980; US Department of Labor, 1979; Whitehead, 1981) questioned the outcomes achieved by participants in these programmes. Bellamy *et al.* (1986) reviewed these studies and identified several problems with the structure and outcomes associated with sheltered workshop programmes. The first and most serious of these problems is the degree to which individuals with disabilities are segregated from non-disabled peers and coworkers, as most sheltered workshop programmes serve only individuals with disabilities. A second problem cited by Bellamy et al. (1986) is the low rate (about 12%) of entry into competitive employment by individuals served in sheltered workshop programmes. The majority who entered competitive employment placements would do so within three months after placement in a workshop compared to 3% of those who had been in a sheltered workshop for more than two years. Thus, these authors concluded that the longer an individual was placed in a segregated employment setting, the less his chances of achieving integrated employment.

A third problem was the fact that very few individuals, only 3% (US Department of Labor, 1979) progressed from one level of the sheltered workshop programme structure to a higher level. In addition, Bellamy *et al.* (1986) pointed out that, on the average, it took 37 years to move from the lowest level of the sheltered workshop programme structure (i.e. day activity) to the next level on the continuum (i.e. work activity). Another 10 years were required, on the average, to graduate from a work activity centre to the regular workshop programme. To move from a regular workshop programme to competitive employment required an average of yet another nine years. Therefore, on the average, it would take someone starting at the lowest level 56 years to be competitively employed in an integrated setting. An overwhelming majority of individuals with mental retardation were served in day activity and work activity programmes. This implies that movement into competitive employment for individuals with the most significant disabilities was virtually non-existent.

The fourth problem was that to the wages received by the majority of individuals in these programmes were well below the poverty threshold. In addition, the number of hours worked per day was extremely low. There was a rising level of dissatisfaction among consumers and rehabilitation service providers with the outcomes achieved by traditional adult vocational and employment service programmes.

Emergence of supported employment

Demonstration projects

Rusch and Hughes (1990) in their historical overview traced the emergence of supported employment. Early studies documented the ability of persons with severe disabilities to learn complex vocational tasks, such as assembly of cable harnesses, cam switches, and bicycle brakes (Bellamy, Horner & Inman, 1979; Gold, 1980; Hunter & Bellamy, 1976). These 'illustrations of competence' were followed by research conducted in integrated competitive employment settings (Rusch & Mithaug, 1980; Wehman, 1981).

More recently, the majority of studies are conducted in natural settings. As a result, a body of knowledge has emerged that addresses the development of individual competence (Hughes, Rusch & Curl, 1990), natural supports (Nisbet & Hagner, 1988), and social acceptance of individuals (Chadsey-Rusch, 1990) with all types and degrees of disability. In addition to addressing the learning of new skills, specific technologies have been developed that focus on generalisation and maintenance of skills (Horner, Dunlap & Koegel, 1988; Mithaug *et al.*, 1988) and the ability to adapt and change as conditions require (Martin, Mithaug & Husch, 1988).

As research findings tended to support that individuals with severe disabilities could learn complex vocational and social skills, demonstration projects were funded that focused on alternatives to segregated sheltered workshop programmes (Rusch & Schutz, 1979; Wehman, 1981; Vogelsberg, 1986; Ellis *et al.*, 1990; Boles *et al.*, 1984). The success of these programmes led to the development of a systematic methodology for achieving and maintaining successful competitive job placement of individuals with disabilities (Rusch & Mithaug, 1980) which gradually evolved into a model of vocational and employment services referred to as 'supported employment' (Rusch, 1990).

Legislation

A critical factor in the emergence of supported employment was legislation passed by Congress authorising supported employment services. The first statutory reference to supported employment in national legislation was made in the Developmental Disabilities Assistance and Bill of Rights Act of 1984 (P. L. 98–527). Subsequent amendments legally incorporated supported employment as an acceptable, desirable, and fundable rehabilitation service and outcome.

Another law, P. L. 99–506, resulted in the development and proliferation of a large number of supported employment programmes and services throughout the United States focusing on achieving integrated employment outcomes for persons with severe disabilities. It allocated funding for states to develop and implement supported employment programmes funded by state and local vocational rehabilitation agencies.

Basic assumptions underlying supported employment programmes

The concept of supported employment is based on four assumptions. First, the best way to get 'ready' to work is to work under actual employment situations. Unfortunately, the concept of 'work readiness' has been employed to limit the access of individuals with disabilities to competitive and remunerative employment. This practice is untenable by today's standards.

Secondly, individuals with disabilities have the right and responsibility to work alongside non-disabled coworkers. Integration is the hallmark of supported employment (Brown *et al.*, 1990).

Thirdly, individuals with disabilities have the right to be paid a decent wage. This assumption recognises the right of individuals with disabilities to achieve social, personal, and financial independence and opportunities.

Fourthly, given the proper types and ranges of support, individuals with disabilities are capable of achieving successful employment. However, to ensure durability and effectiveness, such supports must be developed in conjunction with the natural conditions and expectations of the work environment.

Critical elements of successful supported employment programmes

Numerous professionals have described the essential components required to achieve successful supported employment outcomes (Bellamy *et al.*, 1988; Gardner *et al.*, 1988; Kiernan & Stark, 1986; Moon *et al.*, 1990; Rusch, 1986, 1990; Rusch & Mithaug, 1980; Wehman, 1981; Wehman & Moon, 1988). Trach (1990) identified five essential components of supported employment: (a) community survey and job analysis, (b) job match, (c) job placement and training, (d) job maintenance, and (e) related job services and interagency coordination. These components have been used to evaluate the quality and performance of supported employment services throughout the US (Trach & Rusch, 1989). Each component is discussed below.

Community survey and job analysis

The job development process should include (a) surveying community businesses and employers via telephone to identify job openings, (b) correspondence with and visits to employment sites, (c) negotiation with employers to obtain a commitment to hire an individual with a disability, and (d) analysis of the employment setting in terms of environmental, social and cultural characteristics, and work requirements (McLoughlin, Garner & Callahan, 1987).

The first three elements may include more global marketing strategies such as public relations tactics, employer negotiation strategies, and strategies to increase the visibility of an organisation's employment services, including radio, television, and other public media (Kiernan, Carter & Bronstein, 1989; Shafer, Parent & Everson, 1988). The fourth component is conducted to identify areas where employees will require training and support and its availability locally.

Job match

Potential employees' preferences, interests, and skills should be matched to actual employment demands and conditions. Job analysis must include an assessment of training and support services that may be provided by coworkers, employers, family members, friends, and others in the settings in which the potential employees typically live, work, and play.

The next step is to assess individual preferences, interests, and skills in relation to employment opportunities and settings. Discrepancies between the actual conditions and demands of a specific work setting and the skills of the individual can then identified and the necessary support and training provided.

Kregel, Banks & Hill (1991) using the client job compatibility screening instrument, ' ... a microcomputer-based assessment instrument and job placement tool that determines the extent to which the demands and supports available in a specific employment setting match the strengths and abilities of a potential employee' identified 19 variables that significantly correlated with employment retention at 12 months. They suggested that an effective job-matching instrument may promote long-term employment retention and reduce the costs of employment services.

Job placement and training

Different levels and types of training may be required depending on type of disabilities. Individuals experiencing mental retardation may require skill acquisition, generalisation and maintenance training on both employment and social skills from the first day of employment (Rusch, Chadsey-Rusch & Lagomarcino, 1987). However, the training needs for individuals experiencing chronic mental illness may be minimal in areas related to task performance, with greater emphasis placed on areas related to personal responsibilities and social interaction with coworkers and supervisors (Anthony & Blanch, 1987).

Two primary goals are related to the job placement and training component of supported employment. The first is to extend individual competence required for the new employee to perform all work responsibilities to the employer's and his/her own expectations and satisfaction (Hughes *et al.*, 1990). The second goal is to develop and implement natural support strategies and mechanisms that provide the means for an individual to continue to be successful in those areas in which individual competence may not be adequate.

The literature is replete with examples of training strategies applied in integrated employment settings. Such strategies typically include systematic instruction (Snell, 1987), behaviour–analytic and management strategies (Rusch & Mithaug, 1980), generalisation and maintenance programming (Horner *et al.*, 1988), adaptability training (Mithaug *et al.*, 1987), self-advocacy and social skills training (Chadsey-Rusch, 1990), and withdrawal and fading procedures (Mithaug et al., 1988; Rusch & Kazdin, 1981).

Additional strategies found to be successful for promoting individual competence and employment success for employees with severe disabilities include adaptations and modifications to physical and social factors on the job site (Sowers & Powers, 1990; Wood, 1988), development of natural supports (Griffin, 1992; Nisbet & Hagner, 1988), and the use of rehabilitation engineering and assistive technology (Mueller, 1990; Stack, 1988).

Job maintenance

The primary goal of job maintenance is to achieve job stabilisation so that the primary responsibility for training and support may be transferred to the employee, family, friends, coworkers and others who support the employee at work, home, and in the community (Johnson & Rusch, 1990).

Job maintenance focuses on the development of support mechanisms to maintain long-term employment (Flynn *et al.*, 1991).

'Natural supports' (Nisbet & Hagner, 1988) have received national attention with the funding of six research projects focusing upon the development and evaluation of such support systems. Common examples of natural supports include assistance typically provided by families, friends, and coworkers. Others include adaptations and modifications of physical aspects of an environment, organisation of job tasks and assistance provided by individuals in the community (e.g. bus drivers, grocery store clerks, health professionals).

Job maintenance also involves ongoing contact between employers and rehabilitation staff to identify any training or support needs that may develop. In many cases, supported employees require additional training or upgrading of their skills, revisions in their support systems, or access to additional employment services in the event of job separation.

Related job services/interagency coordination

The last component of an effective supported employment programme relates to the relationship among rehabilitation programme staff and other organisations and agencies. For example, the Social Security Administration (SSA) plays a major role in the lives of people with disabilities in the US. Many individuals who experience serious disabilities are eligible for income maintenance programmes and state and federally subsidised health care. Rehabilitation personnel involved in securing supported employment for individuals with disabilities work closely with SSA staff to ensure that the individual retains, after employment, all benefits to which he or she is entitled. In addition, rehabilitation personnel work closely with individuals in the community to ensure that individuals gain access to, and use of, generic public services available to the general public such as the public library, public transportation, and various community services. Use of generic services may be considered natural supports and are effective means of decreasing the costs associated with the development or use of specialised and technical services. For example, generic employment service programmes may serve as a valuable source of identifying potential job openings through job development activities.

Organisational and implementation factors

Type of placement

Several supported employment placement models have evolved. Individual, enclave, work crew and entrepreneurial placement approaches (Rusch & Hughes, 1990) will be discussed.

The individual placement model typically involves the employment of one individual at one site or several individuals dispersed in various locations or departments at a single site. This '...(a) allows the target employee maximum choice in selecting a job that meets his or her individual preference; (b) offers the greatest opportunity for target employees to be optimally integrated in the workplace; and (c) allows the individual to earn competitive wages' (Kregel *et al.*, 1990). Within this model, it is expected that the presence of the employment specialist will substantially decrease as the supported employee gradually gains greater independence. In addition, greater emphasis is placed on developing natural supports to increase opportunities for integration and independence.

The remaining placement types may be referred to as 'group' placements. For example, in enclave placement a group of no more than eight persons with disabilities are employed to work in the same area on the same task (Rhodes & Valenta, 1985). Opportunities for integration are provided through interaction with coworkers and supervisors during work and breaks. Training and supervision are provided on a continuous basis by an employment specialist.

Similar to enclave placements, work crews are transported to various locations in the community to complete subcontract work (e.g. building maintenance, janitorial work, and grounds-keeping). Training, supervision, and transportation are provided by an on-site work supervisor.

The entrepreneurial model is similar to the enclave approach except that individuals are employed by manufacturing companies to provide very specific services, typically benchwork activities to assemble, package, or sort products. Manpower is provided by an agency serving persons with disabilities to the company who subcontracts the sponsoring agency. Training and supervision are provided on a continuous basis by an employment specialist who is employed by the sponsoring agency.

Funding

Typical supported employment programmes in the US are organised and implemented by private non-profit adult service and rehabilitation agencies that provide a full range of adult day programming, rehabilitation, residential, and sheltered employment services. These agencies receive funding from a variety of sources including local and State Departments of (Vocational) Rehabilitation Services, Mental Health, and Developmental Disabilities. Funding may also be received from charities. In most cases, supported employment services are funded by multiple sources including monies allocated by PL 99–506 and grants to local and state agencies.

Referrals

Referrals come from local offices of the State Department of Rehabilitation Services, schools, hospitals, and other organisations that have contact with or provide services to individuals with disabilities. Relatives, friends, and individuals may seek services independently. Many organisations educate the general public about the availability of these services and encourage families and employers to use supported employment services.

Staffing

Supported employment programmes frequently have a programme director and employment training specialists (also referred to as 'job coaches'). Programmes with sufficient funding also have marketing and job development specialists. The programme director is responsible for administering and managing supported employment services and developing funding resources. Employment training specialists and marketing and job development specialists are responsible for delivering supported employment services to individuals with disabilities (Rusch *et al.*, 1989; Sale *et al.*, 1989).

Supported employment programmes tend to be understaffed, need more qualified staff, generally underpay staff, and experience high turnover rates (Winking *et al.*, 1989). As a result, a number of professionals have called for the increased professionalsation of supported employment staff (Brooke & Armstrong, 1992).

Programme standards

Minimal standards have been established governing the quality of supported employment programmes by the Commission on the Accreditation of Rehabilitation Facilities (CARF, 1990). In addition, a number of states are in the process of developing statewide standards to monitor and evaluate supported employment services. To date, no national standards to guide the type, quality, and duration of supported employment have been established.

Outcomes achieved in supported employment

Research and analysis has concentrated on evaluation of outcomes. Factors studied to determine the success of supported employment in the US include the number of individuals placed in supported employment, type of disabilities experienced, type of placement, wages earned, hours worked, and types of jobs. This section reviews a sample of findings from state and national studies conducted in the US.

Placement rate and type of disability

Recent studies have shown that the majority of supported employees experience mild and moderate mental retardation. The next most common, but much smaller group, experience chronic mental illness.

A small percentage with severe and profound mental retardation, autism, cerebral palsy, and traumatic brain injury have also been successful in supported employment (Vogelsberg, 1990; Kregel *et al.*, 1990; McGaughey *et al.*, 1991; Shafer, Revell & Isbister, 1991).

Type of placement

Shafer *et al.* (1991) reported that 52% of the individuals in their survey ($n = 25,109$) were employed using the individual placement model. The next most common types of supported employment were the enclave (15.3%) and the mobile work crew (12.8%). The remainder of the survey sample were employed using the entrepreneurial model (7.3%), transitional employment (5%), and other (7.5%) types of supported employment placement. The proportion of individuals employed in various types of placements may vary substantially by state, depending on demographic and economic factors.

Wages

Numerous studies have reported that wages earned by supported employees are substantially higher than those earned by individuals in segregated/sheltered employment. Shafer *et al.* (1991) reported average hourly wages ranged from $2.54 to $3.91 for supported employees.

Employees in individual placements received the highest hourly wage ($3.91), while those in entrepreneurial settings earned the lowest wage ($2.54). Individuals in enclave, mobile crew, and other types of placement earned an average of $2.69, $2.85, and $2.85 per hour, respectively.

Individuals, however, in supported employment have the potential of earning six to ten times more per month than their counterparts in segregated employment programmes (i.e. regular workshop, work activity, and day activity programmes) (Kregel *et al.*, 1990; Shafer *et al.*, 1991).

In addition, Kiernan, McGaughey and Schalock, (1986) reported employment outcomes from their national survey of adults with developmental disabilities. They found that individuals in sheltered employment who worked an average of 30.5 hours per week earned × 1.47 per hour and individuals who worked an average of 23.3 hours per week earned $1.24 per hour. These authors also noted that 50% of the individuals in sheltered employment earned $1.09 per hour or less, 75% earned $1.67 per hour or less, and less than 5% earned more than $3.00 per hour. These data indicate that supported employment is a substantially better paying alternative to segregated employment.

Hours worked

In their national survey of supported employment, Shafer *et al.* (1991) reported that over half (51.3%) of the individuals for whom hours worked was reported ($n = 31,319$) worked 30 or more hours per week, 24.4% worked 20 to 30 hours per week, and the remainder (24.3%) worked fewer than 20 hours per week. These data suggest that the majority of supported employees are working on a full-time basis (35 or more hours per week).

Ellis *et al.* (1990) reported that persons employed in individual placements worked the highest number of hours per month (87.4), followed by persons in enclave placements (77.4). In contrast, persons in mobile crews worked the fewest hours per month (65.2). According to Ellis *et al.* (1990), the average hours worked per month by all supported employees in the State of Illinois was 80.8. Again, these data suggest that, on the average, supported employees are working a full 40-hour week.

Types of jobs

The majority of supported employees were placed in jobs such as food service, janitorial-maintenance, factory type work, and housekeeping (e.g. hotels, motels) (Shafer *et al.*, 1991; Kiernan *et al.*, 1986).

Research in supported employment

Research has focused on analyses of employment outcomes. Additional areas include: (a) evaluation of training and support strategies in employment settings (McDonnell *et al.*, 1989; NARF, 1989); (b) cost–benefit analyses (Tines *et al.*, 1990); (c) job tenure and separation (Lagomarcino, 1990); (d) programme assurance, evaluation and standards (Mank, Sandow & Rhodes, 1991; Trach & Rusch, 1989); (e) disincentives and barriers to integrated employment (Noble & Collignon, 1987; Noble & Conley, 1989); (f) coworker involvement (Rusch, Johnson & Hughes, 1990); (g) social ecology of the workplace (Chadsey-Rusch *et al.*, 1989); (h) level of integration at the work site (Lagomarcino, 1989; Parent *et al.*, 1991); (i) level of training and supervision (Johnson & Rusch, 1990); (j) staff-related issues (Everson, 1991; Renzaglia & Everson, 1990); (k) quality of life (Heal *et al.*, 1990; Mank & Buckley, 1989); and (l) issues specific to the employment of persons experiencing mental illness (Bond & McDonel, 1991), traumatic brain injury (Wehman *et al.*, 1989), physical disabilities (Sowers & Powers, 1990), and other disabilities. Review of published studies in these areas is beyond the scope of this chapter. Briefly, the research has demonstrated that integrated employment is achievable and is more consistent with respect for the dignity, value, and potential of individuals with disabilities than segregated services.

However, a word of caution is in order. While research has demonstrated that supported employment is a successful and viable option that is endorsed by thousands of employers, a major barrier to integrated employment remains to be addressed. This barrier involves individuals, agencies, and organisations including state and federal governing bodies, that remain committed to preserving the status quo. For example, Braddock (1987) reported that 41% of federal spending during federal fiscal year 1985 for mental retardation and developmental disability services supported approximately 100000 persons in public institutions, while the remainder (59%) helped finance services for a much larger population in community-based settings. More recently, and of greater concern, are the findings of McGaughey *et al.* (1991), who reported that 80% of all state funds from state mental retardation and developmental disability agencies were allocated for segregated vocational and employment programmes, while 95% of the remaining funds (composed primarily of federal monies) were allocated for segregated services. The implication of these findings is that state and federal government agencies and rehabilitation professionals may represent the most significant barriers to the full employment enfranchisement of Americans with disabilities by promoting the spending of taxpayers' money on segregated vocational services.

Summary

This chapter was focused on the supported employment movement in the United States. A brief historical overview of supported employment was followed by a discussion of problems and resultant dissatisfaction associated with traditional segregated vocational services. The emergence of supported employment was traced to demonstration projects and legislation that ultimately resulted in the funding of this model. An in-depth discussion of the critical elements of supported employment was followed by a brief overview of organisational and implementation elements. Finally, the chapter concluded with a brief discussion of some outcomes achieved in supported employment by Americans with disabilities and an overview of major research issues addressed in the supported employment literature.

   Closely linked to the employment of adults with disabilities is another issue that has come to the forefront of American education: the transition from school to adulthood for students with disabilities (Rusch *et al.*, 1992). This issue has clear implications for vocational and employment systems developed for adults, since a primary outcome of transition is the acquisition of postschool employment. Successful transition requires a cooperative interface between school-based services and agencies providing adult employment services.

   Work is a natural adult life activity. It presents opportunities and challenges for growth and participation that can only be found at work. With this in mind, several limitations were noted including a lack of commitment and resolve to allocate substantial resources to integrated employment opportunities. Full inclusion in the workforce is not just a fad or a dream. It is a reality supported by hard data. For persons with disabilities no amount of rhetoric, legislation, or research can take the place of a well-paying job. Supported employment is one way of achieving that goal.

References

Anthony, W. A. & Blanch, A. (1987). Supported employment for persons who are psychiatrically disabled: an historical and conceptual perspective. *Psychosocial Rehabilitation Journal*, **11**, 5–23.
Bellamy, G. T., Horner, R. H. & Inman, D. P. (1979). *Vocational Habilitation of Severely Retarded Adults: A Direct Service Technology*. Austin, TX: Pro-Ed.

Bellamy, G. T., Rhodes, L. E., Bourbeau, P. E. & Mank, D. (1986). Mental retardation services in sheltered workshops and day activity programs: Consumer benefits and policy alternatives. In F. R. Rusch, ed. *Competitive Employment Issues and Strategies*, pp. 257–271. Baltimore: Paul H. Brookes.

Bellamy, G. T., Rhodes, L. E., Mank, D. M. & Albin, J. M. (1988). *Supported Employment: A Community Implementation Guide*. Baltimore: Paul H. Brookes.

Boles, S. M., Bellamy, G. T., Horner, R. H. & Mank, D. M. (1984). Specialized training program: the structured employment model. In S. C. Paine, G. T. Bellamy & B. Wilcox, eds. *Human Services that Work: From Innovation to Practice, pp.* 181–205, Baltimore: Paul H. Brookes.

Bond, G. & McDonel, E. (1991). Vocational rehabilitation outcomes for persons with psychiatric disabilities: An update. *Journal of Vocational Rehabilitation* **1**(3), 9–20.

Braddock, D. (1987). *Federal Policy Toward Mental Retardation and Developmental Disabilities*. Baltimore: Paul H. Brookes.

Brooke, V. & Armstrong, A. (1992). What to do about a lack of professional identity: a call to action!. *The Advance (Association for Persons in Supported Employment)*, **3**(2), 6–7.

Brown, L., Udvari-Solner, A., Frattura-Kampschroer, E. *et al.* (1990). Integrated work: a rejection of segregated enclaves and mobile work crews. In L. H. Meyer, C. A. Peck & L. Brown, eds. *Critical Issues in the Lives of People with Severe Disabilities*, pp. 219–228, Baltimore: Paul H. Brookes.

Buckley, J. & Bellamy, G. T. (1984). National survey of day and vocational programs for adults with severe disabilities. Unpublished report, Eugene: University of Oregon, Specialized Training Program.

Chadsey-Rusch, J. (1990). Teaching social skills on the job. In F. R. Rusch, ed. *Supported Employment: Models, Methods, and Issues*, pp. 161–180, Sycamore, IL: Sycamore Publishing.

Chadsey-Rusch, J., Gonzalez, P., Tines, J. & Johnson, J. R. (1989). Social ecology of the workplace: Contextual variables affecting social interactions of employees with and without mental retardation. *American Journal on Mental Retardation*, **94**, 141–51.

Commission on Accreditation of Rehabilitation Facilities. (1990). *Standards Manual for Organizations Serving People with Disabilities*. Tucson, AZ: Author.

'Developmental Disabilities Act of 1984.' (PL 98–527, 19 October 1984). United States Statutes at Large, 98, 2662–2685.

Ellis, W., Rusch, F. R., Tu, J. & McCaughrin, W. (1990). Supported employment in Illinois. In F. R. Rusch, ed. *Supported Employment: Models, Methods and issues*, pp. 31–44, Sycamore, IL: Sycamore Publishing.

Everson, J. M. (1991). Supported employment personnel: An assessment of their self-reported training needs, educational backgrounds, and previous employment experiences. *Journal of the Association for Persons with Severe Handicaps*, **16**, 140–5.

Flynn, T. H., Wacker, D. P., Berg, W. K., Green, K. & Hurd, R. (1991). Long-term retention of workers placed in supported employment. *Journal of Vocational Rehabilitation*, **1**(1), 25–34.

Gardner, J. F., Chapman, M. S., Donaldson, G. & Jacobson, S. G. (1988). *Toward Supported Employment: A Process Guide for Planned Change*. Baltimore: Paul H. Brookes.

General Accounting Office. (1980). *Better Reevaluations of Handicapped Persons in Sheltered Workshops could increase their Opportunities for Competitive Employment.* Washington, DC: General Accounting Office.

Gold, M. W. (1980). '*Did I say that?*'. Champaign, IL: Research Press.

Griffin, C. (1992). Typical, generic, in vivo, in situ, normal, informal, typical (a.k.a. natural) supports. *The Advance (Association for Persons in Supported Employment)*, 3(2), 1–3.

Heal, L. W., Gonzalez, P., Rusch, F. R., Copher, J.l. & DeStefano, L. (1990). Comparison of successful and unsuccessful placements of youths with mental handicaps into competitive employment. *Exceptionality*, 1, 181–95.

Horner, R. H., Dunlap, G. & Koegel, R. L. (1988). *Generalization and Maintenance: Life-style Changes in Applied Settings.* Baltimore: Paul H. Brookes.

Hughes, C., Rusch, F. R. & Curl, R. (1990). Extending individual competence, developing natural support, and promoting social acceptance. In F. R. Rusch, ed. *Supported Employment: Models, Methods, and Issues*, pp. 181–197, Sycamore, IL: Sycamore Publishing.

Hunter, J. D., & Bellamy, G. T. (1976). Cable harness construction for severely retarded adults: a demonstration of training technique. *MESPH Review*, 1(7), 2–13.

Johnson, J. R., & Rusch, F. R. (1990). Analysis of hours of direct training provided by employment specialists to supported employees. *American Journal on Mental Retardation*, 94, 674–82.

Kiernan, W. E. & Bruininks, R. H. (1986). Demographic characteristics. In W. E. Kiernan & J. A. Stark, eds. *Pathways to Employment for Adults with Developmental Disabilities*, pp. 21–50, Baltimore: Paul H. Brookes.

Kiernan, W. E., Carter, A. & Bronstein, E. (1989). Marketing and marketing management in rehabilitation. In W. E. Kiernan & R. L. Schalock, eds. *Economics, Industry, and Disability: A Look Ahead*, pp. 49–56, Baltimore: Paul H. Brookes.

Kiernan, W. E., McGaughey, M. J. & Schalock, R. L. (1986). *Employment Survey for Adults with Developmental Disabilities.* Boston: The Children's Hospital, The Developmental Evaluation Clinic.

Kiernan, W. E. & Stark, J. (1986). *Pathways to Employment for Adults with Developmental Disabilities.* Baltimore: Paul H. Brookes.

Kregel, J., Banks, D. & Hill, M. (1991). Effective job matching in supported employment: the client-job compatibility screening instrument. *Journal of Vocational Rehabilitation*, 1(1), 51–58.

Kregel, J., Wehman, P., Revell, W. G. & Hill, M. (1990). Supported employment in Virginia. In F. R. Rusch, ed. *Supported Employment: Models, Methods, and Issues*, pp. 15–29, Sycamore, IL: Sycamore Publishing.

Lagomarcino, T. R. (1989). Assessing the multidimensional nature of integration in employment settings. Unpublished doctoral dissertation, University of Illinois at Urbana-Champaign.

Lagomarcino, T. L. (1990). Job separation issues in supported employment. In F. R. Rusch, ed. *Supported Employment: Models, Methods, and Issues*, pp. 301–316, Sycamore, IL: Sycamore Publishing.

Mank, D., & Buckley, J. (1989). Strategies for integrated employment. In W. E. Kiernan & R. L. Schalock, eds. *Economics, Industry, and Disability: A Look Ahead*, pp. 319–335, Baltimore: Paul H. Brookes.

Mank, D., Sandow, D. & Rhodes, L. (1991). Quality assurance in supported employment: New approaches to improvement. *Journal of Vocational Rehabilitation*, **1**(1), 59–68.

Martin, J. E., Mithaug, D. E. & Husch, J. F. (1988). *How to Teach Adaptability in Community Training and Supported Employment.* Colorado Springs, CO: Ascent Publications.

Martin, J. E. & Mithaug, D. E. (1990). Consumer-directed placement. In F. R. Rusch, ed. *Supported Employment: Models, Methods, and Issues*, pp. 87–110, Sycamore, IL: Sycamore Publishing.

McDonnell, J., Nofs, D., Hardman, M. & Chambless, C. (1989). An analysis of procedural components of supported employment programs associated with employment outcomes. *Journal of Applied Behaviour Analysis*, **22**, 417–28.

McGaughey, M. J., Kiernan, W. E., Lynch, S. A., Schalock, R. L. & Morganstern, D. R. (1991). *National Survey of Day and Employment Programs for Persons with Developmental Disabilities: Results from State MR/DD Agencies.* Boston: Children's Hospital, The Developmental Evaluation Centre.

McLoughlin, C. S., Garner, J. B. & Callahan, M. (1987). *Getting Employed, Staying Employed: Job Development and Training for Persons with Severe Handicaps.* Baltimore: Paul H. Brookes.

Mithaug, D. E., Martin, J. E. & Agran, M. (1987). Adaptability instruction: the goal of transitional programming. *Exceptional Children*, **53**, 500–5.

Mithaug, D. E., Martin, J. E., Husch, J. V., Agran, M. & Rusch, F. R. (1988). *When will Persons in Supported Employment Need Less Support?* Colorado Springs, CO: Ascent Publications.

Moon, M. S., Inge, K. J., Wehman, P., Brooke, V. & Barcus, J. M. (1990). *Helping Persons with Severe Mental Retardation Get and Keep Employment.* Baltimore: Paul H. Brookes.

Mueller, J. (1990). *The Workplace Workbook: An Illustrated Guide to Job Accommodation and Assistive Technology.* Washington, DC: The Dole Foundation.

National Association of Rehabilitation Facilities. (1989). *Exemplary Supported Employment Practices.* Washington, DC:

Nelson, N. (1971). *Workshops for the Handicapped in the United States: An Historical and Developmental Perspective.* Springfield, IL: Charles C. Thomas.

Nisbet, J. & Hagner, D. (1988). Natural supports in the workplace: a re-examination of supported employment. *The Journal of the Association for Persons with Severe Handicaps*, **13**, 260–7.

Noble, J. H. & Collignon, F. C. (1987). Systems barriers to supported employment for persons with chronic mental illness. *Psychosocial Rehabilitation Journal*, **11**, 25–54.

Noble, J. H. & Conley, R. W. (1989). The new supported employment program: Prospects and potential problems. In W. E. Kiernan & R. L. Schalock, eds. *Economics, Industry, and Disability: A Look Ahead*, pp. 207–222, Baltimore: Paul H. Brookes.

Parent, W., Kregel, J., Wehman, P. & Metzler, H. (1991). Measuring the social integration of supported employment workers. *Journal of Vocational Rehabilitation*, **1**(1), 35–49.

Renzaglia, A. M. & Everson, J. M. (1990). Preparing personnel to meet the challenges of contemporary employment service alternatives. In F. R. Rusch, ed. *Supported Employment: Models, Methods, and Issues*, pp. 395–408, Sycamore, IL: Sycamore Publishing.

Rhodes, L. E. & Valenta, L. (1985). Industry-based supported employment: An enclave approach. *Journal of the Association for Persons with Severe Handicaps*, **10**, 12–20.

Rusch, F. R. (1986). *Competitive Employment Issues and Strategies*. Baltimore: Paul H. Brookes.

Rusch, F. R. (1990). *Supported Employment: Models, Methods, and Issues*. Sycamore, IL: Sycamore Publishing.

Rusch, F. R., Chadsey-Rusch, J. & Johnson, J. R. (1991). Supported Employment: Emerging opportunities for employment integration. In L. H. Meyer, C. A. Peck & L. Brown, eds. *Critical Issues in the Lives of People with Severe Disabilities*, pp. 145–169, Baltimore: Paul H. Brookes.

Rusch, F. R., Chadsey-Rusch, J. & Lagomarcino, T. (1987). Preparing students for employment. In M. Snell, ed. *Systematic Instruction for Persons with Severe Handicaps*, 3rd edn., pp. 471–490, Columbus, OH: Charles E. Merrill.

Rusch, F. R., DeStefano, L., Chadsey-Rusch, J., Phelps, L. A. & Szymanski, E. (1992). *Transition from School to Adult Life: Models, Linkages, and Policy*. Sycamore, IL: Sycamore Publishing.

Rusch, F. R. & Hughes, C. (1990). Historical overview of supported employment. In F. R. Rusch, ed. *Supported Employment: Models, Methods, and Issues, pp.* 5–14, Sycamore, IL: Sycamore Publishing.

Rusch, F. R., Johnson, J. R. & Hughes, C. (1990). Analysis of co-worker involvement in relations to level of disability versus placement approach among supported employees. *Journal of the Association for Persons with Severe Handicaps*, **15**, 32–9.

Rusch F. R. & Kazdin, A. E. (1981). Toward a methodology of withdrawal designs for the assessment of response maintenance. *Journal of Applied Behavior Analysis*, **14, 131–40.**

Rusch, F. R. & Mithaug, D. E. (1980). *Vocational Training for Mentally Retarded Adults: a Behavior Analytic Approach*. Champaign, IL: Research Press.

Rusch, F. R. & Schutz, J. P. (1979). Nonsheltered employment of the mentally retarded adult: research to reality? *Journal of Contemporary Business*, **8**, 85–98.

Rusch, F. R., Trach, J., Winking, D., Tines, J. & Johnson, J. (1989). Job coach and implementation issues in industry: The Illinois experience. In W. E. Kiernan & R. L. Schalock, eds. *Economics, Industry, and Disability: A Look Ahead*, pp. 179–186. Baltimore: Paul H. Brookes.

Sale, P., Wood, W., Barcus, J. M. & Moon, M. S. (1989). The role of the employment specialist. In W. E. Kiernan & R. L. Schalock, eds. Economics, Industry, and *Disability: A Look Ahead*, pp. 187–206. Baltimore: Paul H. Brookes.

Shafer, M. S., Parent, W. S. & Everson, J. M. (1988). Responsive marketing by supported employment programs. In P. Wehman & M. S. Moon, eds. *Vocational Rehabilitation and Supported Employment*, pp. 235–250, Baltimore: Paul H. Brookes.

Shafer, M., Revell, W. G. & Isbister, F. (1991). The national supported employment initiative: A three-year longitudinal analysis of 50 states. *Journal of Vocational Rehabilitation*, 1(1), 9–17.

Snell, M. (1987). *Systematic Instruction for Persons with Severe Handicaps*, 3rd edn. Columbus, OH: Charles E. Merrill.

Sowers, J. & Powers, L. (1990). *Vocational Preparation and Employment of*

Students with Physical and Multiple Disabilities. Baltimore: Paul H. Brookes.

Stack, R. P. (1988). The rehabilitation engineer and technological services. In P. Wehman, W. Wood, J. M. Everson, R. Goodwyn, S. Conley, eds. *Vocational Education for Multihandicapped Youth with Cerebral Palsy.* Baltimore: Paul H. Brookes.

The Supported Employment Evaluation Project. (1990). *Supported Employment in Michigan: Thirteenth Quarterly Statistical Summary Statewide Report.* Kalamazoo: Western Michigan University, The Supported Employment Evaluation Project.

Tines, J., Rusch, F. R., McCaughrin, W. & Conley, R. W. (1990). Benefit–cost analysis of supported employment in Illinois: A statewide examination. *American Journal on Mental Retardation*, **95**, 44–54.

Trach, J. (1990). Supported employment program characteristics. In F. R. Rusch, ed. *Supported Employment: Models, Methods, and Issues*, pp. 65–81, Sycamore, IL: Sycamore Publishing.

Trach, J. S. & Rusch, F. R. (1989). Supported employment program evaluation: Evaluating degree of implementation and selected outcomes. *American Journal on Mental Retardation*, **94**, 134–40.

US Commission on Civil Rights (1983). *Accommodating the Spectrum of Disabilities.* Washington, DC: Author.

US Department of Labor (1977). *Sheltered Workshop Study: a Nationwide Report on Sheltered Workshops and Their Employment of Handicapped Individuals*, vol. I. Washington, DC: US Department of Labor

US Department of Labor (1979). *Study of Handicapped Clients in Sheltered Workshops*, vol. II. Washington, DC: US Department of Labour.

Vogelsberg, R. T. (1986). Competitive employment in Vermont. In F. R. Rusch, ed. *Competitive Employment Issues and Strategies*, pp. 35–49. Baltimore: Paul H. Brookes.

Vogelsberg, R. T. (1990). Supported employment in Pennsylvania. In F. R. Rusch, ed. *Supported Employment: Models, Methods, and Issues*, pp. 45–63. Sycamore, IL: Sycamore Publishing.

Wehman, P. (1981). *Competitive Employment: New Horizons for Severely Disabled Individuals.* Baltimore: Paul H. Brookes.

Wehman, P. & Moon, M. S. (1988). *Vocational Rehabilitation and Supported Employment.* Baltimore: Paul H. Brookes.

Wehman, P., West, M., Fry, R., Sherron, P., Groah, C., Kreutzer, J. & Sale, P. (1989). Effect of supported employment on the vocational outcomes of persons with traumatic brain injury. *Journal of Applied Behavior Analysis*, **22**, 395–405.

Whitehead, C. (1981). *Final Report: Training and Employment Services for Handicapped Individuals in Sheltered Workshops.* Washington, DC: Office of Social Services Policy, Office of the Assistant Secretary of Planning and Evaluation, US Department of Health and Human Services.

Winking, D. L., Trach, J. S., Rusch, F. R. & Tines, J. (1989). Profile of Illinois supported employment specialists: an analysis of educational background, experience, and related employment variables. *Journal of the Association for Persons with Severe Handicaps*, **14**, 278–82.

Wood, W. (1988). Supported employment for persons with physical disabilities. In P. Wehman & M. S. Moon, eds. *Vocational Rehabilitation and Supported Employment*, pp. 341–364, Baltimore: Paul H. Brookes.

24

Quality assurance for adults with mental retardation and mental health needs

SHAUN GRAVESTOCK

Introduction

People with mental retardation were historically feared, segregated and denied access to quality services. Hospital scandals, deinstitutionalisation and community care programmes have brought their care into public focus. However, specialist services to meet their mental health needs are still of varying quantity and quality. This chapter reviews quality assurance (QA) trends in relation to service objectives, structure, process, outcomes, quality of life and consumer satisfaction.

Quality assurance trends

Over the past four decades, service providers have been concerned with cost containment and accountability through QA activities. This has been related to the rising costs of health care services, increasing consumer rights and governmental concerns about the wide variations in costs, quantity and quality of care provided. Since the 1960s, the USA federal government and the independent Joint Commission on Accreditation of Health Care Organisations (JCAHO) have developed quality standards for providers. Such standards are used in accrediting providers as eligible to receive federal and third party funding and purchasing contracts.

The emphasis shifted from cost containment by resource utilisation reviews (1960s) to professional standards review organisations (1970s) determining the necessity, appropriate delivery and acceptable quality of service provision. The required large-scale retrospective casenote audits, patient care evaluation and diagnosis-related group studies proved costly and time consuming. Record keeping improved and there was a reduction in costs due to unnecessary or lengthy admissions and polypharmacy.

However, overall quality of care was unchanged as little attention was paid to ongoing reassessment (monitoring) and resolving identified problems.

In the early 1980s, USA legislations established peer review organisations whilst JCAHO required identification and monitoring of important problems associated with quality of care processes against established standards. Community Mental Health Centres were legally required to conduct multidisciplinary QA reviews (Fauman 1989).

Since the mid-1980s service providers in Canada and the Netherlands have also been required to operate QA programmes (Garden, Oyebode & Cumella, 1989). Meanwhile the Australian and New Zealand Quality Assurance Project (1982) developed standard treatment outlines for psychiatric disorders based on meta-analyses of outcome studies, practice surveys and expert consensus conferences. More recently the emphasis has shifted towards clinical outcome indicators for mental health service providers (Fauman, 1989).

In the UK, recent White Papers (Department of Health 1989*a,b*) emphasised professional participation in regular local audit activities and possibly total quality management (Berwick, Enthoven & Bunker 1992). However, to implement QA in mental health services and relate client outcomes to structure and care processes poses several problems. These include:

- Agreeing measurable quality care objectives and standards relevant to service users chronic and complex needs.
- Poor quality client records and information systems.
- Wide variations in care processes, not always explained by local service users needs and available resources.
- Defining the casemix factors (sociodemographic, comorbidity, severity, chronicity, etc.).
- How and when to measure outcomes, quality of life and consumer satisfaction, given that several service users may be unable or unwilling to participate.
- Staff resistances/fears about changing working patterns to integrate ongoing data collection and monitoring.

Mental health service researchers have been increasingly concerned with the complex issues of evaluating resettlement programmes (Freeman & Henderson, 1991), consumer satisfaction (Lebow, 1982), quality of life (Roberts, 1990), outcomes (Mirin & Namerow, 1991) and cost-effectiveness (Wilkinson *et al.*, 1990.)

Mental retardation service researchers have also evaluated resettlement (Wing, 1989) reprovision costs (Glennerster, 1990) and quality of care as conceptualised by normalisation principles (Wolfensberger, 1983) or client 'accomplishments' (O'Brien, 1987). Qualitative research also addressed the quality of community life and client satisfaction (Edgerton & Bercovici, 1976; Flynn, 1986). Jenkins (1990) discussed the need for specific outcome indicators to evaluate the quality and effectiveness of mental health services in the context of recent UK health service reforms.

Methodological issues

QA activities in community services for adults with mental retardation and mental health needs should include the following:

Setting quality objectives

These are agreed explicit statements of what a quality service aims to accomplish for its users. Objectives should be related to service values, principles and philosophies but also operationalised. Effectiveness and user outcomes should then be more easily assessed against pre-set objectives. Such QA objectives include:

- monitoring service planning, management, training,structure and pro-cess to ensure care provided to users is: accessible, appropriate, socially acceptable, coordinated, cost-effective, equitable, ethical, proactive and relevant to continuing care needs (McClelland 1992).
- Monitoring service users outcomes in terms of: improving or main-taining mental, social and physical functioning (morbidity and mor-tality), quality of life and consumer satisfaction; preventing and minimising unmet needs, adverse outcomes, additional handicaps and burdens (Gravestock, Holt & Bouras, 1991).

Identification of quality problems

Quality problems should be related to quality objectives and within the local service organisation's control. Ideally, all providers should agree a few problems most relevant to service users and likely to be improved by the QA approach (Morosini & Veltro, 1991).

Specific quality problems

These relate to high-risk (most severe/chronic/disabling), high-volume (most common) or high-cost (to client/carers/ service) client 'conditions', diagnoses or treatments (Fauman, 1989). High-risk quality problems might concern: challenging behaviour; diagnosis of schizophrenia, dementia, autism or personality disorder; use of aversive/restrictive behavioural treatments; psychotropic medication side effects and toxicity; or use of formal detention. High-volume quality problems might concern: minor behaviour problems; 'social care' needs; diagnosis of neurotic/ adjustment disorders; use of oral neuroleptic drugs; or availability of behavioural therapies. High-cost quality problems might concern: ageing or dementing conditions; adolescents with mental retardation and mental health needs; physical, sexual and emotional abuse; offenders with mental retardation and mental health needs; clients with severe mental retardation and mental health needs requiring day/inpatient treatment; exclusion from local services and resettlement; or family/systemic and long-term psychotherapies.

Agreement of methods and standards

For each specific quality problem selected for monitoring, quantitative data collection methods and explicit measurable quality standards should be agreed. Methods should be reliable, valid, sensitive and economical. Ideally, standards should be based on agreed local priorities and specified before practice observation (Jenkins, 1990).

Various QA (Beswick, Zadik & Felce, 1986; James, Howell & Abbott, 1989) or audit (Royal College of Psychiatrists, 1989; Gath, 1991) methods may be used such as: random/selected peer/external review of client records, medication charts, letters, care plans and minutes of individual/ house programme planning meetings (Gravestock & Bicknell, 1992); client assessment data (Anness *et al.*, 1991); written, verbal and non-verbal users feedback from diaries, checklists, questionnaires, interviews, observation, participation events, quality circles, complaint analyses etc. (Sheikh & Meakin, 1990; Hall & Pieri 1992,); case management (Department of Health, 1989*b*) and service information systems (Farmer, Holroyd & Rohde, 1990).

Service-user outcomes

QA monitoring structure and process aspects of care should be related to service user outcomes in terms of avoidable mortality, morbidity, relapse/readmission rates, functioning, unmet needs, quality of life and consumer satisfaction (Jenkins, 1990). Comprehensive information systems are required to measure reduction in the incidence and prevalence rates of mental health needs due to developmental/prevention care processes. Admission, discharge, relapse and readmission rates should be related to local service structure and process factors, including the availability of inpatient beds.

Adverse outcomes may be monitored by 'sentinel events' i.e. those adverse client outcomes which should always result in further enquiries to determine possible avoidable factors. Examples might include: deaths due to status epilepticus, dementia, suicide or challenging behaviours; lithium or anticonvulsant toxicity and tardive dyskinesia; physical, sexual or emotional abuse; frequent or failed admissions and discharges; assaults against staff or other service users; use of physical restraints and seclusion; being sent to prison; prolonged exclusion from local service facilities/ systems; not leaving their room for over a month; and service users' complaints. Morosini & Veltro (1991) also suggested 'positive' sentinel events to determine possible repeatable factors such as clients achieving: open/sheltered employment; independent living; stability following withdrawal from long term psychotropic medication or discharge from long-term inpatient/daypatient treatment or care.

Given the chronic, complex needs of many adults with mental retardation and mental health needs, functional outcome assessments must be multidimensional and ongoing. Complementary service user-orientated outcome monitoring approaches are also required including consumer satisfaction, quality of life and needs assessment.

Consumer satisfaction

Increasingly, adults with mental retardation are being consulted for their subjective views about services using a variety of interviewing methods (Flynn, 1986). Consumer satisfaction is important as it relates to service users quality of life and quality of care by influencing their attendance, acceptance and compliance with care offered. Given their cognitive, sensory, communication and emotional disabilities, to achieve meaningful representation of clients views about specific services requires careful attention to methodological issues including: type/content of questions and interviews; pilot studies; cross-checks; consent, privacy, responsiveness, social desirability and acquiescence; ensuring users valued feedback results in service changes (Atkinson, 1988; Crocker, 1989).

Quality of life

Whilst most agree that multidimensional subjective and objective quality of life indicators are needed (Landesman, 1986), debate continues about how best to define and measure service users quality of life. Central to the debates are the relationships between indicators of individual service users experiences/needs, social/environmental factors, quality of care provided and their relative importance in determining quality of life (Roberts, 1990).

Subjective quality of life measures concern values, happiness, satisfaction and wellbeing in relation to life experiences such as: physical/ mental health; severity and chronicity of symptoms; health and social care received; physical environmental, housing and financial circumstances; physical safety; social networks and integration; meaningful activities, work and leisure; personal functioning, development and independence; relationships and sexuality. More objective quality of life outcome measures attempt to measure the 'goodness of fit' between group/ individual service users experiences/needs and quality of care provided by service staff/environments (Schalock *et al.* 1989; Leonard, 1989).

Physical, cognitive, affective social and economic dimensions of quality of life should be related to individual assets, impairments, disabilities and handicaps (World Health Organisation, 1980). Adults with mental retardation and mental health needs are often further disadvantaged by additional impairments (physical, sensory, communication, epilepsy etc.) in fulfilling survival roles such as mobility, physical independence and social integration. Quality of life should also be related to their additional burdens (Nirje, 1976) including: lack of occupational and social skills; inadequate resource provision by society; attitudes encouraging rejection, segregation and isolation; and personal awareness of their handicaps. It should be remembered that for adults with mental retardation and mental health needs, their mental health needs may be the most important determinant of service setting and quality of life.

If quality of life is used as an outcome measure, service providers must agree what value will be attached to providing users with information, supporting their choices and then assessing subjective quality of life. Such data can be more valid though possibly less reliable than the similar, supposedly more objective social, environmental and quality of care indicators preferred by many service providers (Stanley & Roy, 1988; Whitaker, 1989).

The biases of individuals and methods must be considered when assessing innovations and changes, emphasising the need for long-term subjective and objective monitoring. The major challenge remains how to relate individual quality of life to the value systems, objectives and quality of care provided by specialist and other services, given the limited resources (Knapp, 1991).

Needs assessment

Needs can be defined as 'the requirements of individuals to enable them to achieve, maintain or restore an acceptable level of social independence or quality of life as defined by the particular care agency or authority' (Department of Health Social Services Inspectorate, 1991). This normative definition does not consider the expressed needs of service users nor their degree of disability and level of risk. Needs assessment should allow service providers to consider these issues in relation to access, changing service priorities, rationing and equity across client groups.

Explicit values, criteria and rules are essential for needs assessment linking client functioning, effectiveness of interventions and service user outcomes in terms of no need, met need or unmet need (Brewin *et al.*, 1987). Ideally 'bottom-up' users needs assessment data should be integrated with 'top-down' service monitoring systems (Wing, 1991).

Summary

QA is a necessary component at all levels of services for people with mental retardation and mental health needs. Service information systems are required to identify the people with mental retardation and mental health needs as well as the structures and processes deployed to meet their needs. Successful implementation of QA programmes will depend on addressing methodological problems and improving communication between service users and providers. QA should be integrated with ongoing service activities so regular feedback and staff training can influence improvements.

Service providers should set quality objectives and identify priority quality problems to monitor against agreed standards. Increased emphasis on monitoring service users outcomes and unmet needs should avoid cost and volume issues predominating. Despite limited resources,well-managed QA programmes offer providers positive and creative opportunities to build on service strengths and address service needs.

Acknowledgements

I wish to thank Andrea Hughes and Dr Mary Lindsey for their advice and correspondence enclosing papers and QA documents.

References

Anness, V., Bhat, A., Bouras, N., Callias, M., Hollins, S., Rohde, J. & Sacks, B. (1991). A multi-aspect assessment for people with mental handicap. *Psychiatric Bulletin*, **15**, 146.

Atkinson, D. (1988). Research interviews with people with mental handicaps. *Mental Handicap Research*, **1**, 75–90.

Berwick, D. M., Enthoven, A. & Bunker, J. P. (1992). Quality management in the NHS:the doctor's role-1. *British Medical Journal*, **304**, 235–9.

Beswick, J., Zadik, T. & Felce, D. (1986). *Evaluating Quality of Care*. Kidderminster: British Institute of Mental Handicap.

Brewin, C. R., Wing, J. K., Mangen, S. P., Brugha, T. S. & MacCarthy, B. (1987). Principles and practice of measuring needs in the long-term mentally ill:the MRC Needs for Care Assessment. *Psychological Medicine*, **17**, 971–81.

Crocker, T. M. (1989). Assessing consumer satisfaction with mental handicap services;a comparison between different approaches. *British Journal of Mental Subnormality*, **35**, 94–100.

Department of Health (1989a). *Working for Patients*. London: Her Majesty's Stationery Office (HMSO).

Department of Health (1989b). *Care in the Community: Community Care in the Next Decade and Beyond*. London: HMSO.

Department of Health Social Services Inspectorate (1991). *Care Management and Assessment–Managers Guide*. London: HMSO.

Edgerton, R. B. & Bercovici, S. M. (1976). The cloak of competence: years later. *American Journal of Mental Deficiency*, **80**, 485–97.

Farmer, R., Holroyd, S. & Rohde, J.(1990). Differences in disability between people with mental handicaps who were resettled in the community and those who remain in hospital. *British Medical Journal*, **301**, 646.

Fauman, M. A. (1989). Quality assurance monitoring in psychiatry. *American Journal of Psychiatry*, 146, 1121–30.

Flynn, M. C. (1986). Adults who are mentally handicapped as consumers: issues and guidelines for interviewing. *Journal of Mental Deficiency Research*, **30**, 369–77.

Freeman, H. & Henderson, J. (1991). *Evaluation of Comprehensive Care of the Mentally Ill*. London: Gaskell.

Garden, G., Oyebode, F. & Cumella, S. (1989). Audit in psychiatry. *Psychiatric Bulletin*, **13**, 278–81.

Gath, A. (1991). Audit. *Psychiatric Bulletin*, **15**, 23–25.

Glennerster, H. (1990). The costs of hospital closure: reproviding services for the residents of Darenth Park Hospital. *Psychiatric Bulletin*, **14**, 140–3.

Gravestock, S., Bouras, N. & Holt, G. (1991). Outcome indicators in mental handicap. *British Journal of Psychiatry*, **159**, 294–5.

Gravestock, S. & Bicknell, J. (1992). 'Emergency' referrals to a South London community mental handicap team (CMHT). *Psychiatric Bulletin*, **16**, 475–7.

Hall, D. J. & Pieri, L. F. (1992). Providing a community mental handicap service. *Psychiatric Bulletin*, **16**, 20–1.

James, J., Howell, H. & Abbott, K. (1989). Quality Matters 1. 'Slicing the apple': maintaining and improving quality in mental handicap services. *Mental Handicap*, **17**, 156–9.

Jenkins, R. (1990). Towards a system of outcome indicators for mental health care. *British Journal of Psychiatry*, **157**, 500–14.

Knapp, M. (1991). The direct costs of the community care of chronically mentally ill people. In H. Freeman and J. Henderson, eds. *Evaluation of Comprehensive Care of the Mentally Ill*, pp. 142–73, London: Gaskell.

Landesman, S. (1986). Quality of life and personal life satisfaction: definition and measurement issues. *Mental Retardation*, **24**, 141–3.

Lebow, J. L. (1982). Consumer satisfaction with mental health treatment. *Psychological Bulletin*, **91**, 244–59.

Leonard, I. (1989). Quality of life in a residential setting. *Psychiatric Bulletin*, **13**, 492–4.

McClelland, R. (1992). The quality issue. *Psychiatric Bulletin*, **16**, 411–13.

Mirin, S. M. & Namerow, M. J. (1991). Why study treatment outcome? *Hospital and Community Psychiatry*, **42**, 1007–13.

Morosini, P. & Veltro, F.(1991). Process or outcome approach in the evaluation of psychiatric services. In H. Freeman & J. Henderson, eds. *Evaluation of Comprehensive Care of the Mentally Ill*, pp. 127–41, London: Gaskell.

Nirje, B. (1976). The normalisation principle and it's human management implications. In R. J. Flynn and K. E. Nitsch, eds. *Normalisation, Social Integration and Community Services*. Baltimore:University Park Press.

O'Brien, J. (1987). A guide to personal future planning. In G. T. Bellamy & B. Wilcox, eds. *A Comprehensive Guide to the Activities Catalog: an Alternative Curriculum for Youth and Adults with Severe Disabilities*. Baltimore: Paul H. Brookes.

Quality Assurance Project. (1982). A methodology for preparing 'ideal' treatment outlines in psychiatry. *Australian and New Zealand Journal of Psychiatry*, **16**, 153–8.

Roberts, G.(1990). Estimating quality of life. *Psychiatric Bulletin*, **14**, 586–9.

Royal College of Psychiatrists. (1989). Preliminary report on medical audit. *Psychiatric Bulletin*, **13**, 577–80.

Schalock, R. L., Keith, K. D., Hoffmam, K. & Karan, O. C.(1989). Quality of life: its measurement and use. *Mental Retardation*, **27**, 25–31.

Sheikh, A. J. & Meakin, C. (1990). Consumer satisfaction with a psychiatric out-patient clinic. *Psychiatric Bulletin*, **14**, 271–4.

Stanley, B. & Roy, A. (1988). Evaluating the quality of life of people with mental handicaps: a social validation study. *Mental Handicap Research*, **1**, 197–210.

Wilkinson, G., Croft-Jeffreys, C., Krekorian, H., McLees, S. & Falloon, I. (1990). QALYs in psychiatric care? *Psychiatric Bulletin*, **14**, 582–5.

Whitaker, S. (1989). Point of view. Quality of life and people with a very profound handicap. *British Journal of Mental Subnormality*, **35**, 3–7.

Wing, J. K. (1991). The broad context of health care. In H. Freeman & J. Henderson, eds. *Evaluation of Comprehensive Care of the Mentally Ill*, pp 18–23.

Wing, L. (1989). *Hospital Closure and the Resettlement of Residents*. Aldershot: Gower.

Wolfensberger, W. (1983). Social role valorisation: a proposed new term for the principle of normalisation. *Mental Retardation*, **21**, 234–9.

World Health Organization. (1980). *International Classifications of Impairments, Disabilities and Handicaps*. Geneva: WHO.

25

The challenge of providing high quality services

JIM MANSELL

Introduction

A major challenge faced by services for people with learning disabilities (mental retardation) is the care of the small number of people who, in addition to their learning disability, show really serious problem behaviour. With the wider development of community-based services, it is these people who are most difficult to place and who are most likely to be returned to institutions (Sutter *et al.*, 1980; Intagliata & Willer, 1982) where they are likely to remain unpopular patients, avoided by staff (Grant & Moores, 1977; Raynes, 1980). There continues to be considerable uncertainty in the UK about the extent to which community care is feasible for this client group (Department of Health 1984; 1989).

A large-scale hospital replacement programme in South East England faced this problem (Korman and Glennerster, 1985; 1990). A small proportion (about 20) of the 660 people living in the hospital in 1984 were widely regarded as presenting such serious problems that it had been planned to move them to new institutions rather than community services. In 1983 and 1984 this policy was reexamined in the light of growing experience of community-based alternatives within the region (Mansell, 1988; 1989). In a major departure from previous policy, the Regional and District Health Authorities opted for community services following the 'ordinary life' model for people with severe or profound learning disability who presented very challenging behaviour (Kings Fund Centre, 1980). Services for people with mild learning disability were developed on a different model (Dockrell, Gaskell and Rehman, 1990).

Recognising the lack of expertise in developing supported housing services for these clients, the Regional Health Authority established a special development team based at the University of Kent, to help local agencies develop appropriate services. Using a process of individual service planning with the local health authority, coupled with extensive practical help and some transitional financial incentives, the team helped establish and support community placements (Special Development Team, 1988; Toogood *et al.*, 1988). This support was available for up to 18 months, after which time the local service agency assumed full responsibility for the service.

This study was commissioned to evaluate the community-based residential services set up with support from the Special Development Team. The main measure of effectiveness used was direct observation of how clients spent their time. This approach was adopted because directly accessing the experience of service users avoids inadvertently confounding measures of process and outcome. Where evaluations have used measures of, for example, individual programme goals achieved, it may be that the result owes more to staff activity (in this case, in setting achievable goals) than to real differences in client experience (de Kock *et al.*, 1988; Repp & Barton, 1980). Activity patterns have been widely studied in British learning disability services (Felce, Kushlick and Mansell, 1980; Mansell *et al.*, 1984; Rawlings, 1985; Felce, de Kock & Repp, 1986; Joyce, 1988) and are beginning to be used in routine service monitoring (Hewson, 1991; Hughes & Mansell, 1990). There is therefore a good basis for comparison of results with other studies.

Although activity patterns do not themselves provide information about such qualitative goals as the choice open to an individual, or the respect in which they are held, improvements in these areas should be reflected in the variety of activities and the extent of the person's participation in them. If low levels of engagement in meaningful activity are found, this reflects a genuine problem whatever other measures may indicate, for example, if people say they are content but observation shows them to be inactive for most of each day (Mansell *et al.*, 1987). Although attempts have been made to measure client activity patterns using interview (O'Neill *et al.*, 1981), direct observation provides the most accurate way of measuring client activity patterns (Joyce, Gray & Mansell 1989) in a study population who are mostly unable to speak authoritatively for themselves.

Study participants

Details of the Special Development Team's full caseload, in terms of the location of people at the point of referral, the nature of the challenging behaviours and progress with the implementation of individual service plans for people in each of the referring districts is available elsewhere (Special Development Team, 1988; Emerson *et al.*, 1987; 1988). This paper presents results for 18 people on the team's caseload, who were living in NHS mental handicap hospitals at the time of referral. At the time of writing, 11 of these people have moved to staffed houses in the community.

The most common form of challenging behaviour amongst this group, and hence the most likely reason for referral, was serious violence towards other people and the material environment. Typically, problems included scratching, punching, kicking, biting and the throwing of objects (chairs, tables, crockery) at people. Fig. 25.1 summarises the characteristics of the people included in the study including scores on the Adaptive Behavior Scale (Part 1) (Nihira et al, 1974) and challenging behaviours identified by interview and/or observation during the study.

These data show that this is indeed a very disabled group of people. In addition to severe or profound learning disability, every individual in the study had multiple self-stimulatory behaviours, made inappropriate vocalisations (such as moaning or screaming) and very challenging behaviour. Five people also had epilepsy, two were suspected of autism, two were thought to have psychiatric disorders and one had phenyl-ketonuria. Two people had, at some point, been detained under the Mental Health Acts. The average age of the people in this study was 31 and on average these individuals first received institutional care at the age of 10.

All people involved in this study lived in two large hospitals in Kent. Ten people lived on ordinary wards at the beginning of the study, and eight lived in special units reserved for those with the most challenging behaviour. These were either specially designated wards in the hospitals, including houses on the edge of the hospital campus (Emerson *et al.*, in press) or places in specialist private hospitals. Each community service was individually designed for one or two people in the study group, usually living with one or two people with less severe disabilities in a staffed house or apartment. Three people (GF, MM and MS) lived in houses which were on the same site as other residential facilities (called 'campus' houses in the remainder of this paper). For two people this was a temporary placement. The third moved to a house which was not supported by the Special Development Team but where the home leader had been trained by the Team and was receiving further training in the same department at the University. These services require substantial management and specialist support beyond the initial setting-up period, which has often proved difficult to provide. Several placements have broken down, including that for one person in this study (WG), who was returned to hospital at the last datapoint (but who has since returned to a staffed house in her home district).

Person	Sex	Year of birth	ABS total score	Challenging behaviour			
				Self-injury	Aggression	Damage	Other
HM	M	1958	80			✓	Rummages in rubbish
BF	F	1950	86	✓	✓	✓	Strips
SS	M	1958	154	✓		✓	
WG	F	1955	70	✓	✓	✓	Smears faeces, pica, strips
PH	F	1954	123		✓	✓	Steals, strips
ST	M	1956	78		✓	✓	
JK	M	1956	54	✓		✓	Strips, climbs
MM	M	1949	87	✓	✓	✓	Hoards, strips, absconds, non-compliance
MS	M	1957	52	✓	✓	✓	Steals, absconds
GF	M	1957	211	✓	✓	✓	Pica, steals, absconds, inappropriate sex
SM	F	1954	49	✓	✓	✓	Non-compliance, strips, smears faeces
PA	F	1960	80		✓		
RV	M	1964	110		✓	✓	Smears faeces
MT	F	1958	80	✓	✓	✓	Smears faeces, strips
KP	M	1971	94		✓	✓	Strips, pica, sprawls
HK	M	1961	86		✓	✓	Smears faeces, strips, pica, steals
MK	M	1954	45	✓		✓	Smears faeces, strips, pica, steals
FP	M	1973	108	✓	✓	✓	Non-compliance, vomits

Fig. 25.1. Characteristics of study participants

Measurement and design

The evaluation used repeated observational measures (Bijou, Petersen & Ault, 1968) and a combination of experimental-control group comparison and single-case design methodology to determine clinically significant relationships between client activity and the environment. This has been a productive methodological approach in other studies of innovative learning disability services (Felce, de Kock and Repp, 1986; Rawlings, 1985). The particular benefits of this approach for this study were that it provided quantitative data on important treatment/intervention issues in a population where group-comparison studies alone would be inappropriate, because of the individual nature of each person's challenging behaviour and the small number of potential subjects.

The study was planned as a multiple time-series design across subjects, in which individuals form their own controls and staggered transfer to new services would control for confounding variables (Campbell & Stanley, 1966). People could therefore join the study after its onset and could move at whichever point in time their new services were ready.

Since an earlier study (Wing, 1988) had reported no improvement in client experience of some of the first people to move out of one of the hospitals concerned, in services which themselves turned out to replicate many of the organisational features of the hospital, it was decided to include some measures of the physical and social environment as well as of client experience. It was important to know whether, if client experience did not change, this was a result of the failure of the experimental service to work, or a failure to properly create the experimental service.

The principal measure was a 20-second momentary time-sample (Beasley, Hewson & Mansell, 1989) which measures how much time the individual handicapped person spends in various categories of behaviour. For example, time spent in leisure activities; personal or self-help type of skills; using complex equipment; other practical tasks or domestic chores; work or formal educational activities; going for walks; in seclusion or time spent doing nothing at all. Attempts on the part of the client to interact with other people as well as the nature of other people's contact to them (positive, negative, conversation or assistance) and each person's challenging behaviour was also recorded, using individually specified definitions. The number of staff and clients within the same room was also recorded every five minutes.

The data collected represent 'composite days' in the lives of each individual. Observations were taken over three weekdays within a few days of each other to cover the period between 8.00am and 7.00pm, so that at each datapoint there were 1980 (11 hours x 60 minutes x 3) observations of activity for each individual. Information was collected for on seven occasions over three years. Interrater reliability was assessed across codes, individuals and data-points; mean weighted occurrence/non-occurrence reliability was between 84% and 95% on each occasion.

The material richness and space of the physical environment were recorded once in each condition. Staff allocation to the living unit was recorded on each visit by examining duty rotas.

Results

The first results presented concern the overall differences in the types of environment included in the study. In these comparisons, all observations in a particular environment have been averaged.

Physical environment

The small staffed homes were very different to the institutional settings they replaced. The institutional wards provided more space than houses, but this space was shared with large numbers of people. The typical living

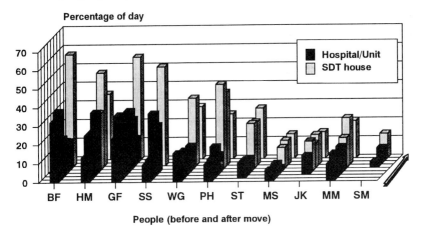

Fig. 25.2. Engagement in constructive activity

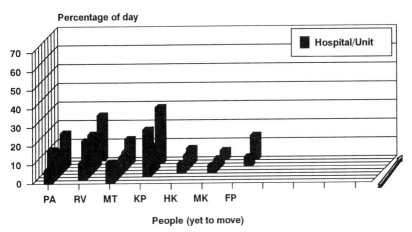

space available to people in institutions in this study was 173 m² shared by 19 people, compared with 31 m² shared by two to four people in a typical house. Moreover, no rooms were locked in the houses, whereas in hospital environments, and in particular in the special units, between 15–35% of the living unit was likely to be unavailable to people. Amongst others, these included the kitchen (in almost all cases), bedrooms, bathrooms, staff rooms (office and rest), cleaners' cupboards, laundry and other storerooms. In hospital environments cooking, laundry and other basic services were organised centrally and cleaning was undertaken by domestic staff. In the homes these activities were intended to be a major source of participation by the people served, with appropriate levels of help from the support staff.

The material environment of the wards of hospitals and special units was often barren and sometimes bizarre (for example, one ward had 17 sideboards and wall-units in the 'lounge'). The physical condition of some of these living units were dilapidated. There was usually literally nothing for people to do but sit, watch television or walk about. The houses were much richer environments, decorated and equipped with the wide range of furnishings and domestic items one would expect to find in an average household.

Staffing

The staffed houses each served many fewer people and had much higher staffing ratios than the other kinds of service. The number of staff on duty (as recorded at the same time as the observations) show that, on average, the staff/client ratio in hospital wards was 1:3.5, in special units 1:1.6 and in the houses 1:0.9. Not only were the staffing ratios higher in community-based services but the observational data also suggests that the staff were 'delivered', in that they actually spent more time physically in the presence of clients (staff were present in 91% of observations in the houses and 86% in the three 'campus' houses compared with 74% in the hospital settings).

People living in the houses were also less likely to be with individuals who had competing needs to their own; people living in staffed houses were likely to be the only service user in the room for 63% of the time (and mostly with just one other for the remainder), compared with 42% in the three 'campus' houses, 33% in ordinary hospital wards and 27% in special units.

Client activity pattern

Fig. 25.2 represents graphically the overall level of participation in meaningful activity of everyone included in the study at each of the seven datapoints. Averaging the observations in each condition, the group that moved to houses almost doubled their level of participation in meaningful activity, from 16 to 28%. The one person whose placement broke down (WG) moved to a large institution and then to a small private home at the last datapoint, where her level of participation shows some decrement. Similarly, three people in houses (MM, HM and PH) show declining levels of participation after the initial move. The people who had not yet moved out of hospital showed no clear trend in their level of participation in meaningful activity, strengthening the case for attributing changes in the group that moved to the community services rather than passage of time or general improvement in all services.

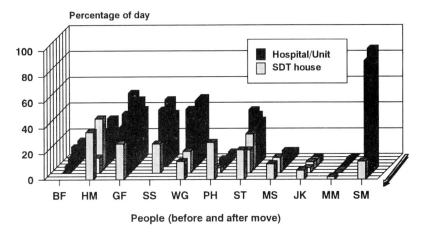

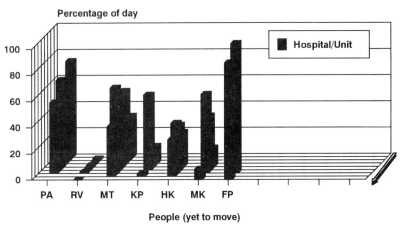

Fig. 25.3. Minor problem behaviour

More detailed analysis shows that these increases consist of participation in practical housework tasks, including assisted use of relatively complex equipment like irons and microwaves, and longer meal times.

Minor problem behaviours (mainly self-stimulation) showed an inverse relationship with engagement for everyone except MS (Fig. 25.3). This suggests that self-stimulation can often be competed out by engagement in purposeful activities. Serious problem behaviour (Fig. 25.4) decreased overall in nine cases after transfer to community settings, although this data should be interpreted with caution because it is highly variable, reduction does not always coincide with transfer and momentary time-sampling does not necessarily detect infrequent but very serious problems. Nevertheless, it does appear possible to conclude at least that the higher

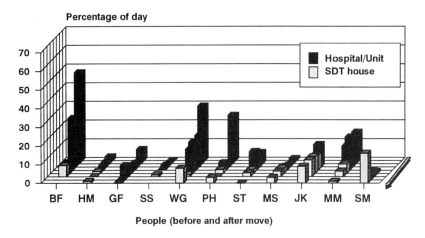

People (before and after move)

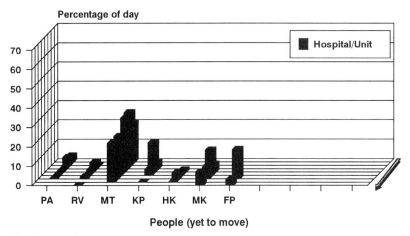

People (yet to move)

Fig. 25.4. Major problem behaviour

levels of participation in meaningful activity were achieved without worsening their problems.

In terms of social contact received from other people, individuals in hospitals and special units received contact from staff for a relatively small proportion of the day. The total contact received was 7% in hospital and 9% in special units (i.e. equivalent to 46 minutes and 59 minutes, respectively in an 11 hour day). In the campus houses total contact received was 13% (equivalent to 86 minutes) but in the other houses it was 26% (172 minutes). In these houses the form of contact was also different in that 42% of the contact was in the form of assistance rather than conversation. The houses therefore delivered much more contact and more of the contact was directly therapeutic.

Most people never received contact from other clients. Six of the 18 people who participated in the study were recorded as being contacted by other clients for approximately 7 minutes' worth in the 11 hour day observed on only one of the datapoints; one person received this level of contact on two datapoints; and one other received 26 minutes in 11 hours on one datapoint. This reflects the degree of handicap of the people served and suggests that, for this group at least, the idea that large facilities provide important social relationships with other handicapped people is mistaken.

Discussion

Although the participants in this study may not necessarily be representative of those in other areas, they were those identified by service agencies as among the most difficult people with severe or profound learning disability to serve in the region. The results of this very detailed, long-term study do therefore make a significant contribution to the policy question of the relevance of different treatment approaches as hospitals are replaced by alternative services. The results show that it has been possible to set up small-scale staffed housing placements in the community which offer much richer social and material environments than the hospitals they replace. Given the extreme nature of the problems experienced by this client group and the long history of failure by services to do more than provide custodial care, this is no mean achievement.

The findings about staff ratio and staff contact are of interest. The not inconsiderable amount of time clients spend in hospital and campus services without supervision in part reflects the option for people to wander off into the dormitories unnoticed. However, in group care situations, particularly in special units, individuals may be placed at some risk when left among people who also have severe problem behaviour. That nearly a quarter of the time observed these people had no staff present is surprising and should cause managers to reexamine ward organisation and staff morale. Although the houses show higher levels of staff contact, there is still considerable room for improvement and this has implications for management and training. What data there is on campus-based units and special treatment units suggests these are not very different from the large hospitals they were intended to replace.

In terms of client activity patterns, the overall results suggest that, even for people who, in addition to their severe or profound learning disability, have very serious challenging behaviour, small staffed homes can provide improved client experience as measured by engagement in meaningful activity; but that to do so requires attention to the quality of staff performance as well as to basic material and social resources. The simple enrichment of the social and physical environment by transfer from institutions to staffed houses does not in itself ensure greater involvement by the person served in meaningful activity. In line with other research on community-based residential services, which has shown generally favourable but variable results, the data highlights the importance of staff performance as a key factor in placement success. While community services may provide a richer material environment and wider opportunities for constructive activity than institutions, the patterns of staff behaviour which have been shown to be important in enabling active participation by people with severe or profound learning disabilities can be overlooked or ignored in the pursuit of 'homeliness'. Models for the delivery of good staff performance in ordinary housing have been developed (Mansell *et al.*, 1987; Felce, 1989).

Summary

The results of community studies point up the problem of maintaining the standards reached in the new services. Some are beginning to show evidence of decay in the activity levels achieved and the associated staff performance. Other work in progress has examined this issue in one district where it seems that the other community services are so much less well organised than the special service that managers have found it impossible to prevent that service being undermined by lack of staff, continuity, training and good practice leadership (Hughes & Mansell, 1990). Thus the success of specialised staffed housing for people with challenging behaviour may ultimately depend on the extent to which mainstream community services are effective.

Acknowledgements

The author would like to thank Fran Beasley, Research Fellow on this project; the service users and staff who participated in the study; and colleagues in the Centre for the Applied Psychology of Social Care who helped with data collection.

References

Beasley, F., Hewson, S. & Mansell, J. (1989). *MTS: Handbook for Observers*. University of Kent at Canterbury, Centre for the Applied Psychology of Social Care. Canterbury: CAPSC.

Bijou, S., Petersen, R. & Ault, M. (1968). A method to integrate descriptive and experimental field studies at the level of data and empirical concepts. *Journal of Applied Behavior Analysis*, **1**(2), 175–91.

Campbell, D. & Stanley, J. (1966). *Experimental and quasi-experimental Designs for Research*. Boston: Houghton-Mifflin.

de Kock, U., Saxby, H., Felce, D., Thomas, M. & Jenkins, J. (1988). Individual planning for adults with severe or profound mental handicaps in a community-based service. *Mental Handicap*, **16**(4), 152–5.

Department of Health and Social Security (1984). *Helping Mentally Handicapped People with Special Problems: Report of a DHSS Study Team*. London: Department of Health and Social Security.

Department of Health (1989). *Needs and Responses: Services for Adults with Mental Handicap who are Mentally ill, who have Behaviour Problems or who Offend*. Report of a DoH Study Team. London: Department of Health.

Dockrell, J., Gaskell, G. & Rehman, H. (1990). Challenging behaviours: problems, provisions and 'solutions'. In A. Dosen, A, Van Gennep, & G. J. Zwanikken, eds. Treatment of mental illness and behavioural disorder in the mentally retarded. *Proceedings of the International Congress*. Amsterdam. Leiden: Logon Publications.

Emerson, E., Beasley, F., Offord, G. & Mansell, J. (1992). All evaluation of hospital-based specialised staffed housing for people with seriously challenging behaviours. *Journal of Intellectual Disability Research*, **36**, 291–307.

Emerson, E., Cummings, R., Barrett, S., Hughes, H., McCool, C. & Toogood, A. (1988). Challenging behaviour and community services: 2. Who are the people who challenge services? *Mental Handicap*, **16**, 16–19.

Emerson, E., Toogood, A., Mansell, J., Barrett, S., Bell, C., Cummings, R. & McCool, C. (1987). Challenging behaviour and community services: 1. Introduction and overview. *Mental Handicap*, **15**, 166–9.

Felce, D. (1989). *The Andover Project: Staffed Housing for Adults with Severe or Profound Mental Handicaps*. Kidderminster: British Institute of Mental Handicap.

Felce, D., de Kock, U. & Repp, A. (1986). An eco-behavioral comparison of small community-based houses and traditional large hospitals for severely and profoundly mentally handicapped adults. *Applied Research in Mental Retardation*, **7**, 393–408.

Felce, D., Kushlick, A. & Mansell, J. (1980). Evaluation of alternative residential facilities for the severely mentally handicapped in Wessex: client engagement. *Advances in Behaviour Research and Therapy*, **3**(1), 13–18.

Grant, G. & Moores, B. (1977). Resident characteristics and staff behavior in two hospitals for mentally retarded adults. *American Journal of Mental Deficiency*, **82**(3), 259–65.

Hewson, S. (1991). The evaluation of quality in a mental handicap service. International Journal of Health Care Quality Assurance, **4**(3), 18–22.

Hughes, H. M. & Mansell, J. (1990). *Consultation to Camberwell Health Authority Learning Difficulties Care Group: Evaluation Report*, Vols. 1–3. Canterbury: Centre for the Applied Psychology of Social Care.

Intagliata, J. & Willer, B. (1982). Reinstitutionalization of mentally retarded persons successfully placed into family care and group homes. *American Journal of Mental Deficiency*, **87**, 34–9.

Joyce, T. A. (1988). Individual and environmental determinants of normalisation-related outcomes for mentally handicapped people living in

hospital, hostels and staffed houses. PhD thesis, United Medical & Dental
Schools, Guy's Hospital.

Joyce, T., Gray, H. & Mansell, J. (1989). Evaluating service quality: a
comparison of diaries with direct observation. *Mental Handicap Research*,
2(1), 38–46.

Kings Fund Centre, (1980). *An Ordinary Life*. London: Kings Fund Centre.

Korman, N. & Glennerster, H. (1985). Closing a hospital: the Darenth Park
project. *Occasional papers in Social Administration No. 78*. London:
Bedford Square Press.

Korman, N. & Glennerster, H. (1990). *Hospital Closure*. Milton Keynes: Open
University Press.

Mansell, J. (1988). *Staffed Housing for People with Mental Handicaps: Achieving
Widespread Dissemination*. Bexhill: South East Thames Regional Health
Authority.

Mansell, J. (1989). Evaluation of training in the development of staffed housing
for people with mental handicaps. *Mental Handicap Research*, **2**(2), 137–51.

Mansell, J., Felce, D., Jenkins, J., de Kock, U. & Toogood, A. (1987). *Staffed
Housing for People with Mental Handicaps*. Tunbridge Wells: Costello.

Mansell, J., Jenkins, J., Felce, D. & de Kock, U. (1984). Measuring the activity
of severely and profoundly mentally handicapped adults in ordinary
housing. *Behaviour Research and Therapy*, **22**, 23–9.

Nihira, K., Foster, R., Shellhaas, M. & Leland, H. (1974). *AAMD Adaptive
Behavior Scale*. Washington, DC: American Association on Mental
Deficiency.

O'Neill, J., Brown, M., Gordon, W., Schonhorn, R. & Greer, E. (1981). Activity
patterns of mentally retarded adults in institutions and communities: A
longitudinal study. *Applied Research in Mental Retardation*, **2**, 367–79.

Rawlings, S. (1985). Behaviour and skills of severely retarded adults in hospitals
and small residential homes. *British Journal of Psychiatry*, **146**, 358–360.

Raynes, N. (1980). The less you've got the less you get: functional grouping, a
cause for concern. *Mental Retardation*, **18**, 217–20.

Repp, A. C. & Barton, L. E. (1980). Naturalistic observations of
institutionalised retarded persons: a comparison of licensure decisions and
behavioural observations. *Journal of Applied Behavior Analysis*, **13**, 333–41.

Special Development Team, (1988). *Annual Report 1987*. Canterbury: Centre for
the Applied Psychology of Social Care.

Sutter, P., Mayeda, T., Call, T., Yanagi, G. & Yee, S. (1980). Comparison of
successful and unsuccessful community placed mentally retarded persons.
American Journal of Mental Deficiency, **85**(3), 262–7.

Toogood, A., Emerson, E., Hughes, H., Barrett, S., Cummings, R. & McCool,
C. (1988). Challenging Behaviour and community services: 3. Planning
individualised services. *Mental Handicap*, **16**, 70–4.

Vitello, S. J., Atthowe, J. M. & Cadwell, J. (1983). Determinants of community
placement of institutionalised mentally retarded persons. *American Journal
of Mental Deficiency*, **87**(5), 539–45.

Wing, L. (1988). *The Darenth Park Project, 1980–1985: The Effects on the
residents*. MRC Social Psychiatry Unit. London: Institute of Psychiatry
(mimeo).

Part VI
International perspectives

26

Services for people with dual disgnosis in the USA

FRANK J. MENOLASCINO

Introduction

Services in the United States for all persons with mental retardation have evolved and expanded during the last three decades. Beginning with the Community Mental Health Retardation Facilities Construction Act of 1963, profound and far-reaching changes have occurred in the integration of persons with mental retardation into the mainstream of community life. As a consequence, a revolution has come to pass in the programmes and technological aspects associated with serving these individuals. Nirje (1969) defined a major ideological shift in service delivery in the principle of normalisation which not only encouraged the habilitation of persons with mental retardation but also called for radical changes in how society related to individuals with special needs. This paradigm shift from warehousing to community integration resulted in a three-decade process of deinstitutionalisation, the establishment of community-based alternatives, and a fuller understanding, appreciation and acceptance of people with mental retardation. By helping these individuals become integrated into the life of the community, normalization led to the establishment of family-like residences, the fostering of acceptance and the weaving of each person as thoroughly into social fabric as possible (Fletcher & Menolascino, 1989; Kugel & Wolfensberger, 1969; Wolfensberger, 1991).

In concert with this process of social change, service delivery has changed as well. Individuals living in relatively small community group homes (i.e. 15 and fewer residents) increased from 40000 to 125000 between 1977 and 1988. In addition, public institutions for persons with mental retardation decreased their populations from approximately 195000 in 1968 to 87000 in 1989, and the number of individuals with a primary diagnosis of mental retardation in state psychiatric facilities declined from 37 000 to 2 000 between 1960 and 1988 (Amado, Lakin, & Menke, 1990). This number can be somewhat misleading, however, since these 2 000 individuals constitute a high percentage of the seriously disturbed. Persons without complex mental retardation are typically discharged to the community while those who are mentally ill remain institutionalised. The result of this state of affairs has been the establishment of what are essentially chronic mental hospitals for persons with mental retardation (American Psychiatric Association, 1991). Further, there are a significant number of individuals with mental retardation who had been hospitalized in the past and subsequently 'forgotten'. Although clear data on this population remain inadequate, the state of Massachusetts, for example, with a population of under 6 million, has 'found' an estimated 220 such individuals in its state mental hospitals. In a single five-county area in the state of Nebraska, 170 persons with mental retardation remain in public institutions, many of whom are less severely disabled than those presently living in community settings. However, as a result class action suits, comprehensive assessments have been mandated and special mental health units for the provisions of appropriate programmes are emerging (American Psychiatric Association, 1991).

Although the residents in small community programmes are, on average, less severely impaired than the residents of large public and private institutions, there are growing numbers of individuals with a dual diagnosis who are progressing well in community settings (Lakin *et al.*, 1989). Yet some doubt still persists regarding the ability, or perhaps the desire, of leaders of community programmes to meet the needs of all persons with complex mental retardation. Many questions remain regarding the quality of care and capability of communities to offer a wide spectrum of services to all persons regardless of the severity of their handicaps.

Thus, many persons with mental retardation still remain poorly served in both institutional and community-based settings, particularly those with concomitant mental illness. Scheerenberger (1987) describes the deinstitutionalisation trend as a mixture of success and failure since approximately half of the individuals involved in the process have merely been relocated to nursing homes, county homes, private homes or correctional facilities. The number, quality and diversity of residential programmes are inadequate. Most community agencies pick and choose whom they will accept, often screening out the more complex individuals or retaining the option of expelling those regarded as too challenging. Although the transition is neither perfect nor complete, the modern array of services available in the United States is impressive.

Planning the future

Late in 1985, The President's Committee on Mental Retardation sponsored a National Strategy Conference on mental illness in persons with mental retardation in Washington, DC. The major purpose of the conference was to delineate the state of the art and to chart a national course of action and support. Major national themes and trends were analyzed and critically questioned and a significant amount of consensus emerged relative to basic issues and strategies for change.

In terms of epidemiology, it was unanimously agreed that the incidence rate of mental illness in persons with mental retardation is significantly higher than in the non-retarded population and that there are psychiatric syndromes unique to this group. It was accepted as a unanimous challenge to define and develop strategies to prevent the institutionalisation of individuals with dual diagnosis and to find ways to bring those who are currently institutionalised back into the community (Scheerenberger, 1988; Fletcher & Menolascino, 1989). The array of services that are currently being developed throughout the United States to facilitate this challenge include models for care and treatment of acute psychiatric disorders, specialised education and vocational programmes, group homes and supportive services such as day hospitals, counselling and family support programmes.

It was clearly pointed out during this conference that America's states and communities need to include persons with mental retardation and mental illness within their entire range of currently available programmes and services. For example, it was suggested that an individual with mild retardation and schizophrenia would live in a group home with other non-psychiatrically involved mentally retarded persons as long as there was active and ongoing community-based backup support for the treatment and management of this person's mental illness. This approach is in contrast to the lingering practice of establishing separate programmes for the dually diagnosed in both institutional and community-based systems of service. While it is true that behavioural disorders continue to constitute a major barrier to community placement (Gardner & Moffatt, 1990), the creation of segregated settings stands in direct contrast to the ideology of normalisation. The trend accepted by conference participants was that mental health centres should engage in both acute and follow-up psychiatric care, while mental retardation programmes should focus on the residential, educational, vocational and recreational needs of the dually diagnosed.

As previously mentioned, the needlessly high number of persons with mental retardation and mental illness in state institutions was viewed as another national challenge. A corollary problem dealt with the dually diagnosed being shuffled from institutions for the mentally retarded to institutions for the mentally ill in a lifelong cycle of non-treatment. Conference participants agreed that this cycle of despair had to be brought to an end. It was emphasised that these individuals have long held the same rights and privileges as all other US citizens (United Nations, 1971), yet when diagnoses are combined, such rights are often obscured, resulting in interagency conflicts which leave the dually diagnosed poorly served by both systems. The best approach advocated was to treat the acute psychiatric needs of persons with mental retardation in psychiatric settings and to meet their long-term needs in community programmes with secondary support provided by the mental health system. Generally, psychiatric services in the United States for citizens with mental retardation tend to be provided: 1) in institutions by visiting consultants rather than full-time professionals; 2) as active aspects of an outpatient clinic; 3) as part of a University Affiliated Programme, usually via a multidisciplinary team; and 4) in special inpatient/outpatient service systems for complex retarded citizens.

It was agreed by all in attendance at the president's committee on Mental Retardation that major strides have indeed been made over the past 20 years regarding psychotherapeutic intervention techniques, the application of the principles of applied behavioural analysis, the use of psychoactive drugs and the evolution of models of care. Basic recommendations for the future targeted new and improved services, more innovative basic and applied research and more relevant and in-depth training.

Current service challenges

Individuals with a dual diagnosis who currently present the most complex sets of clinical challenges have behavioural or personality problems as one of their core problems. Although their primitive behaviours often emanate from their extremely restricted ability to deal with the external world, it is important to remember that these limitations have direct repercussions on their families, their caregivers and society in general. These complex individuals tend to exhaust their caregivers, both physically and emotionally. Those with severe retardation and mental illness forcibly demand careful rethinking of where they should be served. For example, should they be served within their family, a community-based facility, an institution? Also, how should they be served: full day programmes, individually tailored partial day programmes, daily treatment programmes involving recreational rather than developmental or vocational goals? Far from being resolved, the relevant allocation of society's resources remains a challenge to all professionals in both the mental retardation and mental health fields.

The array of programmes and services that are currently being developed in the United States include models for care and treatment of acute psychiatric disorders, specialised education and vocational programmes, group homes and supportive services such as day hospitals, individual and group therapy and family support programmes. Recognising the need for decent and responsive programmes and services for persons with mental retardation and mental illness, whether institutional or community-based, is one thing, but putting our values into practice can be quite another, as is evident from the persistent professional issues which surrounded the institutional versus the community based array of services. Nevertheless, persons who are mentally retarded and mentally ill do require quite a full range of programmes and supports. The two extremes in this continuum are prevention and acute care, and both are greatly needed. Prevention includes simple, low-cost supports, such as respite care, in-home services and parent training, which serve to lessen the impact of mental illness or prevent it entirely (Butterfield & Berkson,1991). At the other end of the continuum is acute care; short-term inpatient psychiatric treatment such as that provided at the University of Nebraska Medical Centre. The average length of stay for persons with mental retardation and mental illness admitted to this centre was two weeks, after which they typically return to their community programmes.

Although the vast majority of service systems for persons with mental retardation are not saturated with persons with a concurrent mental illness, there will exist a relatively small number of such individuals who require specialised services. There are no easy answers for meeting the requirements of these individuals, but certain treatment practices and settings are unacceptable, including locked doors, locked windows, alarm systems, increased use of punishment, mechanical and chemical restraint and prohibition of movement outside the unit itself. We also need to explore options regarding community placements and support for the dually diagnosed who are elderly, individuals who challenge the legal system, those who live in rural areas and persons who have severe to profound mental retardation and multiple physical handicaps (Lakin *et al.*, 1991; Menolascino & Potter, 1989*a,b*).

By far the most important issue for individuals with dual diagnosis in the decade ahead, however, is entitlement to services. On the whole, persons with mental retardation are not competent enough to seek services on their own and most have some form of publicly funded health insurance, such as Medicaid or Medicare, which pays for basic health care but limits reimbursement for mental health services. Further, the regulations which govern the manner in which this population is to be cared for are often vague and occasionally disturbing. To quote from the American Psychiatric Task Force Report:

> The Accreditation Council on Services for People with Developmental Disabilities promulgates standards [which] refer to drugs only in the context of 'controlling behaviour', to be recommended by 'a physician or psychopharmacologist' (who is not defined further and in practice is often a pharmacist) and approved by behaviour management and human rights committees. The word 'psychiatrist' is mentioned only in the index of that publication...On the other hand, if an individual has more than five seizures yearly, examination by a 'qualified neurologist' is mandated.

> This state of affairs is most disturbing. While the right of people with mental retardation to medical care is recognised and while all available data indicate that mental disorders are virtually the most handicapping condition associated with mental retardation, there is no requirement for providing them with professional psychiatric care. Moreover, psychopharmacological agents are treated a priori as restrictive, to be used under non-medical control, for nonspecific 'behavioural control', rather than for treatment of mental illness.

Overview of a successful model of community care

Despite the shortcomings that remain in caring for people with mental retardation, models of excellence do exist, such as those associated with the Wrentham State School in Massachusetts, the University of California at Los Angeles and the Children's Hospital in Boston (American Psychiatric Association, 1991). The Eastern Nebraska Community Office of Retardation (ENCOR) in Omaha, Nebraska was recognised in 1985 as an outstanding American model for the provision of modern community-based services by the president's committee on Mental Retardation and continues to demonstrate that it is both possible and cost-beneficial to serve individuals with mental retardation and mental illness in their home communities (Casey *et al.*, 1985).

The fact that almost one-fifth of the ENCOR population has a dual diagnosis means that the agency has had to develop a wide range of services to meet their unique needs. Outside of the university-based inpatient service, ENCOR has no special facilities for the dually diagnosed. An early lesson was learned when the agency decided to establish a special group home for individuals with severe aggression and self-injury. It became obvious that congregating persons with similar behavioural needs was not an effective treatment approach. Although it made administrative sense to concentrate similar individuals and specialised staff, the long-term results were deteriorating behaviours, increased use of aversive interventions and increased staff turnover. Other non-normalising phenomena also crept into this setting such as locked doors, locked windows and mechanical restraint devices. The homogenous grouping approach was, therefore, abandoned in favour of a more integrated, normalised model.

The offender with mental retardation

Whether found guilty or not, these individuals present major service challenges to the system. ENCOR currently serves 25 individuals (2.2% of the total ENCOR population of 1140) who have transgressed the law and entered the criminal justice system. Their past offenses or charges have included shoplifting, assault, indecent exposure, arson and sexual assault.

Although they do not comprise a large percentage of clients, this particular group presents major integration challenges because of anti-social behaviours. Even though such behaviours occur infrequently, they can pose a threat to the public welfare. The key to success has been the provision of adequate supervision, plus the recognition that in some cases certain individuals will require life-long support and supervision. Staff have had to learn that, in some instances, movement into less restrictive settings does not depend on 'functional skills' but on antisocial tendencies.

General recommendations

Over two decades of programme development, community involvement, citizen advocacy and clinical experiences with ENCOR have produced several lessons which might be useful to other communities in the process of developing comprehensive services for persons with mental retardation and mental illness. The first lesson is that it takes time, political commitment and a willingness to reflect on and put into practice those values which centre on community integration. Another lesson is that the service system has to be prepared to serve all individuals regardless of the level of mental retardation or the extent of allied disabilities if it hopes to be responsive to the needs of families. This commitment to zero rejection necessitates the practice of a number of basic values such as the concept of community and human interdependence; the vigilance of parents, family members and other citizens; the acceptance of the principle of normalisation; the assumption that all individuals are capable of change over their lives; the practice of nonviolence; and the constant questioning of the nature of the service system and the values that propel it. The community must also be responsive to presenting needs and this can take considerable effort. For example, one must find sensitive and competent physicians, psychologists; encourage industries to open their doors to integrated work alternatives; create a number of family support services; and discover ways to teach direct caregivers the complex task of serving these challenging individuals. It is also recommended that existing community resources be utilised. This not only keeps costs down, but does enable clients to receive high quality care.

In addition to the driving force of clear values, managerial system with public accountability is recommended. ENCOR is governed at the community level by five elected county commissioners. These elected officials provide a direct link to parents, neighbours, employers and the public at large for both compliments and criticism. Because this governing body is controlled locally and has a well-organised and active Parent Advisory Committee, the agency is open to continuous monitoring and community input. In essence, the programme belongs to the people, not to some distant and faceless bureaucrats. This facilitates and produces constant improvements in service models, quality of care and opportunities for integration.

Summary

The potential and ongoing needs of a subpopulation of citizens with complex mental retardation have presented a continuing challenge to the US systems of services for nearly three decades. Although there have been no easy answers for meeting the unique requirements of these individuals, there are principles which have been espoused from the beginning: normalisation, the developmental model and cost/benefit considerations.

While the services available to persons with dual diagnosis in America are impressive, the question still remains: Are individuals with mental retardation and mental illness who were heretofore 'protected' in an institutional environment actually better off within communities whose citizens often devalue their presence? In response, it can be stated that appropriate habilitation services are rare and antipsychotic medications are chronically utilised in the typical public institution. Individuals with complex mental retardation typically receive mental health treatment from psychologists, social workers or 'counsellors', many of whom lack the training necessary to provide adequate care. Yet while an enhanced quality of life following deinstitutionalisation is possible, it is not inevitable (Allen, 1989; Mallory & Herrick, 1987; Schalock *et al.*, 1989). Certainly the 'dumping' of persons into the community in the name of normalisation must be utterly rejected since it only fuels the risk for mental illness to develop. We need to do more to ensure that community placement of individuals is without trauma and that supportive structures are in place and remain active. Initial and ongoing support is vital to success.

Services for the dually diagnosed are throughout most of the nation, but a more energetic outreach posture will be needed in the future. Keeping in mind the demonstrated difficulties associated with motivating citizens with mental illness but without mental retardation to attend community resource settings, the dually diagnosed individual is in need of a far more direct linkage. We thus foresee an increase in mobile mental health services to provide outreach programmes in group homes or sheltered places of employment. We also foresee an enhanced focus on the training of skilled personnel in mental health treatment techniques so that they can utilise their new skills as an ongoing part of their daily work in education, training and residential facilities throughout the United States. Direct and indirect components of modern mental health consultation practice can and should be accomplished concurrently.

References

Allen, D. (1989). The effects of deinstitutionalisation on people with mental handicaps: a review. *Mental Handicap Research*, **2**, 18–37.

Amando, A. N., Lakin, K. C. & Menke, J. M. (1990). *1990 Chartbook: Services for People with Developmental Disabilities*. Minneapolis, MN: University of Minnesota Press.

American Psychiatric Association (1991). *Psychiatric Services to Adult Mentally Retarded and Developmentally Disabled Persons: Task Force Report 30*. Washington, D. C.: American Psychiatric Association.

Butterfield, E. & Berkson, G. (1991). The Milwaukee project clarified. *American Journal of Mental Retardation*, **95**, 477.

Casey, K., McGee, J., Stark, J. & Menolascino, F. J. (1985). *A Community-based System for the Mentally Retarded: The ENCOR Experience*. Lincoln, NE: University of Nebraska Press.

Fletcher, R. & Menolascino, F. J. (1989). *Mental Retardation and Mental Illness: Assessment, Treatment and Service for the Dually Diagnosed*. Lexington, MA: Lexington Books.

Gardner, W. I. & Moffatt, C. W. (1990). Aggressive behaviour: definition, assessment and treatment. *International Review of Psychiatry*, **2**, 91–100.

Kugel, R. & Wolfensberger, W. (1969). *Changing Patterns in Residential Services for the Mentally Retarded*. Washington, DC: US Government Printing Office.

Lakin, K. C., Anderson, D. J., Hill, B. K., Bruininks, R. H. & Wright, E. A. (1991). Programs and services received by older persons with mental retardation. *Mental Retardation*, **29**, 65–74.

Lakin, K. C., Hill, B. K., Chen, T. & Stephens, S. A. (1989). *Persons with Mental Retardation and Related Conditions in Mental Retardation Facilities: Selected Findings from the 1987 Medical Expenditure Survey*. Minneapolis, MN: University of Minnesota for Residential and Community Services.

Mallory, B. L. & Herrick, S. C. (1987). The movement of children with mental retardation from institutional to community care. *Journal of the Association of Persons with Severe Handicaps*, **12**, 297–305.

McGee, J., & Menolascino, F. J. (1991). *Beyond Gentle Teaching*. New York: Plenum.

Menolascino, F. J. (1974). The mentally retarded offender. *Mental Retardation*, **12**, 7–11.

Menolascino, F. J. & Stark, J. (1984). *Handbook of Mental Illness in the Mentally Retarded*, New York: Plenum.

Menolascino, F. J. & Potter, J. (1989*a*). Delivery of services in rural settings to the elderly mentally retarded–mentally ill. *International Journal on Ageing and Human Development*, **28**, 261–75.

Menolascino, F. J. & Potter, J. (1989*b*). Mental illness in the elderly mentally retarded. *Journal of Applied Gerontology*, **8**, 192–202.

Nirje, B. (1969). The normalisation principle and its human management implications. In R. Kugel and W. Wolfensberger, eds. *Changing Patterns in Residential Services for the Mentally Retarded.* Washington DC: US Government Printing Office.

Schalock, R., Keith, K., Hoffman, K. & Karan, O. (1989). Quality of life: its measurement and use. *Mental Retardation*, **27**, 25–31.

Scheerenberger, R. C. (1987). *A History of Mental Retardation: A Quarter Century of Promise*. Baltimore, MD: Brookes Publishing.

Scheerenberger, R. C. (1988). Past, present and future roles for institutional settings in the care of mentally retarded/mentally ill persons. In: J. Stark, F. Menolascino, M. Albarelli, V. Gray, eds. *Mental Retardation and Mental Health: Classification, Diagnosis, Treatment, Services*. New York: Springer-Verlag

Stark, J., Menolascino, F., Albarelli, M. & Gray, V. (1988). *Mental Retardation and Mental Health: Classification, Diagnosis, Treatment, Services*. New York: Springer-Verlag.

United Nations (1971). *Declaration on the Rights of Mentally Retarded Persons*. New York: United Nations General Assembly, 2027th Plenary Meeting.

Wolfensberger, W. (1991). Reflections on a lifetime in human services and mental retardation. *Mental Retardation*, **29**, 1–16.

27

Developing services in Canada: Ontario vignettes

ALICE PUDDEPHATT AND SAM SUSSMAN

Introduction

Canada is a federation of provinces each with individual responsibility for health and social service programmes. Across Canada, it is difficult to form a unified picture of services to the population with mental illness and mental retardation (dual diagnosis). British Columbia, Alberta, and Ontario offer specific dual diagnosis programmes; Saskatchewan includes this population in its 'generic' mental health programmes. We were unable to discover what programmes are available in the rest of Canada.

In Ontario there is a paucity of community-based programmes outside Toronto, the capital city of the province. Mental retardation institutions maintain behavioural units to treat the most seriously disabled dually diagnosed individuals, while there are also dual diagnosis units in five of the province's psychiatric hospitals. An initiative to provide funding for community programmes seems likely to founder on the rocks of recession.

Background

Canada's population is approximately twenty-six and a half million. It is made up of ten provinces, which have exclusive jurisdiction in many areas, and two territories, which are under closer federal control. The constitution of Canada provides for provincial responsibility in many areas, including health, social services and education. The federal government retains some influence in provincial activities with its systems of federal grants. The funds are earmarked for particular applications; hence policies are frequently shaped by the size of the federal grants allowed in any area.

The history of dual diagnosis

In the early years of Canada's development, there were no services for the dual diagnosis population. Although the condition had been recognised as early as the mid-nineteenth century, both mental illness and mental retardation were thought to be incurable until about the 1830s and thus there was no perceived need to differentiate between individuals with one or other condition or both. Asylums became repositories, as had the jails and workhouses before them, for any individual who could not be cared for in the community.

As early as the seventeenth century, the province of Quebec (then New France) established hospitals which served 'the impoverished, the disabled and the helpless' (Griffin & Greenland, 1981). These 'disabled' included the physically disabled, the mentally ill, and the developmentally disabled. Despite its pioneering of services this province is slow to move toward deinstitutionalisation. In the eighteenth century, a workhouse was built in Halifax, Nova Scotia, which housed social misfits and those who were guilty of certain misdemeanours like gambling and fortune telling. Developmentally disabled and mentally ill people were included in this population, but were not forced to work if they were found incapable (Francis, 1977). By the nineteenth century, lunatic asylums were built in both New Brunswick and Nova Scotia, to which at first developmentally disabled individuals were admitted. There was still no mental retardation institution in Nova Scotia by 1914 (Stead, 1914), and only a training school by the mid-1960s (Gibson, Frank & Zarfas, 1963). In New Brunswick and Newfoundland, institutions were only in the process of being constructed by 1963, while Prince Edward Island had a small residential unit (Gibson *et al.*, 1963).

It soon became obvious to the government and asylum administrators that the presence of 'incurably' ill people was burdening the asylums to the extent that those who might be cured were in jeopardy of not receiving services. In Ontario this realisation came about in the middle of the nineteenth century, when the Directors of the Provincial Lunatic Asylum decreed: 'It has been found necessary to exclude all idiotic and paralytic cases – one of which class might occupy the room which in a year, might suffice for three or four patients who, in succession might be received and cured – but of these incurable idiots there is now a large number in the Institution' (Simmons, 1982). However, this exclusion was theoretical, since the asylum inspectors would not refuse admission to people in need of shelter, many of whom were mentally retarded rather than mentally ill.

The crying need for institutional accommodation finally led to the establishment in 1876 of Ontario's, and Canada's, first separate Asylum for Idiots. Through 1888, this was still the only one of its kind in the country (Wilbur, 1888). This was the first instance of an administrative distinction being made between people with mental retardation and those with mental illness. However, although people with the two different conditions were now housed separately, their governmental responsibility lay with the same Provincial Secretary, a position which would later become the Minister of Health.

Institutional treatment of dual diagnosis

When the developmentally disabled population began to be considered as a separate group from the mentally ill or indigent categories, governments built institutions initially to shelter and protect these 'unfortunates'. Later the philosophies were to be turned on their heads, with the institutions being used to rid society of its 'undesirable' or 'dangerous' members. In both cases, the residents of the government facilities were comprehensively cared for during their lifetimes. This 'cradle to the grave' spectrum of care included services for people with mental retardation who were also mentally ill. Usually these services would consist of a separate ward or unit in the mental retardation institution where disturbing patients could be segregated from their more 'normal' peers, and as psychiatric theory developed, so did active treatment for the dually diagnosed in place of passive custodial care.

The Asylum for Idiots at Orillia formed the basis of the eventually Ontario-wide system of residential facilities for people with mental retardation, which remains in existence today with twelve wholly government-run facilities still in operation. The rest of Canada provided twelve additional provincial establishments in the 1960s, some of which have now been closed (Gibson *et al.*, 1963).

Ontario with its population of nine and three-quarter million is the most populous province in the Dominion of Canada. It provides a good example of the embryonic stage of development of services to the dual diagnosis population throughout Canada. Due to the provincial responsibility for both health and social services, services vary from province to province.

In 1974, in Ontario, services for people with mental retardation were segregated from those to the mentally ill. With the passage of the Developmental Services Act 1974 all institutional and community services for people with mental retardation came under the jurisdiction not of the

Ministry of Health but of the Ministry of Community and Social Services. This realignment of provincial departments took place throughout Canada at about this time, partly due to a restructuring of the federal support payments in the area (Zarfas, 1988).

At about the same time, 'normalisation' philosophies contributed to the attitudes of both government and social service workers that people with developmental disabilities were not 'ill', and did not belong under the aegis of the Ministry of Health. Normalisation also contributed to the massive deinstitutionalisation programmes which were created at about the same time in a planned movement of individuals from government-operated institutions to community residence. The decision in Ontario to move individuals from institutional settings to the community was made by the government in cooperation with community agencies, people with developmental disabilities and their parents.

On December 31, 1974 there were 7028 individuals with mental retardation in institutions in Ontario and currently there remain approximately 3150. Those dually diagnosed persons still residing in government-run institutions have the benefit of several behaviour management units which aim to treat their psychiatric disorders.

Ontario psychiatric hospitals' dual diagnosis units

While it has been argued that Wolfensberger's principles of normalisation have been achieved for the majority of the people with mental retardation in Ontario, the dually diagnosed in the community have been relegated to a psychiatric service netherworld. Few psychiatrists are willing to accept clients with mental retardation. Psychiatric hospitals are reluctant to admit people with a dual diagnosis and community residential homes, as a consequence, view the psychiatric hospitals as being uncooperative and not understanding of their plight. Because of their commitment to deinstitutionalisation, the government institutions for mental retardation are reluctant to readmit individuals who have been living in the community, even though they would benefit from the type of treatment offered in the behaviour management units. In Ontario, the transfer of services from the Ministry of Health to the Ministry of Community and Social Services left the dually diagnosed 'between the cracks' of the two ministries because the division of responsibility was based on a diagnosis of having exclusively either mental retardation or mental illness. Any individual who presents symptoms of both conditions may be 'bounced' around from one agency to another with no one willing to act on his/her behalf (Griffiths, 1986).

The Metropolitan Agencies Representatives' Council in Toronto (MARC) in a report entitled 'A Continuum of Service for Persons with Dual Diagnosis' (1989), said:

Confusion or failure to differentiate between symptomatology and etiology in determining a proper response to requests for treatment perpetuates several service issues:

1) it allows the shifting of responsibility for people with dual diagnosis back and forth between the mental health [i.e. the Ministry of Health] and the developmental service systems [i.e. the Ministry of Community and Social Services];
2) it leads to misdiagnosis and missed diagnosis; and,
3) it leads to inappropriate treatment for many dually diagnosed persons who continue to clog the system when crises erupt (MARC, 1989).

Beds in Ontario psychiatric hospitals presently number approximately 3500 and there are fears (as in the nineteenth century) – not unfounded – that the occupancy of beds by the dually diagnosed will lead to bed blockages. The rationalisation that the problems are behavioural rather than 'psychiatric' is also utilised by professional institution staff. Additionally, the institutions have found that once the client is ready for placement the original referral source, usually a community agency, will sometimes refuse accommodation.

Against this backdrop there is the issue of clinical expertise or lack thereof in dealing with this group of people. Thus in the multidisciplinary setting which characterises all of Ontario psychiatric hospitals, there is in many institutions an aura of therapeutic/professional nihilism which permeates the atmosphere when dealing with the dually diagnosed. The psychiatrist is frustrated from a clinical/therapeutic perspective and the social worker from a community and familial placement perspective. These anxieties are directly traceable back to the administrative dichotomy created in 1974. Psychiatric hospital personnel, being employed by the Ministry of Health, have not perceived themselves as being responsible for the treatment of the dual diagnosis population. As a result the therapeutic programme in the psychiatric hospital is decidedly lacking in the necessary resources to treat the dually diagnosed patient.

In a provincial psychiatric hospital in Ontario (London Psychiatric Hospital), serving a catchment area of over a million, with 320 inpatients (1991 figures), only 28 patients have been dually diagnosed. The average length of stay of a dually diagnosed patient was ninety days, compared with an average length of stay of two weeks for patients admitted to general treatment wards. The majority of the dually diagnosed patients are admitted for physical aggression, when the community setting was unable to cope with these problem behaviours (Edwards, 1991, personal communication). For some of these patients placement remains a problem even after a considerable stay in hospital because of the likelihood of physical aggression. In other words, the structured programme of the hospital may temporarily contain or abate the aggression but it may resurface in a less structured environment.

Scant attention has been paid in the past to the psychiatric problems of people with mental retardation by the psychiatric hospitals, with little research or data gathering. In 1990 the Ministry of Health commissioned a survey on the status of dual diagnosis services in Ontario psychiatric hospitals. Five programmes of dual diagnosis were described, in the hospitals of Brockville, Hamilton, Penetanguishene, St Thomas and Whitby, Ontario, providing 118 beds (Kazdan, 1990). Kazdan states that these five hospitals operate as five separate solitudes, with almost no communication between them. Lack of psychiatric diagnosis for a substantial number of clients and staffing issues were also of major concern. He has this to say about his experiences:

'The treatment of patients as well differs from hospital to hospital. Some hospitals base their treatment on behaviour theory using restraints and other behaviour techniques rather than drugs. Other hospitals use more traditional psychiatric approaches administering drugs to control behaviours. Still other hospitals use an eclectic approach to treatment using whatever seems to work for a particular patient.'

Although the five psychiatric hospitals which have dual diagnosis units represent a start, this disadvantaged group requires far more than the 118 currently available inpatient beds. The authors estimate that, given a population of close to ten million in Ontario, 210 beds and many more community services are required to service this population adequately.

In addition to the resource shortage, many health professionals in Ontario are ill-equipped to work with the dually diagnosed and as a result become easily frustrated. In Ontario we know of no Faculty of Social Work where mental retardation is a core component of the curriculum, yet many social workers are employed in the developmental handicap field. In psychiatry there are only two residency programmes in developmental handicap, one of which is located at Queen's University in Kingston, Ontario and the other at the University of Western Ontario in London, Ontario.

Community services for dual diagnosis

Across Canada, community services to the dual diagnosis population vary widely. Most community programmes in dual diagnosis are funded largely by government grants. Because of the provincial responsibility for this area, there is no unified data source for the whole country.

British Columbia has one of the most complete networks of service in the nation. The BC Mental Health Society has developed a 'Protocol for Services' for 'persons with a mental handicap' (Morrison & Foulis, 1991), which, with its team of psychiatrists, psychologists, nurses and social workers, will provide assessment and diagnosis, consultation with care professionals, treatment in the community if possible, and training for other professionals. The province has been divided into four areas, of which one is now providing a complete client service, while the other three are in various stages of development.

In Alberta there have been moves toward specialised services for the dual diagnosis population, but most of the services available are aimed at the general population. Community Behavioral Services in Edmonton have published a directory of agencies who are willing to serve dually diagnosed individuals (Community Behavioural Services, 1991). Also in Edmonton, the Alberta Hospital Edmonton runs a Special Adult Assessment Unit. In Calgary, the Calgary SCOPE (Support, Coordination, Operation, Planning, Evaluation) Society provides 'community-based outreach services for individuals with mental handicaps who are experiencing behavioural or emotional problems' (Calgary Outreach Services, n.d.). It offers outreach services, a residential support programme and a counselling therapist programme. The Western Human Resource Alberta Corp. offers residential and alternative day programmes to dually diagnosed individuals in Calgary, with the goal of moving clients from group homes into independent living or 'community partner' situations.

In Saskatchewan, there remains only one large institution for persons who are developmentally disabled, Valleyview Centre, with a few hundred residents. Developmentally disabled persons in the community 'with psychiatric problems are seen by regular mental health workers, and if required, are admitted to regular psychiatric inpatient units. Occasionally behaviourally difficult patients are returned to Valleyview Centre' (Thorpe, 1991). In a survey of group home operators and psychiatrists, both groups stated that the overwhelming need in Saskatchewan is for community support services for the dual diagnosis problem. Psychiatric care for the acutely mentally ill is not usually difficult to obtain for this population, except in cases of persons with very severe problems (Thorpe, 1991).

The Manitoba government does not fund any dual diagnosis programmes (Sourisseau, 1992, personal communication). There are presently no programmes for the dual diagnosis population in Quebec either (Roth, 1992, personal communication).

Ontario has several community programmes for the dual diagnosis population, but many of them are centred in Toronto. Professional centres such as the J. D. Griffin Adolescent Centre, York Behaviour Management Services, the Muki Baum Treatment Centre, the Reena Foundation and Surrey Place Centre each offer therapeutic and behavioural services to dually diagnosed individuals. However, they are usually not accessible to people outside of Toronto due to space limitations and travel difficulties.

The Metro Agencies Representatives' Council in Toronto has implemented its 'Continuum of Service for Persons with Dual Diagnosis'. They have received government funding for a two-year pilot project for assessment and treatment planning and a 5-bed residential programme for persons with dual diagnosis. However, the ideal situation in which the dually diagnosed individual receives services from prevention and early intervention through assessment and treatment planning, crisis intervention and long-term care and support (MARC, 1989), is still far from fruition.

Outside of Toronto, programmes are rather fewer. In the Kitchener–Waterloo region a 'Support Clusters' programme has been initiated for the family, caregivers, or any concerned persons, as well as for the client. The programme aims at allowing the support group to work out where its needs lie, whether in education, social support, or counselling. Then the programme coordinators help each group to access the services they require in order to form a cohesive and stable network around the dually diagnosed individual. This programme works on the principle of 'empowerment' of the individual and her/his support system, each member achieving whatever level of involvement to which he/she wishes to commit (Support Clusters, 1990).

In Stratford, Ontario, the Association for Community Living (supporting developmentally disabled clients) has developed a project called 'Community Connection'. This programme has been successful in placing developmentally disabled people in community work and leisure situations, with the assistance of 'natural supports' given by people in the general population without special training in mental retardation (Leavitt, 1991). While this programme is not aimed specifically at dually diagnosed clients, they are frequently the beneficiaries of it. Because Stratford is relatively small (population 27 000), community ties tend to be stronger, and word-of-mouth publicity more effective. This programme has been able to reintegrate many of its clients into a truly communal work and social life, thus breaking the isolation so often experienced by developmentally disabled people in the community.

The government of Ontario has provided a support network for residents of its facilities discharged into the community. Most institutions now have a 'community services' team. These teams work with the developmentally disabled people and their community care staff to ensure a smooth transition to the community. These teams, made up of psychologists, behaviour specialists and social workers, frequently become the only 'psychosocial' resource available to many dually diagnosed people. Unfortunately, as with most other services, they are limited by time and resources in the number of clients with whom they can work. It is all too often the case that 'the squeaky wheel gets the grease'. In practice, severe behaviour disorders may receive immediate attention, since they are very disruptive to a living or working situation, while an individual with symptoms of depression may not receive needed attention at once.

Community Living London of London, Ontario, houses 200 developmentally handicapped people in group homes some of which have staffing levels of three staff to four clients. The Executive Director has said that their clients require a total of approximately 365 inpatient days in a secure treatment facility, in order to treat their periodic eruptions of violence, at either the psychiatric or remaining developmental handicap institutions (Hudson, 1991, personal communication).

The Ministry of Health operates a 1700-bed 'Homes for Special Care' (HSC) community residential programme for discharged psychiatric patients which no person with a dual diagnosis or mental retardation label may now enter. In the early 1980s, due to community and advocacy group pressure to remove developmentally disabled persons from the perceived less than optimal therapeutic conditions in the HSC programme, the government decreed that the dually diagnosed were no longer to be admitted. However, as of this writing, over ten per cent of the HSC population is dually diagnosed; they are the remnants of the previous policy. The living conditions and supervision in the Homes for Special Care Programme, at least in one jurisdiction (London, Ontario), have dramatically improved since the early 1980s, but the administrative order and advocacy group resistance still stands. Appropriate housing and therapeutic services to the dually diagnosed remain perennially problem-

atic and create severe difficulties for the clients, their families and the
system as a whole.

Recent developments in Ontario

In 1984 the Ontario Ministry of Community and Social Services established
a unique professional programme at Queen's University, called the
Developmental Consulting Programme (DCP). This programme was set
up 'to provide consultation and programme development services on a
contract consulting basis to agencies and organisations in the province...
In addition, the programme...focuses attention at the university on the
developmental handicap field so that faculty and students...have enhanced opportunities to direct their attention to the challenges and issues
that confront us' (Exchange Journal, 1985). The DCP acts for the benefit
of all developmentally disabled people, including those who are dually
diagnosed.

In 1988 the government of Ontario, seeing the success of the DCP, chose
the University of Western Ontario, in London, Ontario, to become its next
partner in an academic liaison in the field of developmental disabilities.
The Developmental Disabilities Programme was established to: 1) act as a
catalyst to promote the increase of skills acquisition of community
professionals, 2) to encourage even more research into the causes and the
treatment of developmental disabilities and 3) to promote a high quality of
health and social services. It is a professional education and research
organisation which provides consultation to government-operated
facilities, group homes, agencies, and families of individuals with
developmental disabilities.

A government-endorsed document, commissioned by the Ministry of
Health and entitled 'Building Community Support for People: A Plan for
Mental Health in Ontario', July 1988, specifically targets the dually
diagnosed as one of the groups most in need of community health services
(Graham, 1988). It is hoped that this report's recommendations will soon
be implemented.

In 1990 the Ministries of Health and of Community and Social Services
in Ontario announced a joint funding initiative over a four-year period to
support the development of community programmes for the dual diagnosis
population. Models are currently being proposed in areas such as crisis
prevention, education, case management, assessment, medication monitoring, therapeutic intervention, and caregiving support. Unfortunately,
Ontario presently finds itself in a severe recession and it seems probable

that this funding is in jeopardy. Although the government of Ontario has been attempting to provide community services to the dual diagnosis population, as the institutions are being phased out, economic reality is likely to intrude on the further development of community resources.

A beginning has been made in the provision of services to the dual diagnosis population in a number of the provinces of Canada. However, anything short of full equality for the dual diagnosis population in terms both of distribution of and access to services is anathema. The incremental increase in both the knowledge base and its application in the hospital and community, however, is proceeding in many Canadian provinces.

Summary

Services to the dual diagnosis population in Canada vary by province, due to the federated structure of the country. Those offered in British Columbia, Alberta and Ontario have been described, but others across the country may have been omitted. As with all government-supported programmes, proposed future services to the dual diagnosis population may not come about, due to recessionary budget constraints.

References

Alberta Hospital Edmonton (n.d.) *Can We Help You?: Special Adult Assessment Unit.* Edmonton, Alta.: Alberta Hospital Edmonton.

Calgary Outreach Services (n.d.). The Calgary SCOPE Society. Calgary, Alta.: Calgary Outreach Services.

Community Behavioral Services (1991). *Dual Diagnosis Resource Manual.* Edmonton, Alta.: Community Behavioral Services.

Developmental Disabilities Program (n.d.). *Developmental Disabilities Program.* London, Ontario: University of Western Ontario.

Exchange Journal (1985). New program is expected to deal with a wide variety of projects. *The Exchange Journal*, **1**(1), 1–2.

Francis, D. (1977). The development of the lunatic asylum in the Maritime provinces. *Acadiensis*, **6**(2), 23–38.

Gibson, D., Frank, H. F. & Zarfas, D. E. (1963). Public mental retardation services in Canada: evolution and trends. *Canadian Psychiatric Journal*, **8**(5), 337–43.

Graham, R. (1988). *Building Community Support for People: A Plan for Mental Health in Ontario.* Toronto, Ontario: Ontario Ministry of Health.

Griffin, J. D. & Greenland, C. (1981). Institutional care of the mentally disordered in Canada: a 17th century record. *Canadian Journal of Psychiatry*, **26**, 274–7.

Griffiths, D. (1986). *Psychiatric Pinball: Impact of Deinstitutionalization on the Dual Diagnosed Individual.* Toronto: Behavior Management Services, York Central Hospital.

Kazdan, A. (1990). *Dual Diagnosis: Dual Dilemma*. Toronto, Ontario: Ontario
    Ministry of Health.
Leavitt, B. (1991). Community connection. *University of Western Ontario
    Clinical Bulletin of the Developmental Disabilities Program*. **2**(1), 1–2.
MARC (Metro Agencies Representatives' Council) (1989). *A Continuum of
    Service for Persons with Dual Diagnosis*. Toronto, Ontario: Metro Agencies
    Representatives' Council.
Morrison, B. & Foulis B. (1991). *Protocol for Services: Mental Health Services
    for Persons with Mental Handicaps*. Surrey, B. C.: British Columbia Mental
    Health Society.
Simmons, H. G. (1982). *From Asylum to Welfare*. Downsview, Ontario:
    National Institute on Mental Retardation.
Stead, Mrs. (1914). The Nova Scotia league for the care and protection of the
    feeble-minded. *Public Health Journal*, **5**(4), 219.
Support Clusters (1990). *Support Clusters Mission Statement*. Kitchener-
    Waterloo, Ontario: Support Clusters.
Sussman, S. (1992). From Institution to Community: An Historical and
    Evaluative Study of Services for Mentally Ill People in Ontario, Canada.
    Loughborough University. Ph.D. Thesis.
Thorpe, L. U. (1991). *Psychiatric Problems and Services for the Adult Mentally
    Retarded: Saskatchewan Survey*. (In press).
Wilbur, C. T. (1888). Institutions for the feeble-minded. In M. Rosen,
    G. R. Clark and M. S. Kivitz, eds. *The History of Mental Retardation*,
    vol 1, pp. 293–301, Baltimore: University Park Press.
Zarfas, D. E. (1988). Mental health systems for people with mental retardation:
    a Canadian perspective. *Australia and New Zealand Journal of
    Developmental Disabilities*, **14** (1), 3–7.

28

The prevention and management of seriously disruptive behaviour in Australia

TONY ATTWOOD AND RON JOACHIM

Introduction

A contemporary issue facing service providers is the prevention and management of seriously disruptive behaviour which can result in injury to clients, staff and members of the public. In this context behaviour includes aggression, damage to property, assault or when someone has been severely frightened.

Disruptive behaviour has a cost in both human and economic terms. The human costs for clients include the misery of living in damaged and spartan environments, reduced opportunities for appropriate recreational, occupational and social activities and the fear of harm. The human costs for staff include the risk of injury, working in a less than satisfactory environment, and the frustration of not being able to provide appropriate care and management. In economic terms, disruptive behaviour is expensive in terms of higher staff ratios, time off as result of injuries, higher staff turnover with recruitment and training expenses, and the provision of replacement possessions and security. Thus, there is a strong incentive for service agencies to ensure effective means of reducing disruptive behaviour. A further incentive in some jurisdictions is government legislation which imposes a legal requirement upon employers to provide a safe working environment for staff.

The issue of appropriate services for people with mental retardation and severely disruptive behaviour is becoming more acute with the policy of replacing large institutions with ordinary housing dispersed throughout the community. As the deinstitutionalisation process is gathering momentum, there remains the problem of appropriate services for those who may have:

a) remained in the institutions because their behaviour was considered disruptive, which delayed their selection for discharge. However, they will eventually be transferred to community facilities.
b) lived at home yet their challenging behaviour is such that their parents are requesting permanent care admission, but it is unclear whether they should be admitted to an institution, a special unit, or whether, a community facility could cope with their behaviour.
c) been resident in a community facility, but circumstances lead to the development of severe challenging behaviour and an alternative placement is considered.

In the past, special units have been used to manage the behaviour in a secure environment in addition to developing staff expertise. However, evaluation of these units has shown considerable disadvantages, modelling of inappropriate behaviour, difficulty finding subsequent accommodation and poor generalisation of appropriate behaviours (Blunden & Allen, 1987; Hoefkins & Allen 1990; McBrien, 1987; Vischer, 1982).

An alternative approach has been adopted by several agencies in the United Kingdom (Emerson *et al.*, 1987), United States (Donellan *et al.*, 1985), and Canada (Vischer, 1982). A decentralised model with an intensive intervention team provides practical support to the person in their natural home. Of people with an intellectual disability identified as having challenging behaviour 70% could be maintained in their present house if there were extra resources to cope with the behaviour (Vischer, 1982). One of the main reasons often given on admission to residential unit is not that the behaviour could not be managed in an ordinary house but that the disruption to other people's lives was too severe (Maher, 1986). An intervention team could work with the other residents as well as the client to decrease this disruption.

Over the last 20 years a range of successful procedures have been developed and evaluated to reduce the incidence and severity of disruptive behaviours, but many of these were developed in institutional settings or special units. The problem is how to apply these procedures to people living in ordinary homes in the community where there may be only four or five residents with only one or two staff on duty, and it may take some time for assistance to arrive.

The service organisation may not provide a clear policy on staff roles and responsibilities (especially in legal terms) in relation to disruptive behaviour where someone is at risk of injury and staff are then left in a quandary. Staff also need some means of emotional debriefing after a disruptive incident as the process can be quite traumatic for all those concerned including the client. In addition, staff may need some positive means of examining why the behaviour occurred and what strategies can be used to prevent its recurrence and how to manage any similar situation more effectively.

Behavioural technology can analyse why disruptive behaviour occurs and provide ways of reducing its severity and frequency. However, direct care staff with knowledge of the individual and continuous contact, may lack training in behaviour analysis and intervention for serious disruptive behaviour. A solution is to provide a staff training programme specifically on seriously disruptive behaviour that emphasises prevention, management and review. The training should also be linked to a clear organisational policy and procedures on seriously disruptive behaviour.

Current service models

In Australia, some service models include staff training in the prevention and management of seriously disruptive behaviour. Western Australia could be regarded as the pioneer State, having started their programmes in the mid-1980s (Batini *et al.*, 1987). Queensland adopted and modified their service model and that of Smith and Read (1983 unpublished manuscript) who developed ' Professional Assault Response Training' in California. However, the Queensland model provides more emphasis on prevention, emotional debriefing and psychiatric disorders, and used less intrusive self-defence procedures. The other States have a more conventional approach for managing disruptive behaviour, using local teams who develop individual management programmes and special residential units, much as in other countries.

The Queensland model

In 1989, a survey was conducted to provide information on the nature and distribution of disruptive behaviour amongst the 2621 registered clients of Intellectual Disability Services, the main State Government agency for people with mental retardation in Queensland.

The survey identified disruptive behaviour in people of all ages, from under 5 years to over 80, but the majority were between the ages of 10 and 40 years (73%). They lived in a range of accommodation, with roughly a third living at home, a third in community-based houses, and a third in three residential centres in Brisbane. There were just over 100 people with extremely severe and multiple disruptive behaviours. The data indicated a large range of causes, including environmental factors (overcrowding and lack of privacy), frustration due to poor communication skills and lack of stimulation, lack of attention and affection, poor interpersonal skills, the effect of living in a large institution since childhood, and behaviour associated with certain diagnoses such as autism. Thus, any effective intervention for disruptive behaviour needed to include staff training in a considerable range of causes.

A small working party was formed to provide recommendations on the prevention and management of seriously disruptive incidents (SDI). It recommended a training and management programme be developed for all staff of the organisation that would include training in protective actions to minimise injuries to staff, an administrative review process after an SDI and strategies to reduce the risk of a similar incident occurring again.

The training programme

A serious disruptive incident was defined as follows.

1. Whenever someone sustains substantial injury, or requires hospital treatment through violent action of another person while in the care of a staff member or volunteer.
   Whenever a staff member completes an accident report form in which the injury was apparently caused by the deliberate action of a client.
2. Whenever a client or staff member has been severely frightened. For example, when a client upturns furniture, or starts pushing other people around and threatens them.
3. Whenever a client is sufficiently disruptive to require the emergency intervention of medical/psychiatric services or the police.

A standard procedure was to be implemented every time an SDI occurred based on the following rationale.

1. Create safer places for clients and staff.
2. Facilitate the learning by clients of more effective and less distressing ways of managing their experience, expressing their needs, and manipulating their environments.
3. Improve the quality of staff/client interactions by increasing the knowledge, skills and confidence of staff in potentially disruptive situations.

The above rationale was based on the principles that:

1. Seriously disruptive behaviour is a reality in most areas of life and not unique to people who have an intellectual disability.

2. Aggression is a way of expressing a need or attempting to solve problems.
   There are many other appropriate and less distressing ways of solving problems.
3. Disruptive behaviour is the result of a collection of contributing factors.
4. Some contributing factors can be changed so that incidents become less likely to occur, and may even be prevented.

A comprehensive staff training package was developed based on the above rationale and principles. With classroom and practical instructions and the use of a specially devised manual for each participant, the course covered areas of prevention, management and analysis of an SDI. The course was conducted by two instructors who adopted a variety of presentation styles and role playing, and consisted of five sessions each taking half a day.

Session 1

The first session starts with the definition of seriously disruptive behaviour, case studies of clients and examples from participants in their personal and professional lives. These studies illustrate that disruptive behaviour is not an exclusive phenomenon to people with intellectual disability and that there is a sequence of stages preceding and following the incident. This session examines the build-up of relevant background factors.

a) Factors in the current environment, e.g. disturbing noise level
b) Medical factors, e.g. complex partial seizures
c) Emotional factors, e.g. fear, grief
d) Communication skills
e) Previous experience, e.g. living in an institution
f) Developmental level, e.g. problems associated with adolescence
g) Psychiatric disorders

Participants write in their manual the background factors relevant to their clients. At the end of the session a detailed analysis of the background factors of one client known to several participants, takes place.

Session 2

This session is concerned with 'triggers', i.e. events which precipitate disruptive behaviour. The training material outlines common triggers such as provocation, miscommunication, unmet expectations and failure, and includes ways of avoiding or minimising 'trigger' events.

Session 3

The programme looks at the escalation of disruptive behaviour, how to recognise and reduce levels of stress and agitated behaviour. Specific strategies are described for dealing with behaviour that is due to frustration (F), the need for attention (A), non-compliance (N), a threat (T), or anxiety (A). The FANTA strategies are described and demonstrated in a series of role playing by instructors and then the participants.

Session 4

The disruptive incident is examined, including relevant legal concepts such as the duty of care and reasonable force. Practical skills to avoid injury are taught, including methods of release, e.g. when someone is pinching you avoiding being hurt and methods of intervening when a client is injuring another person. These methods were designed to be effective, simple and easy to demonstrate and practice photographs and descriptions of the techniques are also included in the participants manual.

Session 5

This last session examines the person's recovery to normal behaviour and possible remorse for the consequences of the disruptive incident. The programme also includes information on how to avoid further triggers (e.g. inappropriate use of time out, prn medication). Staff are also trained in the administrative procedures for the reviews that occur after the incident. Participants then undertake a role play of a formal incident review based on a client known to several participants. This provides an opportunity for the instructor to assess their understanding of the sequence of stages involved in disruptive behaviour and their ability to design an effective intervention strategy. The course material also includes evaluation of the participants' intervention and management strategies in order for the participants to be awarded a certificate of attendance and satisfactory performance.

Administrative procedures and review of the incident

The service organisation introduced two reviews, initial and formal, to be undertaken after an incident. Instructions and practice in running these reviews were included in the staff training programme.

Initial incident review: This review occurs as soon as practicable after an incident, preferably within several hours. The purpose of the initial incident review were to:

Ensure all injuries, if any, were adequately treated, assess all ongoing risk to all people present and take appropriate action, deal with the emotional reaction of those involved, ensure short term management guidelines, fill out an SDI report and ensure involved members of the public, staff from other agencies, or community services were contacted for debriefing.

Persons who should attend include staff immediately involved, a senior staff member, the client if appropriate and a person knowledgable about behaviour management and SDI procedures.

Formal review of the incident: The preparation for the formal review was the responsibility of the nominated senior officer who was to ensure that within two days of the incident an appropriate person (a staff member, friend or relative) consulted with the client(s) involved (including any injured party) in the SDI.

This person would assess if it was appropriate for the client(s) to attend the formal review or part thereof. It would be appropriate for the client to attend if their expressive and receptive language was sufficient to ensure that the review was a learning experience. A client should not attend if he or she perceives it as a devalued, punitive, or an attention-gaining experience. It may be appropriate for other clients to give information and/or attend the review.

The formal incident review should occur not later than two weeks after the incident. It was the responsibility of the nominated senior officer to arrange the time and ensure the appropriate people attended. The review should be held to:

1. facilitate collaborative problem solving;
2. help resolve residual feelings;
3. analyse the incident;
4. review short-term guidelines and select a longer term management strategy;
5. recommend any act of restitution, if appropriate;
6. complete any outstanding issues relating to members of the public and staff of other agencies and services.

Persons who attended the initial incident review should also attend the formal incident review along with the client's programme coordinator, other significant caregivers, client's advocate, if appropriate, and a psychologist, if available. The review should be conducted fairly for all relevant parties. It should never be a blame-seeking or punitive experience for anyone including staff. The chairperson would be responsible for the implementation and monitoring of agreed strategies and in particular:

1. Review any injuries sustained. Encourage the expression of residual feelings, but ensure no one is victimised.
2. Analyse the incident to ascertain how future incidents can be avoided.
3. Select an intervention strategy to deal with future incidents. This process is facilitated by using a needs intervention grid which lists the concerned parties in the incident, e.g. disruptive client, staff, public etc. and the needs/interests or motivation of each of these parties. Alongside the list is a series of options with a column for each management suggestion generated during the formal review. The most effective and least restrictive option is then identified by a tick, cross or question mark in the grid as to whether the option meets the needs of each party.

    Any intervention must comply with the organisations's procedures on behaviour management and should be written up by the programme co-ordinator or psychologist and implemented by all persons involved with the client.
4. Recording
    Any intervention aimed at reducing SDI should be documented and include regular reviews in accordance with the standard procedures on behaviour management.
5. Further Reviews

    It will not always be necessary to have another formal review if a similar incident occurs again. If the same person engages in a different type of disruptive behaviour, another review and intervention strategy may be necessary. In addition, the situation should be reviewed by nominated senior officers six months following the initial incident.

The logistics of training all staff

Queensland is the most decentralised State in Australia, with services needing to span some 2000 km. In order to provide training for 1300 staff, a 'train the trainer' approach was adopted.

Initially, 33 staff from all service regions in the State were given training which included the basic course, as well as instruction and practice on how to train staff in their regions. Trainers were given a manual which contained methods on: how to run group training, how to stimulate discussion on particular topics, how to present specific material to participants, and how to deal with those who may be hostile or apathetic.

Because of the practical nature of SDI training, particularly the passive self-defence training, two instructors were required to present the material to staff. Each region therefore had a minimum of two staff attending the course. During the 'train the trainer' course, staff were assessed on attitude, knowledge and skill to determine if they would be suitable to run regional courses.

One of the regional trainers would coordinate the region's training, as well as implement the review process. These people received further training in conducting the initial and formal incident review meetings. Regional coordinators would typically have a good knowledge of behaviour management procedures and the training process. Finally, a divisional committee consisting of all regional coordinators and the senior clinical psychologist who convened the working party maintained an overview for training in SDI and the implementation of the procedures.

At the end of 1992 just over half of the 1300 staff have undergone the training programme.

With experience, the manual and methods of presentation have been improved. Staff have been extremely positive in their feedback and a reduction in the frequency and severity of disruptive behaviour is anticipated. This will be measured by repeating the original survey, and comparing previous and current staff injury statistics.

Summary

Although seriously disruptive behaviour may be a rare occurrence in people with an intellectual disability, its impact is great for the individual, staff and service agency. Effective strategies need to be developed for the prevention and management of such behaviour. They should be appropriate for relatively small, community-based services and the first option should be to support the person in their home environment rather than transfer them to a special unit. One strategy is to design a staff training package that includes an explanation for the factors that lead to disruptive behaviour and means of reducing their impact on the person, as well as information on the legal responsibilities of staff and how they can protect themselves and others from injury. Service organisations also need unambiguous policies and procedures to provide an administrative framework to support clients and staff.

Many agencies are now examining the value of staff training in the prevention and management of seriously disruptive behaviour. A model has been developed in Queensland that may prove appropriate for other service providers. Although the effectiveness of this model needs evaluation, our impression is that it has great potential to reduce the problems and consequences associated with seriously disruptive behaviour.

References

Batini, P., Elliot, J., Jones, G., Michelson, D. & Payton, N. (1986). *The Prevention and Management of Seriously Disruptive Behaviour*. Authority for Intellectually handicapped persons, WA.

Blunden, R. & Allen, D. (1987). *Facing the Challenge: An Ordinary Life for People with Learning Difficulties and Challenging Behaviour*. London: Kings Fund.

Donnelan, A., La Vigna, G., Zambito, J. & Thredt, J. (1985). A time-limited intensive intervention programme model to support community placement for persons with severe behaviour problems. *Journal of the Association for Severe Handicap*, **10**, 123–31.

Emerson, E., Barrett, S., Bell, S. *et al.* (1987). The Special *Development Team: Developing Services for People with Severe Learning Difficulties and Challenging Behaviours*. Institute of Social and Applied Psychology, University of Kent.

Hoefkins, A. & Allen, D. (1990). Evaluation of a special behavioural unit for people with mental handicaps and challenging behaviour. *Journal of Mental Deficiency Research*, **34**.

Maher (1986). Ensuring quality services for people with challenging behaviour. In L. Ward, ed. *Getting Better all the Time?* London: King's Fund.

McBrien, J. (1987). The Haytor Unit. *Mental Handicap*, **15**, 77–80.

McDonnell, A., Dreardon, B. & Richens, A. (1991). Staff training in the management of violence and aggression. 1) Setting up a training system. *Mental Handicap*, **19**, 73–6.

McDonnell, A., Dreardon, B. & Richens, A. (1991). Staff training in the management of violence and aggression. 2) Avoidance and escape principles. *Mental Handicap*, **19**, 109–12.

McDonnell, A., Dreardon, B. & Richens, A. (1991). Staff training in the management of violence and aggression. 3) Physical Restraints. *Mental Handicap*, **19**, 151–4.

Vischer, J. (1982). Problem analysis in planning a community-based behaviour management programme. *Practical Approaches to Developmental Handicap* **6**, 22–28.

29

The European scene

ANTON DOSEN

Introduction

Psychiatric disorders and behaviour problems in people with mental retardation have been receiving greater attention over the last two decades. The diagnostic and treatment advances together with the development of community services have contributed to a more rigorous scientific and professional approach in this field. Despite the fact that most European countries have adopted the principles of normalisation and social integration for the services for people with mental retardation, differences exist between them in their approach to care. There is still a paucity of published work describing international developments with a few exceptions mainly, the USA, UK, Netherlands, etc. International conferences organised by the World Psychiatric Association and other bodies have highlighted these problems and the need for better care.

Sweden

In most Scandinavian countries and especially in Sweden, the care for people with mental retardation is firmly based on the principle of normalisation. People with mental retardation have the same rights as other members of society and if they suffer from mental illness or behaviour problems they are treated by ordinary psychiatric services. The fear is that special settings and facilities may lead towards some form of segregation, separation and discrimination (Melin, 1988).

Similarly, offenders with mental retardation who are dealt with by the forensic psychiatric service. However, there is a small specialised national unit for the most dangerous and difficult offenders. There are still people with severe mental retardation in the few remaining small institutions. As a consequence no specialised psychiatric services have been developed and doctors and nurses receive very little training, if at all, on the psychiatric aspects of mental retardation (Day, 1991). The need for specialised facilities is increasingly being discussed. There is a growing body of concern among professionals that some kind of specialisation is required for people with severe mental retardation with severe behaviour problems and/or psychiatric illness. Some specialised group homes have already appeared on an experimental basis.

Netherlands

The deinstitutionalisation movement in the 1970s together with the adoption of normalisation principles has brought to attention the shortage of psychiatric help for people with mental retardation. Government, community agencies and professional groups are focusing on working out priorities of care for people with mental retardation and the organisational framework of appropriate services. Behaviour problems and psychiatric disorders have been the subject of discussions. (Dosen, Van Gennep & Zwanikken, 1990). The idea for special 'centres' for the care of people with mental retardation and psychiatric problems has been gaining popularity (Dosen, 1988). Such a centre would provide inpatient care, day treatment and ambulant service. In addition, it could become a resource for training and research and be linked with mental health services for the general population. In practice this plan is restricted only to a particular region of the country.

Germany

Controversial views among professionals in Germany over the past few decades have delayed development of services geared towards people with mental retardation and mental health problems. The traditional psychiatric associations have been rather indifferent to this situation, resulting in lack of specialist training and research. Current initiatives have, however, stimulated a dialogue and cooperation among interested bodies and professionals and the creation of specialised services and training are actively considered (Bradl & Hennicke, 1992).

Italy

The Italian Psychiatric Revolution in 1978 produced significant reforms in the care of people with mental retardation. All institutions for children younger than 15 year old were closed and, until recently, adults with mental retardation were not admitted to psychiatric hospitals. Their care was provided entirely by their families. Some recent changes in the legislation have allowed admissions of people with mental retardation to psychiatric hospitals for treatment of severe acute psychiatric disorders (Cocchi, 1992). There is no governmental central organisation to co-ordinate management, planning and service developments. However, there exist several private institutions and clinics run by religious organisations. The situation is even more complex if one takes into account the stigma attached to the diagnosis of mental retardation by Italian society (Cocchi, 1992).

The situation in other European countries

In countries such as Belgium and Switzerland, the main problem is the resettlement of people with mental retardation to community from the long-stay institutions. Lack of central planning, leadership, professional disagreement and rivalries have resulted in delaying development of community services (van Walleghem, 1988). Cultural aspects in accepting the coexistence of mental retardation and mental illness in some countries might also be responsible for the lack of specialised services, as for example, in Spain (Salvador & Martinez-Maroto, 1992).

In Eastern European countries, strong ideological issues prevail, focusing only on the teaching of people with mental retardation without allowing the development of mental health services. The current social and economic problems faced by these countries have added considerably to their shortcomings for planning and developing specialist services (Igric, 1992; Vetro, 1992).

Summary

The following problems appear to characterise the current European scene as far as psychiatric services for people with mental retardation is concerned:

Organisational problems
Professional ideology and approach
Cultural aspects and believers.

Perhaps with the exception of the UK (Part V), where there has been an organised system of services for people with mental health problems and mental retardation, none of the other European countries has achieved an optimum level of care so far. Instead there have been rather isolated initiatives pioneered either by individuals or organisations. Professional ideologies and social attitudes have added to difficulties while economic and fiscal consideration have been another major factor for lack of appropriate services. International collaboration with joint programmes and projects supported by the European Community are urgently required to ameliorate the problems, bridge the gaps among the different parts of Europe and stipulate the necessary developments. The formation of the European Association of Mental Health in Mental Retardation which held its inaugural meetings in the Netherlands in 1992, should become a forum of exchange of ideas and pressure group to advocate for the necessary service provision.

Further collaboration, not only within Europe but also with North America and Canada and organisations such as the National Association for the Dually Diagnosed would be beneficial.

References

Bradl, C. & Hennicke, K. (1992). Current Issues in Germany. In *Mental Health Care for People with Mental Retardation: European Experts Conference Proceedings*, pp. 130–136, Veldhoven.

Cocchi (1992). Mental handicap today in Italy. In *Mental Health Care for People with Mental Retardation: European Experts Conference Proceedings*, pp. 40–42, Veldhoven.

Day, K. (1991). The need for specialist psychiatric services. In *Proceedings of the Ninth Conference of the Asian Federation for Mental Retardation*, pp. 383–390, Bangkok.

Dosen, A. (1988). Community care for people with mental retardation in the Netherlands. Australia and New Zealand. *Journal of Developmental Disabilities*, **14**, 15–18.

Dosen, A., Van Gennep, A. & Zwanikken, G. J., eds. (1990). *Treatment of Mental Illness and Behaviour Disorder in the Mentally Retarded*. Leiden: Logon.

Igric, L. (1992). Report on the care for mentally retarded persons in Croatia. In *Mental Health Care for People with Mental Retardation: European Experts Conference Proceedings*, pp. 14–20, Veldhoven.

Melin, L. (1988). Services and provisions for persons with mental retardation in Sweden. *Australia and New Zealand Journal of Developmental Disabilities*, **14**, 37–42.

Salvador, L. & Martinez-Maroto A. (1992). Current situation in Spain. In *Mental Health Care for People with Mental Retardation: European Experts Conference Proceedings*, pp. 48–58, Veldhoven.

Van Walleghem, M (1988). Survey of principal care facilities for people with mental retardation in Belgium. *Australia and New Zealand Journal of Developmental Disabilities*, **14**, 31–5.

Vetro, A. (1992). Situation for mentally retarded people in Hungary. In *Mental Health Care for People with Mental Retardation: European Experts Conference Proceedings*, pp. 30–38, Veldhoven.

30

Availability and gratification of services in Japan

AKIHIKO TAKAHASHI

Introduction

Over the past two decades, there has been a proliferation of programmes on treatment and supportive services for people with mental retardation in Japan. However, the question remains, how much do these treatments and programmes really satisfy the needs of clients?

Treatment and supportive programmes are often planned from a professional point of view, and focus mainly on the function or behaviour of the individual. The tendency is to ignore other problems individuals with disabilities and their families have to overcome. A holistic approach to service delivery is needed. This chapter considers some aspects of planning and delivery of service in Japan.

Disadvantages of the present services

In services for people with mental retardation, the term 'service' has a dual meaning, covering: (1) systems of assisting diagnosis and treatment, counselling and guidance, economic and social support and (2) individual methods for each of the above components in the service system.

Our survey on parents of children with mental retardation in Japan highlighted various shortcomings in the system of services (Takahashi, & Ooshima 1990a,b). The main findings were as follows.

1) In about 60% of children their abnormality was first noted before the first year of age. Over half (57.9%) of the surveyed parents had suspected their child's condition and had sought advice, but 25.3% were unsuccessful and spent years without help.
2) As for the explanation given by doctors, 47% of parents were satisfied, 42% felt it was inadequate and 6% denied receiving any explanation on

the diagnosis or treatment. Many parents claimed that suggestions and recommendations given were often far beyond their comprehension and practically were difficult to apply. Words used by professionals were often too generic and scientific. Mothers did not want to hear scientific and technical terms on diagnosis and treatment for their children. Instead, they wanted someone who would listen to their complaints and worries, be sympathetic and offer them simple suggestions on matters of daily life.

3) Many parents were inclined to choose day-care centres suggested by the parents' association of handicapped children rather than government agencies and hospitals.

Thus, there appears to be some discrepancy between parents' needs and professional views, resulting in discontentment and distrust, by parents, of professional and government agencies.

Similar issues apply to individual components of service systems, e.g. treatment methods. There are, in Japan, many clinics and centres using a variety of treatment approaches for children with mental retardation. Parents, however, cannot compare the effectiveness of each method in selecting the best for their child and this often leads them to feel embarrassed and confused.

Service planning

Effective planning of service programmes require the following sequence of activities (Ager, 1990).

(a) Assessment of need
(b) Identification of strategies to meet this need
(c) Consideration of these alternative strategies with regard to various key factors
(d) Implementation of the favoured strategy, and
(e) Evaluation of the impact of the adopted strategy.

Services currently provided in Japan have been found to be disconnected from the recipient and hence the need. Takayama (1991) suggested the following key issues in planning a comprehensive rehabilitation system in mental retardation.

(i) Supportive service available from the stage of early medical intervention to social rehabilitation.
(ii) Cooperation between rehabilitative services in the community.

(iii) Resources for consultation and counselling in the community co-ordinated.
(iv) Provision of information service and
(v) Promotion of research and training.

Evaluation of the service programmes for people with mental retardation should take into consideration the following points.

1. Are there enough programmes and systems of treatment and support?
2. Is the programme widely known to those who need help and support?
3. Does the programme respect the clients needs?
4. Is the programme easy to access?
5. Does the method of treatment and training adapt to individual needs?
6. Do clients have a choice?
7. Does the programme evolve as the client ages?
8. Are instructions and explanations given in an easy and comprehensive way?
9. Is the aim of the service to meet the real needs of the client and not only to satisfy professional interest?
10. Does the service provide a 'Key-person' and 'Coordinator' on a primary care level for the client?

Summary

Service programmes for people with mental retardation in Japan have been examined to assess client satisfaction. Crucial discrepancies between clients' needs and service were found. In order to improve effectiveness of services, Ten Point Evaluation Guidelines are proposed to support clients' and parents' views, and respect clients' choice.

References

Ager, A. (1990). Planning sustainable services: Principles for the effective targeting of resources in developed and developing nations. In W. I. Fraser, ed., *Key Issues in Mental Retardation Research*, pp. 385–394, London & New York: Routledge.
Takahashi, A. & Ooshima, M. (1990a). Consumer's view of a community care programme. In W. I. Fraser, ed. *Key Issues in Mental Retardation Research*, pp. 203–208, London & New York; Routledge.
Takahashi, A. & Ooshima, M. (1990b). On the planning of community care system for handicapped children (II). *Psychiatria et Neurologia Paediatrica Japonica*, **30**, 119–30. (Japanese text).
Takayama, T. (1991). *Position Paper for the Planning of Comprehensive Rehabilitation System of the KITA-KYUSHU City*, pp. 64, Kita-Kyushu City Office. (Japanese text).

31

Strengths and difficulties in developing countries: the case of Zimbabwe

JACK PIACHAUD

Introduction

We should all feel some discomfort when we consider the problems of developing countries. We use the word 'developing' euphemistically as it protects us from thinking about poverty. Tables 31.1 and 31.2 outline some disparities in resources and consumption between the poor and rich nations. The term 'developing' implies that western industrial economies are developed, as if they have reached an endpoint in growth. In our field it is often important to view individual human development as a continuous process with no endpoint and, perhaps more importantly, that those who have developed further have no moral advantage and have some duty to help those less well off.

We should ask ourselves whether we are concerned about mental retardation as an abstract concept, as it applies to a particular part of the globe, 'our patch', or whether we can be concerned about all people with mental retardation, the vast majority of whom live in the poor countries of this world. It is a matter of our own resources. We can spread ourselves or the resources so thin that we feel they will disappear, so most of us have a behavioural streak in our makeup and we find it comfortable, and more profitable, to focus on aims and objectives that are achievable, but it is important that we look out from time to time from our usual systems and ponder on some less achievable objectives.

This chapter examines some issues of the developing countries, referring anecdotally to the author's experience in Zimbabwe, asking two general questions: what are the strengths that we might learn from? what are the difficulties that we might help with?

Table 31.1. *Grain consumed per capita and total energy consumed, per year, for different parts of the world.*

	Pop Mil	Grain Kg/Capita	Grain consumption Mil Ton Coal Equiv
DCs	1100	700	6509
East Asia	906	286	661
Latin America	333	262	311
Africa	413	169	158
South Asia	1292	225	363
World	4043	365	8002

Source: Gilland, B. (1979). *The Next Seventy Years.* Abacus Press.
DCs = Western Europe and North America.

Table 31.2. *Wealth and Health Indicators*

	GNP US×	LE Yrs	IM	CD	AW %
Low income Developing economies	260	57	94	12	32
Middle income Developing economies	1400	60	80	11	69
Industrial market economies	10320	74	11	1	100
Zimbabwe	630	55	74	12	52

Source: Carrin, G. (1984). *Economic Evaluation of Health Care in Developing Countries.* Croom Helm.
GNP = Gross national product per capita.
LE = Mean life expectancy.
IM = Infant mortality per thousand births.
CD = Child deaths before the age of 5 years.
AW = Percentage of the population having access to clean water.

Attitudes, beliefs and values

In a review of anthropological data (Edgerton, 1970) it is suggested that in tribal and third world cultures a whole range of possible attitudes to people with mental retardation exist. There are some societies that value the handicapped and look after their disabled members, yet within these cultures there would be individuals who reject their disabled children. There are cultures that place little or no value on the disabled and let such children die, yet within these societies there would be individuals who protect and care for their disabled offspring.

The main conclusion drawn by Edgerton was that there is no stereotype of so called more primitive societies and that values arise in a complex and ill-understood way; he also concluded that the attitude taken by a social group did not reflect its economic status; poor societies could be protective whilst wealthy societies could be rejecting. In our own cultures, where we may work hard to develop particular values, yet find these values opposed, it is interesting to reflect on this global pluralism as it allows us to move away from ideas of personal antagonism and see it rather as part of human nature for there are conflicting values, which reflect the peculiar pressures that shape the individual. Indeed it is sometimes difficult to know what values underlie attitudes and actions.

In a study carried out by Wig *et al.* (1980) case vignettes were used to estimate people's attitudes to various mental health problems, one case briefly described was that of a child with moderate mental retardation. These descriptions were given to community leaders in three different locations, rural areas in three different countries, and the informants were then asked to give their opinion as to the seriousness of the problem and the possibility of such a child working, marrying, and being able to stay at home. The attitudes varied considerably. Two of the three centres in the trial reported quite favourable attitudes to the idea of this child working, marrying, being able to stay at home, whilst the third centre gave a very different, more negative view of the future.

The values of the two centres with the more favourable outlook may seem more humane and more in keeping with the welfare of the disabled. However, these different attitudes may reflect different levels of survival rather than issues of value. The cultures with the more favourable prognosis may arrive at this because of the limited survival of severely handicapped children, whilst the community with the more negative view of the future may care for and protect the most profoundly disabled and thus have a different sense of the possible outcomes for disabled children. Such speculation needs verification but data on such matters are lacking.

In Zimbabwe, there does not seem to exist a traditional view. There is general acceptance within the community that disabled people need looking after. There is, however, a stoical attitude to death and misfortune which is a necessary defence mechanism when 10% of children die before the age of five. Parents might discuss the possibility of their hyperactive, severely retarded child falling in the river and drowning, which is a risk with relatively high odds and is of the same order of problem as parents in the UK discussing the risks of their child running into the road and being knocked down; yet the acceptance in the former situation seemed greater than in the latter. The author is not aware of any direct acts to kill disabled children, and this was never spoken of as an acceptable event.

The notions of causality are mainly spiritual, even in people with knowledge of the biological causes. The question is 'Why me, why my child'? Such questions are common in the UK also. The spiritual causes include the 'Child of God', and such families saw the child as a gift to be looked after. More commonly the cause was seen as a result of the action of ancestral spirits, and the birth of a handicapped child meant that the ancestors were making some point which might be about past relationships within the family or a sense of grievance that the spirits have about present actions. The meaning for the family would be worked out in consultation with a spirit medium and this would bring the family together and in some instances help in the bonding of the child to the family. The most divisive cause is that of witchcraft whereby someone, even the mother, maybe accused of deliberately or inadvertently bringing an evil spirit into the child and the family. As such, the stigma of the child for the family could be great.

What is most impressive is the tolerance to the range of possible beliefs and explanations which can be incorporated into a group's thinking and there is a strength here for us to learn from. Too often arguments arise in our services over minor disagreements, yet, within workshops organised for parents and workers in Harare, it was possible to combine biological and spiritual explanations as well as solutions; a behavioural approach was not seen as contradictory to caring, to taking medication or visiting a spiritual healer. As in most cultures the burden falls on the women and there is a stigma attached, that woman feel it more. There is a greater stigma attached to some of the associations of the mental retardation, especially epilepsy,which is seen as having bad spiritual causes as well as being contagious.

A case here illustrates the difficulties of making judgments and giving advice. Tendai was six years old, living with her mother who was a peasant farmer; she had a mild right-sided hemiplegia, mild mental retardation, and epilepsy; otherwise she was a bright and likeable child who made good social contact. Her mother was concerned that Tendai was not going to school, so we, and the clinic staff, talked to her mother who eventually talked to the headmaster and Tendai went to school accompanied by her brothers. One day she had a fit on the way to school, everybody ran away from her, there was great concern and she stopped going to school. Her mother was very upset but when we suggested going to mediate with the headmaster, explain about the epilepsy and try to get her back to school, her mother disagreed and did not want to follow this up. It became clear that the mother was responding to the community stigma. If she had continued sending Tendai to school, she would have drawn the anger of the community and not only Tendai but the whole family would have become stigmatised and isolated. There seemed no solution in the short time we had to work with this family, but there was a need to reflect on how far we should push other people to become champions of the rights we believe in and to wonder whether change in social systems always requires sacrificial lambs.

The overall sense of the attitudes of parents with disabled children within Zimbabwe, as compared to attitudes within the UK, is one of similarity. They worry about the causes, they feel the social stigma, they look all over for cures but eventually they come to some acceptance and ask the practical questions: 'Who will care for my child, who will feed and cloth my child, how shall I bring him or her up, what should I expect him or her to be able to do, what should he or she do during the day, will he or she be able to look after him or herself?'

Epidemiology

There are problems in defining the boundaries of mental retardation in developing countries. Are the skills required for independence in rural Africa the same as those required for a South American urban slum? All societies appear to identify those people who are deemed backward or slow in development, and it seems that most languages differentiate between those who are born mentally disordered and those who acquire it later in life; however, whilst the lack of a particular skill may create a problem in one place it may be of little relevance in another. For the more severe, biologically determined types of retardation, however, there will be less cultural influence in definition.

There are also methodological/practical problems, such as: gaining hard data about any phenomena in developing countries is difficult due to lack of adequate resources; there are difficulties with transport, difficulties in communicating with people over distances, agreeing on terms and meanings, finding people able to perform complicated tasks reliably, finding people at home at the right times. These issues are well discussed in the International Pilot Study of Severe Childhood disability (Belmont, 1984). The other reference which reviews most aspects of mental retardation in developing countries is the WHO Publication '*Mental Retardation: Meeting the Challenge*' (WHO, 1985).

Pursuing the issue of prevalence the general statement that mental retardation is at least as common in the developing world seems the safest (WHO, 1985). Reliable data which can be generalised are not available from many sites. In the study coordinated by Belmont, ten centres took part in piloting two screening questionnaires, using both a house to house survey method and a key informant method. They were particularly interested in testing the questionnaires for sensitivity and specificity and had not selected representative samples for population studies. The prevalence in seven of these centres ranges from 5 to 16 per 1000.

In a South African study of urban coloured children, a prevalence of between 2.64 and 3.36 was found, somewhat lower than expected (Power, 1977). This study made use of key informants working within the urban services rather than doing a house-to-house survey.

In Zimbabwe, the National Disability Survey, performed in 1981, reported a prevalence 2.3 per 1000 but this was essentially concerned with physical disabilities which were the result of the Independence War and its classification of mental disorders was not very precise. In 1989, the Community Based Rehabilitation project, funded by the Swedish De-velopment Agency, undertook a survey in six locations throughout the country and reported a prevalence of 2.2–2.8 per 1000, it is suggested that the prevalence figures arrived at were an underestimate in the order of 50 % (Finkenflugel, 1991).

Some epidemiological work suggests that making use of local people is a less effective method of case finding than bringing in trained and impartial staff. Perhaps people are less likely to tell someone who lives quite close and is well known in the area that there is a problem which reflects badly on the family. The effectiveness of local case finders can greatly be enhanced by training courses (*ibid*).

Another important point about using local people is that, whilst the prevalence may be less well identified, those people willing to come forward for treatment are identified and there is a general increase in community awareness, both important effects if the objective is to improve services. The incidence of mental retardation would be expected to be greater in developing countries and for there to be an association between the general level of health care and the level of childhood disability. This is linked to the causes of mental retardation, particularly its associations with malnutrition, infections and poor ante-natal and perinatal care.

Whilst mildly retarded children may grow up in a rural environment and find some social niche, the more severely retarded and the profoundly retarded may succumb early to the rigours of life, through malnutrition and infection. The prevalence may not then reflect incidence. Areas of higher prevalence may have better childcare services but are still not preventing some forms of mental retardation. Surveys of aetiology also face methodological problems such as poor access to health service, difficulty in keeping and finding records, etc. Most surveys are hospital based and therefore do not necessarily give a full picture of the community morbidity.

Zimbabwe: demography and services

Zimbabwe is described as being a Southern African and Central African country. It has no coastline and most of the country is on a reasonably fertile plateau, though there are areas of drought and very poor productivity. In 1890, a group of British entrepreneurs, under the leadership of Cecil Rhodes, decided to turn this fertile plateau into an area of commercial farmland, which they did in a systematic way, moving the local population off into the less fertile tracts of land, within 30 years they converted the country into a large farm with commercial products for the European market. Tobacco is still a major export as is cotton, maize, soya and citrus fruits. There are also large mining interests. In 1981, after many years of struggle, the local people took back political independence from the Europeans and are at present trying to form a viable mixed economy.

Culturally, there is a mixture of old and new, African and European. Harare, the capital city, has areas which are quite European, with private hospitals, schools and all modern conveniences; it is in many ways like an English provincial town. The southern suburbs and a large dormitory town are African; they are poor and becoming overcrowded with a steady urban drift of population from rural areas. Fifty miles out of town, past the largely European-owned commercial farms, rural Africa begins.

Of the population, 60% live in rural areas and are peasant farmers; some areas quite productive, whilst others dry and desolate; there are few services and it may be a 10 mile walk to see a nurse and a 100 miles, with little available transport, to see a doctor.

Of the population, 15% live in commercial farms, some of which care very well for their workers, while others rely on migrant labour and offer very little. About 25% live in towns and cities where the hospitals and clinics are quite accessible, particularly in Harare.

Rehabilitation technicians are based in some hospitals providing a network of trained staff throughout the country with some responsibility for disability. The 'rehab tech' has a two-year training, the focus being on physical disability, but their work includes mental retardation. The present rate is one 'rehab tech' to about 200000 people.

In addition, each district has at least one hospital with an occupational therapist and/or more likely, a physiotherapist. The two central hospitals have larger departments and in Harare there is the Children's Rehabilitation Unit, which acts as a central referral point for childhood disability. It was set up in 1987 by the Ministry of Health with help from UNICEF. Over 2500 children have been seen by there, over 1000 of whom had mental retardation. These children are then referred back to the districts with assessments and treatment plans, and the staff from the CRU make visits into the provincial centres to follow up. The outreach work has recently been severely hampered by transport and personnel shortages.

The University has degree courses in physiotherapy and in occupational therapy, whilst the Departments of Paediatrics and Psychiatry undertake service, teaching and research in this field. There is a teacher training course in special education. There is a reliance on overseas lecturers in the Medical School and other higher education centres.

The Ministry of Education has a special needs section run by the School Psychological Services. Each Province has an Educational Psychologist and there are a number of special classes, integrated into local primary schools.

There is an active voluntary body, the ZIMCARE TRUST, which runs several special schools for all types of mental retardation, it runs some residential and day services for adults as well as an outreach community service in rural areas.

There are two poorly resourced hospitals offering residential services for adults with mental retardation. The number of places is small, and most mentally retarded people are cared for in the community by their family.

Strengths and difficulties

A clear strength is the range of services and the cooperation between the ministries, the University, the different professional groups and the NGOs (non-government organisations). The main difficulty is the unmet need. The country's population is 10 million; with half this under the age of 15, taking a conservative prevalence of 0.3% for severe mental retardation would suggest that there are about 15000 children in need of services.

About 1000 school places for the severely retarded exist in specialist schools, principally in the cities (ZIMCARE, 1990); there are about 2500 places at special classes in ordinary schools, many rural, which will cater for a wide variety of learning disorders, some severe, but mostly mild (School Psychological Service, 1990).

There are community-based rehabilitation schemes which take services to rural homes assessing and teaching. One such scheme had been in contact with over 3000 families in a 5 year period (Mariga & McConkey, 1987). However, this is now stopping due to shortage of funds.

The principal system of care is the extended family, which is a network through which relationships between a wide number of people are defined by social rules, contracts and language, emerging as 'the community' in rural areas. This network based on social rules reflects the role of institutions, the primary purpose being to care for its members by directing the individuals to think of others, to have communal thoughts rather than just think of themselves and their own goals. An example of the way language is used to cement these relationships is in the use of the word 'amai', meaning mother. Many women within the extended family can become 'amai', including aunts and first and second cousins, which must convey to the child a wider sense of belonging.

The extended family is a strength, keeping someone within that family is a normal way of valuing them. The family provides a nurse, a watcher, a helper, a feeder, giving identity and a role to the disabled person.

The extended family, however, like the 'community' and the welfare state in the West, like any institution, has its faults. It forces people into relationships not of their own choosing. It makes demands on individuals and restricts freedom. For a middle-aged woman whose children have grown up, it may not be unpleasant to move in with a sister to help look after a disabled child, but for a girl in her teens being taken out of school to look after the handicapped younger brother, may represent a tragedy.

Seeing third-world poverty tests ideas of normalisation, but also clarifies them. The central concept of normalisation is not a relative but an absolute judgment. Treat all people in the way that is customary to value people in the culture; it is the content, not the concept, itself which is relative. By keeping them part of the family, by giving them a purpose and tasks to do, people become valued.

There may be little material valuing other than being fed; happiness and caring do not have to depend on wealth. Surveys on mental health problems tend to rate depression in a similar order of magnitude in rich and poor countries (Orley & Wing, 1979; Reeler, 1991). Taking the converse then, there is something within the social fabric, that is happiness, which is not directly related to wealth; it does not necessarily depend on an extra member of staff, or more outings to the park, or going down to the pub, or a bigger and better television.

Great difficulties lie ahead for most developing countries with the urban drift and the possible breakup of family without the backup of a welfare state but the family, however, need not be lost if certain social pressures can be applied to promote it. The mobility of people whilst fostering the nuclear family also allows children to move and to spend time with different parts of the family; so even if small nuclear bits of the extended family locate themselves in the cities, the network can be retained through the children, though this requires the emphasis to be on communal thinking rather than the individualistic thinking which seems so central to Western philosophy. Once the child's education and the passing of exams becomes more important than the family network, then the extended family will decline.

At this time, there can be little place for residential care as a major plank of mental retardation services in Zimbabwe; those places that exist are legacies of the colonial era. Those with private resources may develop such places, but it must be uncertain whether central government should put its scarce resources into such ventures. The provision of assessment services, the screening out of those with more remediable disabilities, the prevention of disabling conditions, the provision of day services, work opportunities and school places are the most crucial elements of services.

The welfare state, private enterprise and the family as models of care all have their limitations; it is of interest to speculate that future development of social systems may lead to a synthesis of these differing approaches and greater interchange between the so-called developed and developing countries might provide new solutions to the problems faced by disabled people.

Summary

Mental retardation in poor countries has political, economic, spiritual, social, psychological and biological aspects which are of interest to our own learning and amenable to our consideration. There must be a mutuality in any interaction which considers local needs and concerns; there is a common human pragmatism which is interested in knowledge that is helpful.

As defined by a Western psychobiological approach there are clearly preventable causes of mental retardation and at present there is little written data as to the needs of the handicapped. There are examples of good care in a range of different settings but a very large unmet need that is worthy of our attention.

There are local 'traditional' systems which manage issues such as causality, cure and care, though there is a great danger of these systems breaking down, as societies move to an urbanised and individualistic mode of living.

Observation of different systems of care leads to the conclusion that the welfare of people with severe disabilities relies on the quality of inter-personal relationships between them and those around them, rather than on wealth, location and the social systems available. We should all be sensitive to opportunities to work in developing countries and promote such opportunities for others.

References

Axton, J. & Levy, L. (1974). Mental handicap in Rhodesian African children. *Developmental Medicine and Child Neurology*, **16**, 350–5.

Belmont, L. (1984). The international pilot study of severe childhood disability. Final report: screening for severe mental retardation in developing countries. *Bishop Bekkers Foundation and Institute Research Series*, No. 1. Utrecht, The Netherlands. (Mimeo)

Carrin, G. (1984). *Economic Evaluation of Health Care in developing countries*. London: Croom Helm.

Edgerton, R. (1970). Mental retardation in non-Western societies. In H. C. Haywood, ed. *Social and Cultural Aspects of Mental Retardation*, pp. 523–559, New York: Appleton Century.

Finkelflügel, H. J. M. (1991). Identifying people in need of rehabilitation in rural Zimbabwe. *Central African Journal of Medicine*, **37**, 105–10.

Gilland, B. (1979). *The Next Seventy Years*. London: Abacus Press

Mariga, L. & McConkey, R. (1987). Home based learning programmes for mentally handicapped people in rural Zimbabwe. *International Journal of Rehabilitation Research*, **10** (2), 175–83.

Morley, D. & Lovel, H. (1986). *My Name is Today*. London; MacMillan.

Orley, J. and Wing, J. K. (1979). Psychiatric disorder in two African villages. *Archives of General Psychiatry*, **36**, 513–20.

Power, D. J. (1977). A study of the prevalence of severe mental retardation among coloured children in an urban community. *South African Medical Journal*, **52**(1), 30–4.

Reeler, A. P. (1991). Psychological disorder in primary care and the development of clinical services: an African perspective. *The Psychologist: Bulletin of the British Psychological Society*, **4**, 349–53.

School Psychological Service (1990). *Annual Report*. Ministry of Education and Culture, Harare, Zimbabwe.

WHO (1985) Mental retardation: meeting the challenge. *WHO offset Publication No. 86*. Geneva.

Wig, N. N., Suleiman, M. A., Routledge, R. *et al.*, (1980). Community reactions to mental disorders; A key informant study in three developing countries. *Acta Psychiatrica Scandinavica*, **61**, 111–26.

Zimcare Trust (1990). *Annual Report*. Harare, Zimbabwe.

Index